LAURANCE A. MASON,

3563

HIDDEN PROPHECIES IN THE PSALMS

By J. R. Church

Editorial and Research
Jack Jewell
Patricia Berry

All scripture references are from the King James Version unless otherwise stated.

Hidden Prophecies in the Psalms
First Edition, 1986
Copyright © 1986 by **Prophecy Publications**
Oklahoma City, OK 73153

Printed in the United States of America

Published by:
Prophecy Publications
P.O.Box 7000
Oklahoma City, OK 73153

ISBN 0-941241-00-9

Dedicated to. . .

"The rising again of ... Israel"
(Rabbi Simeon)

Acknowledgments

I wish to express my sincere appreciation to Patricia Berry, of Oklahoma City, who originally discovered this unique prophetic emphasis: Psalms 17 alluding to the British general, Allenby, taking Jerusalem in 1917; Psalms 39-44 giving the story of the Holocaust from 1939 to 1944; and Psalm 48 presenting the birth of Israel in 1948. Her assistance in research over the years has been a real help and blessing to me.

Also, I want to express my appreciation to Jack Jewell of Carrollton, Georgia, for his diligence and expertise in helping me pour over the writings of Jewish scholars and historians. His research was invaluable. Jack has an excellent background for the work he put into this book. For several years he was a college professor and specializes in the field of writing.

He lived in Israel during 1978-79, taught at the Anglican School in Jerusalem, and traveled widely across Israel doing research on the history of the land. He presently writes a syndicated column for the Times-Georgian Newspaper. He also gives himself to the ministry of reaching convicts through his work as Chaplain in the Georgia Department of Corrections.

Jack spent literally months pouring over hundreds of books on Jewish history. Along with his help, we have been able to add ancient rabbinical concepts to our study. *Hidden Prophecies in the Psalms* is documented with historical facts to show how the Psalms present the ebb and flow of each year in this century.

I would also like to thank the many friends who wrote or called from time to time with suggestions about the prophetic nature of the Psalms. I have been able to incorporate many of their finds into this study. They were so numerous, I would not be able to name all who helped to make this book possible. However, I am very grateful for their help.

Finally, I would like to thank the following friends for helping to underwrite the publication of this book. It is with grateful appreciation that I acknowledge their assistance. They felt the importance of our research in the Psalms and prayerfully stood by our commitment to share the book with others. They include:

Tom, Anna and Beth Ables, Tyler, TX
Myrtle Adams, Rye, TX
Sherry Allison, Kendall Allison, Roger Casey,
    Redlands, CA — In memory of Lucy Ann Cooksey
Roland, Sherri, Amber and Eric Austin, Stillwater, OK
Chris and Martha Barden, Layfayette, LA
Jean M. Bell, Melbourne Beach, FL
Mr. and Mrs. Kenneth L. Berry, Buford, GA
Kathleen Birkett, Canada
Richard and Ruth Bolt, University Park, IL
Rev. and Mrs. Burton L. Bonn, Edina, MN
James and Ruth Booth, Bulverde, TX
R. L. and Ola Borden, Portales, NM
Ralph Burrs, Oklahoma City, OK
Leo Cadenhead, Clyde, TX
Mr. and Mrs. Steve Carnes III, Jonesboro, GA — In memory
    of Thomas Stephen Carnes, Sr.
Ardella Casteel, Spruce Pine, NC
William and Socorro Churbe, San Antonio, TX
Joanna Clardy, Austin, TX
Arthur Coffman, Grady, NM
Mr. and Mrs. Herbert W. Colson, Greensburg, IN
Stephen and Cynthia Conner, Edmond, OK
Howard G. Crum, Oklahoma City, OK
Mr. and Mrs. Bill Daniel, Floydada, TX
Mr. and Mrs. Con C. Davis, Willows, CA
Don and Geraldine Deibler, Oklahoma City, OK
Mr. and Mrs. Dock Dorrell, Diamond, MO
Richard Dulaney, Oklahoma City, OK
Jessie Edgecomb, Midwest City, OK
Mr. and Mrs. Robert Elliott, Lubbock, TX
Martha Espander, Pueblo, CO
Dale and Janice Fain, Enid, OK
Faith Baptist Church, Hutchinson, KS
Joseph E. Felt, Mt. Perry, OH
Bruce Patrick French, Houston, TX
Jimmy and Misun Gardner, Oklahoma City, OK
Ruby Garner, Brownfield, TX
Dorothy and Erwin Glover, Lubbock, TX
Mr. and Mrs. Harold L. Griffith, Oklahoma City, OK
Mr. and Mrs. Robert Guidry, Lake Charles, LA
Mr. and Mrs. Phil Haberer, Earth, TX
Ruth A. Hamilton, Grand Ledge, MI
William C. Hart, Jr., Newport Beach, CA

Jesse and Elizabeth Herrian, Choctaw, OK
Floyd Hildreth, Sterling, KS
Etta Hill, San Antonio, TX
A. C. Holland and Rev. Kenneth Carroll, Dimmitt, TX
Russell and Aaron Hollenberg and Family, San Diego, CA
John and Jo Ann Hulen, Nashville, TN
Steve and Janice Hulen, Nashville, TN
Marian Hunsberger, Baltimore, MD
Melvin E. Hutton, Spur, TX
Harry Ray Jesko, Texico, NM
Mrs. Louise Jewell, Carrollton, GA
Mr. and Mrs. Lloyd A. Jordan, Lubbock, TX
Frank Keener, Dewey, OK
Mrs. Lucile F. Keller, Oklahoma City, OK
Keneke, Milolii, HI
Mrs. Judy Kennedy, Long Beach, CA
Mr. and Mrs. Estel Ketchum, Mesa, AZ
Mary L. Kienlen, Canadian, OK
Anthony Koshay, Port Huron, MI — In memory
    of his mother, Maxine V. Koshay (1910-1986)
Milton Lakey, Fallon, NV
Dean and Jean Lampman, Loveland, OH
Lloyd G. Lammers II, Lubbock, TX
Fred and Helen Lipham, Floydada, TX
Mr. and Mrs. Julius J. London, Oklahoma City, OK
Mr. and Mrs. Robert Long, Caldwell, OH
Mr. and Mrs. Sidney Lord, San Antonio,TX
Jim and Tina MacArthur, Bryan, TX
Jerry and Dottie McCall, Clearwater, FL
Mae McClain, Oklahoma City, OK — In memory
    of Morgan-Davis-Turpin-McClain
Robert McWethy, Wichita, KS
Edward Madole, Claremore, OK
Ellen Webb Massengill, Littlefield, TX
Modena Mayfield, Abilene, TX
Mrs. Annie R. Mendenhall, High Point, NC
Margaret Miller, Clovis, NM
Mr. and Mrs. W. J. Miller, Fayetteville, GA
Dr. Felix K. Milton, Allen Park, MI
Dr. T. H. Monnier, Clearwater, FL
Mary Murphy, Seattle, WA
Gladys Murray, Canada
Mr. and Mrs. Sam L. Muse, Newalla, OK
Cmdr. Bill and Beth Neel, Lubbock, TX
Samuel Orlando, Houston, TX
Merle and Ramona Palmer, Blythwood, SC
Clarence Poisal, Oklahoma City, OK — In memory
    of his wife, Sonja Poisal

Mr. and Mrs. Eric Prove, Ganado, TX
Mr. and Mrs. Donald Putnam, Newberry Springs, CA
A. and G. Schirrmacher, Canada
Harold, Verna, and Mary Schmidt, Canada
Mrs. Regina Schoettlin, San Antonio, TX
Mr. and Mrs. Kenneth Sherman, Pevely, MO
Carolyn, Connie, Mike, and Shonna Skarda,
   Clovis, NM: Plano, TX; and El Paso, TX
Mr. and Mrs. Paul Smith, Oklahoma City, OK
Wendell H. Smith, Windom, MN
Edward and Betty B. Snipes, Aiken, SC
Joe and Tracye Stettheimer, Lubbock, TX
Marie Stewart, Lubbock, TX
Lawrence, Martha and Matthew Stice, Garden Grove, CA
Mr. and Mrs. Dwight T. Still, Lawrenceville, GA
Mr. and Mrs. Richard Stroud, Kennesaw, GA
Barbara Szettella, San Antonio, TX
Gary A. and Sue Taylor, Lubbock, TX
Shirley Totsch, St. Peters, MO
Margaret Trayser, Plain City, OH
Dale and Brenda Travis, Lubbock, TX
Sidney Tuggle, Midwest City, OK
Arthur and Susan Valladao, Lubbock, TX
Mr. and Mrs. H. T. Woods, Lebanon, MO
A Friend of Israel, Pt. Orange, FL
Friends of Israel, Millersburg, OH

TABLE OF CONTENTS

The Numbers Psalms

The Deuteronomy Psalms

THE ADVENTURE BEGINS!

It was September, 1983. I had made a study of Psalm 102, which contains some fascinating prophetic references to the science of archaeology. After producing a television program on the subject, my interest was stirred. "Perhaps there are other psalms," I thought, "which contain prophetic passages geared for this generation." My attention turned to Psalm 90. I knew the psalm had been written by Moses and was convinced that it also contained prophetic material.

Thinking it would make an appropriate study for our television program, Prophecy in the News, I began to pour over the verses and ponder their possibilities. However, I couldn't seem to put the message together. I laid aside the material for a while and directed my thoughts elsewhere hoping that when I returned to the study, my mind would be more organized. Later that day, I mentioned my frustration to Patricia Berry, research assistant. "Patty," I said, "would you take a look at Psalm 90 and give me your assessment? There must be something prophetic there, but I can't seem to put my finger on it."

Days went by. Passing her desk one morning, I asked, "Did you come up with anything on Moses?"

"No," she replied, "but I have something that might be of interest to you." Turning to Psalm 48, she asked, "Will you read verses 4-6?"

Pausing for a moment, I read, *For, lo, the kings were assembled, they passed by together. They saw it, and so they marvelled; they were troubled, and hasted away. Fear took hold upon them there, and pain, as of a woman in travail.*

She asked, "Doesn't that sound like the United Nations giving birth to the state of Israel?"

The description seemed obvious. The assembled *kings* could imply a group of representatives from various governments and the *woman in travail*, the rebirth of the state of Israel. After I acknowledged the prophetic implication of Patty's find, she said, "Did you notice in which psalm that prophetic reference was made?"

I replied, "Psalm 48."

"Well," she reminded, "in what year did the United Nations give birth to the state of Israel?"

"1948."

"Doesn't it seem a bit more than just coincidence that the birth of Israel in 1948 should be described in Psalm 48?" she asked.

To which I whimsically replied, "Cute."

"Well," she continued to prod, "will you read a couple of verses in Psalm 17?"

By this time I had become suspicious. Turning to the psalm, I read, *Keep me as the apple of the eye, hide me under the shadow of thy wings, ... Like as a lion that is greedy of his prey, ...* (vv. 8,12).

"Doesn't that," she asked, "sound like a description of the British general, Allenby, taking Jerusalem in 1917?"

"It sure does!"

Allenby captured Jerusalem on behalf of Great Britain, the symbol of which is a lion (v. 12). The British commander had used airplanes to buzz the city, frightening the occupation forces of the Turks into surrender. The *wings* (v. 8) might be a reference to those World War I biplanes.

The implications were overwhelming! If, indeed, Psalm 17 describes an event occurring in 1917 and Psalm 48 an event in 1948, what about other psalms? Do they also describe events which have befallen the Jewish people in this century? I immediately found a quiet place where I would not be disturbed. With my Bible in one hand and a yellow marking pen in the other, I studied the Psalms with an expectation never felt before.

To my delight, I was also told that the Psalms happen to be the 19th book of the Old Testament! Could God have placed it there to tell the story of the 1900's? It appeared as if book 19, chapter 1 introduced 1901; book 19, chapter 2 alluded to 1902; book 19, chapter 3 caught the ebb and flow of 1903; etc. Wow! Furthermore, the 19th book of the New Testament happens to be the book of Hebrews! Perhaps God has positioned that book as well to say that the 1900's would be the century of the Hebrews!

As I embarked upon my new adventure, two potential problems

had to be considered. First, I had to ask myself, "Am I trying to read into these verses something which is not there? Am I twisting Scripture in order to make it fit into a mold of my own making?" And secondly, "If I proceed past the psalm numbered according to the current year, will I not be accused of setting dates?" These are two things which I fear in my prophetic research ministry and avoid judiciously.

I have always held to traditional views and still do. I do not know the future and cannot prognosticate. Furthermore, I refuse to allow myself to believe that future events are etched in stone and thus have no alternative but to come to pass in the year numbered according to each psalm. I can go no further than to say that the later psalms seem to set a TREND for those events which the Bible's prophets say will someday come to pass.

It was not I who put a reference to the resurrection in Psalm 88:10, nor would I dare to suggest that the resurrection must occur in 1988. I am not the one who wrote that Psalm 88 is the "gloomiest psalm found in the Scripture." That assessment was recorded by H. C. Leupold in the ZONDERVAN PICTORIAL ENCYCLOPEDIA OF THE BIBLE.

The words of Psalm 88:3, ... *my soul is full of troubles: and my life draweth nigh unto the grave* are not my words. The psalmist wrote that. Neither would I dare to suggest that the Tribulation Period must begin in 1988. I merely point out that Psalms 88-94 appear to describe the major events of seven dreadful years — in chronological order.

It was not I who described the *abomination of desolation* in Psalm 91. It was the psalmist who wrote, *Surely he shall deliver thee from the snare of the fowler,* ... (v. 3). Other commentaries have described this verse as a prediction of that dreadful time when the antichrist will appear and the Jewish remnant will flee to the mountains.

Nor was I the one who wrote in Psalm 94, *O LORD God, to whom vengeance belongeth;* ... *shew thyself* (v. 1). The statement implies a prophetic prayer for Christ to appear on the day of His vengeance. Though Psalm 94 describes the devastation to be wrought at Armageddon, we cannot say with any degree of certainty that those events will occur in 1994. I must approach those later psalms only with the suggestion that they seem to set a TREND for those events which I feel will someday come to pass.

Though the prophetic scenario appears to be described in chronological order and conforms to the biblical sequence of predicted events, it is by no means necessary for those events to occur in the immediate future. Jonah's predicted destruction of Nineveh after forty days was held in abeyance for over a hundred years. Daniel's *seventy weeks* representing 490 years (Daniel 9) were fulfilled down to the end of 483 years. But the last seven years were put on hold and are yet to come to pass. John the Baptist preached *the kingdom of heaven* is at hand, but ended up in prison and was beheaded, instead.

Were these men mistaken? Obviously not, but God was both touched by the repentant Ninevites and angered by an unbelieving Israel. Perhaps the main reason Jesus said, *No man knoweth the day nor the hour,* was because he knew the Father could not be held to the mere expectations of men. We cannot put God in a box. He is sovereign!

It is with some degree of reluctance, then, that I even approach the subject for fear of being labeled as a date setter. I do not wish to be classified in such a manner. On the other hand, if I were to shelve this entire study on the uncanny twentieth century chronology apparent in the Psalms, would I not then be remiss in my calling?

In Psalm 49 the Lord promised to open His *dark saying upon the harp.* He thus implied that prophecies (dark sayings) were hidden in Israel's ancient songbook. The passage in Psalm 49:4 follows a description of the birth of Israel (Psalm 48), indicating that those *dark sayings* would not be discovered until after the return of the Jews to their homeland. We now live in that predicted era. The Jew has returned. We must conclude that His *dark sayings* are thus being revealed.

THE TORAH IN SONG

"Moses gave to the Israelites the five books of the Law; and corresponding with these David gave them the five books of the Psalms" (Midrash Psalm 1:1).[1] David compiled the first and fourth books of the Psalms; Solomon, books two and three; and the fifth is believed to have been compiled by Ezra after the Babylonian captivity. The Psalms are divided as follows:

Genesis Book — Psalms 1-41
Exodus Book — Psalms 42-72
Leviticus Book — Psalms 73-89
Numbers Book — Psalms 90-106
Deuteronomy Book — Psalms 107-150

Though scholars have long noted the comparison between the Psalms and the Torah (Genesis-Deuteronomy), it seems none have considered the prophetic design suggested in this book. In 1893, the noted author E. W. Bullinger wrote in his introduction to the Psalms: "Manuscript and Massoretic authorities, the Talmud (Kiddushin 33a) as well as the ancient versions, divide the Psalms into five books. Many attempts have been made from ancient times to discover the reason for the classification of the Psalms into these five books; but none of them is ... satisfactory."[2]

Why are the Psalms divided into five parts? The mystery has eluded even the world's most celebrated theologians. Bullinger's attempt at explanation stops short of our suggestion, for he wrote in 1893. He could not have foreseen the year by year progression of the twentieth century. Nevertheless, he addressed the dilemma: "There must be a reason why the second psalm is not (for example) the seventy-second; and why the ninetieth (which is the most ancient of all the psalms, being a prayer of Moses) is not the first."[3]

In his frustration he posed the question, but did not provide the answer. It is possible, however, that we have discovered the answer in this century! The Psalms happen to be the 19th book of the Old Testament. Also, each psalm appears to be chronologically designed to describe events in each successive year (at least the first eighty-six) — Psalm 1 referring to 1901, Psalm 2 to 1902, etc. To put it another way, we may say book nineteen, chapter one, introduces 1901. Book nineteen, chapter two alludes to 1902, etc.

Another noted theologian, H. A. Ironside, in his commentary on the Psalms wrote: "It is a new thought to some people that we have not only one book of the Psalms, but in reality there are five books. Our Bible begins with the Pentateuch, from Genesis to Deuteronomy; and the entire Bible, it has been pointed out by others, seems to be built upon that Pentateuchal foundation. The book of Genesis is the book of life and the book of election; the book of Exodus is the book of redemption; Leviticus is the book of sanctification; Numbers is the book of testing and experience; Deuteronomy is the book of divine government. It is a very interesting fact that the book of Psalms consists of five books also and that these five link perfectly with the five books of Moses."[4]

Fascinating!

Ironside compared the five divisions of the Psalms with the five books of Moses and declared, "We have a progressive line of truth in accord with the subjects treated in the five books of the Pentateuch, and the remarkable thing is that in the first book of the Psalms the great outstanding themes are Divine Life and Electing Grace — God's wonderful provision of grace, just the same as in the book of Genesis."[5]

"In the second book of the Psalms the great outstanding theme is redemption, as in Exodus. In the third book of the Psalms we are occupied with sanctification, communion with God, the way into the sanctuary, as in the book of Leviticus. The fourth book is the darkest one, for it is the book of testing, the book of trial, as in Numbers. Many of these psalms have to do with bitter, hard experiences that the people of God often have to go through in this world. And then the last book of Psalms is the book that brings God in as overruling in all the trials, the difficulties, and perplexities — the divine government, as in the book of Deuteronomy — God bringing everything out at last to His honor and glory and to

His people's eternal blessing."[6]

Ironside outlined the concept found in the Mosaic divisions and yet missed entirely the prophetic scenario. It is obvious that the five books of Moses outlined the chronology of events. There must be a Genesis period when the Promised Land is prepared for the return of the Chosen People. There must follow an Exodus period when the *wandering Jew* returns. Once in his land, there must be a Leviticus period when Temple Worship is restored. A Numbers period will introduce seven dreadful years of tribulation followed by the coming of Messiah to establish a Deuteronomy period — the kingdom of heaven on planet earth.

The first forty-one psalms of this nineteenth book of the Old Testament not only compare with Genesis, they also appear to describe the first forty-one years of this century. Considering those events which led to the birth of Israel, we could even call 1901 through 1941 the Genesis period. The turn of the century appears to represent the beginning of a new work by the Great Creator. Just as He called Abraham, Isaac, Jacob, and Joseph in the book of Genesis, so He chose men like Theodor Herzl, Chaim Weizmann, and others to develop the World Zionist Movement for the purpose of reclaiming the Promised Land.

After the death of Joseph, the children of Israel fell into Egyptian bondage — until God chose Moses to lead them out. Ironically, in 1942, the Jewish people were suffering a Nazi persecution comparable to that inflicted by Pharaoh of Egypt. Thus began the Exodus period. The loss of six million Jewish lives shocked the civilized world. The nations were forced to realize the need for a Jewish homeland, preparing the way for a modern exodus and the rebirth of Israel in 1948.

Psalm 73 marks a new division ushered in by the Yom Kippur War of 1973. The sacrifice would prepare the way for development toward Temple Worship — the theme of Leviticus. That was the year a symbolic "half-shekel offering" was received from Jews the world over with which they built the Jerusalem Great Synagogue. Though it may not be a temple, the edifice has the characteristics of a temple, with perhaps two exceptions: First, it was not built on the Temple Mount; and secondly, the rabbis do not offer animal sacrifices in it. The Jerusalem Great Synagogue, like the Temple, however, has been declared a "beit tefillah," a house of prayer. It is a "world" synagogue, the first central house of Jewish worship since the destruction of the Temple nineteen centuries ago.

Since Temple Worship would be impossible without priests, a special school has been organized to prepare a twentieth century priesthood for the ceremonial duties required. It is called "Yeshiva Ha Cohenim" — "yeshiva" meaning school and "cohenim" meaning priesthood. Will the priesthood be reinstituted soon? And will Temple Worship be restored? Well, those are questions which must remain unanswered until the fulfillment of each event predicted.

The fourth division (Psalms 90-106) finds the children of Jacob in the midst of their Numbers period. The Mosaic book by that title describes the troubles of Israel during its 40-year sojourn in the wilderness. Likewise, these psalms imply a future time of heartache, called by Jeremiah *Jacob's trouble* (Jeremiah 30:7). It will culminate at Armageddon with the glorious appearing of their long-awaited Messiah!

The final book (Psalms 107-150) corresponds to Deuteronomy. The term means "repetition of the law" and seems to represent just that — as Messiah comes to establish His millennial kingdom. He will teach the world for 1,000 years how to obey His law. The word Deuteronomy was derived from the Septuagint (a Greek translation produced in Alexandria, Egypt, circa 300 B.C.) The term comes from a phrase in Deuteronomy 17:18, "a copy of this law." In ancient Hebrew, however, the book was not called Deuteronomy; rather, it was known by a title taken from its opening statement, *These be the words* ... (Deuteronomy 1:1). Originally, the book was called DABAR meaning "WORD." Had the Hebrew title (Dabar) been directly translated into Greek, the name of the fifth book of Moses would have been LOGOS (WORD)! The Greek translation of the book was obviously not the original. Therefore, it was called "a copy" (Deuteronomy) rather than the direct Greek translation "Logos."

Is it any wonder John wrote in the introduction of his Gospel, *In the beginning was the WORD, and the WORD was with God, and the WORD was God.* Jesus Christ is the WORD! In Revelation 19 John described Christ's return at Armageddon, *And he was clothed with a vesture dipped in blood: and his name is called the WORD of God* (Revelation 19:13). Yes, the fifth division of the Psalms implies the LOGOS period of world history — the millennial reign of Christ! That is the prophetic plan laid out in the Pentateuch. It is detailed in the Psalms and is being fulfilled in this twentieth century.

The five books of Moses also represent a prophetic scenario for the entire history of man. There was a Genesis period as described in the book which bears its title. It outlined the history of God's chosen people from Adam to Moses. Then came the Exodus period from Moses to David. It was a time when the Israelites possessed their promised land and established the kingdom. Next came the Leviticus period, with the establishment of Temple Worship. It reached its glory with the building of Solomon's Temple and covered a period of history which climaxed when the Son of God came to *dwell* (tabernacle) among men (John 1:14).

With His rejection at Calvary, the people of Israel entered their Numbers period — 2,000 years of heartache. They were driven from their land to suffer among Gentile nations. One day, however, their Messiah will return in power and great glory to establish the Deuteronomy period of history — His millennial reign!

Either way you look at it, the five books of Moses tell a prophetic story. That is why our study in the Psalms is so fascinating. Those five ancient songbooks were compiled at a time when no human could have known the sequential development of history, much less the events of the twentieth century. Yet, they compare perfectly with what we now know has happened to the Jewish people since 1901. And of the future? Well, let us read on.

HOW LONG?

It has been the desire of every Jewish mother to bear the Messiah. Each generation longed for Him, particularly in times of national dilemma. Nowhere in Jewish literature, however, is that yearning more poignantly expressed than in the Psalms.

In the original Hebrew scriptures the question, *How long?* appears eighteen times in twelve passages. Twelve is the number of "governmental perfection" and compares to the twelve tribes of Israel. Eighteen is made up of three sets of six (6+6+6) — six being the number of man. Why does the question appear eighteen times? Perhaps as a balance to counter the difficulties and heartaches inflicted upon the Chosen People by the antichrist whose number is *six hundred threescore and six* (Revelation 13:18).

The first *How long?* is found in Psalm 4. It begins with the Lord asking of the sons of men, ... *how long will ye turn my glory into shame?* (Psalm 4:2). It is noteworthy that God, Himself, asks the question this first time — it is also the only time. In every instance afterward, the question emerges from an anguished soul.

In Psalm 6, David returns the query, *My soul is also sore vexed: but thou, O Lord, how long?* (Psalm 6:3). In the first instance (Psalm 4) the Lord is vexed, and in return (Psalm 6) His Chosen People are vexed. The question is reminiscent of that posed by the disciples in Matthew's Gospel, ... *when shall these things be? and what shall be the sign of thy coming, and of the end of the world?* (Matthew 24:3). Those asking about the future were not scolded; they simply were told ... *of that day and hour knoweth no man* (Matthew 24:36).

Assuming the first six psalms represent the initial six years of this century, please note that in 1906 the nations were moving furiously toward war. It would be the first global war of mankind. In Russia, the Jews were under severe persecution. November, 1905, witnessed Russia's worst "pogrom" (massacre of helpless Jewish people) to date. During the four "pogrom" years

(1903-1906), nearly a half million people fled in fear for their lives. No wonder Psalm 6 records the lamentation, *How long?* The devout wanted to know when they could expect deliverance. Following the query, the psalmist cries, *Return, O Lord!* (Psalm 6:4). Yet, the Jews do not believe Messiah has ever come the first time. It is a prophecy veiled from Jewish eyes.

Political insanity ran rampant in 1913, setting a course for war — *nation against nation, kingdom against kingdom.* Therefore, it may be significant that the question appears again in Psalm 13. This time, David uses it to introduce the psalm — emphasizing its prophetic importance on the eve of World War I: *How long wilt thou forget me, O Lord? for ever? how long wilt thou hide thy face from me? How long shall I take counsel in my soul, having sorrow in my heart daily? how long shall mine enemy be exalted over me?* (Psalm 13:1-2).

It may be inappropriate to set dates for the conclusion of this age, but it appears to be altogether appropriate to ask, *How long?* Presumably, it was not enough for the psalmist to know WHAT the future held. He also wanted to know WHEN those events would occur.

The question does not resurface until Psalm 35. Did God have 1935 in mind? Germany's Dr. Joseph Goebbels, the Minister of Propaganda, put the matter quite bluntly in an interview he gave to a London journalist on July 7, 1935: "Jewry must perish!"[1] At no time did the Nazis attempt to cover their crazed desire to destroy the Jews. On September 15, 1935, the Nuremberg Racial Laws declared, "... anyone with as much as one-quarter 'Jewish blood' was not to be considered German and was to be ejected from German national life."[2] ... *they gnashed upon me with their teeth,* wrote the psalmist, *Lord, how long wilt thou look on? rescue my soul from their destructions* ... (Psalm 35:16-17). How appropriate for the Jews to be concerned with the subject of "when" in light of chaotic world conditions in that year!

Though the terminology *How long?* is not used in Psalm 39:4, the Holocaust appears eminent and the heartache of the national tragedy can be felt as the psalmist prays, *Lord, make me to know mine end, and the measure of my days* ... There is no *How long?* at this point for that contains hope for deliverance. Certain death approaches for six million of the world's Jewish population. There is no deliverance ahead for them — no need for a query draped in hope, only the pitiful prayer, ... *to know mine end.*

The question is not restated until Psalm 62. *How long will ye imagine mischief against a man?* (Psalm 62:3). This time, the question appears to be leveled at those who plot acts of terror. Psalm 62 compares with Arab attacks in the early 1960's which led to the formation of the PLO in 1964. Their mischief-making has become a thorn in the side of Israel. The "Jeduthun," an instrument upon which Psalm 62 was played, suggested a chant of the victim of persecution and oppression. So it was in 1962 with innocent civilians becoming the target of terrorism.[3]

The next *How long?* is recorded in Psalm 74. It seems to appear as the result of the Yom Kippur War. *We see not our signs: there is no more any prophet: neither is there among us any that knoweth how long. O God, how long shall the adversary reproach?* (Psalm 74:9-10). In these verses the Jewish people seem to despair. We are told in I Corinthians 1:22, ... *the Jews require a sign,* but in Psalm 74 they cannot see those signs. If the psalm marks the events of 1974, then we can understand the mindset of those Jewish leaders who greatly desired a negotiated peace treaty.

From this point in the Psalms the question appears more frequently. In fact, the question is asked in seven passages from Psalms 74 through 94. Only five psalms later: *How long, Lord? wilt thou be angry for ever? shall thy jealousy burn like fire?* (Psalm 79:5). And again in the following psalm: *O Lord God of hosts, how long wilt thou be angry against the prayer of thy people?* (Psalm 80:4). May we be reminded that in 1979 and 1980, Prime Minister Begin and President Sadat were trying to thrash out a peace treaty. Things weren't going well. It looked hopeless for awhile, until President Jimmy Carter broke the deadlock.

In 1982, Israel grew tired of PLO attacks and launched an offensive called "Peace for Galilee." Could that be why the question appears again in Psalm 82? *How long will ye judge unjustly, and accept the persons of the wicked?* (Psalm 82:2).

Psalms 88 through 94 describe seven dreadful years wherein the wrath of God will be poured out upon an unbelieving world. Why the question appears again in Psalm 89 may be understood in light of *Jacob's trouble.* It is a descriptive phrase indicative of heart ache and trouble — the kind which will come in the day of God's wrath, *How long, Lord? Wilt thou hide thyself for ever? shall thy wrath burn like fire? Remember how short my time is* ... (Psalm 89:46-47).

Next, the question arises in Psalm 90. But this time, it is posed by Moses, *So teach us to number our days, that we may apply our hearts unto wisdom. Return, O Lord, how long?* (Psalm 90:12-13). At this point in the prophecy, it seems, the Jewish people are digging into the Word. They are desperately trying to number their days, and from all indications their question is about to be answered.

The question reaches a climax in Psalm 94. The psalmist wrote: *Lord, how long shall the wicked, how long shall the wicked triumph? How long shall they utter and speak hard things? and all the workers of iniquity boast themselves? They break in pieces thy people, O Lord, and afflict thine heritage. They slay the widow and the stranger, and murder the fatherless* (Psalm 94:3-6).

The question appears for the last time in Psalm 94 — for a wonderful reason. The query is answered with the appearing of the great King to declare the *day of vengeance of our God.* How long? No longer! The glorious appearing of Messiah is the theme which opens Psalm 94, *O God, to whom vengeance belongeth* ... *show thyself* (v. 1).

How long? It was asked first by the Lord, then was taken up by God's Chosen People and repeated over and over until the question was brought to a glorious conclusion in Psalm 94. It never appears again in the Psalms. If the question is to be asked at all, it is at least the prerogative of the Jews. They are the Chosen People. Though they have suffered as no other people, they have not been forever forsaken. The promise of deliverance will come. Messiah will appear to establish a millennium of peace. God will keep His promise.

MYSTERY OF THE NUMBERS REVEALED!

I asked a Jewish friend one day to decipher the Hebrew number for 88. I was curious about Psalm 88 and the possibility of a mystical significance of the number. Hebrew numbers are taken from their alphabet. Our numbers have no relationship with the letters of the English alphabet, but in many of the more ancient alphabets, numbers are derived from their letters.

For example, Roman numerals correspond to certain letters in Latin. "I" becomes one, "V" becomes five, "X" becomes ten, "L" becomes fifty, "C" becomes one hundred, etc. In a similar fashion, Hebrew numbers are taken from their alphabet. The first ten letters become 1 through 10. The eleventh letter becomes 20, the twelfth becomes 30, etc.

As you may recall, in the Roman alphabet, a bar placed at the top and bottom of a Latin letter makes that letter a number. If the letter "V" has a bar across the top and bottom of it, it becomes the number five. In a similar fashion, the Hebrew numbering system also has a special method by which letters are made to represent numbers.

Sometimes the symbol has the appearance of an apostrophe and at other times quotation marks. Often both are used. These marks are called in the Hebrew language "avi-ka-dabar," meaning "as my father would have said it." Perhaps you do not recognize the term "avi-ka-dabar," but are familiar with its more modern pronunciation — abra-ca-dabra.

So I asked my friend to remove the "abracadabra" from Psalm 88 and tell me what that Hebrew number 88 would be if it were a word instead. He reached into his desk, pulled out his Hebrew copy of the Psalms (Tehillim), and turned to Psalm 88.

After a moment, he looked at me and said, "It is the word "pach."

I asked him, "What does it mean?"

He replied, "It is, how you say, a trap — like a pit. It is like a man who dug a pit for a trap and then fell in it."

The meaning is obvious. The Jewish people will one day enter upon a seven-year period of unparalleled trouble. There has never been anything like it before in history. The life of the Israeli nation will draw near to the grave.

This antichrist will lay a trap through which he will plot the genocide of the Jews and the enslavement of the rest of the world. In a manner similar to that of Adolf Hitler, he will deceive the whole world.

I asked my friend, "What Hebrew word is used in Psalm 91:3 which is translated 'snare' of the fowler?" He turned to it in his Hebrew Scriptures, then looked up excitedly and said, "It is pach! It is the same word!"

Not only was he excited, I was elated! It is a theme which appears to be laid in Psalm 88 and sprung in Psalm 91. But that's not the end of it, for you see, the one who laid the trap will fall into his own trap, and that is found in Psalm 94, the last of these seven psalms, the theme of which is built around the "pach" — the trap, the snare, the pit. Psalm 94 describes the Battle of Armageddon on the day of God's vengeance.

After a study of the number 88 (See Psalm 88), another friend pointed out the Hebrew definition of the number 87. The two Hebrew letters "peh" and "zayin," which make up the number 87, also happen to make up the Hebrew word "pahz" meaning "refined gold." The ordinary Hebrew word for gold is "zahab." But, according to the Gesenius Hebrew-Chaldee Lexicon to the Old Testament, "pahz" comes from a root word "pahzaz" meaning, "to separate, to distinguish ... specifically, to separate and purify metals from dross, by means of fire." The word also means "to leap, to bound, or to flee as a gazelle.[1]

This ancient rendering, however, seems to have almost fallen into disuse among the Hebrews. These meanings are all important when considering the future Jewish remnant (144,000) who will be separated and sealed in their foreheads, as opposed to the "mark of the beast" in the foreheads of wicked men (representing the ordinary gold of Mystery Babylon). The Jewish remnant will be tried in the fires of the Tribulation Period. When they restore Temple worship, they will "leap for joy," but when the "abomination of desolation" occurs, they will "flee as a gazelle."

By the way, the melting point of gold is 1948 degrees Fahrenheit!

A study of the two numbers (87 and 88) set my mind to thinking. What about the numbers 90 through 106? How many of them are made up of words in the Hebrew language? Do they tell the story of the Tribulation Period and the Second Coming of Christ?

Are you ready for this? They do! Out of 17 chapters in the NUMBERS division of the Psalms, there are 12 numbers which make up words in the Hebrew Lexicon. Six of them describe Armageddon and the glory of Christ's return, followed by another six which portray God's vengeance upon the wicked! No wonder this section of the Psalms is called NUMBERS! And no wonder Moses wrote in Psalm 90:12, *So teach us to NUMBER our days, that we may apply our hearts unto wisdom.*

Be sure to read the INTRODUCTION TO THE NUMBERS PSALMS which preceeds our commentary on Psalm 90. Also note the meanings of various numbers throughout the book. You will be fascinated by the prophetic story they have to tell!

DIVIDING THE DISPENSATION

On the evening of His resurrection, Jesus emphasized the prophetic importance of the Psalms. Having startled the disciples, He said, ... *all things must be fulfilled, which were written in the law of Moses, and in the prophets, and in the PSALMS, concerning me* (Luke 24:44). According to the resurrected Christ, there are prophecies in the Psalms!

As I studied that verse, I realized that it contains a description of that which would begin the era, and of that which would end this dispensation. Jesus said there are prophecies which must be fulfilled in *the Law of Moses and in the Prophets*. That part of the statement was fulfilled in the first century. But then Jesus said there are prophecies in the Psalms; and as I study the New Testament, I find very few references to the Psalms.

Jesus revealed what He meant to the disciples, but His explanation is not recorded for us. *Then opened he their understanding that they might understand the scriptures* (Luke 24:45). We can only look into the events in the years following for an understanding of His statement. There are prophecies in the Law, prophecies in the Prophets, and prophecies in the PSALMS which must be fulfilled.

For example, in his epistle to the Romans, the Apostle Paul wrote concerning the Law and the Prophets: *But now the righteousness of God without the law is manifested, being witnessed by the law and the prophets* (Romans 3:21). He did not say that the righteousness of God is witnessed by the Psalms. He spoke only of the Law and the Prophets. His first century letter fulfilled only the first half of our Savior's prophecy that night in the Upper Room. Perhaps the Psalms were put on the shelf in God's closet of secret things until the far future — to the days of that last generation which would see the Second Coming of Jesus Christ.

When Paul arrived at Rome a few years later, he met with the elders of the synagogue and tried to convince them that Jesus was the Messiah, but only out of the Law and the Prophets: *And when they had appointed him a day, there came many to him into his lodging; to whom he expounded and testified the kingdom of God, persuading them concerning Jesus, both out of the law of Moses, and out of the prophets, from morning till evening* (Acts 28:23). The Apostle Paul reasoned with them out of the LAW and the PROPHETS; but it does not say he reasoned with them out of the Psalms.

From such statements as these, we may consider the possibility that the words of Jesus in the Upper Room on the night of His resurrection were in themselves a prophecy, giving details of those things which would introduce the dispensation — namely the fulfillment of the Law and the Prophets — and concluding with that which would occur at the end of the dispensation — namely the prophecies given in the Psalms.

The Bible often contains broad statements which describe both the beginning and the ending of an era. The finest example and most recognized is the reading of Isaiah by Jesus in the synagogue at Nazareth. It is recorded in Luke 4:16-21. Here is a perfect example of a prophecy describing both the beginning and the ending of this dispensation. Jesus opened the book of Isaiah (61:1-2) and read, *The spirit of the Lord is upon me, because he hath anointed me to preach the gospel to the poor; he hath sent me to heal the broken-hearted, to preach deliverance to the captives, and recovering of sight to the blind, to set at liberty them that are bruised, To preach the acceptable year of the Lord. And he closed the book, and he gave it again to the minister ...* (Luke 4:18-20).

Please note that our Savior did not finish the sentence. He read that part of the prophecy which declared the *acceptable year of the Lord,* but He did not read the rest of the prophecy which concerned the end of the dispensation, namely the *day of vengeance of our God.* Many commentaries have suggested that the verse is a clue to the understanding of prophecy. The *acceptable year of the Lord* opens the dispensation, and the *day of vengeance of our God* will close it. There are at least 2,000 years intervening between the beginning of the *acceptable year of the Lord* and the concluding *day of vengeance of our God.* There are many such verses in the Bible which deal with the beginning and the ending of the era.

Isaiah gave another prophecy in which he described both the first and the second coming of Christ in the same passage: *For unto us a child is born, unto us a son is given: and the government shall be upon his shoulder: and his name shall be called Wonderful, Counselor, The mighty God, The everlasting Father, The Prince of Peace. Of the increase of his government and peace there shall be no end, upon the throne of David, and upon his kingdom, to order it, and to establish it with judgment and with justice from henceforth even for ever. The zeal of the LORD of hosts will perform this* (Isaiah 9:6-7). The prophet described both the first coming of our Savior, as he wrote, *For unto us a child is born ...* and the Second Coming of our Savior, as he continued, *and the government shall be upon his shoulder ...*

Another example occurred on the day of Pentecost, when Peter explained the coming of the Holy Spirit and the appearance of what the Bible described as *cloven tongues like as of fire* that sat upon each of them. Peter explained by quoting the prophet Joel: *But this is that which was spoken by the prophet Joel; And it shall come to pass in the last days, saith God, I will pour out of my Spirit upon all flesh: and your sons and your daughters shall prophesy, and your young men shall see visions, and your old men shall dream dreams: And on my servants and on my handmaidens I will pour out in those days of my Spirit; and they shall prophesy* (Acts 2:16-18).

At this point Peter has described the beginning of the dispensation. But the rest of Joel's prophecy describes those events which shall conclude the dispensation. There is at least two thousand years between the description given of the Spirit being poured out upon all flesh and the following description which will occur yet in the future: *And I will shew wonders in heaven above, and signs in the earth beneath; blood, and fire, and vapour of smoke: The sun shall be turned into darkness, and the moon into blood, before that great and notable day of the Lord come* (Acts 2:19-20).

That part of Joel's prophecy was not fulfilled on the day of Pentecost. The sun did not turn into darkness, nor the moon into blood. Those events will come to pass at the conclusion of this dispensation. Peter, however, did not know that. When he preached on the day of Pentecost, he probably thought the sun was about to go out. He did not know where to conclude the reading. The world is still awaiting the fulfillment of the last part of the prophecy. Yet it is found in the same passage. It is another example of those many prophecies which describe both the beginning and the ending of the era.

In later years Peter wrote of those ancient prophets and how they were unable to discern the time factor separating their prophecies: *Of which salvation the prophets have inquired and searched diligently, who prophesied of the grace that should come unto you: Searching what, or what manner of time the Spirit of Christ which was in them did signify, when it testified beforehand the sufferings of Christ, and the glory that should follow* (I Peter 1:10-11).

The Old Testament prophets could not ascertain the difference between the predictions surrounding the first coming of Christ and the prophecies which should herald His Second Coming. They went back to their own writings and searched in an effort to discover the time difference between the sufferings of Christ, which occurred at His First Advent, and the glory of Christ, which will come at His Second Advent. The sufferings of Christ introduced the era, and the glory of Christ will conclude the era.

In Acts 15 another example is given of those events which would both begin and end the dispensation. A council was held by the church at Jerusalem over the salvation of Gentiles. At the meeting, Peter told about the first Gentile convert, Cornelius, a Roman centurion. This had been frustrating to the Jewish believers, for up until Cornelius all believers were Jews. Cornelius opened a whole new dispensation — that of Gentile Christianity. It was a point of contention among Jewish believers. Thus, the meeting at Jerusalem was convened to discuss the problem.

After Peter told about the first Gentile convert, James declared the conclusion of the matter: *And after they had held their peace, James answered, saying, Men and brethren, hearken unto me: Simeon hath declared how God at the first did visit the Gentiles, to take out of them a people for his name. And to this agree the words of the prophets; as it is written, After this I will return, and will build again the Tabernacle of David, which is fallen down; and I will build again the ruins thereof, and I will set it up: That the residue of men might seek after the Lord, and all the Gentiles, upon whom my name is called, saith the Lord, who doeth all these things* (Acts 15:13-17).

According to this passage, the dispensation of Gentile Christianity began with the conversion of Cornelius, the Roman centurion, and will be concluded one day when the Tabernacle of David is set up on the Temple Site. Here is a prophecy of that for which we can look — to let us know that the *fullness of the Gentiles* has come. I believe it is a prophecy which will see the completion of the Bride of Christ. It is another example of a prophetic passage describing those events which both open and close the era.

Yet another example of this can be seen in the Gospel of Luke when, at the Pid Yon Habin of Jesus (a ceremony for the Redemption of the First-born) Joseph and Mary brought the baby to the Temple to offer turtle doves. An old prophet, Simeon by name, took the infant Christ in his arms and gave this prophecy: *And Simeon blessed them, and said unto Mary his mother, Behold, this child is set for the fall and rising again of many in Israel ...* (Luke 2:34). Here is a prophecy of the fall of Israel, which occurred two thousand years ago. But in the same sentence, Simeon predicted the rising again of the Chosen People. This has been under fulfillment since 1948.

Concerning the fall and rising again of Israel, the Apostle Paul gave another example of a prophecy which describes both the beginning and the ending of the era: *For if the casting away of them* [Israel] *be the reconciling of the world, what shall the receiving of them be, but life from the dead?* (Romans 11:15). In this prophecy, we can see both the fall and the rising again of Israel. We can see the casting away, which resulted in the development of Gentile Christianity, but we are also told that one day Israel will be received again. When this occurs and reconciliation is made, the dispensation of Gentile Christianity will come to a glorious conclusion. This spectacular event is called in this verse, *life from the dead.* We call it rapture and resurrection.

The prophets themselves were confused as to the timing of the resurrection. One such example of this confusion can be found in Daniel: *And many of them that sleep in the dust of the earth shall awake, some to everlasting life, and some to shame and everlasting contempt* (Daniel 12:2). On the surface, it would appear that someday a general resurrection will take place of both the saved and the unsaved. But according to the book of the

Revelation, we know that is not the case. This theme, by the way, was repeated by Christ: *Marvel not at this: for the hour is coming, in the which all that are in the graves shall hear his voice, And shall come forth; they that have done good, unto the resurrection of life; and they that have done evil, unto the resurrection of damnation* (John 5:28,29). Again, we find the verse deals with the beginning and the ending of an era. The resurrection of the saved will occur at the beginning of the millennial reign of Christ, and the resurrection of the lost will take place at the end of the kingdom age.

The explanation of the prophecy is given in Revelation: *And I saw thrones, and they sat upon them, and judgment was given unto them: and I saw the souls of them that were beheaded for the witness of Jesus, and for the word of God, and which had not worshiped the beast, neither his image, neither had received his mark upon their foreheads, or in their hands; and they lived and reigned with Christ a thousand years. But the rest of the dead lived not again until the thousand years were finished. This is the first resurrection. Blessed and holy is he that hath part in the first resurrection: on such the second death hath no power, but they shall be priests of God and of Christ, and shall reign with him a thousand years* (Revelation 20:4-6).

Here is a prediction divided by a thousand years. Daniel's prophecy does not concern a general resurrection, nor does that New Testament passage spoken by Jesus refer to a general resurrection. Those who are saved will be raised at the beginning of the millennial reign of Christ — that they might rule and reign with Him for a thousand years. And those who have rejected Christ down through the centuries will be raised at the end of His glorious millennium to be judged at the Great White Throne Judgment, after which, they will be thrown into the lake of fire.

There are many similar passages in the Bible which deal with the beginning and the ending of an era. Another such verse is found in Peter's second epistle. Peter first wrote that a day is with the Lord as a thousand years, and a thousand years explains the meaning of the term *the day of the Lord.* Two verses later, he explained the events which would introduce the Day of the Lord and the events which would conclude this 1,000-year period. *But the day of the Lord will come as a thief in the night; in the which the heavens shall pass away with a great noise, and the elements shall melt with fervent heat, the earth also and the works that are therein shall be burned up* (II Peter 3:10).

The meaning becomes clear when we understand that Peter is describing a thousand-year period. At the introduction of this millennium, the Lord will *come as a thief* in the night. At the end of the thousand years, after the kingdom has been concluded, the Lord will renovate the universe and produce new heavens and a new earth, at which time the holy city New Jerusalem will descend from God out of heaven.

It is the end of the millennium that Peter has in mind when he says, *The heavens shall pass away with a great noise, and the elements shall melt with fervent heat.* In this verse we can see both the introduction and conclusion of the millennial reign of Christ. If we did not understand that the "day" refers to a thousand years, we could not understand the prophetic division in the verse. It is another example of those many prophecies which describe both the beginning and the ending of an era.

Another example can be found in the New Testament book of Revelation. A description is given of that event which will introduce the seven years of the Tribulation Period. The Savior said, *Behold, I come as a thief. Blessed is he that watcheth, and keepeth his garments, ...* (Revelation 16:15). On the other hand, the next verse records the event which will conclude the seven year Tribulation Period: *And he gathered them together into a place called in the Hebrew tongue, Armageddon* (Revelation 16:16). Here is another example of a passage which includes a description of the beginning and the ending of a predicted time period. I believe the verse implies that the resurrection will introduce the Tribulation Period and the Battle of Armageddon will conclude those seven years.

These are just a few of the many prophetic passages in the Bible which describe both the beginning and the ending of an era. And the one that intrigues me most is that statement made by Jesus the evening He walked through the wall of the Upper Room. This was the first day of His resurrection, and this was the most important thing on His mind as He met with His disciples.

Jesus said in Luke 24:44 ... *all things must be fulfilled, which were written in the law of Moses, and in the prophets, ...* That part of the statement was fulfilled in the first century. But it seems as if the second part of the statement describes the end of the era.

Jesus concluded by saying there are *prophecies in the psalms, concerning me.* It is as if God took the prophecies in the Psalms, put them on the shelf in His closet of secret things and closed the door until the last generation.

Paul reasoned with the Jews out of the Law and the Prophets, and they did not believe. But in the last generation, it seems, God will reason with His Chosen People out of the Psalms. That could well result in the fulfillment of the prophecy *life from the dead.* Many first century references cited only the Law and the Prophets. Therefore, we may consider the possibility that the message given by Jesus in the Upper Room on the night of His resurrection was in itself a prophecy, giving details of those things which would introduce the dispensation — namely the fulfillment of the Law and the Prophets — and concluding with that which would occur at the end of the dispensation — namely the prophecies given in the Psalms.

In A.D. 70, the Temple was destroyed. Sixty-five years later the Jews were scattered to the slave markets of the world. Over the next twenty centuries they were to become *the wandering Jew* — without a nation, without a king, without a Temple, without a priesthood, and without a sacrifice — until the long winter of world history was over and the prophetic fig tree (Matthew 24-32) was replanted on Israeli soil.

These past twenty centuries have witnessed the growth of Gentile Christianity. However, we are living in an age which not only has seen the rebirth of Israel, but could see the return of Christ, as well. The Psalms may have been irrelevant to the Apostle Paul as those ancient songs awaited a future century when their prophetic descriptions would begin to unfold. Have we arrived at that special time in history? Many are convinced we have. I think you will be astounded as you read the unveiling of those incredibly cryptic Psalms.

THE
GENESIS
PSALMS

PSALM 1

Blessed is the man ... (v. 1).

"Man will discover that the Psalms we sing today are a rehearsal for the perfect symphony of tomorrow," wrote Rabbi Avrohom Feuer in his exhaustive commentary on the Tehillim (Psalms).[1] Reflecting on ancient rabbinical thought, he continued, "David observed life from a universal vantage point; never was his scope constricted. In every event he was able to detect the broad spectrum ... which emerged. In his personal misfortunes he saw a reflection of the tragedies plaguing the nation down through the pages of history. In his victories David caught a glimpse of the ultimate triumph and redemption of his people. He had the ability and genius to be stimulated and inspired so profoundly by events that he could soar above the boundaries of time; and sing of past, present, and future in the same breath, with the same words " (Talmud, Pesahim 117a).[2]

To many Gentile Christians, the Psalms appear to be little more than the simple songs of an ancient Jewish culture. To the Jew, however, the Psalms enjoy a very special position. They comprise a major portion of Jewish liturgy. David, to whom many psalms are ascribed, is considered on the same exalted plane with Adam and Messiah. According to the Talmud, the three Hebrew letters of Adam's name represent the initials of three men: Adam, David and Messiah. What Adam began, David continued, and Messiah will complete (Sanhedrin 107a).[3]

"The sweet singer of Israel" began his psalms with Moses' last words, *Blessed is the man!* thus placing the Psalms on the same level with the Torah. Where Moses left off, David began. The scene takes us back in time to the foot of Mount Nebo. It's the last day of Moses' life. He blesses the twelve tribes and, in the words of the King James Bible, concludes with this benediction, *Happy* [blessed] *art thou, O Israel: who is like unto thee, O people saved by the Lord, ...* (Deuteronomy 33:29).

When David took up that Mosaic term *Blessed* [happy] *is the man,* his thoughts and prophecies were directed toward the house of Israel. Israel is the man! Psalm 1, therefore, introduces the prophetic story of the nation, not merely that of an individual. Israel, the nation, is the subject of the Psalms. If they tell the story of anyone, it is not the British, the French, the Italians nor the Chinese; it is the story of the Jews. Psalm 1 appears to describe the mind-set of world Jewry in 1901.

"It was ... at the fourth conference of the Bund (the Jewish Socialist Union) in Russia in 1901, that it was decided for the first time that the term NATION be ... applied to the Jewish people."[4] It has to be more than a coincidence that 1901 marked the year when, after nearly twenty centuries of dispersion, the Jews desired to resurrect the spirit of nationalism. No longer were they content as a fragmented entity, it was time to revive the man!

Under the inspiration of the Holy Spirit, David enlarged upon the subject when he wrote about the birth of the baby (Israel), "All the days ordained for me were written IN YOUR BOOK before one of them came to be" (Psalm 139:16 NIV). This rendering of the psalm in the New International Version (NIV) appears to be an accurate description of the prophetic purpose of the Psalms. Here is a verse which prophetically symbolizes Israel, declaring that "all the days" were written in the book! The Jerusalem Bible is equally astounding: "You had scrutinized my every action, all were recorded in your book, my days listed and determined, even before the first of them occurred."

In the King James translation, the words *my members* are in italics which means they were not part of the original Hebrew Scriptures. They were added by the translators. Other versions treat the phrase as "my days." Therefore the verse could read, ... *in thy book all* [my days] *were written, which in continuance* [chronological order] *were fashioned when as yet there was none of them* (Psalm 139:16 KJV). Those events in the development of Israel appear to be listed *in continuance* or chronological order, suggesting Psalm 1 for 1901, Psalm 2 for 1902, etc.

The symbol of the baby is used of Israel many times in the Bible. God instructed Moses, ... *thou shalt say unto Pharaoh, Thus saith the LORD, Israel is my son, even my firstborn* (Exodus 4:22). The symbol was used by Isaiah, Jeremiah, Micah, John,

Paul, and Jesus. Also, down through the centuries, rabbis and Christian scholars have considered the symbolic baby as a picture of the rebirth of Israel. The commemorative coin for 1948 struck by the Israeli government (see picture) shows a woman, Rachel, with a new baby boy — Israel! No wonder David, archetype of Israel, declared: *I will praise thee; for I am fearfully and wonderfully made.*

> *And he shall be like a tree planted* [replanted] *by the rivers of water, that bringeth forth his fruit in his season; his leaf also shall not wither; and whatsoever he doeth shall prosper* (v. 3).

Not only does the commemorative coin show Rachel with her new baby boy, it also depicts a man planting a tree as well. Both symbols are used in the Scriptures to portray the return of the Jews to their land in the last generation. Ezekiel prophesied ... *O mountains of Israel, ye shall shoot forth your branches,* ... (Ezekiel 36:8). Like a symphonic crescendo of expectation the question builds — could the tree on that coin be the famous fig tree predicted to come to life again?

Early Monday morning as rays of the rising sun danced along the limestone walls of Old Jerusalem, Jesus and His disciples started up to the Temple from the Mount of Olives. Before them lay Jerusalem the golden! The magnificent Temple radiated the glory of a thousand prisms. Yesterday, He had received the accolades of the triumphal entry.

It was about breakfast time. Mark records the incident: *And on the morrow, when they were come from Bethany, he was hungry:*

And seeing a fig tree afar off having leaves, he came, if haply he might find any thing thereon: and when he came to it, he found nothing but leaves; for the time of figs was not yet. And Jesus ... said unto it, No man eat fruit of thee hereafter for ever. And his disciples heard it (Mark 11:12-14).

The next day: *And in the morning, as they passed by, they saw the fig tree dried up from the roots. And Peter calling to remembrance saith unto him, Master, behold, the fig tree which thou cursedst is withered away. And Jesus answering saith unto them, Have faith in God* (Mark 11:20-22).

Later that evening when they returned to the Mount of Olives, the disciples asked Jesus about setting up the kingdom. *Tell us, when shall these things be? and what shall be the sign of thy coming, and of the end of the world?* (Matthew 24:3). In reply, Jesus told of several signs which would attend the end of the dispensation.

The highlight of the discourse came when He reminded them of the fig tree, symbolic of the nation of Israel. He indicated that one day the prophetic fig tree would come to life again. *Now learn a parable of the fig tree; When his branch is yet tender, and putteth forth leaves, ye know that summer is nigh: So likewise ye, when ye shall see all these things, know that it is near, even at the doors. Verily I say unto you, This generation shall not pass, till all these things be fulfilled* (Matt. 24:32-34).

As the fig tree is symbolic of Israel, we must observe that the nation died in the years following the crucifixion. It seems as though a special judicial curse was placed upon God's Chosen People. The Romans scattered them among the gentile nations where they have wandered for almost two thousand years. The faltering fig was to lie dormant through the long winter of world history. One day, however, that tree was destined to be "replanted" on sacred soil! The wintertime of history would someday be turned into the spring and summer of the kingdom age.

Most significant is the term "replanted" as literally translated from the original Hebrew language. The tree in this psalm flourishes only as it is replanted by streams of water. From the time of its replanting that tree is destined to yield its fruit in due season and has the promise that its leaves will never wither.

For twenty centuries, the Jewish people have not been allowed to forget their national tragedy. At every Jewish wedding the groom breaks a glass beneath his foot as a reminder of the destruction of the Temple. Not for one day is he allowed to forget. He must pray three times each day while facing Jerusalem.

Every year on the 9th of Av (late July or early August) a Jew must observe the anniversary of the Temple's burning by sitting on the floor or on an overturned bench, with his shoes off, as one would mourn the death of a son, while reciting the Psalm of Lamentation. This same psalm (Psalm 137), *By the rivers of Babylon,* ... is used in the blessing asked three times daily after meals.

Before putting on any new clothes, the Jew will soil them slightly as a symbol of his never-ending national grief. When remodeling a house, at least one brick is left unpainted for the same reason. "In the shtetls [ghettos] of Eastern Europe it was customary to put a bag of earth from the Holy Land under the head of the corpse, so that he might rest on sacred soil."[5]

Through the centuries the suffering Jew would look beyond the walls of his ghetto and see the walls of Jerusalem. Twice, each year the benediction was repeated, "Next year in Jerusalem." But in all those long centuries, no one succeeded in bringing the dream into reality — until August 11, 1882. On that day, a group of young Russian Jews left Kharkov to make "aliyah" (going up) to the Promised Land. "They went there not to die, but to live ... determined to transform into reality a dream that ... until then had lived only in symbols: broken glasses, unpainted bricks, and the forever repeated abstract wish of 'Next year in Jerusalem' ... The fourteen young Jews ... didn't simply go to Palestine ... they returned to Zion."[6]

The most important prophetic sign to mark that predicted generation was to be the revival of Israel, symbolized by the birth of the baby and the replanting of the tree. That incredible event has occurred! It seems that Psalm 1 refers to the beginning of this century. Furthermore, the entire psalm appears to be a prophetic promise to the future Chosen People which would be endowed with new national life — *BLESSED IS THE MAN!*

One cannot be so bold as to try to decide who among the Jewish people *delight ... in the law of the Lord* (v. 2) and who among them are *like the chaff which the wind driveth away* (v. 4). Many have suffered in this century. Perhaps not all of the righteous have prospered nor have all of the ungodly perished; but the Lord is the righteous judge, and the story is not over.

PSALM 2

Why do the heathen rage, and the people imagine a vain thing? (v. 1).

"The first and second psalms constitute an introduction to the Psalter, announcing a theme which is one of the main motifs that run through this book of the Bible."[1] "The sages taught that this chapter describes Messianic times ... In reality, the two proposed settings past and future, present no contradiction ... David detected the seeds of Gog and Magog."[2]

Furthermore, "... the Sages (Berachos 10a) consider the first two psalms as one. Though technically and physically separated, they complement each other spiritually and thematically (Meiri)."[3] Perhaps for this reason, we find some twentieth century events implied in psalms numbered with one year variance. For example, the military aspects of the 1967 war seem to be continued in Psalm 68, etc.

Those rabbinical concepts form our introduction of Psalm 2, which in turn describes a political insanity among the gentile nations of the world — evident in 1902, and building into one war after another, getting worse with the passing of the years.

The kings of the earth set themselves, and the rulers take counsel together, against the Lord, and against his anointed saying,
Let us break their bands asunder, and cast away their cords from us.
He that sitteth in the heavens shall laugh: the Lord shall have them in derision (vv. 2-4).

A world-wide political unrest after the turn of the century created a climate for the coming global conflict. *Why do the heathen rage?* asked the psalmist. *For nation shall rise against nation, and kingdom against kingdom ... wars and rumors of wars*, said the Savior (Matthew 24:7). *The Lord shall have them in derision,* said the psalmist (v. 4), for there shall be ... *upon the earth distress of nations, with perplexity ...* said the Savior (Luke 21:25).

The Talmud (Avodah Zara 3b) emphasizes that this is no ordinary mockery but rather it is the last laugh. Nowhere does Scripture record God laughing except on this day.

By 1902, conspiracy for world government was already underway. With the French Revolution just over a century before, a climate of political unrest descended upon Europe's monarchies. A so-called "age of enlightenment" emerged to topple thrones.

In his book JEWS, GOD AND HISTORY, Max Dimont wrote, "Napoleon's military defeat came with Waterloo, his political end with the Congress of Vienna (1815), where ... the reactionary rulers of Europe ... arrived with ... a firm resolve to set the clock back. They signed ... the Holy Alliance ... swore they would come to the aid of each other in case any ... tried to overthrow any monarchies. The result was a series of revolutions ... fanning the outbreaks of 1820, 1830, and 1848. Jews fought side by side with the Christians ... as Frenchmen, Italians, Germans, Austrians, Englishmen, all infected with the same slogans of nationalism. While men waved their respective flags, talked of the brotherhood of man, and shot each other ... the world, without knowing it, was rushing headlong into World War I."[4]

It was suspected that this same movement which plotted the downfall of European monarchies planned to establish a one-world monetary system. They hoped to eventually gain control of all governments, enthrone their own ruler, and thus deprive the Lord's *anointed.*

> *Then shall he speak unto them in his wrath, and vex them in his sore displeasure.*
>
> *Yet have I set my king upon my holy hill of Zion. I will declare the decree: the LORD hath said unto me, Thou art my Son; this day have I begotten thee.*
>
> *Ask of me, and I shall give thee the heathen for thine inheritance, and the uttermost parts of the earth for thy possession.*
>
> *Thou shalt break them with a rod of iron; thou shalt dash them in piece like a potter's vessel* (vv. 5-9).

God is determined to set His King upon His holy hill of Zion. Messiah will establish a world-wide kingdom, be given the nations for His inheritance and the uttermost parts of the earth for His possession. He will come at the end of a series of great wars to *break them with a rod of iron* and *dash them in pieces like a potter's vessel* (v. 9).

The second psalm aptly describes a political climate at the turn of the century which has progressively developed through two devastating world wars, a series of Koreas and Vietnams, and today's mad race toward nuclear superiority. The world is rushing headlong toward another series of wars — the prophetic battle of Gog and Magog and the awesome Armageddon!

PSALM 3

Lord, how are they increased that trouble me! Many are they that rise up against me (v. 1).

Psalms 3 and 4 were composed as David fled from Absalom. At this stage in the elderly David's life most of his songs had been written. Why then were these two placed out of sequence at the beginning of the Psalms? Talmudic scholars give the following solution:

"It is written: A Psalm of David when he fled from Absalom his son. And, ... of David when he fled from Saul in the cave. Which event happened first? Did not the event of Saul happen first? Then let him write it first? ... For you who do not derive interpretations from juxtaposition, there is a difficulty, but for us who do derive interpretations from juxtaposition there is no difficulty ... Why is the chapter of Absalom juxtaposed to the chapter of Gog and Magog? So ... you can reply ... Is it possible that a son should rebel against his father? Yet this happened; and so this too [will happen]."[1]

Just as such a shocking rebellion did indeed come to pass when Absalom overthrew David, so too will the uprising of Gog and Magog come about in the future! If a wayward son could rebel, certainly the world could produce an antichrist who will attempt to usurp God's throne.

Why was Psalm 3 not Psalm 103? Was it placed in the Psalms at this point because of its relationship to 1903? Does it not fit the scenario of world events as the century progressed? One rabbi, frustrated over chapters not appearing in their proper order, especially in the Torah, suggested that the order of the Torah was deliberately recorded without proper sequence. Otherwise, whoever read them would be able to raise the dead and perform miracles.[2] Though his assessment of the Torah may be farfetched, it is not impossible that God could prepare the order of His Holy Word to contain a message as profound as its contents. Were indeed the Psalms deliberately compiled in their order to await a special generation?

Psalm 3 compares with the suffering of Russian Jews around the turn of the century. For the previous several decades they had endured dreadful "pogroms," or massacres, unleashed against their villages. Five Romanov czars ruled Russia in the nineteenth century, each progressively worse in their treatment of the Jews. Many were deprived of their professions and driven from the cities. A special military conscription policy made Jewish children between twelve and eighteen years of age eligible for twenty-five years of military service. Once a Jewish youth was drafted his parents never saw him again.[3]

Under Czar Alexander III, the "pogroms" were instituted. His formula for solving the "Jewish problem" called for one-third conversion, one-third emigration, and one-third starvation. Twenty thousand Jews were expelled from Moscow. Jews emigrated by the hundreds of thousands to the United States. But the millions for whom there was no escape lived in fear and poverty. Nicholas II, the last of the Russian autocrats, also met the demands of his people for bread with bullets. In despair, some Russian Jews joined revolutionary movements, including Communism.

In 1903 a Russian Orthodox monk, Sergei Nilus, presented the highly controversial PROTOCOLS OF THE LEARNED ELDERS OF ZION to the czar — a document that supposedly revealed an international Jewish conspiracy. But if Nilus expected the czar's gratitude for his disclosure, he must have been grievously disappointed. The czar declared the document to be an outrageous fabrication and ordered all copies of it destroyed. Nilus was banished from the court in disgrace. Unfortunately, a copy of the document survived.

That year it was serialized in a newspaper but failed to

generate much interest. Published again in 1905, it began to attract attention and for a great many anti-Semites at the time it was convincing proof that the Jews planned to dominate the world. In 1919, the PROTOCOLS were distributed to troops of the White Russian army which, over the next two years, massacred some sixty thousand Jews who were blamed for the 1917 Revolution.[4] In 1919 the PROTOCOLS were also being circulated by Alfred Rosenberg, chief propagandist for the German National Socialist (Nazi) Party. In MEIN KAMPF, Hitler used the PROTOCOLS to fuel his own fanatical prejudice.

> *Many there be which say of my soul, There is no help for him in God* (v. 2).

The 1903 publication of the PROTOCOLS fueled a Jewish persecution which continued to increase throughout eastern Europe until it climaxed in the holocaust of Hitler. Psalm 3:2 corresponds with the mind-set of beleaguered Jews.

> *Arise, O Lord; save me, O my God: ...* (v. 7).

One can understand the despair of the Jews after nearly two thousand years of persecution. They had suffered the destruction of their land at the hands of imperial Rome and had faced the cruelties of the Holy Roman Empire. They had been expelled at one time or another from most of the countries of Europe, had suffered under the Crusades and the Inquisition, and now endured the humiliation of czarist Russia. No wonder they cried unto the Lord, *how are they increased that trouble me!* (v. 1). And no wonder some felt there was no hope in God. One can imagine that in 1903 many of the Russian Jews were crying: *Arise, O Lord; save me, O my God: ...* (v. 7).

PSALM 4

Hear me when I call, O God of my righteousness; thou hast enlarged me when I was in distress; have mercy upon me, and hear my prayer (v. 1).

In Psalm 4, David spoke to the masses which followed Absalom urging them to repent. With clarity of vision, David recognized that his wayward son was not the real culprit. Absalom was but a pawn in the hand of Ahithophel, his prominent political advisor. The young upstart was led to believe that he could succeed in taking the kingdom from God's anointed. Ahithophel urged Absalom to publically violate his father's harem. Afterward, say the sages, he intended to bring the rebel to court for his atrocities. Then he would be free to take the vacant throne. Behind the scenes, Ahithophel was the true spoiler, lying and manipulating — typical of the antichrist.

O ye sons of men, how long will ye turn my glory into shame? (v. 2).

Ahithophel's twentieth century counterpart has probably been working behind the scenes, in the safety of anonymity, trying to plot the course of an emerging Jewish nationalism while planning world domination under his own scepter. It would not at all be surprising if he were the perpetrator of the PROTOCOLS. Scriptures indicate that in the end the antichrist plans to destroy the Chosen People and enslave the world.

The year 1904 saw a number of significant occurrences which seem to be reflected in the prophetic aspects of Psalm 4. The leadership of the World Zionist Movement and other Jewish organizations were split within the rank and file as to precisely which major direction to lead the Chosen People. Several options seemed to be open. They could continue to strive for assimilation within the nations where they were scattered. To do this, they would have to shed the stigma of being a "peculiar people" in an effort to become "like the nations."

On the other hand, Theodore Herzl presented an option to establish a Jewish homeland in East Africa. Meanwhile, Baron

Hirsch, another Zionist, offered support for Jewish colonies to settle in Argentina and elsewhere. Y. L. Pinkster, an influential Zionist leader, seemed to support these notions. "It is not a holy land we need," he said, "but our own land."[1]

> But know that the LORD hath set apart him that is godly for himself: the LORD will hear when I call unto him (v. 3).

Hertzl had submitted the "Uganda Proposal" for consideration. The British government had offered the east African country of Uganda as a homeland for world Jewry. "Herzl's strategy nearly ripped the Zionist Movement asunder," wrote Michael Cohen. "His own movement rebuffed him, telling him that there was but one place where a Jewish state could be built, and that was in the Land of Israel."[2] Had they accepted Uganda as the new Jewish homeland, Entebbe would have been their Jerusalem!

The Uganda Proposal must have taxed the patience of God. *O ye sons of men, how long will ye turn my glory into shame?* (v. 2). Theodore Herzl died that year. He was only forty-four years old. When the World Zionist Congress met, the offer was declined. Is it possible that God was angry with the leadership of the Zionist movement? It is not out of character for the Lord to remove even a Moses when necessary.

Ultimately the World Zionist Organization chose to work toward a Jewish homeland in Palestine. Shortly, the "Second Aliyah" was underway which sent thousands of day laborers to the Holy Land. ("Aliyah" is a term meaning to come up. It is more than merely settling the land. Those who participate actually dedicate the remainder of their lives to bringing about the completed state of modern Israel.) In the years following 1905, newcomers built roads, drained swamps, and began preparing the land for subsequent "aliyahs." Twelve years later the British Balfour Declaration formally recognized Palestine as a "National Home for the Jewish People."[3]

Could the reference, ... *thou hast enlarged me when I was in distress;* ... (v. 1) be a veiled reference to the Zionist decision in 1904 to settle Israel as the official Jewish homeland? Could the declaration, *the Lord has set apart him who is godly for himself:* (v. 3) refer to the Jewish decision of 1905 to resist assimilation into the nations? Could the statement, *There be many that say, Who will shew us any good? ...* (v. 6) be a foreshadow of the "pogroms" of 1903-06?

The First World Zionist Congress met in Switzerland in 1897. Policies were set in motion which would bring about the establishment of a Jewish homeland in Israel a half-century later. Thus were fulfilled the dreams of those sages who saw a predicted Messianic era in David's Psalms. Later Theodore Herzl wrote, "In Basle, I created the Jewish State."

PSALM 5

To the chief Musician upon Nehiloth, A Psalm of David.
Thou shalt destroy them that speak leasing: the LORD will
abhor the bloody and deceitful man (introduction, v. 6).

Psalm 5 concludes a trilogy of songs written by David during Absalom's rebellion. In the first of the three he is stung by humiliation as he flees before a rebellious mob led by his own son. *Many ... say ... There is no help for him in God* (Psalm 3:2). In Psalm 4 David sees through the plot of his enemies and lectures the masses for having blindly followed Absalom. He cries, *O ye sons of men how long will ye turn my glory into shame?* (Psalm 4:2). Finally, he turns his attention to Ahithophel, the one who manipulated the revolt, saying, *... the Lord will abhor the bloody and deceitful man* (v. 6). The wicked advisor to Absalom is comparable to the antichrist whose actions are predicted for the last days.

One cannot presume to know the identity of that future antichrist, but in 1905, his dynasty must have been busy planning for world government while plotting to take over the world's economies. There may be a clue in Psalm 5, however, to link the antichrist with the ancient lost tribe of Dan.

David directed the conductor to accompany this psalm on "Nehiloth." The instrument was to be played in such a way as to sound like a swarm of bees. The song was dedicated to the "time of attack and the droning, buzzing sound captured the mood of the enemy hordes who swarmed around Israel like angry buzzing bees."[1] This sound of bees may be a reminder of Samson's riddle

(Judges 14:12-18). The riddle could have a prophetic meaning.
Since the killer of the lion was Samson, a member of the tribe of
Dan, the bees could be a symbol of Danites making honey in the
carcass of the lion of the tribe of Judah. The Danites were suggested by the sages as the tribe which would one day give birth to
the antichrist. The dying Jacob prophesied that Dan would *judge
his people* (Genesis 49:16).

Psalm 118 also makes mention of the bees. *All nations compassed me about ... like bees; they are quenched as the fire of thorns
...* (vv. 10,12). Midrash Shocher Tov refers to the bees as the time
when God "will gather all the nations of the world and bring them
to ascend against Jerusalem."[2] This symbolism is most appropriate. When the bee gathers honey, it thinks that it is collec-
ting the sweet nectar for its own use, not realizing that the beehive
is under the control and supervision of a beekeeper. Similarly, the
nations will gather around Jerusalem under the impression that
they are fighting for their own gain. In truth, they are mere pawns
manipulated by God to fulfill His design for the world.

The symbol of the bees is used today in mystery religions and
secret societies. In the fifth century, the Merovingian thrones of
Europe used the symbol. When the tomb of Childeric, son of a
Frankish king named Merovee, was excavated in 1653, some
three hundred miniature gold replicas of bees were found. They
were turned over to the Hapsburg dynasty, which provided the
emperors of the Holy Roman Empire for almost five hundred
years. Napoleon abolished the throne in 1806, but married the
Merovingian daughter of the Hapsburg ruler. When Napoleon was
crowned as Emperor of France, he wore those three hundred bees
sewn onto his coronation robe![3]

Could the lost tribe of Dan still be around, working behind the
scenes and pretending to encourage the repatriation of Israel on
one hand while on the other hand planning to declare one of their
own the future messiah?

Ahithophel did not imitate foreign ways as did the majority of
those who followed Absalom, but "took the most authentic of
Jewish concepts, the Holy Torah itself, and grotesquely distorted
it to serve his own ends."[4] Perhaps a dynasty of Danites is
likewise preparing the world for their future king.

Jacob further predicted that Dan, as a snake, would bite the
horse's heel causing the rider to fall backward. This seeming rid-

dle may be explained in light of a fast-developing movement to combine all of the world's currencies producing a global monetary system of exchange. An international banking cartel has effectively employed interest rates to take control of nations. The term "usury" comes from the Hebrew "nashak" which means "the bite of the serpent." Perhaps Jacob's prophecy and Samson's riddle of Dan's future plans present the underlying theme of David's psalm.

The bees may also compare with the hordes of Russians who massacred whole Jewish communities in 1905, in what was described as Russia's worst "pogrom." There were over 660 attacks, the worst being in November of that year. They were perpetrated by more than just soldiers. The masses of Russian peasants were led to believe the Jews were wicked and deserving of death.

PSALM 6

To the chief Musician on Neginoth upon Sheminith, A Psalm of David.
Have mercy upon me, O LORD; for I am weak: O LORD, heal me; for my bones are vexed (introduction, v. 2).

David was gravely ill when he wrote this psalm. He had been bedridden for an extended length of time. Some have suggested that he was vexed with a malady in order to put him in a more spiritual frame of mind. He instructed the chief musician to accompany the psalm with an eight-stringed Sheminith — the number eight heralding the future Messianic age when all illnesses will be healed. "Messiah," wrote one rabbi, "will loosen the bonds which shackle us to this world."[1]

The psalm is regarded as one looking forward to the generation which will introduce the kingdom age. The theme transcends David's personal illness to compare with the condition of national Israel — weak with hurting so as to create a yearning for spiritual renewal. The psalm has been incorporated into the daily prayer ritual of religious Jews.

Jewish suffering in 1906 corresponds with the theme of Psalm 6. World Jewry was being spiritually prepared for a revival of their nation and a longing for the Messianic kingdom. Apart from the lamentation, *how long?* in verse 3, one can feel the agony of their suffering.

> *I am weary with my groaning; all the night make I my bed to swim; I water my couch with my tears.*
> *Mine eye is consumed because of grief; it waxeth old because of all mine enemies* (vv. 6-7).

"Jewish history, beyond all histories," wrote the eminent philosopher Alfred North Whitehead, "is composed of tragedies." The year 1906 certainly was no exception. That was the bloodiest year for Russian "pogroms" against the Jews in Slavic history to that date. Thousands of Jewish families tried to relocate in the United States or elsewhere. The governments of Russia, Germany, and other bordering countries made life untenable for God's Chosen People. If any good came out of this barbaric cruelty it was the "Second Aliyah," in which thousands of Jews relocated in Palestine and set about reclaiming and preparing the land for future generations.

Among those arriving in Palestine on September 7, 1906, was a young man whose life would be forever interwoven in the historical fabric of modern Israel. "Silently," David (Green aka) Ben-Gurion would write later, "I gazed at Jaffa, my heart beat wildly ... I had arrived ..."[2] It was to be forty-two years before the providence of God would select him to be the first Prime Minister of Israel.

PSALM 7

> *Shiggaion of David, which he sang unto the LORD, concerning the words of Cush the Benjamite.*
> *... save me from all them that persecute me, and deliver me:* (introduction, v. 1).

Many think this psalm was written about King Saul. Cush, the Benjamite, could be translated "the black man of the tribe of Benjamin." Was David referring to the king? Though David suffered because of him, he refused to take action against the backslidden ruler, for *he was the Lord's anointed.*

In spite of David's loyalty, Saul hounded him relentlessly. Upon Saul's death, however, David composed Psalm 18 as a song of gladness for his personal deliverance. In this psalm, written later, it is thought David felt that he was wrong by not being totally grieved over the death of one so great as the king. Rashi defined "Shigayon" as "an error" of David (Moed Kattan 16b).[1]

Could this psalm prophetically portray a twentieth century monarch who hounded the Jews in 1907? Could Psalm 18 also be a song of rejoicing over the death of that ruler? The Russian czar certainly compares with the scenario. Jewish complicity in the Bolshevik Revolution also can be described as an error (Shigayon) on the part of Jews. Because of czarist persecution during the late 1800's and early 1900's, many Jews joined organizations against czarist rule.

At the same time, other Jewish eyes were longingly cast toward Palestine. A few thousand Jews were able to emigrate to the homeland. Ironically, many of those who stayed in Russia began to work toward a Jewish nationalism through the Jewish Labor Bund which proposed a program for Jewish cultural and national autonomy.[2]

> God judgeth the righteous, and God is angry with the wicked every day.
> If he turn not, he will whet his sword; he hath bent his bow, and made it ready.
> He hath also prepared for him the instruments of death; he ordaineth his arrows against the persecutors (vv. 11-13).

In this psalm, the beleaguered Jewish soul is assured of God's judgment upon the persecutors. Some of those who plotted against the czar in 1907 were Jews. The Bolsheviks desired to overthrow the czar and set up a republic fashioned after the government of the United States. However, the Bolsheviks were betrayed by the very men who pretended to befriend them. Many of Russia's Jews were duped into thinking Communism was the only alternative to oppressive government. Zionism and Communism eventually were to be set on a collision course — indeed an error (Shigayon) of monumental proportions.

> He made a pit, and digged it, and is fallen into the ditch which he made.
> His mischief shall return upon his own head, and his violent

dealing shall come down upon his own pate (vv. 15-16).

Unfortunately, those Jews who joined the Communist movement to fight the czar also fell into a pit of their own making. Those who helped to create the Russian monster, were they alive today, would be appalled to see its uncontrolled advances across the world. Someday, that mighty Magog will invade Israel.

PSALM 8

To the chief musician upon Gittith, A psalm of David (introduction).

Two possible interpretations for the "Gittith," were debated by Talmudic rabbis. First, the Ark of the Covenant was left at the house of Obed Edom, the Gittith, for three months as a temporary measure before David brought it to Jerusalem. Thus the psalm gives a set of guidelines "leading to the loftiest accomplishments to which man can aspire — the love and fear of God."[1] Being the eighth psalm, denoting a new beginning, it lends itself to the twentieth century and preparations for rebuilding the Temple — dwelling place for the Ark of the Covenant.

Secondly, the Gittith is described as a winepress prepared for the judgment of God. Perhaps the prophetic winepress was being prepared for the wars of this century. Nations were to be thrown into the crucible of God's judgment. God was preparing for the "shaking of the nations." World War I was soon to come. It would be among the first "birthpangs of travail" — part of the Armageddon series of wars. It may have marked the beginning of "winepress" judgments.

> O LORD our Lord, how excellent is thy name in all the earth! who hast set thy glory above the heavens.
> Out of the mouth of babes and sucklings hast thou ordained strength because of thine enemies, that thou mightest still the enemy and the avenger (vv. 1-2).

By 1908, Jews in Slavic lands were enjoying a sort of respite from the brutal "pogroms." Psalm 8 extols the Lord. His glory is ablaze in the heavens and can be seen in the nighttime sky. God is preparing for the birth of a new baby called Israel — among the lowly of earth (*babes and sucklings.*) In 1908, preparations were already underway which would result in the birth of the nation destined to prepare for His descent to the Mount of Olives. At that point in time, He will *still the enemy and the avenger* once and for all. The psalmist continues his amazement with the power of God:

> When I consider thy heavens, the work of thy fingers, the moon and the stars, which thou hast ordained;
> What is man, that thou art mindful of him? and the son of man, that thou visitest him? (vv. 3-4).

Among so vast a universe, what is this new baby called Israel? He was to be born in 1948, a child abused, kicked around by the nations; yet Messiah will visit him. God will make *him to have dominion over the works of thy* [God's] *hands ...* (v. 6). As all of these early introductory psalms imply, the birthpangs are about to begin.

It was on July 30, 1908, when something from outer space invaded earth's atmosphere and exploded over the Russian valley of the Podkamennaya Tunguska River. Passengers on the Trans-Siberian Express reported seeing a "bright blue ball of fire streaking across the sky trailing smoke."[2]

Most scientists agree that a comet blew apart, creating an explosion equal to a medium-sized hydrogen bomb. Though no crater was formed, trees were blown down for miles around — each lying opposite the center of the explosion. "It slaughtered reindeer and scattered tents of nomads camping far away."[3] Fortunately, it occurred in a remote uninhabited region of Siberia. Whether or not it was a "sign from heaven" it, nevertheless, seems to compare with the astronomical references of Psalm 8. And, it happened in 1908!

PSALM 9

To the chief musician upon Muthlabben ... (introduction).

Muthlabben was not a musical instrument. The term is translated as the "death of the son."[1] Because of David's sin with Bathsheba, the son born to them had to die. Its death was not a judgment upon the child, but a sacrifice to cleanse David of his sin. Only in this manner could God forgive and restore the king. God put David's sin upon the sinless son. The child bore the blame. In like manner, Christ, the sinless Son, *died for us* (Romans 5:8). Calvary prepared the way for Israel's spiritual adultery to be forgiven. There was a purpose for Christ's death which can be seen in Psalm 9.

> *O thou enemy, destructions are come to a perpetual end: ...*
> *But the LORD shall endure for ever: he hath prepared his throne for judgment.*
> *The wicked shall be turned into hell, and all the nations that forget God* (vv. 6-7,17).

The psalm sets the pace for that special time which would witness the *perpetual end* of all destruction. The Lord is preparing for the kingdom reign, and for the eternal destruction of the wicked.

> *The LORD also will be a refuge for the oppressed, a refuge in times of trouble* (v. 9).

Moshava Deganiah, which was Israel's first collective settlement and forerunner of the modern kibbutz system, was established in 1909.[2] It was a refuge for the oppressed. Both David Ben-Gurion and Levi Eschol, Israel's first two premiers, had lived and worked at Deganiah located near the southwestern shores of the Sea of Galilee.

> *That I may shew forth all thy praise in the gates of the daughter of Zion: I will rejoice in thy salvation* (v. 14).

Verse 14 contains a reference to the *gates of the daughter of Zion.* It was in 1909 that a group of Jews who had immigrated to

Palestine stood upon the sand dunes along the Mediterranean out-side Joppa (known then as the gate of Zion). They dedicated a new city in their Promised Land — to be known as Tel Aviv,[3] at first a suburb or *daughter* of Joppa. Yes, Tel Aviv was dedicated in the year corresponding to the number of the psalm in which was given the very same terminology used by the Arab world *gates of the daughter of Zion* — 1909!

> *The LORD is known by the judgment which he executeth ...* (v. 16).

The Ha-Shomer, an Israeli defense force made up of Jews, was established in 1909. No longer did they depend upon the ruling Turks, nor hire Arab mercenaries for protection against marauders. The Ha-Shomer was the prototype for the IDF (Israeli Defense Force) of today which has won every war they have fought since 1948, sometimes against odds of one hundred to one. Is it any wonder that Psalm 9 prophetically exclaims: *I will be glad and rejoice in thee ... When mine enemies are turned back, they shall fall and perish at thy presence* (vv. 2-3).

PSALM 10

*Why standest thou afar off, O LORD? why hidest thou thyself
in times of trouble? (v. 1).*

Psalm 10 extends the continuity of the theme which can be seen
in the mind-set of the Jewish people, as well as world events in
1910. Some scholars consider Psalms 9 and 10 to have been
originally written as one psalm. There is evidence of an
alphabetic acrostic in the two and there is no superscription to introduce the psalm. "It seems better to regard Psalm 10 as a later
psalm composed as an appendix, or a continuation of the earlier
under different conditions, rather than as part of a psalm which
from the beginning was one whole."[1]

Psalm 10 should rightly be numbered as a separate psalm.
However, if Psalms 9 and 10 were originally a single Biblical
chapter, it might account for the prophetic aspects of some
psalms relating to events which occurred in years prior to, or
following, its numerical identification. Furthermore, the prophetic implications of a psalm cannot be viewed as beginning in
January and ending in December. Nor can we rely on the Jewish
calendar, which begins each year about three or four months early at the New Moon around the time of the autumnal equinox
(September or October).

For example, Psalm 46 reflects upon the end of World War II
which occurred in 1945. Psalm 68 has a reference to the six-day
war of 1967. Psalm 83 names the combatants of the 1982 "Operation Peace for Galilee." The numbers obviously overlap, but that
does not detract from their credibility for setting the TRENDS on
those events which have come to pass in this century.

Also, though there are 150 psalms, some ancient Jewish versions count only 147. Certain psalms are combined to form three
sets of 49 each, comparing to the number of years in Jubilee.
Before the 7th century BC, however, Jubilee was set at every 50
years — hence, 150 psalms.

Some psalms set trends for events which continue for several
years. Therefore, Psalms 9 and 10 seem to compare with events
which overlapped during the early years of this century. And it is
not unthinkable that they should.

Perhaps this accounts for a seeming reference to Halley's comet, which, though it appeared in 1910, may be described in Psalm 11. ... *the LORD'S throne is in heaven ... his eyelids try ... Upon the wicked he shall rain snares, fire and brimstone, ...* (Psalm 11:4,6).

When the famed comet appeared, some declared the "end of the world." Our planet actually passed through the tail of Halley's comet setting off spectacular displays of "shooting stars."[2]

> *The LORD is King for ever and ever: the heathen are perished out of his land* (v. 16).

It is customary for the Ashkenazi Jews to recite this psalm during the "Ten Days of Penitence," the ideal season for repentance. Prophetically, the High Holy Days (from Rosh Hashanah to Yom Kippur) represent a scenario for end-time events. The resurrection and rapture of believers (Rosh Hashanah, the Feast of Trumpets) will be followed by seven years of tribulation (Seven Days of Awe), concluding with the glorious appearing of Messiah (Yom Kippur, the Day of Atonement) as the great High Priest emerges from the Holy of holies (heaven). On that day, the sacrificial blood will flow to the horses' bridles.

God has been putting the Jewish people through the fires of persecution to prepare them for a return to Palestine, while setting the stage for the destruction of the enemy. World War I was just the beginning of a series of wars, disease, famine, earthquakes, etc., until Messiah comes to establish the kingdom.

PSALM 11

> ... *how say ye to my soul, Flee as a bird to your mountain?* (v. 1).

Rashi, the eleventh century Talmudic scholar, called this passage a Gentile taunt to the wandering Jew. The message is prophetic. "Go home!" Why should such a message be relevant in 1911? Because the wicked were about to wage war, as seen in verse 2.

For, lo, the wicked bend their bow, they make ready their ar-
row upon the string ... (v. 2).

As the world moved toward global war, great men emerged to
help shape the destiny of the Jewish people. Among them were
men like Sir Herbert Samuels, a member of the British Parliament; Chaim Weizmann, a distinguished scientist; Vladimir
Jabotinsky, a noted soldier; and Louis Brandeis, an outstanding
lawyer, a member of President Wilson's cabinet, and a U.S.
Supreme Court justice for nearly a quarter of a century. These
and other outstanding statesmen worked toward the establishment of a Jewish national homeland in Palestine.

Samuels had kept a low profile during Herzl's attempt to
establish Uganda as a Jewish homeland under the direction of the
British. He did not view that plan as practicable.[1] Jabotinsky
realized early on that the Ottoman Empire was destined to fall
and that Jewish interests could be served best by alignment with
the British. Hence, he convinced the British to accept three
Jewish battalions as part of the British Army liberating Palestine
from the Turks.[2] Brandeis recognized the need for American
Jews to rally behind Zionism. "You do not have a nation without a
land," he said, "and you do not have a land without a nation."[3]

Chaim Weizmann believed that the Jews could build the nation
of Israel only in cooperation with the British. Perhaps no more
memorable conversation was recorded during the pre-World War
I period than that between Weizmann and British Lord Balfour.
"I have heard of Dr. Herz, — meaning Herzl," said Balfour, while
questioning Weizmann's insistence that Palestine, and Palestine
alone, could be the basis for Zionism.

"Anything else would be idolatry," Weizmann protested, adding "Mr. Balfour, supposing I were to offer you Paris instead of
London, would you take it?"

"But Dr. Weizmann," Balfour retorted, "we have London."

"That is true," Weizmann rejoined, "but we had Jerusalem
when London was a marsh."[4]

This early conversation was to bear fruit in years to come. Both
Weizmann and Balfour were to play major roles in the
establishing of the state of Israel. The coming war would provide
the catalyst.

*Upon the wicked he shall rain snares, fire and brimstone, and
an horrible tempest: this shall be the portion of their cup* (v. 6).

In each of these incredible psalms the message is the same —
war clouds loom on the horizon. Nations are preparing to rise up
against nations, and kingdoms against kingdoms. Verse 11
records a promise for judgment. World War I was the first of a
series leading to Armageddon.

PSALM 12

*They speak vanity every one with his neighbor: with flattering
lips and with a double heart do they speak.
Who have said, With our tongue will we prevail; our lips are
our own: who is lord over us?* (vv. 2,4).

"This psalm was inspired by a prophetic message foretelling an
era when the wicked would succeed in overcoming the poor and
the helpless. However, the psalm ends on the confident note that
God will surely protect the helpless ... in Messianic times when
evil will vanish ..."[1]

It is "... the 'Song of the Day' for Shemini Atzeres. On the seven
days of the Sukkos Festival [Feast of Tabernacles], offerings
were brought symbolizing the seventy nations who surround
Israel. But on the eighth day, Shemini Atzeres, the offering symbolizes only Israel who will remain alone and exalted in Messianic times as God's Chosen People."[2] Accompaniment was
played on the eight-stringed Sheminith, eight being the number of
new beginning. In the midst of a darkening political climate, hope
in the future Messianic kingdom was stirred.

The world was closer to war than most realized in 1912. Politicians were plotting clandestine activities in smoke-filled back
rooms. Armies were gearing up for confrontation. The psalmist
described it accurately. In the months ahead nations would fail to
avert war. Peace talks would not succeed.

*For the oppression of the poor, ... now will I arise, saith the
LORD; I will set him in safety ...* (v. 5).

Five times David asked God to rise (Psalm 3:7; 7:6; 9:19;

10:12; 17:13). Each time God refused, according to Rabbi Pinchas; but he declared that when God sees the poor plundered and hears the screams of the needy, He will arise. He will say (whisper) to the poor, "I will grant safety." The translation "whisper" means God has not yet publicized His plans to take revenge on the wicked.[3]

PSALM 13

> *How long wilt thou forget me, O LORD? for ever? how long wilt thou hide thy face from me?*
> *How long shall I take counsel in my soul, having sorrow in my heart daily? how long shall mine enemy be exalted over me?* (vv. 1-2).

David repeats the query four times, one for each of four national servitudes; Babylon, Media, Greece, and Rome (Midrash Schocher Tov).[1] Both Rashi, an eleventh century rabbi, and Radak, a twelfth century rabbi, wrote that the psalm was dedicated to the misery of national exile.[2] There is no suffering like the agony of an extended exile. It drains the tenacity and endurance of the beleaguered Israel. As they sink in despair, they cry, *How long?* Though it may be inappropriate to set dates for the conclusion of the age, it appears to be altogether appropriate to ask *How long?* (See chapter entitled "How Long?").

In 1913, the Federal Reserve Act was passed through both houses of Congress. With it came the establishment of the Federal Reserve System. Control of America's currency passed into private hands. Upsetting the delicate balance of world finance made war on a world-wide scale inevitable. That year marked an epoch of political insanity — nation against nation, kingdom against kingdom. No wonder the psalmist agonized, *How long?*

PSALM 14

The fool hath said in his heart, There is no God. They are cor-
rupt, they have done abominable works, there is none that doeth
good (v. 1).

Amidst the embattled nations in 1914 stood Joseph Stalin, a man
who was to gain control of Russia and build the backward country
into an ominous Soviet empire. Perhaps the psalmist characteriz-
ed him when he wrote, *The fool hath said in his heart, There is no*
God (v. 1). Lenin, in 1917, became the first ruler of Russia's communist government, but upon his death in 1924, Joseph Stalin rose
to power. Stalin double-crossed his comrades to become the sole
dictator of the Soviet Union. In 1953, he died. Could that be why
the same statement is repeated in Psalm 53? *The fool hath said in*
his heart, There is no God (Psalm 53:1).

One cannot know if the verses referred to Joseph Stalin. It
seems more than coincidental that the same statement is
repeated in the psalms numbered according to the year which
witnessed his revolutionary rise to power and the year of his
death (Psalms 14 and 53).

In the opinion of Jewish sages, David wrote Psalms 14 and 53 as
prophecies of the Babylonian destruction of Solomon's Temple
and the Roman razing of Herod's Temple. With the advent of
World War I, Israel embarked upon its Third Temple Period.

They are all gone aside, they are all together become filthy:
there is none that doeth good, no, not one (v. 3).

The world's first apocalyptic war began in 1914! It brought the
most dreadful destruction ever to come upon the human race to
that time. Nation rose against nation, kingdom against kingdom.
The battles were so numerous and extended that for the first time
in history the expression "World War" was employed. On June
28, 1914, the Hapsburg heir to Austria-Hungary's throne, Ferdi-
nand, and his wife, Sophie, entered their touring car for a trip
through the southern province of Bosnia. A man jumped on the
running board and shot them both point-blank. The assassination
enraged Francis Joseph, the reigning monarch. He declared war

on Serbia. Germany joined him and the war was on.[1]

Over the next four and one-half years, some eight million people died. The elderly Francis Joseph died in 1916, leaving the throne to his grandnephew, Charles. When Austria-Hungary lost the war in 1918, the Hapsburg monarch had to abdicate the throne and go into exile.[2] In World War II, Otto Von Hapsburg, son of Charles I, tried to regain the title, but failed. When the new EEC Parliament met in 1979, however, Otto Von Hapsburg was there as a leading delegate.

The Hapsburg dynasty provided the emperors for the Holy Roman Empire, beginning with Rudolph in 1273. Before that, however, other branches of the family tree served as emperors. The lineage goes all the way back to Merovee(447-458), a Frankish ruler whose grandson, Clovis, was chosen by the Bishop of Rome in 496 as the "New Constantine" emperor of the Holy Roman Empire. This Merovingian dynasty has been regarded by some historians as the family of the Holy Grail, offspring of Mary Magdalene and fathered by none other than Jesus Christ! This dreadful heresy is wicked, but is, nevertheless, believed in some secret societies to this day, and has provided the emerging "Revived Roman Empire" with several candidates for world ruler.[3] It is remarkable that the first world-wide war was sparked by the death of a Merovingian royal heir.

> *Oh that the salvation of Israel were come out of Zion! when the LORD bringeth back the captivity of his people, Jacob shall rejoice, and Israel shall be glad (v. 7).*

The term *Oh that* is an idiomatic Hebrew expression of a yearning for the event to occur very soon.[4] For the verse to be found in this Psalm lends to the prospect of 1914 and the First World War to be in that series of events which will see the total fulfillment of the prophecy concerning the ingathering of Israel.

PSALM 15

> *LORD, who shall abide in thy tabernacle? who shall dwell in*
> *thy holy hill?* (v. 1).

Moses received ten commandments as Israel prepared to enter the Promised Land, four of which dealt with one's relationship with God and six with one's relationship toward others. David, on the other hand, goes beyond those precepts, giving eleven additional commandments for those of Israel who would prepare to re-enter the Promised Land, all of which dealt with one's relationship with his fellow man.

The previous psalms are referred to as "persecution psalms." The text of this psalm changes abruptly to principles for grooming those who were to dwell ... *in thy* [God's] *holy hill* [mountain]. The following psalms (16 and 17) show a progress toward possession of their *goodly heritage* (Psalm 16:6). They compare with those twentieth century events of 1915-17 which led to the Balfour Declaration and Allenby's taking of Jerusalem.

Abraham Shulman described the period in his book, COMING HOME TO ZION. "The history ... of the revived land is the history of five ... waves of immigrants ... The First Aliyah (1882-1903) possessed tenacity and will power ... The Second Aliyah (1904-14) consisted of many young Russian revolutionaries who ... brought their socialist ideas ... inhumanly high ... many couldn't stand the strain. They broke under the self-imposed discipline, and a great number, almost 80 percent, left ... The Second Aliyah turned out to be a 'survival of the fittest,' not necessarily the fittest in muscle but in a power stronger than any physical strength, that of innocence. And those who survived became the core of the future state."[1]

> *He that walketh uprightly, and worketh righteousness, and*
> *speaketh the truth in his heart.*
> *He that backbiteth not with his tongue, nor doeth evil to his*
> *neighbour, nor taketh up a reproach against his neighbour.*
> *In whose eyes a vile person is contemned; but he honoureth*
> *them that fear the LORD. He that sweareth to his own hurt, and*
> *changeth not.*
> *He that putteth not out his money to usury, nor taketh reward*

against the innocent (vv. 2-5).

David's eleven rules for dwelling in Zion must have been too much for many of those in the Second Aliyah. Even Baron Edmond de Rothschild toured the Jewish settlements in Palestine in 1914, but did not stay. The tenth principle condemns those who would violate the Mosaic covenant against charging interest on loans. They shall have no part in Zion.

When Jesus made His first triumphal entry, He overthrew the moneychangers' tables and drove them from the Temple. When He returns, the moneychangers will be driven out again — once and for all. The present international banking cartel prospers on a principle of usury. When antichrist makes his bid for world domination, he will control the world's currencies, requiring his "mark" for buying and selling. Perhaps Moses and David foresaw that generation which would yield to the control of the moneychangers.

PSALM 16

> But to the saints that are in the earth, and to the excellent, in whom is all my delight.
> The LORD is the portion of mine inheritance and of my cup: thou maintainest my lot.
> The lines are fallen unto me in pleasant places; yea, I have a goodly heritage (vv. 3,5,6).

A special kind of people are mentioned here, those who will live to return to the land of their forefathers. The lines or boundaries of the Promised Land are kept by God. Even though the Sikes-Picot treaty of 1916 tried to undermine Jewish rights to the land, the Chosen People are yet to prevail.

The term, *thou maintainest my lot* has been also translated, "you guided my destiny." Through twenty long centuries, the wandering Jew thought he was alone, but God was there — behind the scenes guiding the course of events. The Lord had every intention of bringing the Jews back to their land. God was obliged to benefit Israel because of the *saints* who are buried *in the earth* (v. 3). The Great Creator must keep His promises to Abraham,

Isaac, Jacob, and David.

In 1917, the British Parliament passed the "Balfour Declaration" which stated in part, "His majesty's government views with favor the establishment in Palestine of a national home for the Jewish people and will use their best endeavors to facilitate the achievement of this objective ..."[1]

Lord Balfour had written the declaration as a reward to Chaim Weizmann for his discovery of the raw material for explosives. He solved the problem in only two weeks! He found horse-chestnuts were a perfect source for making acetone and butyl alcohol for explosives. The Balfour Declaration may well be a fulfillment of the passage, *The lines are fallen unto me ... I have a goodly heritage* (v. 6).

> *... my flesh also shall rest in hope.*
> *For thou wilt not leave my soul in hell ...* (vv. 9,10).

Though the verse primarily refers to the resurrection of Christ (Acts 2:27), it also speaks nationally of Israel. Even in the midst of the fires of World War I, the Chosen People were to witness a resurrection of Jewish hopes for their own land. After three thousand years in a political grave, Israel still was preserved from "corruption." Christ's three days in the grave also may have been prophetic of Israel's three millennia exile under Babylon, Media/Persia, Greece, and Rome.

> *Thou wilt shew me the path of life: in thy presence is fulness of joy; at thy right hand there are pleasures for evermore* (v. 11).

According to Rashi, "this is neither a prayer nor a request. It is a prophetic statement about the future ..."[2] God was unfolding His plan to deliver the Jewish people, return them to their land, and send Messiah to establish His millennial kingdom. The following year, 1917, was to see a major development toward the fulfillment of that prophecy.

PSALM 17

*Keep me as the apple of the eye, hide me under the shadow of
thy wings,* (v. 8).

In 1917, the British general, Edmund Allenby, led his troops to
surround the city of Jerusalem. It is reported that the night before
his impending invasion, Allenby prayed that he might take the city
without destroying the holy places. He had wired London for instructions and had received a simple reply — a scripture verse!
*As birds flying, so will the LORD of hosts defend Jerusalem;
defending also he will deliver it; and passing over he will
preserve it* (Isaiah 31:5).

The exciting prospects of such a thing led him to have the verse
read aloud before all his troops positioned in the foothills of
Jerusalem. Allenby commandeered every available aircraft for a
fly-over. On the morning of December 10, what seemed like hundreds of planes skirted low from just over the "Hill of Evil Council" which lays to the south of the Temple site. The sky was
covered from wing tip to wing tip and from nose to tail with
airplanes — British biplanes — captured German aircraft —
everything that would fly!

As they flew low over Jerusalem and the Eastern Gate, one of
the pilots dropped a note demanding surrender — signed by
General Allenby. The Turks had never seen airplanes before, and
were frightened by the strange crafts. According to reports, the
name of Allenby further frightened them, for the word "Allah" in
Arabic means "God" and "beh" is Arabic for "son." The Turks
were looking at a demand for surrender signed by Allah-beh, the
son of God! In response, they hoisted a white flag and surrendered the city without firing a single shot. Psalm 17 seems to
describe that historic event of 1917. ... *hide me under the shadow
of thy wings* could be another cryptic reference to the wings of
those British planes.

In his book "The Remarkable Jew," Dr. L. Sale-Harrison inter-
preted the term "Allah-beh" as "prophet of God." He wrote that
Allenby "arrived on horseback outside the Jaffa Gate, but at
some distance from the gate he alighted and walked on foot, and
bare-headed, towards the city."[1] Later, Allenby told why he

entered Jerusalem on foot. "It seemed to me," he said, "the obvious and natural thing to do. The only alternative to entering on foot by the Jaffa Gate, was to enter on horseback through the enormous hole in the wall surrounding Jerusalem, made specially to permit the German Kaiser to make what he regarded as a triumphant and spectacular entry into Jerusalem. That was a procedure I naturally shrank from repeating."[2]

Wrote Sale-Harrison, "The sacred city, which had been under the Gentile yoke exactly 2,520 years ... was freed on December 9, 1917, which was the first day of the feast Chanuka, or the 24th day of Chisleu. About 2,000 years before, according to the Jewish calendar, Judas Maccabeus, having taken possession of Jerusalem, re-dedicated the Temple and celebrated this remarkable victory. Is it not remarkable that, upon the anniversary of this great victory, this same city should be freed ... [again]?"[3]

It seems that God has a flare for fulfilling prophecies on the anniversaries of similar events which occurred in the pages of the Old Testament. Perhaps the taking of Jerusalem by Allenby fulfilled a prophecy given to Haggai: *Consider now from this day and upward, from the four and twentieth day of the ninth month, even from the day that the foundation of the LORD's temple was laid, consider it ... from this day will I bless you* (Haggai 2:18-19). The time reference of this chapter places it in the generation which will see the shaking of the nations: *And I will shake all nations, and the desire of all nations shall come: and I will fill this house with glory, saith the LORD of hosts* (Haggai 2:7).

World War I and the taking of Jerusalem on the 24th day of the ninth month marked the beginning of the fulfillment of these prophecies. They will conclude with the coming of the *desire of all nations* to establish the *house with glory*. One further note: not only did Great Britain take Jerusalem on the 24th day of the ninth month, they entered the war against Germany on August 4, 1914, which, in the Jewish Calandar, was on the 9th of Av, the anniversary of the destruction of Solomon's Temple by the Babylonians and the destruction of Herod's Temple by the Romans!

Like as a lion that is greedy of his prey, ... (v. 12).

The statement in verse 12, *Like as a lion that is greedy of his prey ...* could well represent the British! A lion is the symbol of Great Britain. It must be more than just a coincidence that Psalm 17 appears to contain a cryptic description of that which occurred in the seventeenth year of this century! Furthermore, the British became greedy of their new protectorate and would not allow the Jews to return with dignity. After promising to establish a "home" for the Jewish people, Britain collaborated with the Arabs while treating the Jews with disdain.

PSALM 18

... A Psalm of David, the servant of the LORD, who spake unto the LORD the words of this song in the day that the LORD delivered him from the hand of all his enemies, ... (introduction).

World War I was over and the psalm alludes to the victory! It also rejoices over the deliverance of the Jewish people. The Promised Land had been prepared for the return of the Chosen People.

In 1918, "Chaim Weizmann, the future first President of the Jewish state, concluded a treaty with Prince Feisal of Arabia (later, King of Iraq) in which Feisal declared that, 'mindful of racial kinship,' Palestine should be opened to Jewish immigration ..."[1]

This psalm is recorded twice in the Bible. The original composition in II Samuel chapter 22 was made by David after the death of Saul. The Talmud (Moed Kattan 16b) says that God was angry with David for not being sorrowful enough over the King's death. Though David mourned, at the same time he was glad to be free from Saul's relentless vengeance. David then wrote Psalm 7 to atone for his error[2] (See notes on Psalm 7).

This version of the song was made near the end of David's life and was recited on the day that his army asked the king not to continue to endanger himself on the battlefield. It was chosen as the "Song of the Day" for the Seventh Day of Passover commemorating the time when God parted the Red Sea. It also represents a prophecy of Israel's future redemption.[3] It was placed as number eighteen because the psalm rejoices over eighteen wars fought by David in his lifetime.

> *He sent from above, he took me, he drew me out of many waters.*
> *He brought me forth also into a large place; he delivered me, because he delighted in me* (vv. 16,19).

The *many waters* may be a reference to the many nations out of which the Jewish people were to return to their homeland.

> *He delivereth me from mine enemies: yea, thou liftest me up above those that rise up against me: thou hast delivered me from the violent man* (v. 48).

In Russia the Czar was dead and a new fledgling government offered freedom for the masses. Little did the Russian Jews know that the promise had a hollow ring about it. The most repressive government in history was in the making. To the relief of European Jewry, Germany and Austria lost the war. Twenty years later, however, Germany would unleash the holocaust!

PSALM 19

The heavens declare the glory of God; and the firmament sheweth his handiwork.

Day unto day uttereth speech, and night unto night sheweth knowledge.

There is no speech nor language, where their voice is not heard.

Their line is gone out through all the earth, and their words to the end of the world. In them hath he set a tabernacle for the sun,

Which is as a bridegroom coming out of his chamber, and rejoicing as a strong man to run a race (vv. 1-5).

Our thoughts are pointed skyward once again as we are reminded of God's Shekinah. The glory of His presence once hovered above the Mercy Seat on the Ark of the Covenant, beyond the veil that covered the Holy of holies. That blue veil represented the sky which veils the universe from our view throughout the day. From sunrise to sunset, the glow of the sun is a symbolic representation of the Shekinah. At night, when the sun has set, we are allowed to see beyond the veil (blue atmosphere) where we behold myriads of stars declaring God's glory.

Day unto day ... implies more than just one coming. It teaches His return as well. The phrase, *The sun is as a bridegroom* ... (v. 5) pictures the second coming of Jesus Christ as the Great Bridegroom. *Night unto night* ... proclaims God's original gospel message written in the ancient constellations. From Virgo to Leo, God had long ago written the story of His son — born of a virgin when He came the first time, yet to return as the *lion of the tribe of Judah* to destroy the many-headed serpent at the conclusion of this dispensation.

At the Tower of Babel, the message was perverted by wicked men, leading God to call Abraham to become the father of a chosen race through which He would give us His written Word, the Bible.

The law of the LORD is perfect, converting the soul: the testimony of the LORD is sure, making wise the simple.

The statutes of the LORD are right, rejoicing the heart: the commandment of the LORD is pure, enlightening the eyes (vv. 7-8).

In the first verses of the psalm, we are told of a magnificent message to be found in the stars, but in verse seven, our attention is drawn to the written Word, *the law of the LORD.* No longer do we depend upon a starry message. We now study the scriptures — *perfect, converting the soul.*

What does this have to do with the twentieth century? Were there "signs in the heavens" at the end of World War I? The winter of 1918-1919 saw mankind's first world-wide disease — a strain of flu which killed 20 million people. Some offered the suggestion that a comet caused the flu, that the "bug" filtered down into our atmosphere from outer space, but no comets were prominent that year.

I am told that when the World Zionist Congress voted to accept the Balfour Declaration, a star appeared in the heavens and remained for forty days — so bright it could be seen in the daytime. I have no documentation for the story but have no reason to doubt the accuracy of its source. Could that be a fulfillment of Psalm 19 though it occurred in early 1918?

"Rabbi Yehuda the son of Rabbi Shimon ben Pazi said: Since David said this verse after eighteen psalms, the rabbis placed it at the end of their eighteen benedictions. Is it then at the end of the eighteenth psalm? It is after the nineteenth! Therefore, we must say that the first two psalms are counted as one [rendering Psalm 19 as, in reality, Psalm 18] (Berachos 9b)."[1]

Perhaps again, we have an instance where a psalm which prophetically describes an event seems to be numbered close to the fulfillment of its prophecy, but not specifically according to the year the event took place. We can only say that the psalms appear to be setting a trend for the twentieth century, else, when we approach Psalms 88 through 94 we could be led to suggest a fulfillment in those years. It is not the purpose of this study, however, to set dates.

The Balfour Declaration had been in place and working for over a year. Jerusalem was no longer under Oriental domination. Surely it was time to proclaim a Jewish national homeland. The eyes of the world focused on Paris in January of 1919. It was the site of the World Peace Conference consummating World War I. Chaim Weizmann was there representing Zionism, as was His Royal Highness the Emir Feisal "representing and acting on behalf of the Arab Kingdom of Hedjac."[2] They drafted an agreement on January 3, 1919, which among other things was to encourage and stimulate immigration of Jews into Palestine on a large scale. Unfortunately, Feisel made the mistake of thinking he spoke for all of the Arabs as many others following him have done. The agreement they worked out was hardly worth the paper it was written upon.

President Woodrow Wilson was hailed as the greatest leader of the world at the time. While in Paris he met with major Jewish leaders for discussions. Rabbi S. S. Wise, perhaps the most able leader of American Jewry of that day, lingered following the conference to talk privately with the president. Here is his account of that visit. " 'Mr. President,' I said, 'world Jewry counts upon you in its hour of need and hope.' Placing his hand on my shoulder, he quietly and firmly said, 'Have no fear, Palestine will be yours.' "[3]

PSALM 20

> The LORD hear thee in the day of trouble; the name of the God
> of Jacob defend thee;
>   Send thee help from the sanctuary, and strengthen thee out of
> Zion; (vv. 1-2).

"This psalm was placed after Psalm 19 in order to express the firm conviction that the salvation of Israel depends not on physical power but on prayer (Berachos 4b)."[1]

The Jewish Midrash explains that this psalm is made up of nine verses to correspond with the nine months of gestation for the birth of a human child. "May He who answers the pregnant mother in labor, answer you."[2] As a prophetic scenario, 1920 was indeed a part of that time which felt those prophetic labor pains — awaiting the birth of Israel. The "day of trouble" had arrived with the turn of the century and was now upon them in full swing.

The psalm alludes to Israel's victorious battles against their Arab enemies in 1920. The year was just one of many filled with conflict. Their Arab neighbors demonstrated the truth of Psalm 20. The Jews in Palestine were forced to maintain their vigilance. The raids against Jewish settlements had to be met with force and the training of those brave settlers laid the groundwork for what eventually became one of the major fighting forces in the world today.

We will rejoice in thy salvation, and in the name of our God we will set up our banners: the LORD fulfil all thy petitions.
Now know I that the LORD saveth his anointed; he will hear him from his holy heaven with the saving strength of his right hand (vv. 5-6).

There is a difference in the scriptural usage of two words "Jacob" and "Israel." In Psalm 20, it is the God "of Jacob" who defends, not "of Israel." At this point in history (1920) there was no Israel, just Jacob, the usurper. Israel would not be established for another twenty-eight years. The state of Israel, not the state of Jacob, was established in 1948. Jacob, the usurper, always tends to claim and consume things that are not yet legally his. So it must have been in Palestine in 1920. Jacob's presence was certainly felt. More than 8,000 Jews made aliyah that year.

There were serious riots in Jerusalem in 1920. Undoubtedly they were fanned from flickering embers to raging flames by the Turkish artilleryman, Aswad, who wrote inflammatory articles and made hair-raising speeches that year. Because his activity incited riots, he received a life sentence to prison. But the British, in typical bureaucratic fashion, let him off the hook. Two years later he emerged as the Mufti of Jerusalem and for over four decades he became a thorn in the flesh of Palestinian Jewry.

Chaim Weizmann was in Jerusalem that year. He describes the situation: "I hasten to warn you of the very serious position which I have found on arrival here. Things have gone from bad to worse. Feisal is, in the long run, a broken reed. I can see other forces coming up which will break all he is connected with."[3]

Concerning the April riots in Jerusalem he wrote: "Jerusalem, where anti-Jewish excesses did not happen since the Crusades has been for three days the scene of wild pogroms, massacres, looting and violation of Jewish women. Lawless bands prowled and raided in our northern hills, and as usual in such cases, banditry took on the aspect of patriotism. [When] one small group of men under Captain [Vladimir] Jabotinsky, had come to defend their quarter, they had been promptly arrested. In the trial that followed before a military court, Jabotinsky received the savage sentence of fifteen years hard labour. He was later amnestied ... but rejected the amnesty with scorn because it included the main instigator of the pogrom, Haj Amin Husseini, the Grand Mufti of later years."[4]

The Third Palestine Arab Congress was held in Haifa in December, 1920. Amongst other things they objected to the present form of government in Palestine as it did not safeguard their best interests. They were leery of Sir Herbert Samuels, the newly appointed High Commissioner of Palestine. Interestingly enough, they objected to the flying of the Zionist flag (banner) the Mogan David or Star of David.[5] Ironic, isn't it? Psalm 20, verse 5 says, ... *we will set up our banners.*

And so it was in 1920, the cry of the Palestinian Jew was for the Lord to *strengthen ... out of Zion.*

PSALM 21

The king shall joy in thy strength, O LORD; and in thy salvation how greatly shall he rejoice! (v. 1).

David composed this psalm just after becoming king. His fledgling government had been temporarily set up in Hebron. He looked forward to that day when he would be firmly established as king. "This psalm was dedicated to two kings, David and Messiah," said Rashi, "for both suffered from enemies who deny their sovereignty: David by those who taunted him about Bathsheba, and Messiah by Gog and Magog."[1]

Thou hast given him his heart's desire, and hast not withholden the request of his lips. Selah (v. 2).

Jewish scholars consider this to be a prophecy for the future, though it is written as if it has already happened. Throughout the centuries the Chosen People have longed for that day when their heart's desire will be met. They look for a return to their Promised Land, the coming of Messiah, and the kingdom of heaven established on earth.

It's hard to believe that the Jews were finally returning to their homeland. For the first time in centuries, 1921 witnessed prosperity in Palestine. Under western dominance the people and the land seemed to respond joyously. "The death rate fell, the birth rate rose, the population grew ..."[2] In 1921 a communal settlement in the Valley of Jezreel was founded by immigrants from Eastern Europe. History confirms this national yearning of the

Diaspora spanning the centuries and fulfilled in this century.

> *Thine hand shall find out all thine enemies: thy right hand shall find out those that hate thee. Thou shalt make them as a fiery oven in the time of thine anger ...* (vv. 8-9).

Could this portion refer to the bloody riots which broke out in 1921? According to Abraham Shulman, Arab nationalism was developing alongside Jewish aspirations for a national homeland. The riots came "like thunder from a blue sky."[3] Men, women and children were slain; whole villages were burned and plundered. The problem was compounded by British promises to both sides. "The British High Commissioner, Sir Henry MacMahon, gave promises of a national state to the Arabs; while Lord Balfour made similar promises to the Jews."[4]

> *Their fruit shalt thou destroy from the earth, and their seed from among the children of men* (v. 10).

Winston Churchill, British Secretary of State for the Colonies, visited Egypt and Palestine to determine the situation first hand. Everywhere he went the Palestinians were eager to convey to him their strong feelings against Zionism. Crowds yelled "Long live the High Commissioner (Samuels) and Mr. Churchill, [but] we won't have the Jews."[5]

Meanwhile, in Jerusalem, Haj Amin Husseini was elevated to the lofty position of Mufti of Jerusalem. As such, he automatically became the spokesman for the Arabs of Palestine. The rest of his life was spent in attempts to expel the Jews from Palestine.

In May 1921, violence broke out in Jaffa and spread across the land. Forty-seven Jews were killed and one hundred forty wounded. Arab casualties were seventy-eight dead and seventy-five wounded. High Commissioner Samuels called a temporary halt to Jewish immigration to Palestine and entered into consultations with the Arabs which eventually lead to the notorious British White Paper of 1922.[6]

> *For they intended evil against thee: they imagined a mischievous device, which they are not able to perform* (v. 11).

Jewish sages tell the story that Titus the Roman was responsible for burning the Temple in 70 A.D. On his deathbed, Titus gave the following instructions: "After death burn my body and scatter the ashes over the seven seas so that the God of the Jews will not be able to find me to bring me before His Tribunal of Justice." The sages say, "Every day, his ashes are gathered and he is judged and burned again and the ashes are scattered over seven seas. This fulfills David's request, 'make them burn like a fiery furnace.' "[7] Rashi commented, "When Titus slashed the sacred 'curtain' which hung before the Holy of holies, with his sword, blood began to flow from it."[8]

The spirit of the psalm is believed to refer to the future defeat of the nations when their spoils will be presented to Israel as its portion. Also, Israel will realize that "... the final victory over the nations is due to His might only, and not theirs (Radak)."[9]

PSALM 22

My God, my God, why hast thou forsaken me? why art thou so far from helping me, and from the words of my roaring? (v. 1).

In 1922, the British further abrogated their commitment to the Balfour Declaration and divided Palestine into two territories, making the Jordan River a boundary. Under the direction of Winston Churchill, the Hashemite Kingdom of Transjordan was established. One can imagine the betrayed Jewish people crying, *My God, my God, why?*

Save me from the lion's mouth: ... (v. 21).

In 1922, the situation of the Jews in Palestine was difficult. Great Britain, the lion, held full sway over the affairs of both Jews and Arabs in the mandated area. Would the lion devour the Jews in favor of the Arabs? Winston Churchill prepared a "White Paper" announcing the lion's position. As it turned out, the document seemed to favor the Zionists but was totally unacceptable to Jews or Arabs.

The idea, garnered by the Jews from the Balfour Declaration of 1917 that they could look forward to Palestine becoming a homeland, was not affirmed in this document of 1922. However,it was not ruled out. Immigration was not to exceed the capacity of the land to support the immigrants. The status of all citizens in

Palestine should be Palestinian. There was to be no imposition of Jewish nationality on the land, neither was there to be subordination of Arab population, culture or language.[1] In pompous British terminology the "White Paper" said almost nothing of significance for either Jew or Arab. The year 1922 passed as a relatively quiet year in Palestine; a year in which political and governmental lines were drawn. In the end it would turn out even as the psalmist uttered:

> *For the kingdom is the LORD'S: and he is the governor among the nations* (v. 28).

Jewish treatment of Psalm 22 readily admits that David "deals with events which were destined to occur hundreds of years after ..." his time.[2] However, they point to Esther and Mordecai as the objects of the prophecy. The psalm is recited as the "Song of the Day" on Purim.

One cannot deny, however, that Psalm 22 is the most descriptive psalm of the crucifixion in the entire Old Testament. To disregard the Messianic aspect of this psalm would be sacrilege.

Psalms 22, 23, and 24 vividly describe the ministry of Christ as the Good Shepherd (22), the Great Shepherd (23), and the Chief Shepherd (24).

The prophetic fulfillment of the Shepherd Psalms was taken and applied by Christ Himself. It was winter time in Jerusalem. People had crowded into the city to celebrate the Feast of Dedication. As Jesus taught in the Temple compound, He hushed His hearers and proclaimed a parable: *I am the good shepherd: the good shepherd giveth his life for the sheep* (John 10:11). The mystery of the Good Shepherd relates to Psalm 22. The message of this prophetic psalm was fulfilled in the life and death of Christ.

The writer of the New Testament treatise to the Hebrews does not use the term Good Shepherd. The context places Christ in His present heavenly position as Great Shepherd. *Now the God of peace, that brought again from the dead our Lord Jesus, that great shepherd of the sheep, through the blood of the everlasting covenant, Make you perfect in every good work ...* (Hebrews 13:20-21). This is basically the prophecy found in Psalm 23. Christ is the Great Shepherd.

The mystery of Psalm 24 is revealed in the first epistle of Peter where the Good Shepherd Who became the Great Shepherd will one day become the Chief Shepherd: *And when the chief Shepherd shall appear, ye shall receive a crown of glory that fadeth not away* (I Peter 5:4).

Here is the order of the prophecy: our Savior came the first time as the Good Shepherd Who giveth His life for the sheep. Presently (in heaven) He is the Great Shepherd Who is perfecting us in every good work. One day He shall appear as the Chief Shepherd to rule and reign over the earth as the *King of glory*.

In order to understand the prophecy of the Shepherd and His sheep, one must apply the rule of "first mention." The setting would be the Garden of Eden and the first sacrifice made by God Himself on behalf of Adam and Eve. The Lord took the skins of a sacrificed animal (thought to be a lamb) and clothed the guilty pair. *Unto Adam also and to his wife did the LORD God make coats of skins, and clothed them* (Genesis 3:21).

The sacrifice thus became the substitute for Adam when judgment was meted out for his sins. The animal died in the place of the sinner. From that day forward the law of sacrifice became a part of the religious service carried out by the human family for the atonement or covering of sin. Year after year, the sacrifice of sheep represented a prophetic picture of that great day when the Shepherd Himself would lay down His life for the human race.

John the Baptist introduced Jesus at the onset of His ministry as the *Lamb of God* (John 1:29) who was to take away the sins of the world. His death on Calvary was the ultimate fulfillment of the prophecy.

My God, my God, why ...? was the cry of the Good Shepherd on that day when He laid down His life for the sheep. The first twenty-one verses of this psalm were fulfilled at Calvary. Every prophetic implication was fulfilled explicitly. It was of the crucifixion that the psalmist wrote:

> *But I am a worm, and no man; a reproach of men, and despised of the people.*
> *All they that see me laugh me to scorn: they shoot out the lip, they shake the head, saying,*
> *He trusted on the Lord that he would deliver him: let him deliver him, seeing he delighted in him* (Psalm 22:6-8).

This is exactly what happened at Calvary that day when the

people gathered to wag their heads at Jesus and laugh Him to scorn. Matthew recorded the account. *And they that passed by reviled him, wagging their heads; ... He trusted in God; let him deliver him now, if he will have him: for he said, I am the Son of God* (Matthew 27:39,43).

> *I am poured out like water, and all my bones are out of joint: my heart is like wax; it is melted in the midst of my bowels.*
> *My strength is dried up like a potsherd; and my tongue cleaveth to my jaws; and thou hast brought me into the dust of death.*
> *For dogs have compassed me: the assembly of the wicked have inclosed me: they pierced my hands and my feet.*
> *I may tell all my bones: they look and stare upon me.*
> *They part my garments among them, and cast lots upon my vesture* (vv. 14-18).

The psalmist described a Roman crucifixion hundreds of years before the Romans even came on the scene. In the days when Jewish executions were made by stoning, the psalmist gave a word picture of crucifixion. He described the profuse perspiration caused by intense suffering when he wrote: *I am poured out like water, ...* He described his bones (those of the hands, arms, and shoulders) as being *out of joint.* And he described the action of the heart affected when he wrote, ... *my heart is like wax; it is melted* ... (v. 14).

The crucified Shepherd exhausted His physical strength: *My strength is dried up* ... He suffered extreme thirst: ... *my tongue cleaveth to my jaws;* ... The method of crucifixion is vividly expressed: ... *they pierced my hands and my feet.* He is shamed as the Savior's unclothed body is reviewed by the jeering crowd: *I may tell all my bones: they look and stare upon me.* These descriptions reveal the mode of death. He was crucified. The circumstances of His crucifixion are also described. There was a period of darkness when the sun refused to shine. *O my God, I cry in the daytime, but thou hearest not; and in the night season, and am not silent* (v. 2). The gambling is predicted: *They part my garments among them, and cast lots upon my vesture.* All of these descriptions were written by David a thousand years before the birth of Christ, and were literally fulfilled at Calvary. It is a picture of the Good Shepherd Who giveth His life for the sheep.

> *I will declare thy name unto my brethren: in the midst of the congregation will I praise thee.*
> *All the ends of the world shall remember and turn unto the LORD: and all the kindreds of the nations shall worship before thee* (vv. 22,27).

Verse 22 marks a pivotal point of history. With the resurrection came the Great Commission to take the Gospel to the ends of the earth.

This concept was not understood by the Jewish people. They thought the blessings of heaven were exclusively theirs, that salvation and forgiveness were to be given only to the Jews. But in fulfillment of the prophecy, the Gospel of Jesus Christ was rejected by the mainstream of Jewish life while welcomed by Gentiles.

> *They shall come, and shall declare his righteousness unto a people that shall be born, that he hath done this* (v. 31).

The last verse reveals the prophetic nature of the psalm: *They SHALL come, and SHALL declare his righteousness unto a people that SHALL be born, ...* (v. 31). For the past two thousand years the Gospel message of Christ's atoning sacrifice has been proclaimed among the Gentiles. The Chosen People have been provoked to jealousy. Jewish pride refuses to consider the Savior's claim to Messiahship.

PSALM 23

> *The Lord is my shepherd; I shall not want.*
> *He maketh me to lie down in green pastures: he leadeth me beside the still waters* (vv. 1-2).

The Jordan River became the eastern border of Jewish territory in 1922-23. Could that be at least one of the prophetic implications of this psalm?

David composed the magnificent psalm during one of the most dangerous and discouraging times of his life. He fled to the God-forsaken forest of Hereth as King Saul and his army dogged his heels attempting to kill him (I Samuel 22:5). Rabbi Avrohom Chaim Feuer describes the Forest of Hereth as "parched and dry-like baked earthenware."[1] The beloved Twenty-third Psalm affirms that God provides and maintains even when the chances of survival seem non-existent.

> *He restoreth my soul: he leadeth me in the paths of righteousness for his name's sake.*
> *Yea, though I walk through the valley of the shadow of death, I will fear no evil: for thou art with me; thy rod and thy staff they comfort me* (vv. 3-4).

Though discouraged by British disregard for the Balfour Declaration, Jews in Palestine remained confident that God would restore the very soul of their national identity some day. They were walking through the proverbial valley. They felt both the "rod" of judgment and the "staff" of comfort. They were used to suffering at the hands of Gentiles over the centuries, yet they were determined to survive.

In London the usual parliamentary proceedings lumbered onward as the pros and cons of establishing a Jewish presence in Palestine occupied legislative chambers. Perhaps typical of the debates was Lord Islington's remarks, "A Zionist home, my Lords, undoubtedly means, or implies, a Zionist government over the district in which the home is placed, and if 93 percent of the population of Palestine are Arabs, I do not see how you can establish other than an Arab government, without prejudice to their civil rights."[2] Others argued in favor of a Jewish homeland in Palestine.

The Targum (a Jewish commentary) says "the valley of death" refers to the exile of the Israelites. In 1923 the exiled people were just beginning their return to the ancient homeland. Jews rushed toward Palestine by the thousands. It was the peak of the Third Aliyah. Thirty-five thousand of them came to Palestine determined to *dwell in the house of the Lord for ever.* They cleared new land, drained more swamps and planted, cultivated and harvested crops. It was backbreaking work with men and women sometimes harnessing themselves like draft animals to pull the plows. But, inevitably they had a table prepared before them in the presence of their enemies.

> *Thou preparest a table before me in the presence of mine enemies: thou anointest my head with oil; my cup runneth over.*
> *Surely goodness and mercy shall follow me all the days of my*

life: and I will dwell in the house of the Lord for ever (vv. 5-6).

A determined Chosen People looked forward in hopes of a complete victory in the Middle East and a homeland restored for those invited to return from the Diaspora. The Targum identifies the *house of the Lord* as the Temple.

Psalm 23 is more than just a prophecy of restored Israel. It is a part of the mystery of the Shepherd. Psalms 22, 23, and 24 present a prophetic picture of the future ministries of the Messiah. In Psalm 22 the Good Shepherd gives His life for the sheep. In Psalm 23 the Great Shepherd, brought again from the dead through the blood of the everlasting covenant, tenderly cares for His sheep. In Psalm 24 the Chief Shepherd appears as the King of kings to reward His sheep.

Psalm 23 must also be considered as a description of this dispensation of New Testament Christianity. It refers to that time when the Gospel will be given to the Gentiles. No wonder then, that among the three psalms, Psalm 23 is the favorite and best-loved by Gentile Christianity.

It is a beautiful picture of the life of the believer, and many sermons have been given on the comfort and care bestowed upon us by our Great Shepherd. It is the picture of the Shepherd Who cares for His flock, leading us through the meadow, feeding us in green pastures, and quenching our thirst beside still waters. Even when we walk through the valley of the shadow of death we need not fear, for He is there to comfort us.

One day He will prepare a table for us. We shall be exalted in the presence of our enemies to rule and reign with Christ for a thousand years! Beyond that, we shall dwell in the New Jerusalem — ... *in the house of the Lord forever.*

PSALM 24

The earth is the Lord's, and the fullness thereof; the world, and they that dwell therein (v. 1).

The psalm was believed to have been composed when David purchased the threshing floor of Araunah, the Jebusite, atop Mount Moriah, on which to build the Temple. David intended to have this psalm recited on the day of dedication for the new Temple. "God's presence, which is spread throughout the entire world, would then be concentrated in the holiest of places, to dwell upon the Holy Ark ..."[1]

The message of Psalm 24 is so important that it was chosen by the rabbis as the "Song of the Day" for the first day of the week, Sunday — a day also observed by Christians for worship. With Psalm 22 revealing the mystery of the "Good" Shepherd and Psalm 23 revealing the mystery of the "Great" Shepherd, Psalm 24 reveals a prophecy yet to be fulfilled. It is the mystery of the "Chief" Shepherd.

The prophecy ultimately will be completed when Jesus Christ returns to earth in power and great glory. In that day He will be known as the Chief Shepherd who owns the sheep. The earth is the Lord's. He is the owner. When He comes, He will establish His throne. We who have served Him will rule and reign with Christ for a thousand years.

> *Who shall ascend into the hill of the Lord? Or who shall stand in his holy place?*
> *He that hath clean hands, and a pure heart; who hath not lifted up his soul unto vanity, nor sworn deceitfully* (vv. 3-4).

In 1924 Palestine's Jewish inhabitants were facing Arab uprisings. The new king of Transjordan had at first extended a hand of friendship, but was having second thoughts. An armed band of Jewish men were chosen to guard and protect their agricultural settlements. Some non-religious Jews who had come from Russia with communistic ideals did not have the inner strength to stay. Disillusioned, many left for Europe and America.

The term, "aliyah," literally means "going up." It is to ascend to the Temple. In modern terminology it has come to mean immigration to Israel. In the middle of 1924 a new wave of immigration began. It was the fourth of five "aliyahs" which brought thousands of Jewish immigrants to Palestine. But, this group was different. Whereas formerly mostly untrained laborers and farmers came, the Fourth Aliyah contained mostly middle class shopkeepers, tailors and industrialists from Eastern Europe and Poland.

Much to the chagrin of David Ben-Gurion they settled in the cities creating ghettos. They showed little or no interest in

Zionism and certainly had no interest in developing the land. Palestine needed pioneers, not landlords. Hence, Ben-Gurion breathed a sigh of relief when they began to leave Palestine en masse during 1927.[2] Nonetheless, the time had come for artisans, bankers and businessmen to "come up" to the land of Israel.

Now as then, it is a question of worthiness, and, of course, no one is worthy but the Lamb. It is the same question seen in Revelation 5 when a search was made throughout the universe for one who is worthy, only to find that the Lamb alone is worthy to become the Chief Shepherd. *And I beheld, and, lo, in the midst of the throne and of the four beasts, and in the midst of the elders, stood a Lamb as it had been slain ... Worthy is the Lamb that was slain to receive power, and riches, and wisdom, and strength, and honor, and glory, and blessing* (Revelation 5:6,12).

The Good Shepherd of Psalm 22 and the Great Shepherd of Psalm 23 now becomes the Chief Shepherd of Psalm 24, for He is worthy. And when will He assume the position of Chief Shepherd? The prophecy is designated for a future generation — perhaps the twentieth century!

This is the generation of them that seek him, that seek thy face, O Jacob. Selah (v. 6).

This century appears to be the one for which the righteous have all been waiting. The mystery of the Shepherd has awaited that special generation described by the psalmist — a people across the world who will seek the face of Jacob. The thrust of that verse is not that men will only seek Him, but will seek the face of Jacob. "His seekers" are those living in this generation who have seen the return of the Jew to his land. The children of Jacob are back home on their ancient soil. The nation of Israel has been reborn among the nations of the world.

They are designated as the generation which will see the mystery of the Shepherd solved. That is what makes this generation so unique in the annals of history. Not only have Christians witnessed the rebirth of Israel, but have actually helped the Jews to return.

Jesus referred to this special generation in Matthew 24:32-34 when He told the parable of the fig tree, another symbol for the restoration of Israel. Like the psalmist, the Savior said, *This generation shall not pass, till all these things be fulfilled* (v. 34).

The generation who seeks the face of Jacob or sees the rebirth of Israel will be the same one to welcome the return of Christ.

Lift up your heads, O ye gates; and be lift up, ye everlasting doors; and the King of glory shall come in (v. 7).

According to rabbinical scholars, "The gates allude to the fact that the Ark was destined to be removed from the Holy of holies and then to be returned through these very same gates at a later time. The Ark was not returned at the time of the Second Temple (Yoma 21b), so this must allude to its return in the days of the Messiah (Ibn Ezra)."[3]

Who is this King of glory? The LORD strong and mighty, the LORD mighty in battle (v. 8).

Christ will come in the midst of history's most destructive battle, the awesome Armageddon. He was the Good Shepherd Who gave His life for the sheep. He is the Great Shepherd Who leads and cares for His sheep, and one day soon He will come as the Chief Shepherd to reward the sheep. When Jesus gave the parable of the Shepherd in John 10, He deliberately veiled its symbolic meaning. But one day soon the mystery of the Shepherd will be revealed.

Though the ebb and flow of Psalm 24 covers more than just 1924, it definitely includes the year as a part of the predicted *generation* (v. 6) which would see the return of the Jews to Palestine, the restoration of the Ark of the Covenant, and the return of Christ — *this King of glory.*

PSALM 25

O my God, I trust in thee: let me not be ashamed, let not mine enemies triumph over me (v. 2).

Arab uprisings continued to increase in 1925. The frustrated Jewish settlers were unable to comprehend the full scope of the situation. Little did they realize that a growing nationalism among the Arab population coincided with their own aspirations of nationhood.

Shew me thy ways, O LORD; teach me thy paths.
Lead me in thy truth, and teach me: for thou art the God of my
salvation; on thee do I wait all the day (vv. 4-5).

This is the first psalm which is arranged according to the Hebrew alphabet. It is not a complete acrostic of the twenty-two letters, implying a need for more learning. The Hebrew alphabet left incomplete is quite significant. Perhaps of even more significance is the plea of the psalmist for teaching. In verse 4, he supplicates, *teach me thy paths. Lead me in thy truth, and teach me:* ... he begs in verse 5. *Good and upright is the LORD: therefore will he teach sinners in the way,* he says in verse 8. *The meek will he teach his way* is enunciated in verse 9. And finally in verse 12 he queries, *What man is he that feareth the LORD? him shall he teach in the way that he should choose.*

Why does there seem to be an emphasis on teaching and learning in this psalm? And what has it to do with 1925? What could it have prefigured? That was the year of the opening of Hebrew University on Jerusalem's Mount Scopus. The new school of higher learning was dedicated on April 1 of that year, along with the establishing of Technion (The Haifa Institute of Technology) a few months earlier! Weizmann counted the opening of the Hebrew University the second most important event after the Balfour Declaration. The aged Lord Balfour along with Baron Edmond de Rothschild attended the ceremonies.[1]

Remember not the sins of my youth, nor my transgressions:
according to thy mercy remember thou me for thy goodness'
sake, O LORD (v. 7).

David asked for guidance and mercy to assist him in his lifelong quest for righteousness. Psalm 25 is considered an introduction to Psalm 26 where David asks to be tested for spiritual perfection.

The *sins of my youth* refer to errors in judgment made before the age of twenty. Though Bar Mitzvah arrives at thirteen, making a Jewish youth answerable to the courts, God does not condemn a young man until he is twenty. All transgressions of the teenager are considered to be errors and misjudgments. After twenty, however, all transgressions are considered to be intellectual rebellion.

*The troubles of my heart are enlarged: O bring thou me out of
my distresses* (v. 17).

The term *troubles* reminds one of the coming Tribulation
Period called by Jeremiah, *Jacob's trouble* (Jeremiah 30:7). God
uses trouble to enlarge the spiritual horizons of His people. One
rabbi suggested that affliction will rid the devout of their lusts for
pleasure and frivolous cares. In 1925, the suffering Jewish immigrants in Palestine were fulfilling at least the spirit of this
verse.

*Consider mine enemies; for they are many; and they hate me
with cruel hatred.*
*O keep my soul, and deliver me: let me not be ashamed; for I
put my trust in thee* (vv. 19-20).

Arab hatred for Jewish settlers caused the newcomers to dig in
with more determination than ever to stay. Those early years
helped to prepare them for the hard decisions which lay ahead. In
a few years, they would press for statehood. They could not be
content to dwell among the Arabs under the control of the British.
They must be driven to greatness which eventually was thrust
upon them. Those early pioneers of the Promised Land could certainly relate to the closing verse of David's prayer for guidance
and protection.

Redeem Israel, O God, out of all his troubles (v. 22).

In August, 1925, Field Marshall Lord Plummer arrived to
replace Sir Herbert Samuels as British High Commissioner of
Palestine. His appointment marked a turning point in British,
Arab and Jewish relations. The old gentleman lost no time in
making it known that he was now in charge. He was a meek
devout Christian who held the land of Jesus in awe. His first official act was to go to the Anglican church for prayers.[2] In a way,
verse 9 seems to sum up Lord Plummer's attitude, *The meek will
he guide in justice.*

PSALM 26

Judge me, O LORD; for I have walked in mine integrity: I have trusted also in the LORD; therefore I shall not slide.
Examine me, O LORD, and prove me; ... (vv. 1-2).

The flow of Psalm 26 compares quite well with the testing of Jewish spiritual stamina in 1926. It was, for the most part, a peaceful time with very little hostility with the surrounding Arabs. Consequently, the military-minded Lord Plummer began cutting and whacking down British armed police and Jewish resistance forces. What might not have been taken into consideration was that the Fourth Aliyah was mostly city dwelling people. The Arabs felt very little pressure on the land. So conflict between Jew and Arab was at an all time low.

Further, the land of Palestine began to suffer an economic slump. There was widespread unemployment and many of the artisans of the Fourth Aliyah left Palestine.[1] As it turned out, in 1928, dire consequences resulted from the failure of the Yishuv (Jewish presence in Palestine) to maintain adequate defense forces despite Plummer's budget cutting.

According to rabbinical thought, David had given a lifetime of service to the Lord. Feeling that he had attained perfection, David asked God to test him that he might prove his worthiness as a devout king. God replied by allowing his temptation with Bathsheba. The test proved that David had not reached a state of perfection after all.

"That I may publish with the voice of thanksgiving, and tell of all thy wondrous works.
Lord, I have loved the habitation of thy house, and the place where thine honor dwelleth (vv. 7-8).

David desired to prove his worthiness that he might be allowed to construct the Temple, the place where the glory resided. This same desire is manifested in this generation by devout Jews. It is said that if any generation have the ability to rebuild the Temple and do not, it is as if they destroyed it! Therefore, all Zionist plans for restoration must include rebuilding the Temple. Though it may be publicly denied, it plays a central part in Jewish life. The old adage "Next year in Jerusalem," repeated by Jews twice a year, is not without special significance.

A. F. Futterer, an Australian born explorer, whose mother was of German descent, was looking for the Ark of the Covenant around Mount Nebo in 1926. Though he did not find it, his search fired the imaginations of many on the possibility of its place in prophecy. The story of German archeologists looking for the Ark in the Hollywood movie, "Raiders of the Lost Ark" was inspired by Futterer's early trips to Mount Nebo in hopes of finding the golden box.

> *Gather not my soul with sinners, nor my life with bloody men:*
> *In whose hands is mischief, and their right hand is full of*
> *bribes* (vv. 9-10).

As alluding to 1926, this might well describe the Arab inhabitants among whom the pioneer Jews must live. There were small but continual provocations and British policy was to placate Arabs while restricting the Jews.

> *But as for me, I will walk in mine integrity: redeem me, and*
> *be merciful unto me.*
> *My foot standeth in an even place: in the congregations will I*
> *bless the LORD* (vv. 11-12).

Here lies a hope for the future — that the Chosen People will commit no falsehood or trickery. David prays for purity of heart and motive. Returning Israel has attempted to maintain such an attitude in the twentieth century. Offers are continually made to negotiate peace with Arab militants. Only Israel manifests a consistent integrity.

PSALM 27

> *The LORD is my light and my salvation; whom shall I fear?*
> *the LORD is the strength of my life; of whom shall I be afraid?*
> *When the wicked, even mine enemies and my foes, came upon*
> *me to eat up my flesh, they stumbled and fell.*
> *Though an host should encamp against me, my heart shall not*
> *fear: though war should rise against me, in this will I be confi-*
> *dent* (vv. 1-3).

Jewish congregations throughout the world recite this psalm at the conclusion of each service throughout the month of Elul and

during the ten Days of Awe (also called Days of Repentance). It is
used to usher in the spirit of those Days of Awe. The prophetic implications of the High Holy Days are apparent. Jewish scholars
believe the Feast of Trumpets (Rosh Hashanah) portrays that
future time when the heavenly trumpet will sound to raise the
dead and set the judgment. The seven intervening days between
Rosh Hashanah and Yom Kippur may represent the seven years
of Tribulation.

The Day of Atonement (Yom Kippur) prophetically speaks of
the coming of Messiah at Armageddon to offer the great sacrifice.
On that day, the blood will flow to the horses' bridles. Psalm 27 is,
therefore, a prophetic psalm which will be fulfilled as the age of
Messiah approaches. That makes it relevant to the twentieth century. The suffering of Jews at the hands of their enemies as
depicted in the psalm must come to pass in the days preceding the
coming of Messiah.

> One thing have I desired of the LORD, that will I seek after;
> that I may dwell in the house of the LORD all the days of my life,
> to behold the beauty of the LORD, and to enquire in his temple.
> For in the time of trouble he shall hide me in his pavilion: in
> the secret of his tabernacle shall he hide me; he shall set me up
> upon a rock (vv. 4-5).

These verses may allude to the future seven year Tribulation
Period which may be a fulfillment of the prophetic scenario laid
out in the Days of Awe. The *tabernacle* may refer to the future
"Tabernacle of David" and the *rock* may be the foundation stone
beneath a cupola atop the Temple site just north of the Mosque of
Omar. On the pavement area stands a cupola called "The Dome
of the Tablets" named after the Ten Commandments kept in the
Ark of the Covenant. The Ark was said to have rested on the rock,
site of the Holy of holies in both Solomon's Temple and Herod's
Temple.

On the other hand, they may refer to the fleeing of the Jewish
remnant to Petra (Rock) when the abomination of desolation occurs in the midst of the Tribulation Period. When the antichrist
establishes his throne in the Tabernacle of David and claims to be
God, the 144,000 will escape to the mountains. God will *hide* them
in His *pavilion.*

Also, the passage may refer to an earthquake which shook

Palestine on July 11, 1927. The city of Nablous (old Shechem) suffered most. Many were killed and almost every building leveled. It is interesting to note that during 1919-21 the Arab inhabitants refused to allow Jews to settle there. Yet, following the quake, the Jewish municipality of Tel Aviv sent two truckloads of bread and financial assistance to their enemies. Nablous residents appreciated the help. The Mosque of Omar sustained $500,000 in damages, prompting speculation that an earthquake would someday remove the Moslem mosque to prepare the way for the rebuilding of the Temple! According to government reports, many Arab lives were lost, but there was not one Jewish casualty.[1]

> *And now shall mine head be lifted up above mine enemies round about me: therefore will I offer in his tabernacle sacrifices of joy; I will sing, yea, I will sing praises unto the LORD* (v. 6).

The main religious service rendered at the Tabernacle of David was music. Most animal sacrifices were offered at the Tabernacle of Moses at Gibeon. The verse lends itself toward the Tabernacle of David which was promised by Amos to be set up *in that day* (Amos 9:11).

> *Deliver me not over unto the will of mine enemies: for false witnesses are risen up against me, and such as breathe out cruelty.*
> *I had fainted, unless I had believed to see the goodness of the LORD in the land of the living.*
> *Wait on the LORD: be of good courage, and he shall strengthen thine heart: wait, I say, on the LORD* (vv. 12-14).

Again, the verse lends itself to 1927 and the conflicts between Arabs and Jews. Growing Arab nationalism posed a threat to Jewish survival in Palestine. During the final year of Lord Plummer's tenure as British High Commissioner of Palestine, he inaugurated land reform measures and continued to cut defense forces. "Had he remained for another two years or had he been followed by some outstanding personality of the same caliber, then the long peace of the 1920's would probably have continued."[2]

The fact that over 5,000 Jews left Palestine while only 2,300 entered in 1927 and the general slowdown of aliyah since 1925 led the Arabs to believe that Zionism was short-lived. The tragic events of the following year proved that the Arab assessment was inaccurate. The Jews were in Palestine to stay. They could say, *And now shall mine head be lifted up above mine enemies round about me.* The comfort rendered by the psalmist to *wait on the LORD* looked past the Holocaust to the birth of the nation and eventually the Messianic Era.

PSALM 28

"Unto thee will I cry, O LORD my rock; ... (v. 1).

In the Jewish Talmud one rabbi commented on the rock, " 'Do not read this word as Rock but as Artist, Sculptor.' A man draws a form on a wall but he cannot endow it with life, but the Holy One, Blessed be He, creates a form within a form [an embryo inside the mother] and bestows it with breath and a soul ... (Megillah 14a)."[1]

As the psalm indicates, the Lord had created the embryo of the nation of Israel and was not about to abort the baby. Israel was due to be born in 1948, but in the 1920's, God would not allow harm to come to the embryo beyond that necessary to bring forth a healthy nation.

> *Draw me not away with the wicked, and with the workers of iniquity, which speak peace to their neighbours, but mischief is in their hearts.*
> *Give them according to their deeds, and according to the wickedness of their endeavours: give them after the work of their hands; render to them their desert.*
> *Because they regard not the works of the LORD, nor the operation of his hands, he shall destroy them, and not build them up* (vv. 3-5).

This psalm has the same theme as given in Psalm 27. David prayed for peace from his persecutors — the Philistines. In like manner, the Palestinians of the twentieth century who derived their name from the ancient Philistines set about to drive the Jewish settlers from Palestine. The underlying theme corresponds with events in 1928. During the twenties and thirties,

Arab raids on Jewish villages, which would discourage the average immigrant, made the Jews even more determined to stay. The continual bloodletting would not drive those who had made aliyah (going up) to their Promised Land. They were the first of four million of the Chosen People who would eventually make Eretz (the land of) Israel their home.

PSALM 29

> *The voice of the LORD is upon the waters: the God of glory thundereth:* ...
> *The Lord sitteth upon the flood; yea, the Lord sitteth King forever.*
> *The Lord will give strength unto his people;* ... (vv. 3,10-11).

This psalm is a vivid description of a raging storm. In it the voice of God is heard granting full assurance that He is in control. The seven voices of God here depict the seven benedictions (prayers) recited by observant Jews on every Sabbath. "To what do the seven blessings said on Sabbath correspond? Rabbi Halefta B. Saul said: To the seven voices mentioned by David (commencing with) 'upon the waters.' God is with His people during the storm and comforts them during the calm that follows."[1]

"Just as the eighth psalm is to be read by moonlight, when the stars are bright, as the nineteenth needs the rays of the rising sun to bring out its beauty," wrote Charles H. Spurgeon a century ago, "so this can be best rehearsed beneath the black wing of tempest, by the glare of the lightning or amidst the dubious dusk which heralds the war of elements. The verses march to the tune of thunderbolts."[2] The psalm closes on a note of peace which comes with the calm following the storm.

Indeed 1929 was a stormy year. On "Black Friday," October 29, the stock market collapsed sending virtually the whole world into economic chaos. "The anti-Semitism of the great depression of 1929 was entirely different," wrote Max I. Dimont. "It was manufactured in Germany and imported by American Nazis of Germany as part of a plot to undermine the American will to fight Hitler's brand of fascism. Many Americans, unable to comprehend the nature of a depression in the world's richest country, fell prey to Hitler's paid propagandists.[3]

Meanwhile, 1929 was a violently stormy year for the Jews in Palestine. After the riots of September, 1928, the Mufti (official title of the Arab ruler of Jerusalem), began to step up Arab resistance. He had been biding his time between 1925 and 1928, because the British High Commissioner of Palestine was Lord Plummer, a seasoned soldier and a polished diplomat. He was experienced in colonial matters having been governor of Malta for five years. Plummer saw his role as peace keeper and held bias toward neither Jew nor Arab. Once when the Jews had scheduled a demonstration, the Mufti advised Lord Plummer that he could give no guarantee on behalf of the Arabs that peace and order would be preserved. The old soldier is said to have "put his eyeglass in his eye in characteristic fashion, given the Mufti an uncompromising stare and said: 'Your eminence, there is no need for you to be responsible. It is I who is responsible for the maintenance of order in Palestine.' "[4]

But in 1928, Lord Plummer relinquished his office and the Mufti immediately began planning and carrying out terrorist activities against the Jews though the British later exonerated him from all blame.[5] The alleyway adjoining the Wailing Wall had long been closed as a thoroughfare. He had it opened to traffic and began the age old hue and cry about the wall belonging to the Temple Mount which was, and is to this day, controlled by the Arabs. "He presented on October 8, 1928, a memorandum to the administration insinuating that the Jews intended to take possession of the Haram es Sharif, the third holiest shrine of Islam."[6] The British investigated and dismissed the allegations. But the storm was building with furious intensity.

In August of 1929, the storm broke. It all started rather innocently. A Jewish boy kicked a soccer ball into an Arab garden. According to an account by Henrietta Szold, a resident of Jerusalem at the time, "On August 17, a Jewish boy kicked a football into an Arab garden and ran to claim it. In the brawl that followed, he was stabbed to death by an Arab."[7] The Zionists seized the occasion of the boy's funeral to make a demonstration. In the days that followed riots swept the land. Ironically, Jews who had fled eastern Europe because of widespread pogroms, now faced merciless pogroms in the Promised Land.

Viscount Edwin Samuel wrote an eyewitness account of the riot in Jerusalem: "That afternoon, Friday, August 23, 1929, I was at the government offices, just outside the Damascus Gate. The first we knew of anything wrong was a faint and distant shouting, like the ominous buzzing of bees. Looking out from the balcony, I could see small groups of men running out of the Old City through the next exit, the New Gate, and pouring down the hill towards the Damascus Gate. Other Arabs came running out of the Damascus Gate itself and attacked any Jewish passers-by they happened to meet. I could see in the sunshine the flash of the daggers that most peasants then carried. Some Jews ran and escaped; others took refuge in nearby Arab houses ... some were attacked indoors and killed."[8]

The most ghastly incident was at Hebron where over 700 Jews lived. Armed Arabs came to Hebron on August 24, 1929, and slaughtered 60 Jewish men, women and children. In one incident 23 Jews had fled to an upstairs room for safety. The Arabs fell upon them with daggers and axes so that the blood of the innocent victims "ran down the stairs and soaked through the ceiling and splashed to the floor below."[9] The riots were most furious in Hebron and Safed. In all, 133 Jews were killed and 339 wounded. Arab losses were 116 dead and 232 wounded,[10] though most of the Arabs were casualties of police forces trying to restore order.

Chaim Weizmann was vacationing in Switzerland where he had recently attended the Sixteenth Zionist Congress in Zurich. Years later he wrote of how the news of the massacres in Palestine reached him. " 'The Under Secretary of State regrets to announce ...' were the first words of the cable which brought me the news of the Palestine pogroms of 1929 ... I was struck as by a thunderbolt."[11] Did his anguished response in 1929 echo the tumult of Psalm 29?

PSALM 30

I will extol thee, O LORD; for thou hast lifted me up, and hast not made my foes to rejoice over me (v. 1).

The opening verse of Psalm 30 seems to resound the thanks of the Jewish people for the turn of events between 1929 and 1930. If 1929 was a crucial year in the history of the entire world (and Israel in particular), then 1930 brought blessed, even though short-lived, relief from stormy times. True enough, the world was plunged into a great economic depression. Pogroms recently had ravaged Palestine. Stalin treated Russian Jews with a heavy hand and the ominous factions of Hitler, Mussolini and Tojo were on the rise. But, 1930 was a brief respite from the raging torrent of the previous year.

> ... *weeping may endure for a night, but joy cometh in the morning.*
> *LORD, by thy favor thou hast made my mountain to stand strong: thou didst hide thy face, and I was troubled* (vv. 5,7).

It's difficult to place this particular psalm in the correct chronology of David's life. It is titled, "A Psalm and the Song at the Dedication of the House of David." Yet, no Scripture is conspicuous indicating that David was in such dire straits at either the dedication of his palace or at the celebration of the purchase of the Temple site. "Modern scholars are agreed that the psalm is a personal testimony of God's mercy in a time of sore distress."[1]

The riots of late 1929 prompted the British to appoint a commission to "determine the rights and claims of Moslems and Jews in connection with the Western, or Wailing Wall in Jerusalem." That commission established certain rules for both Jews and Arabs regarding the Wall. These rules applied until 1948, when Israel became a nation.[2] But, of more serious consequence was the publication of a British White Paper redefining the Zionist political posture of the British government under the newly elected Ramsey MacDonald. The paper was drafted by the office of Sidney Webb who was British Secretary of State for the Colonies. Webb was given the title, Lord Passfield, and the report became known as the Passfield Paper. In essence, it was a pro-Arab document — as Golda Meir put it, "whittling down Jewish settlement and immigration to Palestine."[3] The paper obviously was biased in favor of the Arabs. It seems the Arabs, who had perpetrated the riots, also were to receive special benefits from the British.

When Chaim Weizmann returned to London he found everything changed. The recently elected Ramsey MacDonald government was distinctly cool toward Jewish problems in Palestine. Except with the Prime Minister himself, Weizmann appeared to have none of his former political clout. Passfield, in bureaucratic fashion, refused Weizmann an audience. Instead, his wife, Beatrice Webb granted him an interview. One needs little imagination to fathom the depths of his hurt and humiliation. The wealthy socialite snobbishly uttered, "I can't understand why the Jews make such a fuss over a few dozen of their people killed in Palestine. As many are killed every week in London traffic accidents, and no one pays any attention."[4]

In the parliamentary debates that followed, former Prime Minister Lloyd George accused MacDonald of failing the trust he had inherited with the office and breaking the word of England. Weizmann also conferred with MacDonald, eventually receiving a letter from him repudiating much of the anti-Zionist bias of the Passfield Paper. The Arabs called the letter a "black paper" charging that the MacDonald government had not acted in good faith.[5] "How foolish were the Zionist delegates at the 1931 Congress who blamed Weizmann for being satisfied with a letter!" wrote Weizmann in his autobiography.[6]

> *What profit is there in my blood, when I go down to the pit? ...*
> (v. 9).

The term "pit" is used elsewhere, implying a trap to enslave the Jews. It will culminate in the predicted "abomination of desolation" and will bring world-wide retaliation against the Jewish people. The anti-Semitic cry against so-called Jewish international bankers could bring on the future Armageddon, just as Hitler stirred up the German people in the 1930's. It must be noted that world Judaism is not guilty of plotting the enslavement of mankind. They are victims, used as a diversion by those who are behind the satanic conspiracy (see Psalm 88).

PSALM 31

> *Pull me out of the net that they have laid privily for me: for thou art my strength* (v. 4).

Again the *net* appears with increasing regularity. It is a trap laid by antichrist forces to bring about the extermination of the Jewish race. Hitler used the *net* effectively, but its greater use can be noted for the future (see Psalm 88).

> *I was a reproach among all mine enemies, but especially among my neighbors, and a fear to mine acquaintance: they that did see me without fled from me.*
> *I am forgotten as a dead man out of mind: I am like a broken vessel.*
> *For I have heard the slander of many; fear was on every side: While they took counsel together against me, they devised to take away my life.*
> *But I trusted in thee, O LORD: I said, Thou art my God.*
> *My times are in thy hand: deliver me from the hand of mine enemies, and from them that persecute me* (vv. 11-15).

Thoughts of betrayal by those whom he had befriended and threats of mortal danger from the very government he was dedicated to protect must have raced through David's mind as he composed Psalm 31. He was fleeing from the wrath of King Saul. Having been summoned by the Lord through the Prophet Gad to return to the land of Judah, he saved the town of Keila from destruction by the invading Philistines. However, the ungrateful citizens tried to lock him inside their town's fortress until King Saul could be summoned to capture him. He escaped to the Desert of Ziph only to be betrayed and forced again to elude sudden death from Saul (I Samuel 22:5; 23:1-19).

Similar events occurred in 1931 as the Jews struggled for a homeland in Palestine. Prime Minister of Great Britain Ramsey McDonald's letter to Chaim Weizmann on February 13th had been encouraging, but betrayal of the Zionist cause seemed to be on every hand. Even within the ranks of leadership in Palestine irreparable rifts in leadership were occurring. For example, Vladimir Jabotinsky came to the world Zionist Congress in Basle, Switzerland, that year with specific intentions of unseating Weizmann. Despite the fact that Weizmann resigned, the congress still carried out a humiliating no confidence vote.[1]

However, there were some blessings in disguise. During the Western World's "roaring 20's," Palestine "suffered through an economic blizzard."[2] Therefore, little of the impact of the Great Depression was felt there and the country recovered more rapidly than more highly industrialized nations. Consequently, as the Fifth Aliyah got underway the Zionists were able to absorb vastly more refugees than were anticipated. By 1935, 62,000 Jews were admitted to Palestine, "a figure undreamed of in 1930," wrote Weizmann.[3]

Joel prophesied, ... *your old men shall dream dreams, your young men shall see visions* ... (Joel 2:28). So it was in 1931. Young men like Jabotinsky, Ben-Gurion, Weizmann and Begin were dreaming dreams about a Jewish national homeland. Jews in Germany, Russia and America were dreaming of comfortable assimilation into Gentile populations. But, perhaps the most venerable sage of Judaism at that point in time was seeing what might be called an ominous vision. The Rabbi Chaim Ozer Grodzensky, affectionately known as "the Chofetz Chaim" foresaw the holocaust immediately ahead. "On the first day of Sukkos, 5692 (1931), the Chofetz Chaim ... knocked on the table and said in anxiety: I am not exaggerating. The time is coming when we shall be in danger. I am not talking about making a livelihood, but in danger of life, to our lives and the lives of our wives and children."[4]

Hitler had been pressing for anti-Semitic legislative bills in German national legislature since 1925. There were more than 700 racist and anti-Jewish newspapers cranking out propaganda. The so-called "Protocols of the Elders of Zion" were widely distributed. And as the Jews of Berlin left their synagogues following the Rosh Hashanah services in 1931 they were shocked by the frenzied taunts of truck loads of Blackshirts. "Heil Hitler! Juden raus! Schlagt die Juden tot! (Heil Hitler! Out with the Jews! Beat them to death!)"[5]

The lament of the psalmist in verse 12 seems to be apt for Jewry in the year 1931, *I am forgotten as a dead man out of mind; I am like a broken vessel.*

PSALM 32

When I kept silence, my bones waxed old through my roaring all the day long.
For day and night thy hand was heavy upon me: my moisture is turned into the drought of summer (vv. 3-4).

In 1932 the Nazi Party won a majority in the German national elections. Hitler was soon to become Chancellor of Germany. Prosperous Jewry became the target of ridicule. The Nazi party launched a campaign to accuse them of becoming rich at the expense of the German economy. Thus began an ever-increasing campaign against the Jews.

Germans were led to hate a whole race of people. The psalm aptly describes the heartaches of Jews in Germany during this period. Those who did not actively campaign against Hitler regretted not speaking out against his views of Aryan superiority. Little by little Hitler's insinuations brought recriminations against Jewish investments in the country. Shop owners were driven out of business. Bankruptcies and foreclosures became commonplace.

The Fifth Aliyah, which began in 1929, grew beyond all Zionist expectations in 1932 as Hitler ominously emerged as a beast from the depth. "I happened to be in Palestine when the first stream of German immigrants came in," wrote Chaim Weizmann. "Here they were, those German Jews, used to a regular and sheltered life, mostly in business or professional pursuits, altogether unfamiliar with social earthquakes of this kind, which were more or less commonplace in East European Jewry. They lacked, therefore, the flexibility and adaptability of the Russian or Polish Jews; they took ... their tragedy more desperately to heart. I saw them also in Germany as the shadows were closing in on them."[1]

Yet, in Germany many Jews hailed Hitler as a new leader who would correct the blunders of the Weimar government. Some had their names changed from those sounding Jewish because of their great love for the "fatherland." They actually thought of themselves as Germans first, then Jews — just as some American Jews feel today.[2]

Germany's Jews were, nevertheless, looked upon with scorn — blamed for every fluctuation in the economy. Soon to come were the yellow star patches, the ghettos, and the deportations to concentration camps. However, the world turned a deaf ear. They appeared to be blind to the increasing German persecution of the Jewish community.

PSALM 33

The LORD bringeth the counsel of the heathen to nought: he maketh the devices of the people of none effect (v. 10).

A certain moment, just before noon German time, January 30, 1933, is etched in the annals of infamy. That was the moment

Adolph Hitler was sworn in as Chancellor of Germany. Over the following twelve years he bathed Europe in an unprecedented bloodbath exterminating at least six million Jews and perhaps twice again as many Christians. His final fate was, as this psalm predicted, an ignoble death and a device brought to nought.

"Indeed, with Hitler's rise to power on January 30, 1933, the systematic and 'legal' destruction of German Jewry began."[1] After they had brushed aside the Weimar Constitution which had guaranteed parity in the eyes of the law to all citizens, Hitler and his cabinet had the power to enact laws without parliament. The "Enabling Act" of March 24, 1933, permitted the passage of laws which deviated from the Weimar Constitution. So began the first of four phases of Hitler's plan to annihilate the Jews from the face of the earth. A long series of laws against Jews and minorities were enacted over the following twelve years — the most dastardly, called the "Final Solution," will be discussed at length between Psalms 39 and 44.

Since the appearance of Hitler's MEIN KAMPF in 1926, it should have been evident to the whole world that if he ever rose to power he would systematically destroy the Jews of Europe and possibly all the Jews of the entire world. He spit out venom indicting all Jewry. They were described as "parasites, malignant germs, bloodsucking leeches, the personification of the devil and the very symbol of evil which were out to drag everything really great in the gutter."[2] He charged that the Jews intended to enslave the world. They were alien to Christianity, "the founder of which in holy anger took a whip to drive them out."[3]

PSALM 34

A Psalm of David, when he changed his behaviour before Abimelech; who drove him away, and he departed (introduction).

Alone and persecuted, David fled from the face of King Saul, armed only with the sword of Goliath whom he had recently slain on the battlefield. He fled for safety to the city of Gath where Achish (Abimelech) was king (I Samuel 21:10-15). It is said that the brothers of Goliath (who formed the king's bodyguard) recognized David and were appalled that he was brazen enough to

appear in their city armed only with their late brother's sword.
They demanded that David be executed. Otherwise, they
reasoned, the king must abdicate the throne in favor of David for
"to the victor go the spoils." They reasoned that the people of
Gath were the servants of David as he had single-handedly
defeated their army in the recent war.

But David feigned lunacy and God (according to Jewish
folktales) came to his rescue by causing the king's wife and
daughter also to be afflicted with insanity. Apparently, this threw
the palace into utter chaos. When David was brought forth for
trial the king uttered, "Do I lack madmen, that ye have brought
this fellow to play the madman in my presence?"[1] The king
ordered him to be released. Thus was David saved from the hands
of his enemies. Later he wrote Psalm 34 as an almost perfect
acrostic of the Hebrew language praising God for deliverance.

> *The eyes of the LORD are upon the righteous, and his ears are*
> *open unto their cry.*
> *The face of the LORD is against them that do evil, to cut off*
> *the remembrance of them from the earth* (vv. 15-16).

Lunacy of another magnitude loomed in Germany during 1934.
Hitler was demonstrating the madness of Nazism. As insanity so
long ago had invaded the palace of David's enemies at Gath, so
crazed destructive madness deluded the leadership of Germany.
Like David in ancient times, the Jews of Europe were alone and
persecuted. Even the most imaginative pessimist amongst the
Jews could not have foreknown the insanity of Nazi Germany and
the anguish of blood and tears to be unleashed in the months
ahead.

Thousands of Jews fled Nazi Germany while hundreds of others
committed suicide.[2] Seldom, if ever, has the world witnessed the
wave of madness which swept Germany in 1934. Those within the
palace had the mind-set of an evil power bent on the utter destruction of all God's people.

> *Evil shall slay the wicked: and they that hate the righteous*
> *shall be desolate* (v. 21).

And so it was in the end. But in the interim, millions of in-
nocents would be brutally murdered. It was not the world's finest
hour.

PSALM 35

Plead my cause, O LORD, with them that strive with me:
fight against them that fight against me (v. 1).

It is not known for sure when David wrote this psalm. "Internal evidence seems to fix the date of its composition in those troublous times when Saul hunted David over hill and dale," wrote C. H. Spurgeon, "and when those, who fawned upon the cruel king, slandered the innocent object of his wrath, or it may be referred to the unquiet days of frequent insurrections in David's old age." Spurgeon goes on to characterize the psalm as analogous to Christ's prayer in the Garden of Gethsemane. There is a triple character in the song. "Its complaint, prayer, and promise of praise are repeated with remarkable parallelism three times, even as our Lord in the Garden prayed three times using the same words."[1]

In many ways, the year 1935 was reminiscent of the anguish of both Psalm 35 and the dreadful experience of Jesus in the Garden. The Jews of Europe faced false accusers, traitorous betrayers and isolation from deliverance. From the PALESTINE POST on October 28, 1935, came this headline: "Nazis apply Nuremburg Laws against the Jews in Germany." The article read, "Jews in Germany may no longer participate actively or passively in municipal elections, although they must continue to pay municipal taxes."[2] The announcement explained that since the Jews are no longer citizens of the Reich, they are automatically deprived of their municipal citizenship rights.

As early as "Boycott Day," April 1, 1933, the Jews of Germany had been singled out for persecution. On that day hundreds of non-Jews were legally prohibited from buying in Jewish-owned shops. Three days later, Jews were barred from civil service and public employment at all levels of government on the pretext that it was illegal for "non-Aryans" to hold government jobs.

But it wasn't until 1935 that the Nuremburg Laws were enacted defining who non-Aryans were and defining their status as citizens. These laws legitimated racism and anti-Semitism and provided legal basis for the "purity of German blood." Marriage and extramarital relations between Germans and Jews resulted in the disenfranchisement of the "subjects" or "nationals" living in Germany but not of German blood. It became an obsession with the Nazis to legally define non-Aryans. Basically, the Nuremburg Laws divided them into three categories. (1) A "Jew" was anyone with at least three Jewish grandparents, or anyone who had two Jewish grandparents and belonged to the religious Jewish community as of September 15, 1935, or afterward. (2) A "Mischling, first degree" was anyone with two Jewish grandparents but was not married to a Jew and did not belong to the Jewish religious community. And (3) A "Mischling, second degree" was anyone with only one Jewish grandparent. Thus was set in motion an ungodly plan to seek out, identify and exterminate all Jews dwelling anywhere in the Nazi regime.

Dr. Leo Baeck was the rabbi of Berlin. He was especially gifted with foresight. While most of the Jewish leadership considered the anti-Semitic policies of the Nazis as merely propaganda he stated as early as April, 1933, "The thousand-year-old history of German-Jewry is at an end."[3] He composed a special prayer for the somber Yom Kippur service that year. "We stand before our God," the prayer read, "with the same courage with which we confess our sins, individual and collective, we shall declare with deep aversion that the lies against us, and the defamation of our religion and its teachings, are far beneath our dignity. We stand by our faith and our fate. ... We stand before our God. ... Before Him we bow, but we stand upright before men ..."[4]

It is interesting that the overtones of this pious rabbi's prayer in the troubled times of Germany in 1935, closely parallels David's prayer in times of trouble recorded in Psalm 35.

PSALM 36

The transgression of the wicked saith within my heart, that there is no fear of God before his eyes.

For he flattereth himself in his own eyes, until his iniquity be found to be hateful.

The words of his mouth are iniquity and deceit: he has left off to be wise, and to do good.

He deviseth mischief upon his bed; he setteth himself in a way that is not good; he abhorreth not evil (vv. 1-4).

David could not have produced a more graphic description of

Adolph Hitler and his policies had he been alive in 1936. In the November 15th edition of the publication "Kommende Kirche," the German church was castigated for having the wrong attitude toward the Jewish question. "The Evangelical Church was declared to have disappointed the high hopes that have been placed in its positive contribution to the solution of this life and death issue before the German people. The church had failed to implement within its own society the separation of German blood from Jewish blood and was guilty of the sin of allowing Germans to be ministered to by those of Jewish or mixed blood. This was nothing less than disloyalty and disobedience not only to Adolph Hitler but to God Who had sent Hitler to the German people. ... God was at work through Adolph Hitler. To further his work was to serve God, to sabotage his work was to serve the devil. 'Thou shalt love the German Volk:' this was God's call, and it involved the protection of the German people from its archenemies, the devilish Jews."[1]

In the previous month Karl Holz, an official of the church, had uttered, "If in one night all the Jews in the whole world were in one stroke struck dead, that would be the most sacred red letter day in the whole of world history. No Christian love may be shown to the Jews. Christ showed none toward them. He drove them out of the Temple. The father of the Jews is the devil."[2]

Toward the end of the year the German Evangelical Church encountered increasing difficulty in dealing with the Nazis. The passage of the Nuremberg Laws apparently split the church's leadership. It was dangerous to oppose any of the Nazi party propaganda. Non-supportive members of the liaison between the government and the Evangelical Church were forced to resign. It's not surprising, then, that on February 12, 1937, the new chairman of the Reich Church Committee in his inaugural speech uttered blasphemies. "The recognition of Jesus as the Son of God," he proclaimed, "[is] ridiculously inessential." He stated that the Fuhrer was the purveyor of a new revelation of a twofold commandment to love one's nation above all else and to love one's neighbor — neighbors being those who are one's brother by blood."[3]

Months later when Hitler's forces invaded Russia, the German Christians in Thuringia in a burst of pride issued a pulpit manifesto to be read in the churches. It stated that the fight now

being waged "... in the most profound sense was a conflict between the divine and satanic forces of the world, between Christ
and antichrist, between light and darkness, between love and
hate, between order and chaos, between the eternal German and
the eternal Jew." The policies of Hitler were portrayed as divine
and holy while the policies of the world's churches were evil and
that the churches "once more had betrayed Christ and crucified
Him afresh."[4]

Indeed, 1936 was a hateful and cruel year for both German Jews
and Christians. On February 19th, Friedrich Weissler, a Jewish
Christian attorney, became the first martyr of the German Con-
fessing Church. It was now obvious that not only were the Jews to
be annihilated, Evangelical Christians also would not be tolerated
amongst the so-called "master race."

PSALM 37

> *Fret not thyself because of evildoers, neither be thou envious*
> *against the workers of iniquity* (v. 1).

"Whenever the superscription of a psalm is merely 'to David,'
then it is neither a song nor a prayer," wrote Rabbi Avrohom
Chaim Feuer, "It is the Holy Spirit speaking through David."[1] In
this sequel to Psalm 36, the righteous are urged not to be envious
nor compete with the success of the wicked. "The prosperity of
the wicked," commented G. Campbell Morgan, "has within it the
elements of its own destruction, and cannot last."[2]

> *The wicked plotteth against the just, and gnasheth upon him*
> *with his teeth.*
> *The wicked have drawn out the sword, and have bent their*
> *bow, to cast down the poor and needy, and to slay such as be of*
> *upright conversation* (vv. 12, 14).

Rabbi Obadiah Ben Jacob Sforno (a sixteenth century
Talmudist) commented that David composed this psalm while inspired with a prophetic vision of the forthcoming rebellion led by
Jeroboam against David's grandson Rehoboam. The ten tribes of
the north would be taken away leaving only Judah and Benjamin
as the kingdom of David. According to Feuer, "Sforno relates

every verse of the psalm to an event in the long struggle between the kingdoms of Judah and Israel."[3]

In 1937, the wicked Nazis seemed to prosper and had the upper hand over German Jews and Evangelical Christians. But, as pointed out by Morgan, verses 12 through 20 of this psalm states that the prosperity of the wicked has the elements of destruction built into itself. Nazism was no exception. Hitler had predicted that the Aryan "master race" would rule a thousand years. The devastating attempts to bring about such a regime lasted only twelve dreadful years.

"The wicked have drawn out the sword," and the sword appeared to be polished and ready to begin the slaughter. The plans for the "Final Solution" were already being prepared. Within months the bloody sword would reap a grim harvest. The first phase of Aryanization, from January, 1933, to November, 1938, was more or less a voluntary transfer of Jewish holdings into German hands. Soon the systematic slaughter of the Jews would begin.

By late 1937, the German Jew had no civil rights. He had no freedom of speech and could not defend himself in print. He could not vote or attend a political meeting; be employed as a civil servant; work as a writer, artist, musician, or actor. He could not teach, belong to a professional organization, or receive government aid even if he were starving. He could not buy food and drugs in some stores. More and more he was ostracized by his neighbors. His only hope was to get out of Germany. During 1937, 23,000 emigrated, bringing the number of refugees to a total of 129,000. About one-fourth of the original German Jewish population had fled the country since 1933. Those who remained had little hope of escape.[4] Indeed, the sword was drawn out and the bow bent to slay the upright.

PSALM 38

My lovers and my friends stand aloof from my sore; and my kinsmen stand afar off.

They also who seek after my life lay snares for me: and they that seek my hurt speak mischievous things, and imagine deceits all the day long (vv. 11-12).

The last four psalms of this Genesis section deal with a common theme. David is afflicted with serious illnesses which he acknowledges were caused by his sins. Instead of lamenting in a negative way, he presents lessons and insights which he gained from his suffering. "According to many commentaries," wrote Avrohom Feuer, "this psalm contains a deeper message, as it expresses the feelings of the entire nation of Israel which suffers from the ravages of the long dark exile."[1]

The year 1938 was a crucial period in the development of the emerging holocaust. Hitler dismissed the last moderate leaders from his evil government. The road was cleared for war and for the destruction of the Jews. Since 1933 steady and consistent pressure had been applied to the Jews of Germany. First the Jews were boycotted, then by legislation their citizenship and economic status were stripped away; emigration was encouraged. There was even a plan suggested to move the Jews to Madagascar where it was hoped they would perish due to the tropical climate. So far the Jewish question had seen very little violence.

But in 1938, it became obvious that as many as six million Jews were in danger of annihilation. In March, Austria was absorbed. Under Adolph Eichmann mass arrests of Jews took place as he perfected his "Center for Emigration of Jews, a device which plundered and expelled Jews simultaneously."[2] In July, thirty-two nations sent representatives to Evian, Switzerland, to see what refuge would be offered to the persecuted Jews. Just before the conference met, Hitler ordered mass arrests of Jews and destroyed synagogues in Munich, Nuremberg, and Dortmund. Within a week the delegates returned without having reached any decisions whatsoever. Not one nation, including the United States was willing to change immigration policies for the Jews. Verse 11 seems to describe the world's mood, *My lovers and my friends stand aloof from my sore.*

> But I, as a deaf man, heard not; and I was as a dumb man that openeth not his mouth.
> But mine enemies are lively, and they are strong: and they that hate me wrongfully are multiplied (vv. 13,19).

In October, under the direction of Reinhard Heydrich hundreds of Jews were rounded up like animals and brutally driven into

Poland. Among them was a man named Zindel Grynspann. He wrote to his teenage son in Paris describing the brutalities.

On November 7, the lad, in desperation, walked into the German embassy in Paris intending to shoot the ambassador. He was directed, instead, to a counselor named Ernst vom Rath whom he shot. Vom Rath died two days later. Hitler had become bold enough to disregard world opinion, perhaps due to the lethargic results of the Evian Conference. He ordered mass retaliation on the Jews for the death of the obscure embassy employee.

Mass destruction of Jewish property took place in a pogrom called "Crystal Night." Organized riots led by soldiers in plain clothes swept across Germany on the night of November 10. Heydrich reported that 815 shops, 171 homes and 76 synagogues were destroyed and 191 synagogues were set on fire. The value of shattered plate glass alone amounted to twenty-four million marks and was estimated to equal one-half of the annual glass production of Belgium from which it was imported. Thirty-six Jews were killed and thirty-six seriously injured and 20,000 were sent to concentration camps.

Nazi crimes against the Jewish people were so fierce they were hard to believe. Most of the world turned a deaf ear to the atrocities just as the psalm implies. It seemed that few spoke out against Hitler. On November 11, 1938, however, the PALESTINE POST brandished this headline: "Nazi hooligans vent wrath on the Jews throughout Germany."[3] Two days later the "Palestine Post" published this headline: "New Nazi savagery spells doom of Jewish life in Germany."[4] According to the report, Jews were hiding in the woods outside Berlin. There were reports of torture and murder. Indeed, the heartache of God's Chosen People during the year of 1938 seems to be mirrored in Psalm 38.

PSALM 39

To the chief Musician, even to Jeduthun, A Psalm of David (introduction).

"This psalm," wrote Rabbi Avrohom Feuer, "conveys the dismal mood of a crushed man, or nation, shrouded in the gloom of failure and defeat."[1] He goes on to explain that homiletically, the Hebrew word for Jeduthun refers to "the evil decrees and oppressive laws which the enemy imposes on either the individual or the collective nation of Israel."[2] Psalms 39, 62, and 77 are all dedicated to Jeduthun and represent the chants of the victim of persecution and oppression.

This was certainly the situation of the Jews of Germany in 1939. As early as January 30, Hitler uttered this fearful threat, "Today I want to be a prophet once again: If the international Jewish financial establishment in and outside Europe should succeed once again in plunging the peoples of the world into war, then the result will not be a Bolshevization of the globe and thus a victory for Judaism, but the annihilation of the Jewish race in Europe." [3] That prophecy was reiterated in January and September of 1941. Dr. Joseph Goebbels stated flatly on November 16, 1941, "We are witnessing the fulfillment of this prophecy at this very moment."[4]

> ... I will keep my mouth with a bridle, while the wicked is before me.
> I was dumb with silence, I held my peace, even from good; and my sorrow was stirred (vv. 1-2).

Persecution of Jews worsened. Yet, there was little outcry. They were afraid to protest, hoping that with the turn of each new day relief would come. In some uncanny way, Psalm 39 captures the spirit of the year.

The Nazis were seeking the deportation of all German Jews. There were open threats and indications of a plan to destroy all European Jewry. "Between December 1939 and August 1941, about 50,000 to 60,000 Jews - children and adults - were secretly killed by lethal injections and in gassing installations designed to look like shower rooms. It was a foretaste of Auschwitz.[5] These victim's ashes were shipped to relatives who were warned not to demand explanations or to spread "false rumors".

Meanwhile, Reinhold Heydrich was given the go-ahead to develop the Reich Central Office for Jewish Emigration. It was patterned after Eichmann's operation in Vienna. Ultimately, all Jews within the Reich were to be put into concentration camps or closed ghettos. In the end it fostered the "final solution" to the Jewish problem.[6]

Czechoslovakia was occupied in March bringing over 315,000 Jews under Nazi domination. In September Poland surrendered.

Three and a third million Jews comprised ten percent of Poland's population. At the beginning of 1939, about 270,000 Jews of Germany and Austria were suffering under Hitler's cruel regime. By the end of that year the number approached four million.

> *My heart was hot within me, while I was musing the fire burned: ... (v. 3).*

Could this be a cryptic prediction of those horrifying events which fell upon the Jews of Europe? The "fire" may well be a reference to the ovens of Auschwitz along with those of the other death camps where millions were cremated.

> *LORD, make me to know mine end, and the measure of my days,... (v. 4).*

There is no hope evidenced in that request. There is only a resignation that the end is near. The future proved to be bleak indeed for the persecuted Jews. Death for millions lay ahead in Hitlers concentration camps.

> *Behold, thou hast made my days as an handbreadth; and mine age as nothing before thee: verily every man at his best state is altogether vanity. Selah (v. 5).*

"At this point the persecuted man is overwhelmed by his tragedy, and questions the value of life itself."[7] Eventually, six million precious people — mothers, fathers, children, grandparents — were to be horribly slaughtered.

Also in 1939, the British restricted Jewish emigration to Palestine. The Arab riots of 1936 had intensified the Palestinian situation. There was much debate about partitioning the land between Jews and Arabs. No action was taken, however, leaving the Jews as a minority in an Arab state. Jewish immigration was limited to 75,000 over the next five years. After that there was to be none unless the Arabs agreed. The British once again appeared to have given the edge to the Arabs.[8] From this time forward it was obvious that the Jews of Palestine inevitably would have to fight the British in order to establish a Jewish National homeland.

PSALM 40

I waited patiently for the LORD; and he inclined unto me, and heard my cry.
He brought me up also out of an horrible pit, out of the miry clay, and set my feet upon a rock, and established my goings.
And he hath put a new song in my mouth, ... (vv. 1-3).

In the first eleven of these seventeen verses, one would think that David was enjoying peace and prosperity, but not so. The last six verses reveal that he was surrounded by many dangers and was in desperate need of deliverance. Such was also the case, by the way, for the Jews in Eastern Europe in 1940.

Rabbi Rashi wrote almost a thousand years ago that the psalm also alluded to the future Messianic redemption and "will stimulate unprecedented waves of fresh song and jubilation."[1]

This *new song* compares with that of the Jewish remnant during the Tribulation Period. *And they* [144,000] *sung as it were a new song before the throne ...* (Revelation 14:3). Though 1940 was not the year for a new song, the events of that year will eventually lead to the fulfillment of the prophecy.

Jewish rabbis suggest that when God saves through natural means, an existing song should be used to express gratitude. But when redemption comes by supernatural means, a new song should be written. A *new song* is also called for in Psalms 96:1 and 98:1. They are part of a series of twelve psalms (95-106) which follow the glorious appearing of Messiah, ultimately fulfilling the prophecy alluded to in Psalm 40.

Many, O LORD my God, are thy wonderful works which thou hast done, and thy thoughts which are to usward (v. 5).

Jewish insight into this verse concurs with events as they were in 1940, for as early as the eleventh century, Rashi wrote that God's thoughts were occupied with long term plans for Israel's welfare. The Midrash adds, "God's concern for the ultimate success of Israel is the guiding force behind all events in history, even those which originally seemed to be detrimental. For example, Isaac became blind only so that Jacob should later be able to take the blessings which Isaac had intended for Esau. (All dark spots in history are for the sake of future light.)"[2]

> For innumerable evils have compassed me about: Mine ini-
> quities have taken hold upon me, so that I am not able to look up;
> they are more than the hairs of my head: therefore, my heart
> faileth me (v. 12).

The first twelve verses of this psalm echo a joyous mood depicting the unrelenting faith of David during difficult times. The latter verses show that it was written during many dangers. It is another example of the psalmist's ability to enjoy rapturous joy in the midst of abject despair.

The year 1940 held little joy for the Jews of Europe. For example, in Poland, Chaim Kaplan was a Hebrew teacher and author who became entrapped in the Warsaw Ghetto after November 15th. He kept a meticulous diary. "We are used to seeing the victims of the sword in war. We are used to counting the dead, the wounded, the physically maimed, and the mentally disturbed," he wrote.[3] "In previous wars," he continued, "the front had almost no organic connection with the nation in the rear, its creator ... Not so today: modern war is a people's war. Its front extends from the dwellings of paupers to the halls of princes. Every citizen is a soldier on the battlefield" (February 14, 1940).[4]

"The conquerors," Kaplan reported, "have begun a new political campaign. Gangs of young toughs, Polish youth (you won't find an adult among them) armed with clubs, sticks and all kinds of dangerous weapons, make pogroms against the Jews" (March 28, 1940). These roving bands, directed by some invisible hand, looted, maimed and robbed at will. "These sons of Ham — just a year ago shouted in their patriotic fervor, 'Long live Poland! Long live Smigly-Rydz!' They now shout, in their conquered capital, in the presence of those who conquered their land, 'Long live Hitler! Death to the Smigly-Rydz! We want a Poland without Jews.' Is it possible? Yes, I swear it is so. These accursed youth, walking in the ruins of their homeland, organize demonstrations in honor of the Fuhrer."[5]

"Today," Kaplan lamented, "the frightening news reached us of the expulsion of the entire Jewish community of Cracow, and we are turned as if stone" (July 30, 1940). In his diary for the ninth of Av, Tishe'ah Be'av, a day of fasting (August 12, 1940), Kaplan's entry read, "Public prayer in these dangerous days is a forbidden act. Anyone caught is doomed to severe punishment. If you will it is even sabotage and is subject to execution. But that does not deter us. Jews come to pray in rooms behind drawn curtains ... How good it is to be a Jew! The Lodz Ghetto ... is a prison for 100,000 miserable Jews who depended on miracles and did not leave the city when its gates were still open ..." (August 26, 1940).[6]

On November 15 the conquering Germans closed the Warsaw Ghetto. It had become a virtual prison. Jews were forced to wear the "badge of shame," as he put it, a star of David on an arm band with the name "Jew" emblazoned upon it. Jews were no longer permitted to pass into the Aryan section of Warsaw without special permission. On November 17 he wrote, "What we dreaded most has come to us. We had a premonition that ghetto life awaited us."[7] It was only a matter of time before most Polish Jews were exterminated.

1940 was a busy war year for the Germans. In April, Denmark and Norway were invaded. In the following month, France, the Netherlands and Belgium were overrun. France capitulated on June 21. So sure were the Nazis that France could not hold out, that on June 18, Hitler broached the Madagascar Plan to Mussolini. Madagascar was at the time a colonial holding of France in the Indian Ocean off East Africa. During 1940 millions of Jews came under direct Nazi domination. As a result, most would face tragic and merciless death during the following months.

The number 40 is comprised of a single Hebrew letter "mem," meaning "water"[8] and denotes the upcoming birth of Israel. The nation was to be "born of water" in 1948. Also, the number 46 means "water," adding to the emphasis that the 1940's would see the birth of the nation.

It is quite possible that Jesus had a prophetic message for the nation on the night He met with Nicodemus, a representative of the government. Jesus said, *Except a man* [Israel?] *be born of water and of the Spirit, he cannot enter into the kingdom of God* (John 3:5). Since Israel was born of water in 1948, the nation may be approaching that day when it will be born of the Spirit! Soon after, the kingdom will come!

Psalms 80, 81, 85, and 86 have numbers with Hebrew meanings which lend to the nation's upcoming birth *of the Spirit.* The numbers 80 and 85 both mean "mouth," while 81 and 86 both mean "to blow." Could this multiplicity of numbers mean Israel will be born of the Spirit soon?

The number 80, in the Hebrew alphabet, is a single letter "peh," signifying "a mouth"[9] and may represent a very important turn of events for Israel in the Leviticus period. Compare the number 40 (mem) meaning "water" with 80 (peh) implying the "Spirit." Several examples of this come to mind. First, on the evening of His resurrection Jesus appeared to the disciples, told them about the prophecies in the Psalms, then *breathed on them, and saith unto them, Receive ye the Holy Ghost* (John 20:22). It was as if He were demonstrating that one day Israel would be born of water, then later, of the Holy Spirit!

Secondly, Ezekiel prophesied to the valley of dry bones and they developed into a host of lifeless bodies. Then God said, *Prophesy unto the wind, prophesy, son of man, and say to the wind, Thus saith the Lord GOD; Come from the four winds, O breath, and breathe upon these slain, that they may live. So I prophesied as he commanded me, and the breath came unto them, and they lived, and stood up upon their feet, an exceeding great army* (Ezekiel 37:9-10). This process in the revival of the bones of Israel was made in two steps. As a fulfillment, the 1940's saw the nation born of water. Soon, we should see the nation born of the Spirit.

PSALM 41

> Blessed is he that considereth the poor: the LORD will deliver him in time of trouble.
> The LORD will preserve him and keep him alive; and he shall be blessed upon the earth: and thou wilt not deliver him unto the will of his enemies (vv. 1-2).

This psalm opens with a promise that in the time of trouble God will deliver the man who has stood by the poor. Finis J. Dake comments on this passage, that the Hebrew word for "keep him alive" is "chayah" meaning to restore life, hence, resurrection. Further, in verse 4, the psalmist cries *heal my soul.* This is the only reference in the Bible for soul healing.[1]

> Mine enemies speak evil of me, When shall he die, and his name perish? (v. 5).

Could *he* be Adolf Hitler? His wicked designs against the Jewish people were worse than any other enemy in history. His propaganda campaign engendered hatred of Jews across Eastern Europe. No one else has so deserved to have his name erased from annals of the human race.

The number 41 is made up of two Hebrew letters "mem" and "aleph." They comprise the word "maw" meaning "what?"[2] It denotes consternation and aptly describes the frustration of the Jewish people in 1941. The numbers 45 and 46 also have the same meaning. After going through the Holocaust, the weary Jews were questioning the purpose of it all. They did not understand that those were years of birthpangs for the birth of the nation.

All that hate me whisper together against me: against me do they devise my hurt (v. 7).

All European Jews were in anguish of soul in 1941. In February the deportation of Dutch Jews to the Mauthasen concentration camp began after a small group attacked German police in Amsterdam. "Four hundred thirty Jews were arrested and they were literally tortured to death first in Buchenwald and then in Mauthasen. For months they died a thousand deaths, and every single one of them would have envied his brethren in Auschwitz ..."[3] The intense brutality was designed to keep armed resistance to a minimum.

A plan to resettle European Jews on the island of Madagascar was still under consideration in 1941. However, with the invasion of Russia on June 22 that option was dropped when the Einsatzgruppen operations commenced. These were mobile killing operations carried out by killer squads which ranged across European Russia behind the war zone systematically massacring the entire populations of Jewish villages. "During the first sweep the mobile killing units reported approximately 100,000 victims a month."[4]

Heydrich, who organized the mobile killing units, was given the go ahead to prepare a "total solution" to the European Jewish problem on July 31, 1941. It was to be more secretive than the bloody Einsatzgruppen method. Basically Jews were to be identified, concentrated into groups and transported eastward to death camps.[5]

Meanwhile, the mobile killing units swept through Russia killing Jews "like sleeping flies." Between June and September hundreds of thousands had been slaughtered. At Kamenets Podolski, on September 1, 1941, 26,000 were shot.[6]

On November 28, 1941, Hitler entertained a special visitor from Jerusalem. He was Haj Amin Husseini, the Grand Mufti and titular head of the Arab world. As Germany had occupied no Arabic lands, the Mufti noted that a public declaration of German intentions "would be of immense propagandistic value in the campaign to mobilize the Arab Nations ..." Hitler responded that the fundamental attitude of Germany was self-evident. "Germany," he explained, "had declared an uncompromising war on the Jews. Such a commitment naturally entailed a stiff opposition to the Jewish homeland in Palestine ..."[7] Hundreds of youthful Arab adherents to the Grand Mufti formed an "Arab legion and joined the Axis powers in the War."[8]

On December 8, 1941, just one day after the Japanese attacked Pearl Harbor, the first Jews were herded into an airtight chamber at Chelmno and gassed to death. Simultaneously, 25,000 who had been concentrated in a German ghetto in Riga, Latvia, were murdered by an Einsatzgruppen sweep. The gassing method of annihilation was destined to replace the mobile field operating method of mass killings. "In terms of productivity, secrecy, and psychological costs to the killers," wrote Browning, "the factories of death, processing their victims on an assembly line basis, rendered the old Einsatzgruppen method as obsolete as a cottage industry."[9]

> *An evil disease, say they, cleaveth fast unto him: and now that he lieth he shall rise up no more* (v. 8).

The passage is believed to refer primarily to David who was too sick to stand. It was necessary, however, for him to stand while transmitting orally the Temple Scroll to his son, Solomon.

> *But thou, O LORD, be merciful unto me, and raise me up, that I may requite them* (v. 10).

According to rabbinic scholars, David revealed the reason for his illness. God would not permit him to build the Temple. In this verse, he prays for strength to stand while he gives the details of the Temple Scroll to his son. God had given Moses a detailed description of the future Temple with its many secrets. Moses received the scroll while standing.

Because of the holiness of the document, both the one who transmitted the scroll and the one who received it were required to stand. Moses stood as he gave it to Joshua. Joshua stood as he delivered it to the elders. The elders stood while they imparted it to the prophets. Samuel, the prophet, stood as he gave it to David. Now David must stand to share it with Solomon. That was the problem. David was so sick that he could not stand. This verse was his prayer for strength.

It seems as if the doomed Jewish people in 1941 were denied the privilege of restoring the Temple — though that had been the dream of every generation. In 1947 a "Temple Scroll" would be discovered in the caves near the Dead Sea. Eventually the scroll would be published. Perhaps the famed Temple Scroll which fell into Israeli hands in 1967, published first in 1978 and in English in 1984, is the same scroll spoken of in Jewish history. It is possible that the Temple will be built one day in accordance with the scroll. But those who died in the Holocaust were deprived of its message.

Blessed be the LORD God of Israel from everlasting, and to everlasting. Amen, and Amen (v. 13).

Psalm 41 concludes the Genesis book of the Psalms. It is a somber message which reminds us of the oncoming holocaust. Moses' book of Genesis likewise records the death of Jacob. Afterward, the fearful brethren beg Joseph to forgive their trespass. Joseph reminds them that their rejection of him served a divine purpose. He said, *But as for you, ye thought evil against me; but God meant it unto good, to bring to pass, as it is this day, to save much people alive* (Genesis 50:20).

The enigma of the Jewish Holocaust has engendered the question, "Why?" We may not know all the answers, but one day, we will be told why God let it happen. There had to be a divine purpose.

Amen, and Amen concludes this first book of the Psalms. They represent a prophecy declaring, "So be it! So be it!" (See the chapter, The Prophetic Amen.)

THE
EXODUS
PSALMS

INTRODUCTION TO THE EXODUS PSALMS

Psalms 42-72 comprise the second book of the Psalms. It was compiled by Solomon and compares with the Mosaic book of Exodus. Moses' book opens with the Jews suffering under the slavery of Pharoah. If Psalm 42 compares with 1942, one must note that the Jews were suffering another imposed slavery — brought on by Hitler. The comparison is uncanny and alludes to a prophecy by Micah, *According to the days of thy coming out of the land of Egypt will I show unto him marvellous things* (Micah 7:15). The modern exodus out of Europe compares with Israel's ancient exodus out of Egypt.

Psalms 42-49 are ascribed to the sons of Korah. These eight psalms are added to four others (84, 85, 87, and 88) making a total of twelve. The sons of Korah were Kohathites to whom were given the honor of caring for the Ark of the Covenant. Their father, Korah, had rebelled against Mosaic authority (Numbers 16). The earth opened up and swallowed him, but his sons were loyal to Moses and the service of the Tabernacle. The prophet, Samuel, was a member of their tribe.

The twelve psalms attributed to the Sons of Korah make up a number of governmental perfection. "It is found in all that has to do with rule."[1] With the opening of the Exodus series of the Psalms by those priests who cared for the Ark of the Covenant we may have embarked upon that period which will see its discovery and return to Jerusalem. Perhaps Temple worship will be revived before another generation is gone. (See introduction to the Leviticus Psalms 73-89.)

PSALM 42

My tears have been my meat day and night, while they continually say unto me, Where is thy God? (v. 3).

The psalmist describes the anguish of the long exile for all Israel. Certainly, the sufferings of the Holocaust made a dreadful climax to centuries of Jewish heartache. It is said that a group of Jews in one of the concentration camps put God on trial. They accused Deity of all their problems. There were lawyers for the plaintiffs and lawyers for the defense. A judge and jury heard the case which took several days. Finally, a verdict was brought in. The jury, made up of Jewish prisoners, declared God to be guilty! None ever felt so forgotten as they.

I will say unto God my rock, Why hast thou forgotten me? why go I mourning because of the oppression of the enemy? (v. 9).

Enemy oppression against the Jews was multiplied in 1942. "Blitzkrieg tactics had fizzled out, and the war was behind schedule. The 'lesser races' must be reduced in order that Germany, sustaining a possible defeat in her present struggle, would be certain of victory in World War III."[2] Minor races within the Reich were to be annihilated in order for a master race to ascend.

Accordingly, Reinhard Heydrich was assigned the responsibility of coordinating the "Final Solution" to the Jewish question. He called a ninety-minute conference of fifteen top Nazi leaders on January 20, 1942, in a villa at Waansee, a suburb of Berlin. The meeting was followed by luncheon and drinks.

He unveiled a master plan to exterminate all eleven million Jews in Nazi occupied territories. No longer would Jews be allowed to emigrate. Instead, they were to be evacuated from west to east in columns. "In the course of this labor utilization a majority would 'fall away through natural decline.' The survivors would be treated accordingly."[3] This was a veiled allusion to the planned death camps.

Basically, the eight points of the agenda called for a forced deportation eastward of all Jews in the western part of Europe. The list even included British Jews. Other governments were to be encouraged to pass anti-Semitic legislation similar to Germany's Nuremburg Laws. The execution of the proposed measures was to be done in secrecy and on friendly terms with the Gestapo.[4]

By March 26 twenty thousand Slovak Jews were evacuated in a trial run of the deportation procedure. Two days later the first French trainload of six thousand Jews traveled to Auschwitz to await the gas chambers.

Heydrich was attacked by Czech patriots in Prague, May 27, 1942. He died June 5 and the world was rid of perhaps the most ruthless murderer of all time. Thousands of Jews were rounded up and executed in retaliation and the program of deportation and extermination was stepped up. In fact, just eighteen days after Heydrich's assassination the first selection of victims for Auschwitz's new gas took place.[5] Meanwhile, mobile extermination gas vans traversed occupied territories in Eastern Europe where victims were stripped, placed into airtight bus-like vehicles, asphyxiated by exhaust fumes and buried in mass graves. During 1941-42 more than a million Jews and Soviets were murdered by marauding Einsatzgruppen units on military orders issued by Heydrich's office.

Deportations from France and the Netherlands began July, 17. In order to easily identify Jews in these occupied zones it was decreed that every Jew must wear a yellow Star of David. Country after country caved in to German pressure and deported Jews eastward to concentration and death camps. In August, Belgium and Rumania began deportations, followed by Norway in November. The year ended with a whimper as the Allied nations "pledged punishment for the extermination of the Jews."[6]

As with a sword in my bones, mine enemies reproach me;
while they say daily unto me, Where is thy God? (v. 10).

"On the twentieth of Tammuz, 1941, the Nazis ordered the Jewish inhabitants of Telshe, Lithuania, to dig their own graves. As they stood in the open pits, the Rav and Rosh Yeshiva of

Telshe, HaGaon Rav Avrohom Yitzchak Bloch, led the martyrs of his community in their final declaration of eternal faith, the Shema. 'Hear O Israel, Hashem [the Name] is our God, Hashem is One!' The Nazi beasts gleefully taunted the Rav, 'Where is your God now?' The Rav replied courageously, 'Not only is He my God, He is also your God, and the day will come when you too will realize it!' "[7]

Though the event occurred in 1941 it points up the prophetic impact of Psalm 42. Also, one must note that it is not necessary that the prophetic theme of verse one of each psalm start on January 1 nor for the last verse of a psalm to be concluded on the last day of December. The general prophetic theme is the important thing in these incredible psalms. Nor is it necessary to consider the Jewish calendar which begins each New Year with the first day of Tishri at the New Moon in September or early October. What is important is that we note the ebb and flow of these prophetic psalms.

The number 42 is made up of the Hebrew letters "mem" and "beth" and provide a root for the word "mibdalah" meaning "a separation."[8] It aptly describes the plight of the Jews in 1942 as they were separated from society and from their families — shipped off to the death camps.

PSALM 43

Judge me, O God, and plead my cause against an ungodly nation. O deliver me from the deceitful and unjust man (v. 1).

Psalm 43 continues the theme of the previous psalm, and is also attributed to the Sons of Korah. The first three verses are indicative of Israel's exile. It typifies the tears of Rachel weeping for her children and at least includes the heartaches of world Jewry in 1943.

Could the *ungodly nation* be Germany? And could the *deceitful and unjust man* be Adolf Hitler? A comparison of the psalm with 1943 is at least uncanny, if not prophetic. The Artscroll Translation (Jewish) of this passage reads: "Avenge me, O God, and champion my cause against a people without kindness. Help me to escape from a man of deceit and iniquity."

This translation is reminiscent of events in Warsaw in early 1943. In early January there was an amazing surge of Jewish resistance in the Warsaw Ghetto. Street fighting lasted four days. The uprising continued several weeks. But on April 19 the German army, police, and SS units invaded the ghetto using tanks, artillery and machine guns. After four weeks of continuous fighting the German commander reported that the Warsaw Ghetto "no longer exists."[1] All the Jews of Warsaw were either dead, hiding in the forests, or had been deported to death camps.

Jewish resistance sprung vibrantly alive in many of the ghettos and concentration camps. But it was too little and too late. They fought valiantly with revolvers, grenades, rifles and bricks. "They battled the Nazis," says Meltzer, "in the streets and in the courtyards, from sewers and rooftops, showing a will to resist that electrified the world."[2] In his diary for May 1, Goebbels noted "the exceedingly serious fighting in Warsaw between ... our own Wehrmacht (armed forces) ... and the rebellious Jews. It shows what is to be expected of the Jews when they are in possession of arms."[3]

...why go I mourning because of the oppression of the enemy?
O send out thy light and thy truth: let them lead me; let them
bring me unto thy holy hill, and to thy tabernacles (vv. 2,3).

Did the Jewish show of force attract the attention of God? Was He waiting to see if His people would attempt to rise to their forceful potential? Could Germany or any other nation overrun God's people when they put their trust in Him? Ironically, in a matter of days, the tide of the war turned as the German Sixth Army surrendered to the Russians at Stalingrad on February 2. Still the deportations accelerated all across Nazi-occupied territories with the exception of Denmark where the Gentile Danes rescued seven thousand Jews who had been ordered deported.

Certainly the Jewish ghetto revolts were squelched by the Germans. But an inmate uprising at the Treblinka death camp in August led to the deaths of more than twenty Germans. They seized the armory, burned the barracks and set fire to the gas chambers. Of the 700 inmates engaged in the revolt, between 150 and 200 Jews escaped. They had bravely destroyed a death camp with no outside assistance. Two months later (on October 15) inmates at Sobibor revolted and 300 escaped. The rest were shot to death. Two days later Himmler ordered Sobibor destroyed. Again, Jews, with no outside help, had destroyed a death factory in which over 600,000 Jews had been asphyxiated and cremated.

Despite the millions who were slaughtered in 1943, these brave actions tendered a spark of hope and a greater hope for the survival of Jewry. The success of Jews against overwhelming odds had been demonstrated once more. That trait to win when the odds of victory seem nil carries over to the Israelis of today. Did this turn of events prompt the psalmist to write:

> *Why art thou cast down, O my soul? and why art thou disquieted within me? hope in God: for I shall yet praise him, who is the health of my countenance, ...* (v. 5).

Why art thou cast down, O my soul is a repeat of Psalm 42:5 and 11 and shows that the two psalms have the same theme. They describe a continuation of Hitler's Holocaust.

The number 43 is made up of the Hebrew letters "mem" and "gimel" and comprise the word "mag" which means "magician."[4] How fitting for it to be here, for in the first exodus out of Egypt, there were magicians of Pharoah's court who turned rods into snakes. Adolph Hitler certainly fits the description as one who dealt in black magic. Also, he unleashed the symbolic serpent against the Chosen People.

PSALM 44

> *To the chief Musician for the sons of Korah, Maschil.*
> *We have heard with our ears, O God, our fathers have told us, what work thou didst in their days, in the times of old* (introduction, v. 1).

This is the third psalm attributed to the sons of Korah. It is a *Maschil* for instruction reminding Israel of the *times of old*. According to rabbinic scholars, the events of Israel's ancient past foreshadow their future. The psalmist emphasizes that those were not ordinary times. They were filled with miraculous events which would be repeated in later years.[1]

The phrase *times of old* (days of old) contains the key which will unlock Israel's chains of exile. As Israel contended with the

former inhabitants of the land of Canaan, so again will the Chosen
People have to contend with future inhabitants of Palestine. Jews
will be accused of banditry as they were in days of old, but God
owns the land and can give it to whomever He will.[2]

*How thou didst drive out the heathen with thy hand, and
plantedst them* [Israel]; (v. 2).

Planting Israel like a tree in the Promised Land was a common
term used by the sages. "Just as the tree is permanently rooted in
its soil, the Jews are eternally bound to the Promised Land."[3]

The prophet, Amos, wrote of Israel's return, ... *I will plant them
upon their land, and they shall no more be pulled up out of their
land which I have given them, saith the LORD thy God* (Amos
9:15).

"When a Jew returns to the land of Israel, his soul draws renewed strength as if it had experienced a new birth. In this sense, it
resembles a tree that was transplanted to more fertile soil
(Dorash Moshe)."[4]

These references compare perfectly with the theme of Psalm
1:3: ... *he* [Israel] *shall be like a tree planted* [replanted] *by the
rivers of water, that bringeth forth his fruit in his season;* ... The
replanting of Israel in this century fulfills the promises of God,
realizes the dreams of the prophets and sages, and continues the
theme of the psalms which chronicle the events leading up to the
rebirth of Israel. Psalm 44 is, therefore, considered to be prophetic of the generation which would see a repetition of
miraculous events, comparable to those in their first exodus.

Some 3,430 years ago (490 x 7, or 70 x 7 x 7), Israel was being
prepared for their exodus out of Egypt. They were suffering
under the slavery of Pharoah. In 1944 Israel was being prepared
for their final exodus. They were suffering under the Holocaust of
Hitler.

Thou art my King, O God: command deliverances for Jacob
(v. 4).

How significant of Jewish prayers in 1944! The psalmist is praying for God to please repeat the miracles which He performed in
the ancient past.

*Through thee will we push down our enemies: through thy
name will we tread them under that rise up against us* (v. 5).

In Palestine, Manachem Begin emerged as leader of the Irgun
(Haganah) movement, a Jewish underground operation which
sought to overthrow British rule. Yet, the Jews of Palestine sent
brigades to fight side by side with the Allied forces. Begin, who
later would become a distinguished Prime Minister of Israel, was
a survivor of the Warsaw Ghetto and member of the Polish
forces.[5]

As it became apparent that Germany would lose the war the
struggle for a permanent homeland became an imperative. Since
the beginning of the mandate the British repeatedly had proven to
be untrustworthy in dealings between Jews and Arabs. Obviously,
the British had to go, and an all out war with the Arabs would
have to be won. The survivors of the Holocaust faced an overwhelming task in taking the land and preparing it for settlement.
Begin announced that if the Jews were molested on their way to
the Western Wall or kept from sounding the shofar, the Jews were
prepared to fight.

Was Jacob used instead of Israel because at this point the Jews
were supplanters in the land? In many ways Psalm 44 seems to
prophetically foreshadow the cruelty toward the Jews in Europe
in 1944 and the simultaneous stepped up activities to make
Palestine a permanent Jewish homeland.

*But thou hast cast off, and put us to shame.
Thou makest us to turn back from the enemy: and they which
hate us spoil for themselves* (vv. 9-10).

One commentary renders that passage as "You made us turn
the back of our necks to [the enemy]."[6] Earlier in the war when
open air massacres were carried out, some of the executioners
complained about shooting the victims in the backs of their necks.
They claimed this execution technique reminded them of the Russian NKVD. Sometimes the helpless Jews were lined up on the
edge of a mass grave, shot in the neck and toppled into the trench.
Others were made to lie face down toward the feet of the body
below. Then they were shot in the neck.[7] Such scenes are also
typical of verse 25: *For our soul is bowed down to the dust: our
belly cleaveth unto the earth.*

Just before victims were killed they were forced to hand over all their possessions and strip naked. After death their teeth were knocked out and the gold salvaged, hair was shorn and sometimes even their skin saved to be used in making lampshades. The action lends itself to the prophecy of verse 10: ... *they which hate us spoil for themselves.*

Thou has given us like sheep appointed for meat; and hast scattered us among the heathen (v. 11).

During early 1944, trainloads of Jews continued to steam toward the eastern death camps. Still that spark of hope tendered by revolts like the Warsaw Ghetto was being fanned into a flame. In July, even the inmates at Auschwitz staged a revolt just after the Nazis boasted of gassing and burning 46,000 Jews (the largest number ever) in a single day.

Earlier, in a daring escape, five Jews miraculously fled Auschwitz to bring eyewitness accounts of the atrocities to the Allies. The escapees witnessed to both private and governmental agencies. They hoped to spare the remaining Jews during the Allied offensive. But their efforts were of no avail. Only verbal protests were issued. "The reply of the United States Government, for example, was that the planes for bombing raids on the camps could not be spared in the midst of war. Such an effort," responded U.S. Assistant Secretary of War, John J. McCoy, "even if practical, might provoke even more vindictive [acts] by the Germans."[8]

The Auschwitz inmates devised a scheme in which women who worked in the laundry and other places in the camp smuggled in dynamite from a nearby explosives factory. When the insurrectionists learned that they were next in line to be killed, they hastily blew up Crematorium Number Three killing four Germans and injuring many. Six hundred inmates fled the camp but all were hunted down and killed.[9]

Thou sellest thy people for nought, and dost not increase thy wealth by their price (v. 12).

Yehuda Bauer, in a chapter called "The Mission of Joel Brand," details a daring plan to ransom the Jews doomed for death. Adolph Eichmann offered to exchange one million Jews for

1,000 tons of tea, 1,000 tons of coffee and 10,000 trucks. The Brand Operation failed. Involved in the plan was Moshe Shertok (destined to become Israel's second Premier) who was arrested by the British police and imprisoned in Cairo. Later, the British passed off the Brand Operation as a ploy by the Germans to weaken the Allies.[10]

Thou makest us a byword among the heathen (v. 14).

Even in the midst of history's most tragic hour for the Jews, their race remained the brunt of jokes. The "wandering Jew" has been made the whipping boy for nations. They have been blamed for almost every problem from the bubonic plague to the Great Depression.

Though thou hast sore broken us in the place of dragons, and covered us with the shadow of death (v. 19).

There were reports of wild animals gnawing the bones of Holocaust victims who had been buried in shallow graves.

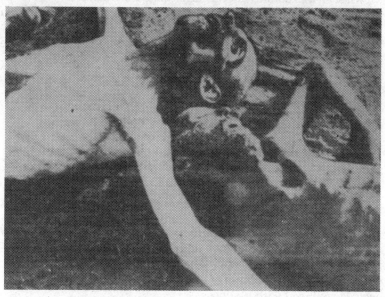

Yea, for thy sake are we killed all the day long; we are counted as sheep for the slaughter (v. 22).

Even as the Russians advanced toward Poland, the bloodthirsty Germans, aware of impending defeat, ran the crematories day and night in order to destroy half a million Hungarian Jews. Over 12,000 were killed every day seven days a week. Auschwitz operated until late October when the Germans blew up the facility, destroyed records and burned warehouses laden with stolen loot.[11] Even then, the hateful guards dumped defenseless prisoners inside Germany where the Nazis were making their last stand. Many died of deprivation.

> *Awake, why sleepest thou, O Lord? arise, cast us not off for ever* (v. 23).

The number 44 is made up of the Hebrew letters "mem" and "daleth." They comprise the word "mad" which in the Hebrew language means "judgment." Also, it provides a root for the word "madbach," which means "a sacrificial altar."[12] We can certainly see a prophetic foreview of that dreadful year of 1944 when so many died.

What an incredible description of the Holocaust! And you know, it seemed that the Lord heard the cry of the distraught Jewish people, for the war was turned against the enemies of God's Chosen People (as noted in Psalm 45) when the Allied force defeated the Axis armies.

PSALM 45

> *My heart is inditing a good matter: I speak of the things which I have made touching the king: my tongue is the pen of a ready writer.*
> *Thou art fairer than the children of men: grace is poured into thy lips: therefore God hath blessed thee forever* (vv. 1-2).

The opening verses of Psalm 45 describe a wedding, possibly the wedding of King Solomon and the Queen of Sheba (according to marginal notes in Dake's Annotated Reference Bible).[1] It exudes the joy and gladness of a Jewish wedding, a time when sorrow is replaced with gladness.

The theme of the psalm coincides perfectly with Israel's exodus out of Egyptian bondage. God brought them, as a bride, to Sinai and established a marriage covenant (the Mosaic Law). Israel became the "wife of Jehovah." In like manner, upon the conclusion of World War II, another exodus was established to bring His wayward wife back to the Promised Land for reconciliation.

Hosea spoke of this future reconciliation: ... *I will allure her, and bring her into the wilderness, and speak comfortably unto her. And I will give her her vineyards from thence, and the valley of Achor for a door of hope: and she shall sing there, as in the days of her youth, and as in the day when she came up out of the land of Egypt* (Hosea 2:14-15). Palestine was just a wilderness in the 1940's but the Jews were brought back and given their *vineyards* in the *valley of Achor* (Jordan River Valley around Jericho).

The Rabbis Radak and Ibn Ezra wrote that this psalm was dedicated to Messiah. Nora Tehillos claims the psalm was "placed after the previous one, which vividly describes the agony of Israel in exile, to foretell Israel's glorious redemption at the time of the Messiah"[2] In the Talmud (Sanhedrin 90b) the verse is rendered "My heart was stirred to compose this song by a spirit of prophecy."[3]

> *Thou art fairer than the children of men: grace is poured into thy lips: therefore God hath blessed thee for ever* (v. 2).

Rabbi Ibn Yachya wrote, "This refers to the all-inclusive excellence of Messiah." Rabbi Meiri said, "The Kingdom of Messiah shall endure forever."[4] In 1945, with an exodus out of Europe underway, the era of Messiah must be only a generation away.

> *Gird thy sword upon thy thigh, O most mighty, with thy glory and thy majesty.*
> *And in thy majesty ride prosperously, because of truth and meekness and righteousness; and thy right hand shall teach thee terrible things.*
> *Thine arrows are sharp in the heart of the king's enemies; whereby the people fall under thee* (vv. 3-5).

This marks the turning point in World War II. Evidently, God heard the cry which concluded the previous psalm. *Arise for our help, and redeem us for thy mercies' sake* (Psalm 44:26). Adolf Hitler committed suicide in April as allied bombers obliterated his military infrastructure. In August, the United States dropped the world's first atomic bomb on Hiroshima, killing 100,000 people with one blow. Two weeks later, another big bomb was dropped on Nagasaki and World War II came to a grinding halt. The devastation of planet earth was ended — at least for the time being.

> *Thy throne, O God, is for ever and ever: the sceptre of thy kingdom is a right sceptre* (v. 6).

Rabbi Radak said, "The prophets always portray the Messianic Era as a time of universal peace only after the terrible war of Gog and Magog."[5] As a reference to 1945, we may be correct to say that the two world wars in the first half of this century are part of the Gog and Magog series of wars which will ultimately bring on the awesome Armageddon.

> *Thou lovest righteousness, and hatest wickedness: therefore God, thy God, hath anointed thee with the oil of gladness above thy fellows* (v. 7).

The rabbis generally agree that the future Messiah will actually be anointed with sacred oil as the verse implies.

> *All thy garments smell of myrrh, and aloes, and cassia, out of the ivory palaces, whereby they have made thee glad.*
> *Kings' daughters were among thy honourable women: upon thy right hand did stand the queen in gold of Ophir* (vv. 8-9).

The eleventh century rabbi, Rashi, suggested that the groom is the Messiah and the *daughters* represent the entire congregation of Israel, described also in Lamentations 2:8 as *the daughter of Zion.*

> *Hearken, O daughter, and consider, and incline thine ear; forget also thine own people, and thy father's house;*
> *So shall the king greatly desire thy beauty: for he is thy Lord; and worship thou him.*
> *And the daughter of Tyre shall be there with a gift; even the rich among the people shall intreat thy favour.*
> *The king's daughter is all glorious within: her clothing is of wrought gold.*
> *She shall be brought unto the king in raiment of needlework: the virgins her companions that follow her shall be brought unto thee.*

With gladness and rejoicing shall they be brought: they shall enter into the king's palace (vv. 10-15).

"According to Rashi, the maidens are the companions of the daughter of the king. This alludes to the future, when the Gentiles will follow in the train of Israel," to which Rabbi Furer added: "They will suddenly relinquish their age-old animosity and become our bosom companions."[6] Rashi's summation is actually under development today. Gentile Christianity is seeing a movement of support for Israel. Many are declaring their love and admiration for the Jews in Israel who have bravely repopulated their ancient Promised Land as the prophets predicted.

Instead of thy fathers, shall be thy children, whom thou mayest make princes in all the earth.
I will make thy name to be remembered in all generations: ... (vv. 16-17).

The carnage of World War II wrought a toll of at least twenty-two million casualties. In the wake of the war a third of world Jewry, six million in all, was dead. The passage explains, *Instead of thy fathers* [they died in the Holocaust] *shall be thy children* [those who survived], *whom thou mayest make princes in all the earth* [they will become politicians and create the state of Israel among the nations]. *I will make thy name to be remembered in all generations:* [a memorial to the victims will be established and a campaign to remind the world continually will be undertaken]. Almost every week a story appears in the news about Nazi atrocities against the Jewish people during those years — a fulfillment of this prophecy. God decreed it should be so.

On May 8, 1945, Germany surrendered. The news brought joy and people danced in the streets. But David Ben-Gurion, in the privacy of his office, wrote in his diary, "V-E Day - sad, very sad." He flew to London and along with Chaim Weizmann, petitioned Prime Minister Churchill to set aside the provisions of the 1939 White Paper and allow one million Jews into Palestine. "He did not know and could not conceive that only about a million non-Russian European Jews had survived."[7]

He went on to New York and asked for a list of "wealthy Jews who will follow me blindly, who will do what I want without asking questions." When the group was assembled, he announced that the British would be leaving Palestine soon and the Arab armies would try to destroy Jewish settlements in Palestine. The Jewish forces had enough manpower to hold off local Palestinian gangs but it would take a great deal of money and manpower to defeat the Arab forces. Wealthy Jews were asked to "mobilize money, arms, machinery, professionals, etc." Though they were taken aback by Ben-Gurion's dark picture of the future, "all agreed to answer the call."[8]

Later, at the first post-war International Zionist Conference, Ben-Gurion did not celebrate with his fellow delegates. Instead, he proclaimed, "Either we stand on the threshold of a state ... or we stand on the threshold of a grave." He warned that if the British Labour Party did not scrap the White Paper, "We in Palestine ... shall fight England!"[9] Though Weizmann recoiled at the thought of fighting Great Britain, he proclaimed "Palestine as a Jewish state should be one of the fruits of victory, and with God's help it will be."

In typical bureaucratic fashion the British intercepted shiploads of Jewish immigrants and interred them in Displaced Persons Camps on Cyprus, Eritrea, Sudan and Uganda. Their illegal White Paper declared these immigrants to be illegal. The struggle against British rule in Palestine was stepped up over the next few months. The outnumbered and ill-equipped Jews successfully fought both the Arab and British forces.

There are too many parallels between the prophecies of these psalms and the events of the years they depict numerically to write them off as mere coincidences. They seem graphically to describe those years in this century which have affected the Jewish people.

The number 45 is made up of the Hebrew letters "mem" and "he" which comprise the word "mah" meaning "what?"[10] It has the same meaning as the number 41 and denotes the frustration of the bewildered Jews. There were so many unanswered questions following so dreadful an ordeal. A third of the world's Jewish population was dead. How sad!

PSALM 46

To the chief Musician for the sons of Korah, A Song upon Alamoth" (introduction).

This psalm was the fifth credited to the Sons of Korah who, wrote Talmudic scholars, "... foresaw occasions in which Israel was destined to be endangered by armies ... during the War of Gog and Magog."[1] Is there a connection with the Jews of 1946 who were saved miraculously from certain death in the Holocaust and the sons of Korah who were spared in the wilderness? Is it prophetically inferred that as the Sons of Korah were the authors of this psalm, they were like the twentieth century Jews snatched from the fires of Auschwitz?

> *God is our refuge and strength, a very present help in trouble.*
> *Therefore will not we fear, though the earth be removed, and*
> *though the mountains be carried into the midst of the sea;*
> *Though the waters thereof roar and be troubled, though the*
> *mountains shake with the swelling thereof. Selah* (vv. 1-3).

Mountains ... carried into ... the sea, said Chazah Zion, "is a figurative description of the re-establishment of Jewish sovereignty. According to this view, we have no fear because there will indeed be a transformation, for the land will change from Arab rule to Jewish rule. The land will become transformed from desolate desert to fertile reconstructed territory. Then the mountains, i.e., the distinguished, righteous men, will uproot themselves from exile and travel over the heart of the sea to make their way to the Holy Land."[2]

Sforno, on the other hand, wrote that "metaphorically, the armies of Gog and Magog will surge forward like a raging sea, only to be defeated and covered with slime and rubble ... The mighty nations who joined Gog and Magog now roar in the anguish of defeat."[3]

Though these were the thoughts of Jewish rabbis many years before, 1946 was to see the fulfillment of the prophecy. World War II appears to be a part of the Gog and Magog series of wars which will bring on the final judgment of God upon a wicked world and the coming of Christ to establish His kingdom. With the conclusion of the war and the rescue of Jews from Nazi death camps, their watchword across the world was, Let's go home! Let us return to the land of our forefathers! There, we shall be safe! Because ...

There is a river, the streams whereof shall make glad the city of God, the holy place of the tabernacles of the most High (v. 4).

The number 46 is made up of the Hebrew letters "mem" and "vav" and comprise the word whose pronunciation is like that of "mah" also used of the numbers 41 and 45, denoting the question "What?" However, it also makes a word which means "water, seed, progeny of a father."[4] Yes, there is a river! The upcoming birth of the baby (nation of Israel) would indeed be the "progeny of a father." God would see to it that Israel should be born of water, to which also the number 40 alludes. It was to Moses that God said, *Israel is my son, even my firstborn* (Exodus 4:22). Holy seed was about to bring forth a nation. Israel would be born of water. In the near future, the nation will be born of the Spirit (which can be seen in the numbers of the 80's).

God is in the midst of her; she shall not be moved: God shall help her, and that right early (v. 5).

The prospects of living in and around Jerusalem seemed to be the safest place for European Jewry. God never promised there would always be a Berlin or London, but there will always be a Jerusalem. Also, according to some calculations, 1945/46 was a year of Jubilee. In the Mosaic Covenant, Jubilee (originally observed every fifty years) was to be a time when all slaves were set free, all debts cancelled, and all land returned to its original owners. The year of release from the death camps fulfilled the prophecy of the slaves set free. Israel's debt of exile was cancelled and events were set in motion to return the land of Palestine to its original owners.

Thousands of war refugees streamed toward British controlled Palestine between 1945 and 1948. However, the infamous and illegal White Paper of 1939 tenaciously was enforced. Those attempting to enter the Promised Land were declared illegal aliens and were either turned back or imprisoned in refugee camps on Cyprus or in Africa.

In April 1946 the British captured two ships, the Fede and the Eliahu Golomb, carrying 1,014 refugees. The passengers vowed to fast until the British allowed them to land. Upon hearing of the declared fast, Golda Meyerson (Meir), along with thirteen other Jewish leaders of the Yishuv, also called a solemn fast in sympathy with the refugees. Golda drank tea but ate no solid food. The others broke the fast just long enough to eat a tiny piece of unleavened bread as commanded by law in observance of Passover. The world press reported the Passover fast.

Meanwhile, to demonstrate how serious their plight was, the refugees on board the two ships vowed that ten men and women would kill themselves each day until the British allowed their entry into Palestine. It was to be a Masada-like standoff on the high seas. Their threats worked and the siege ended after 104 hours. Between 1945 and 1948, only five out of sixty-three refugee ships eluded British interception.[5]

A study commission called the "Anglo-American Committee of Inquiry on Palestine" presented its findings on April 30, 1946. It barred the establishing of a Palestinian state but urged the entry of 100,000 refugees.[6] President Truman called for the admission of 100,000 refugees into Palestine "forthwith."

At this point in time, there was no state of Israel. The fighting forces were fragmented and, for the most part, uncoordinated. A few months earlier the Haganah, the Irgun and the Stern Group had linked in what David Ben-Gurion labeled "an unholy alliance called the Hebrew resistance movement." Manachem Begin was leader of the Irgun. They had freed two hundred "illegal immigrants" from a detention camp, blown up British coast guard vessels and disrupted the transportation industry. Meanwhile, the leftist Palmach forces were dominated by kibbutzniks spearheaded the Haganah movement. In late April, six British soldiers were murdered in Tel Aviv. The British reacted in shocked disgust. But Yishuv leadership seemed to be of one accord in resisting the British while preparing for all out war with the Arabs.

Then came "Black Saturday," June 29, 1946. British tanks and armored cars sped through kibbutzim and city streets in an attempt to crush the Haganah (army) and to intimidate the Yishuv (Jewish presence in Palestine). "All over Palestine," wrote Kurzman, "troops broke into homes, ripped up floors and walls looking for arms, and dragged out Jews by the hair, locking them in cages, then dumping them in detention camps, where some were beaten, tortured, even killed."[7] Jewish leadership was rounded up and imprisoned. Ben-Gurion was in Paris and escaped being jailed. Golda was not locked up probably because the prison had no facilities for women. In Paris, Ben-Gurion reacted in a pensive mood, "I'll tell you what we have to do," he said. "We must establish a Jewish state."[8]

Ho Chi Minh, who was struggling against French rule in Vietnam and living at the same hotel as Ben-Gurion, offered to let him set up a government in exile in his Southeast Asia homeland. Ben-Gurion politely refused. He saw it as his mission to unite all Jewish resistance forces under one leadership. He frantically sought the world over for arms and munitions. It was a frustrating effort because within months Jews were killing Jews in what was tantamount to a civil war.

In the World Zionist Congress of 1946, Ben-Gurion emerged as the leader of the Zionist Movement. Chaim Weizmann agreed to accept the honorary role of president in the future government. Obviously, the British Black Saturday movement had backfired and political prisoners were released.

> *The heathen raged, the kingdoms were moved: he uttered his voice, the earth melted.*
> *The LORD of hosts is with us; the God of Jacob is our refuge. Selah.*
> *Come, behold the works of the LORD, what desolations he hath made in the earth. "He maketh wars to cease unto the end of the earth; he breaketh the bow, and cutteth the spear in sunder; he burneth the chariot in the fire* (vv. 6-9).

What a vivid description of World War II! *The heathen* [Gentile nations] *raged* refers back to Psalm 2 which poses the question, *Why do the heathen rage?* (Psalm 2:1). Both psalms alike predict the wars of Gog and Magog leading up to the final conflict which is yet future. We must note that in World War II the heathen raged and kingdoms were moved (toppled). Looking back we can say that God was preparing the hearts of the Jewish people for their return to Palestine to reclaim their national heritage — for the *God of Jacob is our refuge!*

Verses 8 and 9 are fantastic. *Come, behold the works of the LORD, what desolations he hath made in the earth.* Take a look at Berlin after the bombing. What desolations he had made! Take a look at London after the blitz. What desolations He had made! Take a look at Hiroshima after the big bomb. What desolations He had made in the earth! *He maketh wars to cease ...* — not one local war, but many "wars" worldwide. From the Atlantic to the Pacific, He made wars to cease! From Europe to Asia, He made wars to cease! From Germany to Japan, He made wars to cease! From one end of the earth to the other, He made wars to cease! Perhaps more pointed than any other passage, these verses vividly describe the conclusion of World War II — and in Psalm 46, no less!

PSALM 47

> *O CLAP your hands, all ye people; shout unto God with the voice of triumph.*
> *For the LORD most high is terrible; he is a great King over all the earth* (vv. 1-2).

On the evening of November 29, 1947, David Ben-Gurion lay sleeping at the Kaliya Hotel near the Dead Sea. He was extremely tired and Paula, his wife, did not wish him to be disturbed. A comrade from Jerusalem rushed past her and shook awake the "Old Man" (as he was affectionately called). The exciting news he bore stimulated Jews the world over to dance in the streets — a fulfillment of this psalm: *O CLAP your hands; shout unto God with the voice of triumph.*

"Mazel tov!" he shouted. "We won!" The United Nations General Assembly had voted thirty-three to thirteen for the partition of Palestine into separated Jewish and Arab states.[1] Ben-Gurion rose slowly, slipped on his robe and shuffled to a table and asked for writing paper. With his blue Parker pen he began composing a declaration. When he ran out of paper he scribbled the last few words on blue toilet paper: "... The Jewish people, which has never given way to despair, even at the darkest moments of its history, and which never once lost its faith in itself and in the conscience of humanity, will not fall short at this great hour of opportunity and the historic responsibility that have been given to it. The restored Judea will take an honorable place in the United Nations as a force for peace, prosperity and progress in the Holy

Land, the Near East and the world at large."[2]

A crowd of young people gathered outside singing and dancing. "I cannot be among the dancers," Ben-Gurion noted. "I am like someone in mourning at a wedding, I am filled with an awful fear at the sacrifice that awaits our people."[3]

> *He shall subdue the people under us, and the nations under our feet.*
> *He shall choose our inheritance for us, the excellency of Jacob whom he loved* (vv. 3-4).

"Our inheritance" means the land of Canaan according to the Soncino commentary. Therefore any attempt to drive the Chosen People out is bound to fail.[4] Notice the name *Jacob* is used, which indicates a Jewish presence in the land, perhaps as a usurper. In 1947 the yishuv existed but there was as yet, no officially recognized government.

Yitzhak Rabin described the events as follows: "Early in 1947 events began to move toward statehood for the Jews of Palestine at an even faster pace. Ben-Gurion took over the defense portfolio in the Jewish Agency Executive, bringing a new spirit with him. He summoned all the Haganah officers from battalion commanders upward and for the first time urged us to prepare for war on a scale never before envisioned ... Ben-Gurion asked [Yigal Allon] whether we were capable of standing up to an invasion by the Arab armies. 'We have the basis,' Yigal replied. 'If the present nucleus grows by substantial numbers and if we get suitable equipment, we could indeed face the Arab armies.' But those two if's were cardinal problems."[5]

In April 1947 Ben-Gurion totaled up the arms in the Haganah's possession: 10,073 rifles ... 1,900 submachine guns ... and 444 light machine guns. Heavy equipment consisted of 672 two-inch mortars and 96 three-inch mortars. It goes without saying that there was not one single cannon, heavy machine gun or anti-tank or anti-aircraft weapon, not to mention armor, air or naval force. Nor were there any means of land transportation."[6] "In view of this stock of arms," commented Rabin, "talk of facing up to the regular Arab armies sounded like lunacy."[7]

So it was that the Jews of Palestine found themselves immediately under attack by Arab armies. Psalm 47 "describes the defeat of all the nations hostile to God, which will take place in

Messianic times.''⁸ Could the closing days of 1947 have set in motion a series of battles which eventually will culminate with the Gog-Magog War?

> *God is gone up with a shout, the LORD with the sound of a trumpet* (v. 5).

In the middle of this psalm which heralds the coming of the Messianic age, a reference to the exodus from Egypt and the appearing of God at Sinai is given. Why? Perhaps because 1947 saw the making of a continued confrontation with Egypt. King Faruk was planning a war with the Jews. This was the first of a series of conflicts which ended in 1981 with a peace treaty and the subsequent assassination of Anwar Sadat. Psalm 81 contains the last reference to Egypt in this part of the Psalms. From Psalms 47-81 there are several verses implying these years of Israel's conflicts, confrontations, and negotiations with Egypt (see Psalms 77-81).

It is also important to note that the shofar blast alluded to here occurred at the "transmission of the Second Tablets at Sinai."⁹ The prophetic profile given at Sinai shows that the second forty-day sojourn of Moses in the presence of God foreshadows the Dispensation of Grace, at the end of which the Messiah will descend (as did Moses) with his face shining like the sun. In fact, Moses made seven trips up the mountain, representing generally the great dispensations of human history — Innocence, Conscience, Human Government, Promise, Law, Calvary, and Grace, and concluding with the millennial reign of Christ. Therefore, Psalm 47:5 has an end-time implication as well.

It is a prophecy of the time when the "Dispenser of Strict Justice" rises up and executes His judgment against Gog and Magog; the horn of victory will sound a triumphant blast (Sforno). Radak continued: "That victory will fulfill the prophecy; I shall be exalted amongst the nations ([Psalm] 46:10).''¹⁰ Even Talmudic scholars agree that the passage is a prophecy to be fulfilled during the generation which will see Gog and Magog and the coming of Messiah to establish the kingdom of heaven on earth!

Other Talmudic rabbis say that this sounding of the trumpet has a reference to the Ark of the Covenant, which was concealed as the era of the First Temple drew to a close. "In the future, when the great horn of redemption is blown, this Ark will ascend from its concealment."[11]

The rabbis believe the blast will occur on Rosh Hashanah heralding not only the appearance of the Ark of the Covenant, but the time when the "Dispenser of Strict Justice" sets His judgment and raises the dead. "When the Jew hears the sound of the Teruah [trumpet], he realizes that he deserves shattering punishment for his sins and is inspired to repent. Having felt remorse for his sins, he is forgiven and the verdict is nullified. Thus, God ascends and departs because of the Teruah blast."[12]

What a magnificent picture of the rapture of Gentile Christianity at the beginning of the Tribulation Period. The religious Jews retrieve their Holy Ark and repent, having been left behind as "God ascends and departs" taking us with Him! Question — will the return of the Ark of the Covenant to the Temple Mount occur on a future Rosh Hashanah? Will Russia invade on that day as the divine judgment is set? Will the dead be raised and the saints raptured during that judgment? Will the conversion of the 144,000 occur as a result of those events? Rabbinic thought leans in that direction.

> *The princes of the people are gathered together, even the people of the God of Abraham: for the shields of the earth belong unto God: he is greatly exalted* (v. 9).

The *princes of the people* refer to the nobles of the Gentile nations (United Nations) who helped the Jews, *the people of the God of Abraham* to gather together in the Holy Land (in Messianic times). Rabbinic scholars say, "After the world witnesses God's might in protecting Israel from Gog and Magog, everyone will realize that He truly possesses the power to shield those who trust in Him (Rashi). Thus they will no longer deny God's omnipotence by asking, 'If God is truly All-Powerful, how could He permit heathens [gentiles] to kill the martyrs?' They will realize that although God could have shielded martyrs, He wished to grant them the incomparable privilege of sanctifying His holy name."[13]

Little did the Jewish scholars know, when they expressed this opinion, that the prophecy of the "martyrs" could well be those six million who died at the hands of Hitler's heathens. Nevertheless, the nobles of Gentile nations (United Nations) actually helped the Jews return to their land and reclaim their heritage in 1947.

The number 47 is comprised of the letters "mem" and "zain." The two letters alone do not make a word, but as a root for "mizbeach" they mean "an altar in the holy places as set up by Moses and Solomon." As a root for "mezev" they mean," to gather in."[14] Both were certainly indicative of the year 1947. Six million had been sacrificed while the survivors were gathering in for the birth of their nation.

PSALM 48

Great is the LORD, and greatly to be praised in the city of our God, in the mountain of his holiness.

Beautiful for situation, the joy of the whole earth, is mount Zion, on the sides of the north, the city of the great King (vv. 1-2).

Though no commentaries have ever considered it, Psalm 48 clearly describes the revival of the nation of Israel. It was not the United Nations which was greatly to be praised, but the LORD of heaven. It was He who brought about the circumstances which led to the replanting of the tree and the birth of the baby. Both of these symbols are addressed in this psalm. *Beautiful for situation* (also translated "fairest of sites") comes from a Hebrew term, according to Rashi (an eleventh century rabbi) which means the "branch of a tree." Another rabbi, Yaavetz haDoresh, said it was "not a thin twig, but a very large branch or tree trunk which supports and nourishes many smaller twigs to sprout."[1] This tree is none other than the house of Israel which was cut off and scattered among the nations after the Roman destruction of Jerusalem. It has been replanted in the Holy Land in this generation. Psalm 1 refers to the regathering of Israel as a *tree* [replanted] ... *that bringeth forth his fruit in his season* (Psalm 1:3).

The New Testament book of Matthew records a prophecy made by Jesus concerning this very event. He said, *Now learn a parable of the fig tree; When his branch is yet tender, and putteth forth leaves, ye know that summer is nigh: So likewise ye, when ye*

shall see all these things, know that it is near, even at the doors.
Verily I say unto you, This generation shall not pass, till all these
things be fulfilled (Matthew 24:32-34).

Also, the Apostle Paul spoke of Israel as a tree branch broken
off and to be grafted in again: ... *if some of the branches be*
broken off, and thou [Gentiles], *being a wild olive tree, wert*
grafted in ... because of unbelief they [Israel] *were broken off ...*
if they abide not still in unbelief, shall be grafted in: for God is
able to graft them in again. For if thou [Gentiles] *were cut out of*
the olive tree which is wild by nature, and wert grafted contrary
to nature into a good olive tree: how much more shall these
[Israel], *which be the natural branches, be grafted into their own*
olive tree? For I would not, brethren, that ye should be ignorant of
this mystery, lest ye should be wise in your own conceits; that
blindness in part is happened to Israel, until the fullness of the
Gentiles be come in (Romans 11:17,20,23-25).

Israel is the tree! And Psalm 48 calls its replanting *beautiful!*
Rashi also said that the word was derived from the Greek word
"nymph," meaning bride, hence, "a beautiful bride!"[2] This is
another symbol used to describe Israel — the wife of God, destined to be brought home and reconciled to God.

> *For, lo, the kings were assembled, they passed by together.*
> *They saw it, and so they marvelled; they were troubled, and*
> *hasted away.*
> *Fear took hold upon them there, and pain, as of a woman in*
> *travail* (vv. 4-6).

The *kings ... assembled* alludes to the General Assembly of the
United Nations. *They passed by together* describes the delegation
sent to Palestine to investigate the situation existing in 1947 be-
ween the British, Jews and Arabs. *They marvelled; they were*
troubled, and hasted away. Fear took hold upon them there, and
pain ... remarkably portrays the conclusions of the UN delegation
who returned to New York with the suggestion that a new Jewish
nation be formed. They saw the frustration of the British. They
were well aware of the impending conflict between the Jews and
Arabs. Yet they had felt the pain of two world wars plus the
persecution of European Jewry.

On May 20, 1948, the Swedish Count Folke Bernadote of Wisborg
was appointed by the UN Security Council as mediator between

the Arabs and Israelis. This appointment ended in tragedy.[3] He proposed and revised a plan to make the entire region occupied by the British Mandate into a union of two nations, Israel and Transjordan.

The Arabs distrusted him because they thought he was pro-Israeli. The Jews mistrusted him because they thought he was pro-British. On September 17, the day after his plan had been presented to the UN, he was assassinated.[4] Bernadotte's plan died with him.[5] Indeed, the world felt the pain *as of a woman in travail.* On November 29, 1947, the United Nations voted to give birth to the baby, Israel. And that baby was born on May 14, 1948!

This remarkable psalm refers not only to the tree replanted, but also to the baby born. Psalm 1 carries the same theme. Verse 3 refers to the tree, but verse 1 alludes to the baby: *Blessed is the man!* (Psalm 1:1). The man, according to Talmudic scholars, is Israel. Also, though Jesus referred to the symbol of a tree in his Olivet Discourse (Matthew 24:32-34), He also alluded to the birth of the baby in a previous verse: *All these are the beginning of sorrows* (Matthew 24:8). These *sorrows* are the birthpangs of travail for the birth of the baby, Israel.

On May 14, 1948, the flag of the Israeli nation was hoisted over the land for the first time in 1,813 years. Throughout the Jewish world there was rejoicing and gladness. The emotion of the occasion was electric among the Jews. Not all Gentiles, however, viewed the rebirth of the state of Israel with the same enthusiasm — especially the British, for they had lost their right to rule. It was an awesome and troubling scene as the British witnessed those birthpangs of travail.

The number 48 is made up of two letters in the Hebrew alphabet, "mem" and "cheth" and denotes the condition of the new baby, Israel. The Hebrew word for 48 is "meah" meaning "fat" and "rich" or healthy and wealthy. The connotation of "rich" refers to the fact that God had given the baby it's inheritance — the Promised Land![6]

> *Thou breakest the ships of Tarshish ...* (v. 7).

The term *ships of Tarshish* is an incredibly accurate description of the British. History records that the Phoenician merchants sailed great vessels across the Mediterranean through the straits of Gibraltar and up the western coast of Europe establishing col-

onies. It is safe to assume that they sailed as far north as England
and became the progenitors of the British. In Ezekiel 38:13 their
national symbol is given as a lion. Furthermore, their colonies
were referred to as the "young lions." Harvard University's
Department of Archaeology has found five locations within the
continental United States where the Merchants of Tarshish had
colonies among the Indians at least 2,500 years ago. What better
description of the British occupation of Palestine could have been
given 3,000 years ago?

> Let mount Zion rejoice, let the daughters of Judah be glad,
> because of thy judgments.
> Walk about Zion, and go round about her: tell the towers
> thereof.
> Mark ye well her bulwarks, consider her palaces; that ye may
> tell it to the generation following (vv. 11-13).

The message seemed to be for the Jews to survey the cities,
count the towers, inspect the fortifications — prepare to fight the
Arabs. As the British left the country, the Jews had to turn their
attention to the escalation of the conflict with the Arabs who
blatantly admitted to being the aggressors. Arab nations fought
the fledgling Israeli army with the goal of killing every Jew in
Palestine. The "War of Independence" was unavoidable.

Most significant is the scriptural mandate to *tell it to the
generation following*. Thus begins a special generation — the one
described by Jesus when he told the parable of the fig tree. ... *This
generation*, He said, *shall not pass, till all these things be fulfilled*
(Matthew 24:34). The *generation* began with the birth of the national baby, Israel, in 1948. We now live in what Talmudic
scholars predicted would be "Messianic times" — that special
generation which is preparing the world for the coming of Christ
to establish the promised "kingdom of heaven" on earth.

PSALM 49

Hear this, all ye people; give ear, all ye inhabitants of the world:
Both low and high, rich and poor, together.
My mouth shall speak of wisdom; and the meditation of my heart shall be of understanding.
I will incline mine ear to a parable: I will open my dark saying upon the harp (vv. 1-4).

Psalm 49 enlarges upon that special message given to what Psalm 48:13 described as the *generation following.* And God makes the special announcement Himself. He declared that He will open His *dark saying upon the harp.* His use of the term *harp* reveals that His *dark saying* is to be found in the Psalms! There are hidden prophecies in the Psalms which have not been seen before. There is a secret to be discovered and it was not until after the birth of Israel in Psalm 48 that God announced the possibility of its revelation.

Could that secret be that the Psalms contain a year by year account of the return of the Jews to reclaim their ancient heritage? Does this 19th book of the Old Testament tell the story of the 1900's? Does Psalm 1 introduce the century and 1901? Does Psalm 17 indeed allude to the taking of Jerusalem by Allenby in 1917? Does Psalm 48 actually tell the story of the birth of Israel in 1948? Such was the message given to Daniel ... *shut up the words, and seal the book, even to the time of the end ... knowledge shall be increased* (Daniel 12:4).

We live in that special generation chosen to understand the prophecies. God prepares to impart *wisdom* which, heretofore, has been hidden. The meditation of His heart will open our *understanding* of those things which we have not understood before. Furthermore, the Lord said that He will incline His *ear to a parable.* Which parable? It could be the one given by Jesus on the Mount of Olives when he instructed His disciples, *Now learn a parable of the fig tree; When his branch is yet tender, and putteth forth leaves, ye know that summer is nigh: So likewise ye, when ye shall see all these things, know that it is near, even at the doors. Verily I say unto you, This generation shall not pass, till all these things be fulfilled* (Matthew 24:32-34).

That appears to be the parable, and this the generation. How incredible it is that the promise made in Psalm 49 seems to represent that first year following the birth of the modern state of Israel. Now we can begin to understand the prophecies. God appears to be lifting the proverbial veil from the eyes of His people. Prophecies which previously were not understood are beginning to make sense. The return of the Jewish people to their ancient land represents the key to the understanding of prophecy.

The number 49 is made up of two letters "mem" and "teth." The resulting word is pronounced "metaw" and means "to come, to arrive."[1] It is a beautiful description of the Chosen People coming home to their Promised Land.

In Israel, the year 1949 started on a jubilant note. The cease-fire agreement with the Arab states followed by the armistice agreement hammered out on the Island of Rhodes under the direction of Dr. Ralph Bunch was reason enough for jubilation. In the elections, Chaim Weizmann was elected President of Israel and David Ben-Gurion became Prime Minister. Golda Meir and others traveled extensively in 1948-49 to raise money for the new state.[2]

Theodor Herzl's remains were transported to Jerusalem and buried on Mount Herzl named in his honor. "In Basle," Herzl had proclaimed, "I founded the Jewish state ... Perhaps five years hence, certainly fifty years hence, everybody will perceive it."[3] Sure enough, within fifty years his bold prophecy of a Jewish independent state came true and like Joseph in the Old Testament they carried his bones up to Eretz Israel.

With the war over, Israeli archeologists were anxious to get on with the search for ancient manuscripts. Two years earlier an Arab shepherd lad accidently discovered several cylindrical jars containing Biblical scrolls which were at least 2,000 years old.[4] Dr. E. L. Sukenik (father of Yigael Yadin) set about acquiring the ancient writings. Over the next few years several of the scrolls were translated and published. Indeed God began to open more of His *dark sayings*.

> *They that trust in their wealth, and boast themselves in the multitude of their riches;*
> *None of them can by any means redeem his brother, nor give to God a ransom for him:* (vv. 6-7).

This is the eighth and last in this series of psalms (42-49) credited to the Sons of Korah. Four more later psalms (84-85 and 87-88) are also credited to them, making a total of twelve written by the Sons of Korah. This psalm was written to show that riches can corrupt a man. Korah was said to be the treasurer of pharoah's palace. He held the keys to all of the king's vaults. When leaving Egypt, Korah found the treasure troves full of gold and silver which had been hidden away by Joseph, who had amassed all the world's wealth during the years of famine.[5] Korah used his wealth to challenge Moses' leadership. He even built a tabernacle of his own (Numbers 16:24-27). According to the Talmud, Korah's wealth was so great that hundreds of pack animals were used just to carry the keys to the treasure chests. The wealth was supposed to be used for the public good, but was hoarded by Korah.

When Korah withstood Moses, the earth opened up and fire from Gehinnom leaped out and enveloped him. Korah rolled around helplessly, until he sank into the pit with those who had followed him. His sons also fell in but repented and were spared at the last moment. The treasure also fell into the chasm where it will remain hidden until the Messianic Era. Then it will be discovered and used as it was originally intended. Rabbi Avrohom Feuer wrote, "Their greed backfired, ensnaring them in a trap of their own making."[6]

The prophetic implication alludes to the antichrist who, as Korah withstood Moses' authority, will enter the sanctuary and claim to be Israel's messiah. His vast wealth will be used to spring another trap, but the pit will open up for him instead (see Psalm 88). Whoever this future world dictator will be, he will control the wealth of the world. Is it possible that Psalm 49 is a 1949 reprimand to that mysterious usurper that his money cannot redeem Israel, nor give to God a ransom for the nation? Money did not buy the birth of Israel. God brought about the birth of the nation, Himself.

PSALM 50

The mighty God, even the LORD, hath spoken ... (v. 1).

This psalm introduces us to Asaph, leader of the choir which headed up the processional to bring the Ark of the Covenant to Jerusalem in the days of King David. Asaph wrote twelve psalms. His others (73-83) allude to the future return of the Ark to the Holy Mount (See introduction to Psalm 73).

Gather my saints together unto me; ... (v. 5).

That appears to be a prophetic description of the "Law of Return" passed unanimously by the Israeli parliament on July 6, 1950. David Ben-Gurion described it as a "charter" to the Jews of the world that they might come home to Israel. The law stated, "Every Jew has a right to come to this country as an oleh" (defined in a footnote as: a Jew immigrating to Israel for settlement).[1]

Survivors of the Holocaust were eager to emigrate. Displaced Persons Camps all over Europe were emptied. At first only Czechoslovakia, Bulgaria and Yugoslavia permitted the Jews to leave. Later Poland, Rumania and Hungary followed suit. Thousands of Jews poured into Israel from North Africa and the Middle East. In fact an airlift called "Operation Magic Carpet" brought 48,000 Jews from Yemen. Almost all the Jews of Iraq and Yemen voluntarily came to Israel.

Even while the War of Independence was being waged in 1948, over 100,000 Jews settled in Israel. About 240,000 made aliyah in 1949. In three and a half years 648,000 Jewish immigrants entered Israel. That was one-third more than entered during the entire seventy years of pre-state Zionist aliyahs.[2] Truly the year 1950 witnessed the ingathering of God's people. But it was a difficult time as Israel became a melting pot for the varied backgrounds.

... thou slanderest thine own mother's son (v. 20).

The great influx of Jews into Israel after 1948 created some serious cultural confrontations. Before statehood, most Jewish immigrants were from western nations. During this period there were as many Oriental Jews arriving as there were westerners. The Ashkenazim (European Jews) held the Oriental Jews in disdain.

"From the moment of their arrival in Israel, the North Africans were exposed to a series of grave psychological shocks. In the immigration camps they encountered an almost complete apartheid between European and Maghreb Jews, even as later they discovered a similar wall in the nation at large. The Europeans plainly were obsessed by the danger of levantinization (i.e. the over influence of Oriental Mediterranean customs). By their standards, the backward Easterners had to be 'reformed' -'purified of the cross of Orientalism,' as DAVAR, the Histradrut newspaper had put it in September, 1950."[3]

PSALM 51

> *Have mercy upon me, O God, according to thy lovingkindness: according unto the multitude of thy tender mercies blot out my transgressions* (v. 1).

From a Christian perspective most Israelis, like all nations, do not yet possess a spiritual relationship with God. The Jewish people are not saints by nationality. They have returned to their land, but many have returned in unbelief. And so, wrote the psalmist:

> *Behold, I was shapen in iniquity, and in sin did my mother conceive me* (v. 5).

The psalm could not possibly be fulfilled completely in 1951, but its description reveals that which has developed over the years and will continue to progress until the Messiah comes. It is my opinion that the Jewish people will be returned to a special spiritual relationship with God about the time New Testament Christianity disappears in the Rapture. Furthermore, I believe their spiritual relationship will be revived when the future Elijah appears bearing the ancient ashes of the red heifer. The ashes were once used to sprinkle on the surface of water, which in turn, was applied with a hyssop branch to purify Jews and religious articles rendered spiritually or ceremonially unclean. Looking forward to that future day, the psalmist wrote:

> *Purge me with hyssop, and I shall be clean:* ... (v. 7).

In Psalm 51 David repents with bitter remorse. Some hold that the "I" of Psalm 51 is actually the nation of Israel crying out in repentance.[1] It is a plea for cleansing and purification. Therefore allusion is made to the purification rites involving the Passover and the ashes of the red heifer. In both ceremonies blood was sprinkled by the use of hyssop branches.

"The ceremonies connected with the Passover sacrifice," wrote Louis Ginsberg a generation ago, "had the purpose of conveying instruction to Israel about the past and future alike. The blood put on the two side posts and the lintel was to remind them of Abraham, Isaac and Jacob; and the branch of hyssop for sprinkling the blood on the doors was to imply that, although Israel's position among the peoples of the earth is as lowly as that of the hyssop among the plants, yet this little nation is bound together like the bunch of hyssop, for it is God's peculiar treasure."[2]

The psalm gives the description of a sinful nation seeking the forgiveness of God. The psalm was written by David after his sin with Bathsheba. According to C. I. Scofield, however, the chapter has a dispensational reference. He wrote, "It will be the pathway of returning Israel."[3] He wrote that in 1909, long before the birth of the state of Israel. Yet it is consistent with present developments. God's Chosen People are returning to their land to welcome the Messiah.

In 1951, the tiny nation of Israel enjoyed its first war-free year, though tensions raged within the political ranks of the Knesset over the question of dealing with Germany for reparation payments and the assassination of King Abdullah Ibn Hussein by Arabs on the Temple Mount in July.

> *Do good in thy good pleasure unto Zion: build thou the walls of Jerusalem* (v. 18).

The year 1951 was a time of building throughout the land. State of Israel bonds were issued for the first time and in the first year over $65 million were sold. By the end of 1965 almost $828 million had been sold. "No bond drive in the United States by a foreign government has ever been as successful," boasted Ben-Gurion.[4] Additional loans and grants permitted Israel to build apartment houses, agricultural and mechanical kibbutzim factories as well as an economy that would soon compete in world markets. Truly, God in His good pleasure began building the "walls of Jerusalem" in a big way beginning in 1951.

PSALM 52

Why boasteth thou thyself in mischief, O mighty man? the goodness of God endureth continually.
Thy tongue deviseth mischiefs; like a sharp razor, working deceitfully.
Thou lovest evil more than good; and lying rather than to speak righteousness. Selah (vv. 1-3).

The background of Psalm 52 is plain and simple. A man, perhaps rich and famous, has taken advantage of his position against the house of Israel. In David's time he is easily recognized as Doeg, the Edomite (I Samuel 21 and 22). He was a traitor to David and to Israel.[1] But who is the Doeg of 1952? Who possibly could fit the prophetical description of Psalm 52? Who, in the fourth year of Israel's independence, posed such a threat while having seemingly unlimited support?

For a possible candidate we need to go back a few months earlier and study the behavioral movements of a lowly captain in the Egyptian army. The day after the United Nations decided to partition Palestine in 1947, he paid a rather pompous call on Haj Amin Husseini, the Grand Mufti of Jerusalem. The Mufti earlier had thrown his hat into the ring with Hitler regarding the destruction of Jewry. After World War II he declared a "jihad" (an Islamic holy war) in Palestine against the Jews.[2]

The young Egyptian army captain and his comrades wanted in on the action.[3] For years the army officer had been a leader in the "Free Officers" organization, a subversive group within the ranks of the Egyptian army. On behalf of that organization he proclaimed to the Grand Mufti, "You have need of officers to lead in the struggle and to train volunteers. In the Egyptian army there is a large number of officers who wish to offer their services. They are yours to command whenever you wish."[4]

The young Egyptian captain was destined within a few short months to become a greater leader of the Arab world than the

Grand Mufti could ever have dreamed of becoming. The captain, later colonel, became the first native born ruler of Egypt in over 2,500 centuries.[5] He became a dictator and for a short while was successful in forming a United Arab Republic against tiny Israel and the Western powers.

With the overthrow of King Farouk in 1952, the oldest kingdom on earth became the newest republic. Its leaders were haughty and boastful. Golda Meir tells of a refrain from a song played over and over in Cairo radio. "Weep, oh Israel," were the words, "the day of extermination draws near."[6]

> *Why boastest thou thyself in mischief, O mighty man?*
> *God shall ... destroy thee for ever, he shall take thee away,*
> *and pluck thee out of thy dwelling place, and root thee out of the*
> *land of the living. Selah.*
> *The righteous also shall see, and fear, and shall laugh at him:*
> (vv. 1,5-6).

Could this be a cryptic description of Gamal Abdel Nasser who hated Israel and threatened to drive every Jew into the sea. He aligned Egypt with the Soviet Union and helped get Soviet arms for the Arabs. However, in spite of all his nation's wealth and power and all his anti-Semitic efforts, he suffered at least three humiliating defeats by the hands of the Israelis? *The righteous ... shall laugh at him.*

PSALM 53

The fool hath said in his heart, There is no God (v. 1).

Psalm 53 is an apparent revision of Psalm 14 for it is almost an exact replica of the earlier psalm. Jewish commentaries suggest that Psalm 14 reflects the destruction of Solomon's Temple by Nebuchadnezzar and that Psalm 53 alludes to the Roman destruction of Herod's Temple. Nebuchadnezzar plundered and defiled the sacred place, but the Roman general, Titus not only pillaged the Holy Temple, he actually committed an immoral act with a prostitute in the Holy of holies where the Ark of the Covenant once stood. Jewish scholars say both psalms refer to the exile and future redemption.

Psalm 53 alludes to the climax and conclusion of "the Davidean line, which will occur with the coming of Messiah, who will end the exile and clear the ruins of the Second Temple by dedicating the Third." Further, they say that Messiah will "suffer persecution at the hands of skeptics and scoffers, who will refuse to recognize his sovereignty and will scheme to assassinate him."[1] How ironic that they speak of a rejection of Christ and ascribe it to His future coming, not realizing that those very predictions came true at His first coming two thousand years ago.

Soviet T-64 tanks on parade

Verse 1 speaks of a fool who says in his heart, there is no God. Of all the men in the twentieth century who fit the category, Joseph Stalin gets my vote. The years of 1914 and 1953 mark the rise and fall of the *fool*. On March 5, 1953, Joseph Stalin, an arch enemy of the Jews, died. Verse 1 of Psalms 14 and 53 aptly seem to describe his behavior. Though early in life he attended seminary, he emerged, not as a monk, but as a revolutionary.[2] Until 1911 he was an obscure Russian Georgian. Most of what he had written was still untranslated from the Georgian dialect. The next year he met and impressed Lenin. And in 1913 he advanced Lenin's thinking about the Jews in Russia in an essay called "Social Democracy and the National Question," later renamed "Marxism and the National Question." He wrote that a nation is "a stable community of men, which came into being by historic process and has developed on a basis of common language, territory, and economic life."[3] Hence, the Jews could never be a nation and were doomed to assimilation into the nations of the world. In essence, the Jews would never be allowed a homeland.

Ironic, isn't it? Stalin emerged into the limelight in 1913 and his anti-Semitic writings flourish in 1914, even though he was in Siberian exile. The Jews of Russia responded spontaneously by entering the army in both world wars to defend their homeland as Russians, not as Jews.[4] When Lenin died in 1924, Stalin emerged as the Premier of the Soviet Union. Only the Almighty knows how many people he slaughtered in establishing a power base. He may have killed as many as twenty million people during the 1930's. In the last five years of his life he specifically turned his attention against the Jews and erroneously accused them of attempting to overthrow his regime. He called it the "Doctor's Plot." Fortunately, Stalin died before this tragic lie akin to the "Protocols of the Elders of Zion" could be carried out. Could Psalms 14 and 53 indeed refer to the years of the rise and fall of Joseph Stalin? With his death the attacks on Soviet Jews abated for awhile.

PSALM 54

Save me, O God, by thy name, and judge me by thy strength
(v. 1).

In the years 1954 and 1955 David Ben-Gurion abdicated the office of Prime Minister of Israel for a well-deserved rest. On December 13, 1953, he bade farewell to politics. Packing his books and personal belongings, he and his wife Paula, both in their sixties, went southward from Jerusalem to Sde Boker, a remote and dangerous kibbutz in the Negev Desert. There he became a common day laborer, feeding, shearing and shepherding goats and sheep. Some of his best writings occurred during this two year sabbatical.[1]

In the absence of Ben-Gurion, Moshe Sharett assumed the position of Prime Minister. Golda Meir reflected on the demeanor of the two men. "Sharrett," she said, "was a born diplomat and negotiator. Ben-Gurion was a born national leader and fighter."[2] Consequently, disastrous events occurred in 1954-55 which might have been averted if Ben-Gurion had remained in command as

Prime Minister and Minister of Defense. Unfortunately, Minister of Defense Pinhas Lavon unwittingly allowed an incident to occur in Egypt which eventually played a part in Ben-Gurion's decision to retire permanently from Israeli politics. More on this problem as it unveils in 1955.

For strangers are risen up against me ... (v. 3).

The year 1954 witnessed the unleashing of Arab terrorism in Israel. In the summer of 1953 the Mufti, Haj Husseini (then in his fourth decade of anti-Semitism), along with the Arab nations, organized terrorism raids against Israel. On March 16, 1954, eleven bus passengers were massacred by Arabs on a road near Beersheba. As a result of sneak attacks against Israeli civilians, Israeli Defense Forces Chief of Staff General Moshe Dayan established a bloodhound type battalion called Force 101 under the leadership of Major Ariel Sharon to hunt down and annihilate Arab terrorists. Sometimes these raids appeared too extreme, as in the case of the Jordanian village of Qibya which was reminiscent of the German Einsatzgruppen on innocent European villages during World War II. Perhaps in 1954 extreme measures were necessary to protect the borders of the Promised Land from "strangers who had risen up against [Israel]."

Meanwhile Nasser had been biding his time to oust General Mohammed Neguib from the presidency of Egypt. In November, Nasser became the master of Egypt. The ruling junta had opted for dictatorship rather than democracy. He immediately began a drive to completely rid Egypt of British influence and to gain sole control of the Suez Canal. A group called the Brotherhood of Moslems attempted to assassinate him. The Mufti, being a supporter of this group, found himself on the outside looking in. Within months Nasser became the major spokesman for the Moslem world. He left no doubt that the combined forces of the Arabs would attempt to wipe Israel from the face of the earth.

He shall reward evil unto mine enemies: cut them off in thy truth (v. 5).

In Psalm 52, Doeg plotted against David and in Psalm 54, an entire community of Ziphites betrayed him. Could the treachery of Doeg have foreshadowed the events of 1952 when, as an individual enemy of Israel, Gamal Abdel Nasser began his rise to power in Egypt? Could betrayal by the Ziphites have foreshadowed the 1954 events of the Arab nations who ultimately aligned with Egypt in several attempts to destroy the tiny nation of Israel?

PSALM 55

... Oh that I had wings like a dove! for then would I fly away, and be at rest.
Lo, then would I wander far off, and remain in the wilderness. Selah (vv. 6-7).

The Anglo-Egyptian Agreement was signed in 1954. It called for the withdrawal of all British troops from Egypt over a twenty-month period.[1] Until that time the Israelis felt assured that the presence of British soldiers in Egypt would help avert an all-out attack by the Egyptians. In order to prevent a British pullout, Israeli counter-intelligence agents attempted to blow up several American and British buildings in Egypt. The hope was to show Nasser's "irresponsibility" and convince the British to remain. The plot failed.[2]

It became known as the "Lavon Affair" and broke like a storm over Israel in 1955. Eleven Jews were tried. Six were sentenced to long prison terms and two were hanged by the Egyptians. The incident became a festered sore that would not heal.[3] All of Israel, especially Ben-Gurion, was stung with embarrassment and felt a sense of personal betrayal. How could the Israelis take part in the same kind of terror tactics their enemies were inflicting upon them?

According to Golda Meir, Levi Eschol, the third person to be Prime Minister of Israel once said, "As Prime Minister, Ben-Gurion is worth at least three army divisions to Israel."[4] Accordingly, in February she was dispatched to Sde Boker to tell Ben-Gurion the troubles his colleagues were having keeping the coalition together. He was invited to come back as Minister of Defense. Three days later he arrived in Jerusalem ready to go to work. In the November elections he was returned to the office of Prime Minister. The "Lavon Affair" seemed to be an obsession for him, for he refused to let it be swept under the rug. Six years later it was brought to trial. But, Lavon was never proven to be at fault for the "mishap."

One can imagine David Ben-Gurion saying, *Oh that I had wings like a dove! for then would I fly away,* [back to my sheep farm in the Negev wilderness] *and be at rest. Lo, then would I wander far off, and remain in the wilderness.* Ben-Gurion could not stay in the wilderness raising sheep. He was needed back in the government in the position of Minister of Defense. Why?

> *... for I have seen violence and strife in the city.*
> *Day and night they go about it upon the walls thereof: mischief also and sorrow are in the midst of it.*
> *Wickedness is in the midst thereof: deceit and guile depart not from her streets* (vv. 9-11).

On February 1, 1961, Ben-Gurion tried to resign again but without success, for his government and his people still needed him. Could that be why Psalm 61 says: *Thou wilt prolong the king's life* ...? (Psalm 61:6). By June 17, 1963, however, Ben-Gurion had determined to retire. He resigned for the last time and meant it. That was 1963. Perhaps that's why the psalmist concluded Psalm 63 with these words: *But the king shall rejoice in God* ... (Psalm 63:11). David Ben-Gurion died on November 1, 1973. Perhaps that is the prophetic significance of the passage in Psalm 73: *Thou shalt guide me with thy counsel, and afterward receive me to glory. My flesh and my heart faileth:* ... (Psalm 73:24,26).

> *For it was not an enemy that reproached me;* ...
> *But it was thou, a man mine equal, my guide, and mine acquaintance.*
> *We took sweet counsel together, and walked unto the house of God in company* (vv. 12-14).

David is lamenting over the treachery of his intimate friend and teacher, Ahitophel. He not only encouraged David's own son, Absalom, to rebel but also volunteered to pursue and humiliate David. (see II Samuel 17:1-4). The heartache is so overwhelming that David mourns, *Oh that I had wings like a dove! for then would I fly away, and be at rest* (v. 6). Could David's sense of betrayal over the Ahithophel affair have been a prophetic foreview of the "Lavon Affair" of 1954-55 and afterwards?

PSALM 56

Be merciful unto me, O God: for man would swallow me up;
he fighting daily oppresseth me.
Mine enemies would daily swallow me up: for they be many
that fight against me, ... (vv. 1-2).

In 1956, President Nasser of Egypt, seized control of the Suez
Canal. He also held Sharm el Sheikh, a fortress overlooking the
Tiran Strait leading from the Gulf of Aqaba. In essence he had a
stranglehold on Israeli shipping and marine activity toward the
south.

In August 1955 the world first heard the term "fedayeen" meaning "those who sacrifice themselves." Nasser trained hundreds
of them to make frequent suicide incursions, if necessary, into
Israel to kill, maim and slaughter innocent citizens.[1] Arms from
communist countries flowed into Egypt.

Most notably was the arms agreement with Czechoslovakia in
September 1955. With the Suez Canal firmly in his grip, with
mighty arms (including bombers) at his disposal and with an army inspired by the fedayeen tradition, it was high time to drive
the Jews into the Mediterranean Sea as their forefathers had done
to the Egyptians in the Red Sea so many centuries ago. Jordanian
and Egyptian radio proclaimed daily to Israel, "Egypt will grind
you to dust."[2]

On April 6, 1956, the Egyptian army created a disturbance in the
Gaza Strip. Six Israelis were wounded, and Egypt suffered 140
casualties. In the months that followed, however, it was to ex-
plode into a full-scale war. On October 29 the headline in the
JERUSALEM POST read, "army attacks bases in heart of
Sinai." The next day, the British and the French bombed Cairo.
From the time Israel started the move southward it took only one
hundred hours to reach the Suez.[3]

When I cry unto thee, then shall mine enemies turn back: this
I know; for God is for me (v. 9).

On November 2 Egypt's Sinai army was in full-flight and
Israeli forces sealed off the Gaza Strip. By November 4 the battle
in the Sinai was over. The war lasted from October 29 until

November 6, 1956. Israel was the clear victor. The great Arab boast had been completely squelched. Much of the arms and ammunition supplied by communist countries now resided in depots in tiny Israel. The Egyptian Air Force was almost totally destroyed. Yes, Psalm 56 could very well allude to the 1956 war with Egypt over the Gaza Strip.

PSALM 57

To the chief musician, Al-taschith [do not destroy], *A Michtam of David, when he fled from Saul in the cave.*
Be merciful unto me, O God, be merciful unto me: for my soul trusteth in thee: yea, in the shadow of thy wings will I make my refuge, until these calamities be overpast (introduction, v. 1).

When King Saul heard that David and his band of six hundred men where hiding out in the wilderness near En-Gedi, he gathered three thousand chosen men from the Israelite army and pursued David. But God delivered Saul into the mercies of David. Saul slipped away from his troops to rest and sleep awhile in a large cave. This was David's undreamed-of chance to be rid of the threat of Saul forever. His followers urged him to destroy Saul then and there (I Samuel 24).

My soul is among lions: and I lie even among them that are set on fire, even the sons of men, whose teeth are spears and arrows, and their tongue a sharp sword (v. 4).

The TEHILLIM commentary on this passage says, "Alshich ... identifies those lions as David's own followers who were with him in the cave, for they resembled ferocious lions, roaring to tear Saul apart. David barely succeeded in restraining them."[1]
Compare this statement to the description of the behavior of David Ben-Gurion's cabinet on November 7, 1956, after the smashing defeat of Egypt in the Sinai War. An alarming letter arrived from Soviet leader, Nikolai Bulganin. Ben-Gurion read it in disbelief: "The government of Israel is criminally and irresponsibly playing with the fate of the world. It is sowing hatred of the State of Israel amongst the Eastern peoples ... and place in question the very existence of Israel as a state ... The Soviet government is at this very moment taking steps to put an end to the war

and to restrain the aggressors. The government of Israel should consider before it is too late. We hope [it] will fully understand and appreciate our warning."²

Consternation flooded tiny Israel ... *yea, in the shadow of thy wings will I make my refuge, until these calamities be overpast.* In his victory speech Ben-Gurion had announced that the Egyptian Armistice was dead, Egypt would not be allowed to return the Sinai and Israeli troops would not withdraw. This alarming letter was the response of a humiliated Soviet Union. Ben-Gurion's diary read, "It was a nightmarish day. From Rome, Paris and Washington there is a succession of reports on (Soviet designs against Israel)."³ Never before had the world been so close to the brink of the Gog-Magog War described in Ezekiel 38 and 39.

And how did the *lions* surrounding Ben-Gurion react? Some cried, "Withdraw! Withdraw! Withdraw!" But the real lion, Moshe Dayan was not shaken. "Defy Russia! Defy the world! The Kremlin is bluffing!"⁴ The world will never know whether or not the Soviets were bluffing, for in a dignified way, the dilemma was worked out diplomatically. It should be noted that the Soviets, at the moment, had their hands full in Eastern Europe. There was unrest in Poland and Soviet troops, even at that moment, were invading Hungary.⁵

Could *Al-taschith* [do not destroy] futuristically depict the behavior of Israel in 1957? It seems the prophetic message was, "Do not destroy your enemies, though you have the opportunity." Even when young demented Moshe Dueg threw a hand grenade into the Knesset seriously wounding Ben-Gurion and others in October 1957, he and Israel refused to respond by destruction. Instead he had his longtime friend and trusted personal secretary, Nehemiah Argov fetch him pen and stationery. Even though his right arm was seriously injured and in pain, from his Hadassah Hospital bed he wrote in long hand:

"To the parents of Moshe Dueg: I know that you regret, as do all the people of Israel, the abominable and senseless crime which your son committed yesterday. You are not to blame. You are living in Israel, where justice reigns, and I hope that nothing untoward happens to you or your sons. Would that you succeed in educating the rest of your children to do good deeds and to love Israel (signed — David Ben-Gurion)."

For years Nehemiah Argov had mothered over Ben-Gurion, making sure he wore a sweater or warm socks, organizing his correspondence and seeing that he was not disturbed. Nehemiah was totally dedicated to his job. But within hours he was to accidentally run over a cyclist on the Tel Aviv-Jerusalem Road, after a wasp flew into his car, stinging him on the eyelid. Believing the cyclist dead, Argov fell into an immediate despondency and took his own life. As Ben-Gurion lay in the hospital, not knowing of the death, friends quietly buried the young man. Ironically, the cyclist recovered. But Nehemiah, beloved Nehemiah, was dead. ... *yea, in the shadow of thy wings will I make my refuge, until these calamities be overpast.*

PSALM 58

To the chief musician, Al-taschith, A Michtam of David.
Do ye indeed speak righteousness, O congregation? do ye judge uprightly, O ye sons of men?
Yea, in heart ye work wickedness; ye weigh the violence of your hands in the earth (introduction, vv. 1-2).

Psalms 57, 58 and 59 are a trilogy of *Al-taschith,* meaning "destroy not" psalms. As David refused to destroy Saul, even so, Israel did not pursue the total destruction of Egypt in 1956.

No doubt about it, Egypt's dictator, Gamal Abdel Nasser fully intended to destroy Israel. Instead, his army was routed in utter defeat by the ill-equipped Israeli army. In spite of this, Nasser emerged as a national hero when the Suez Canal was taken over by the Egyptians. His popularity soared in the Arab world to the extent that in February 1958 he was able to form the United Arab Republic (UAR). It lasted about three and one-half years and was composed of Egypt and Syria and sympathizers in Lebanon and Iraq.[1]

The formation of the UAR, with the backing of the Soviets and the communist bloc, meant that now Israel was really on their own. "I used to look around me in the United Nations in 1957 and 1958 and think to myself:" wrote Golda Meir, "We have no family here. No one shares our religion, our language, or our past. The rest of the world seems to be grouped onto blocs that have sprung up because of geography and history [and] have combined to give common interests to their peoples. But our neighbors — and natural allies — don't have to have anything to do with us, and we really belong to no one, except to ourselves."[2]

Back in Jerusalem, Ben-Gurion must have felt some of the same aloneness. He didn't want Israel to take over the West Bank in the event Jordan fell to Nasser and the communists. It would mean that Israel would have to absorb another million Arabs. "We would be encircled again ... Our pressing problem is a lack of Jews, not a lack of territory."[3] And so it seemed to be in 1958.

Ben-Gurion wrote, "Despite our withdrawal to the boundaries that existed before the Suez campaign, Nasser and the other Arab rulers still refused to accept Israel's right to exist ... Day in and day out, the Arab press and the radio denounced the 'Zionist danger' and in Nazi parlance, 'the machinations of international capital.' At mass demonstrations in Cairo, Nasser announced his growing preparations to destroy Israel. These open threats are backed by an incessant flow of arms, especially from the Soviet Union ... while hundreds of officers ... were sent out to the USSR, Czechoslovakia and other Soviet satellites to learn the trade of war."[4] ... *ye weigh the violence of your hands in the earth.* Does not this sound like the activities of the Arabs and the Soviets in 1958?

> *The wicked are estranged from the womb: they go astray as soon as they be born, speaking lies.*
> *Their poison is like the poison of a serpent: they are like the deaf adder that stoppeth her ear;* (vv. 3-4).

Could this be a reference to the birth of the antichrist? Someday, a world dictator will usurp the throne of God. His symbol is the serpent. Moses wrote Psalms 90-100 about the antichrist and dedicated each psalm to a tribe, leaving out the tribe of Simeon. It is remarkable that the name Simeon means, "hearing." Moses left out Simeon and any encyclopedia will confirm the statement in verse 4 that serpents are deaf!

That may be the reason why Revelation 13:9 says, *If any man have an ear, let him hear.* The verse is found in chapter number 13 (a number of ill omen) and in verse number 9 (which means a serpent) in the chapter which describes the dragon or serpent. Serpents are deaf!

PSALM 59

To the chief musician, Al-taschith. A Michtam of David; when Saul sent, and they watched the house to kill him.
Deliver me from mine enemies, O my God: defend me from them that rise up against me.
Deliver me from the workers of iniquity, and save me from bloody men.
For, lo, they lie in wait for my soul: the mighty are gathered against me; not for my transgression, nor for my sin, O LORD.
They run and prepare themselves without my fault: awake to help me, and behold (introduction, vv. 1-4).

Psalm 59 is the third and final of the trilogy of *Al-taschith* [do not destroy] psalms. However, it is based on an earlier episode in which David narrowly escaped being killed by King Saul. Previously, David had slain Goliath and defeated the Philistine army. Obviously God was with HIM in battle — not with Saul. Consequently, Saul grew despondent and called for David to play music to soothe his anguished spirit. While David played the harp, the king grabbed up a javelin and attempted to impale David to the wall. (I Samuel 19:8-10). Fortunately, Saul missed. David fled from the king and escaped into a night which would be filled with terror. His enemies surrounded him and growled like mad dogs. *Saul also sent messengers unto David's house, to watch him, and to slay him in the morning:* ... (I Samuel 19:11).

Psalm 59 details David's anguish that night as Saul's *messengers* surrounded his house uttering terroristic threats and bragging loudly about how David was to be annihilated. David cried out to God: ... *they lie in wait for my soul* ... (v. 3). They wanted not merely to see the death of David, but to annihilate the memory of him from the face of the earth.

Thou therefore, O LORD God of hosts, the God of Israel, awake to visit all the heathen: be not merciful to any wicked transgressors. Selah.
But thou, O LORD, shalt laugh at them; thou shalt have all the heathen in derision (vv. 5,8).

According to verses 5 and 8 these enemies were "heathen" (Gentile nations). So was the year 1959. Seven nations: Egypt,

Syria, Lebanon, Iraq, Iran, and the Soviet Union (Jordan entered later), surrounded the house of Israel uttering threats. It is significant that late in 1959 a crudely produced monthly magazine began circulation from Lebanon. Called OUR PALESTINE, it always addressed its readers as "Children of the the Catastrophe." Its total contents were devoted strictly to Palestinian affairs and threats of "destroying the Jewish presence" or "uprooting the Zionist entity."

"Our Palestine - The Call to Life" was actually the mouthpiece of Harakah al-Tahrir (al Watani) al-Falastini, also known as the Palestine National Liberation Movement. Its common name, Al-Fatah, is derived by reading backward the first letter of each word. Al-Fatah means "opening" or "conquest." Because of OUR PALESTINE's small circulation, five years passed before the Israelis recognized its impact on the Arab world. In 1965 Al-Fatah surfaced as an organized group. Yassar Arafat was one of the founders of the Al-Fatah.[1] His splinter group is now the terrorist oriented Palestinian Liberation Organization. Incidentally, modern terrorists strike at innocent victims in order to tell the world their message. They are neither combat soldiers nor defenders. Fantastic, isn't it? Saul sent *messengers* instead of soldiers to terrorize and try to kill David.

Ironically, years later in the Lebanon war, Israel could have wiped the entrapped PLO from the face of the earth (See Psalms 82 and 83). The young lions of Israel begged for the chance to finish off Arafat and his followers. Instead, Israel declined once again to completely destroy its enemies. That destruction will come later when the wrath of God is poured out at Armageddon.

The two previous Al-taschith psalms dealt with David and Saul in personal one-on-one clashes. In both incidents, Saul himself tried to kill David. For some reason, Psalms 57 and 58 were placed in earlier numerical sequence even though their chronology was of a later date. Further, the two earlier psalms did not implicate the "heathen" Philistines. (Present-day Palestinians derived their name from the Philistines.) Could the implications of this psalm be a veiled prophecy of the rise of twentieth century Palestinian terrorists?

PSALM 60

*To the chief Musician upon Shushan-eduth, Michtam of David,
to teach; when he strove with Aram-naharaim and with Aram-
zobah, when Joab returned, and smote of Edom in the valley of
salt twelve thousand* (introduction).

From the introduction of Psalm 60, it is obvious that David
already had carried out two successful military campaigns. The
object was to rid Israel of foreigners and then to build a Temple
unto God which in time would unite all mankind.

Moab is my washpot; over Edom will I cast out my shoe: ...
(v. 8).

General Joab went to invade Aram. "The Midrash relates ..."
says Rabbi Avrohom Feuer, "that the Arameans confronted him
and asked, 'Are you not the descendant of Jacob, and therefore
does not a covenant exist between us? For Laban, our forebear,
said, *Now therefore come thou, let us make a covenant, I* [Jacob]
and thou; ... And Jacob took a stone and set it up for a pillar
[monument]. *And Laban said, This heap* [stone] *is a witness*
[testimony] *between me and thee this day*" (Genesis 31:44-45,48).
Joab had no answer for their proposal so he went back to
Jerusalem to confer with David. Subsequently, David took off his
crown and went before the Sanhedrin. The seventy elders held
that Aram had nullified the covenant when Balaam attempted to
curse Israel at the request of Balak who brought him from Aram
(Numbers 23:7).[1] As a consequence of the Arameans attempting
to bargain for land that God had promised Israel, David
humiliated them. *Moab is my washpot* (see Psalm 108:9).

Give us help from trouble; for vain is the help of man.
Through God we shall do valiantly: for he it is that shall tread
down our enemies. (vv. 11-12).

It became obvious by 1960 that Israel must prepare for the hundreds of thousands of Jews still waiting to make aliyah, just as
David prepared ancient Israel for the coming Temple. It also
became obvious that as David himself would not build the Temple

in old times, so must the torch be passed to a younger generation in the 1960's. Therefore, David Ben-Gurion began grooming young successors. He brought into the cabinet Shimon Peres, Moshe Dayan, and Abba Eban. They became known as the "Old Man and His Boys." Peres, then as now, became a little too agressive, particularly with Golda Meir. She threatened to resign if he wasn't brought in line.[2]

Also in 1960 Ben-Gurion visited President Eisenhower, Chancellor Konrad Adenauer of Germany, General Charles de Gaulle of France, and Prime Minister Harold MacMillan of England. He sought military aid and confirmed support for Israel. President Eisenhower made only a verbal statement that if Israel were ever attacked the United States would come instantly to her assistance. Ben-Gurion secured a $500 million loan from Germany to develop the Negev. France aided Israel in building a nuclear reactor at Nahol Sorek in Southern Israel. But the fact remained for Israel; *vain is the help of man.*

PSALM 61

Hear my cry, O God; attend unto my prayer.
From the end of the earth will I cry unto thee, when my heart
is overwhelmed: lead me to the rock that is higher than I.
For thou hast been a shelter for me, and a strong tower from
the enemy (vv. 1-3).

Psalm 61 was probably written as David was in exile after Absalom's rebellion.[1] Whenever and wherever it was written, the psalmist was far away from the Tabernacle and longed to worship there. It was a tempestuous time.

For thou, O God, hast heard my vows: thou hast given me the
heritage of those who fear thy name (v. 5).

The trial of Adolph Eichmann (arch enemy of the Jews captured in Argentina a few months earlier), seemed to dominate the news of Israel in 1961. He was a leading Nazi perpetrator of the "Final Solution" under Hitler during the 1940's. He was found guilty and executed in 1962.

Golda Meir was the Israeli ambassador to the United Nations at the time the UN tried to sanction Israel over the trial of Eichmann. Meir pointed out that they had no jurisdiction over Israel in such matters because they had never fully recognized the Jewish state as a sovereign nation. During the course of the debate, the UN voted to cut off financial aid to Israel as "an underdeveloped nation" and to recognize Israel as a "developed nation" — allowing Meir and her entourage a place at the "Table of Nations." The Israeli nation was thirteen years old and was thus recognized as an adult among its peers. That was declared to be Israel's "Bar Mitzvah."

> *Thou wilt prolong the king's life and his years as many generations* (v. 6).

Israel wrestled with enemies from within in 1961. Pinhas Lavon learned of a cover-up in the 1954 diplomatic "mishap" in Egypt. He asked Ben-Gurion in 1960 plainly and simply to clear his name. The Prime Minister wouldn't budge, and Lavon went public resulting in a Knesset vote of confidence in Ben-Gurion the next year. Ben-Gurion survived the election of 1961 but much support had been eroded. "From the party's view," wrote Ben-Gurion, "this is a tremendous victory, after ten months of ruthless slanders ... But from a political viewpoint, these results are a catastrophe."[2] Verse 6 pulses with the ebb and flow of 1961 when Ben-Gurion survived the worst political assault ever of his life (see comments in Psalm 55).

PSALM 62

> *Truly my soul waiteth upon God: from Him cometh my salvation.*
> *He only is my rock and my salvation; he is my defence; I shall not be greatly moved* (vv. 1-2).

It is not clearly known at what time in David's life this psalm was written. More than likely, though, it was during his exile at the time of Absalom's rebellion. Like the previous psalm, there seems to be little significance placed on the when and where of the composition. But prophetically, it could have been written for 1962.

On July 21 of that year terror gripped the heart of every citizen in Israel. Egypt had just launched two types of surface to air missiles. One had a range of 175 miles and the other 350 miles. Nasser told a jubilant crowd in Cairo that his missile could hit any target "south of Beirut" meaning, of course, Israel.[1] The missiles were built under a secret agreement between Nasser and some German scientists. It was reported that the new weapons were being armed with nuclear waste materials and if launched would have deadly effects for months — maybe even years.

> *Trust in him at all times; ye people, pour out your heart before him: God is a refuge for us. Selah.*
> *Surely men of low degree are vanity, and men of high degree are a lie: to be laid in the balance, they are altogether lighter than vanity.*
> *Trust not in oppression, and become not vain in robbery: if riches increase, set not your heart upon them.*
> *God hath spoken once; twice have I heard this; that power belongeth unto God* (vv. 8-11).

As it turned out, Nasser's missiles were equipped only with conventional warheads. The amazing thing was that Israel didn't panic. Nasser's saber-rattling continued to worsen until finally, in 1967, Israel was forced to take pre-emptive measures — the historic Six Day War.

PSALM 63

> *A Psalm of David, when he was in the wilderness of Judah.*
> *O God, thou art my God; early will I seek thee: my soul thirsteth for thee, my flesh longeth for thee in a dry and thirsty land, where no water is;* (introduction, v. 1).

Once David, fleeing for his very life, found himself being chased in the arid, parched, desolate wilderness of Judea. It isn't known for sure who was in pursuit. Nor is it known when this majestic psalm was penned. Was it when Saul and Abner pursued him mercilessly? Was it when Absalom's followers sought to take his life? It doesn't matter. Only David could exult the Lord *in a dry and thirsty land.* It was clearly obvious; David trusted completely in God. He knew his deliverance was at hand.

But the king shall rejoice in God; ... (v. 11).

In 1963 another David of Israel was being pursued; not for his physical life, but for the rulership of Israel. Like the former David, he was tired and weary. This modern day David had already lived longer than his ancient predecessor. As the former David longed for the cool water from his hometown, Bethlehem, this David longed for the solitude of his new homeplace, Kibbutz Sde Boker, in the Negev Desert.

Again the Lavon Affair surfaced. Presumably, this time David Ben-Gurion wouldn't "let sleeping dogs lie." Undoubtedly, the people were growing weary of the long, dragged-out scandal. Who cares if someone made a judgmental error in Egypt over eight years before? Ben-Gurion's former staunchest supporter, Golda Meir, visited David and Paula Ben-Gurion on the evening of June 15, 1963. While munching on Paula's cookies, she and the Prime Minister came to a meeting of the minds. She knew that Abba Eban was waiting in the wings to fill her post as foreign minister. She blasted Ben-Gurion for dealing with Germany.[1] She was tired and had decided to leave politics and become a full-time grandmother.[2]

On June 16, 1963, he resigned and rode silently into the sunset to his beloved Kibbutz Sde Boker. ... *the king ... rejoice*[d] *in God ...* for in the months that followed he remained in the Knesset, attempting a comeback. The final showdown was to come in 1965.

PSALM 64

Hear my voice, O God, in my prayer: preserve my life from fear of the enemy.
Hide me from the secret counsel of the wicked; from the insurrection of the workers of iniquity:
Who whet their tongue like a sword, and bend their bows to shoot their arrows, even bitter words:
That they may shoot in secret at the perfect: suddenly do they shoot at him, and fear not.
They encourage themselves in an evil matter: they commune of laying snares privily; they say, Who shall see them? (vv. 1-5).

Again we encounter a psalm of David while he is in exile. Exactly which exile is impossible to determine. Obviously, he has suffered at the hands of sneaking and unscrupulous men. "[They] have sharpened their tongue like the sword, and aimed their arrow — a bitter word — to shoot in secrecy at the innocent; suddenly they shot, and they were unafraid" (Psalm 64:4,5; Artscroll Translation). The psalmist seems appalled that evil men could so attack the nation of Israel.

Shoot in SECRET smacks of terrorist activity against innocent victims — a political element introduced in 1964. Yasser Arafat organized the Palestinian Liberation Organization. The Al-Fatah movement, led by Yassar Arafat and others, and the older Fedayeen terrorists, organized by Nasser, were poised ready to explode upon a seemingly unsuspecting Israel.

The September issue of OUR PALESTINE boldly asserted: "Our people ask 'when shall we begin?' It feels that the time has come for it to do something, to throw itself — with all the fury boiling up inside it, with all the fighting strength its sinews can muster, with all the anger that it feels in the depths of its being — to throw itself into battle ... Our slogan today is: let the revolution begin."[1]

On New Year's Eve, 1965, Arab terrorism entered a new phase. The Al-Fatah and the Fedayeen flickered alive in a tiny but mushrooming flame of terrorism that is yet to be extinguished. "On the night of Friday 31 December 1964 — 1 January 1965, detachments of our strike forces went into action, performing all the tasks assigned to them, in the occupied territories [Israel] and returning safely to their bases."[2] The Israelis denied that any serious damage had been done and officially seemed to ignore the matter. Nonetheless, Al-Fatah, under the guise of a storm force called "Asifah," finally had surfaced. From that day forward the PLO has been a thorn in the side of Israel.

PSALM 65

Iniquities prevail against me: as for our transgressions, thou shalt purge them away.

Blessed is the man whom thou choosest, and causest to approach unto thee, that he may dwell in thy courts: we shall be satisfied with the goodness of thy house, even of thy holy temple (vv. 3-4).

King David was chosen by God, Himself, to be King of Israel. We read in I Samuel 15:35, ... *the Lord repented that he had made Saul king over Israel.* In the very next verse the prophet Samuel is instructed to go to Bethlehem where God said, *I have provided me a king.* Samuel obeyed and young David was anointed to be the future king.

Unquestionably, David Ben-Gurion was divinely chosen as the first premier of the state of Israel in 1948. He served in this chosen position until June 1963, with the exception of a self-imposed exile to Kibbutz Sde Boker from December 1953 until November 1955.[1] As the Biblical King David's tenure was interrupted when he was forced into exile during the Absalom uprising, so Ben-Gurion's tenure was also interrupted. After their exiles, both were returned to the status of "chosen" leaders.

Again the Lavon affair surfaced to plague Ben-Gurion. This time the "Old Man" overplayed his hand. Golda Meir, Levi Eschol, and Moshe Sharett had been loyal from the beginning. Now, early in 1965, the old warrior from Sde Boker attempted to clear the name of Israel and finish off Pinhas Lavon once and for all. It was a sad affair, with Sharett in a wheelchair, now viciously plagued by cancer, having to openly hurt his old friend. When the final votes were counted Ben-Gurion had lost. He seemed the most hurt by "Golda's venomous speech."

Iniquities also prevailed against the state of Israel that year. Levi Eschol succeeded Ben-Gurion in 1963. In his speech presenting his coalition cabinet of 1965 he proclaimed, "The heads of the Arab states are fostering in the Arab world the idea of preparation for war. They are intensifying the arms race in the Middle East. They are maintaining and stimulating to further activity [of the] Palestine Liberation and Al-Fatah organizations."[2]

Further, Syrian snipers firing from the Golan Heights continually harassed the Eastern Galilee region. Syrian Premier Yusuf Zu'ayin warned, "We shall set the entire area afire and any Israel movement will result in a final resting place for Israel."[3] From January through October, Syria committed sixty-one outrages against Israel. The Al-Fatah organization backed by Syria launched incursions into Israel from Jordan, Lebanon, and the Gaza Strip in order to prevent Israeli reprisals against Syria. Leaders of the organization promised to "liberate the entire Arab land from the Zionist gangs and to drag the Arab nations into war with Israel."[4] And so, 1965 saw the departure of the "Old Man" in a year when *iniquities* from enemies *prevail*[ed] in the midst of threats and insults by enemy leaders.

> *Thou crownest the year with thy goodness; and thy paths drop fatness.*
> *They drop upon the pastures of the wilderness: and the little hills rejoice on every side.*
> *The pastures are clothed with flocks; the valleys are covered over with corn; they shout for joy, they also sing* (vv. 11-13).

All was not gloomy and dreary though; for during the years since 1948 Israelis planted over 150 million trees and turned rocky desolate land into a veritable Garden of Eden. They drained swamps and watered the deserts. They washed the crusty salt out of the soil and scraped away rocks that covered the land in Galilee and other places. In this short period of time, Israel became one of the world's leading exporters of fruits and vegetables. It's as though the psalmist was actually viewing the plains of Sharon, the fields of Galilee, and the pastures of the wilderness.

PSALM 66

> *Come and see the works of God: he is terrible in his doing toward the children of men.*
> *He turned the sea into dry land: they went through the flood on foot: there did we rejoice in him* (vv. 5-6).

In 1966 Egypt began beating the war drums again. The resulting conflicts between Israel and Egypt led to two major wars — the Six Day War of 1967 and the Yom Kippur War of 1973. In 1977 Anwar Sadat came before the Israeli Knesset in Jerusalem with an offer of peace. Menachem Begin and Anwar Sadat signed the resulting peace treaty on the White House lawn in 1979. The Arab world was furious. As a result, Anwar Sadat was assassinated on October 2, 1981.

From Psalm 66 to Psalm 81, Israel is reminded over and over again of their original exodus out of Egypt. Psalm 68:7 says, *O God, when thou wentest forth before thy people, when thou didst march through the wilderness.* Psalm 74:13 continues, *Thou didst divide the sea by thy strength ...* Psalm 77:5 adds, *I have considered the days of old, the years of ancient times.* Psalm 78:12-13 reminds the people, *Marvellous things did he in the sight of their fathers, in the land of Egypt ... He divided the sea, and caused them to pass through; and he made the waters to stand as a heap.* Psalm 80:8,15-16 describes the death of Sadat. *Thou hast brought a vine out of Egypt ... And the vineyard which thy right hand hath planted, and the branch that thou madest strong for thyself. It is burned with fire, it is cut down ...* and Psalm 81:10 concludes all references to Egypt in this section of the Psalms: *I am the Lord thy God, which brought thee out of the land of Egypt ...* These references are placed strategically in the light of Israel's relationship with Egypt. God is reminding the Israeli people that this generation can be likened to the generation of the Exodus.

> *Oh, bless our God, ye people, and make the voice of his praise to be heard:*
> *Which holdeth our soul in life, and suffereth not our feet to be moved* (vv. 8-9).

The author of Psalm 66 is not given in the Scriptures though Rabbi Feuer attributes it to David in the twilight of his career when God released him from the threat of surrounding hostile nations.[1] "A [song] for a safe ending to a national crisis," wrote Rabbi A. Cohen, "rings through this poem."[2] Obviously, it is a picture of Israel surrounded by potential invaders. The nation is reminded that God single-handedly delivered their forefathers from Egyptian bondage. The psalm ends with the affirmation that God's mercy had not been turned from them.

There seem to be prophetic parallels in this psalm to the year

1966. "The Syrians, the Egyptians and the Russians all embarked on new political ventures in the uncertain spring of 1966," wrote a veteran CBS correspondent.[3] He went on to explain that three different levels of danger confronted Israel. The lowest threat was from Palestine "liberation" groups. A higher level of threat was invasion by Egypt and Syria. Of gravest concern was the superpower designs of Russia and communism to dominate the Middle East.

The lowest level of threat, incursions and harassment from liberation movements such as the Egyptian sponsored Palestine Liberation Army (Fedayeen) and the Syrian backed Al-Fatah, was of minimal concern. At that time Israel could handle these with "hands tied behind their backs." As to the higher level of threat, Israeli Defense Forces already had defeated Egypt, Syria and the Arab forces twice, so that threat caused no real panic. But what about the super power, the Soviet Union? Well, perhaps there was nothing to fear from the bear of Gog. After all, the profound warnings of Russia's Chairman Bulganin during the Sinai campaign of 1956 turned out to be nothing but a big bluff.

The Israeli Parliament moved into the new Knesset building in Jerusalem in August, 1966. Led by Prime Minister Levi Eschol, they fearlessly could have proclaimed that God *suffereth not our feet to be removed*.

PSALM 67

> God be merciful unto us, and bless us; and cause his face to shine upon us; Selah.
> That thy way may be known upon earth, thy saving health among all nations. (vv. 1-2).

This is a blessed psalm of thanksgiving for the abundant harvest which came soon after the miraculous victory over Assyria in the days of King Hezekiah. According to Rabbi Cohen in the Soncino commentary on the Psalms, it is a priestly blessing not only for Israel but for all of mankind. Since even Jewish scholars recognize it as a "priestly blessing" one can easily see the importance of a Jewish return to the Western Wall and the Temple Mount which had been denied to Jews since 1948.

During 1967 hostile Arab nations backed by the Soviet Union prepared to launch a major two front attack against Israel. As God had saved Israel from brutal Sennacherib's invasion, so saved He modern Israel from Nasser and the Arabs.

This psalm is a hymn of thanksgiving and praise for God, Who once again has shown He ultimately directs in the affairs of nations. Israel gave thanksgiving and praise for victory which came in only six days of fighting.

> *O let the nations be glad and sing for joy: for thou shalt judge the people righteously, and govern the nations upon earth.*
> *Let the people praise thee, O God; let all the people praise thee* (vv. 4-5).

During the famous Six Day War, the city of Jerusalem was reunited under Jewish control for the first time in nearly 2,000 years. Jews from around the world rejoiced in that most historic and important occasion. Jerusalem had been divided since 1948 with barbed wire cutting off East Jerusalem and the Temple site from Jewish access. Within hours, however, Israeli soldiers had overrun the border and made their way to the Western Wall.[1] Hardened soldiers wept openly with joy and the ram's horn trumpet (shofar) was sounded in triumph.

King Hussein had planned to build an Arab luxury hotel along the site of the Western Wall (also called the Wailing Wall) which would forever close its access to Jewish prayers. To do so, however, he would have to permanently close the Morgrabi Gate. Since there are too few gates into the Moslem mosque area anyway, he decided to open the Eastern Gate — in defiance, I might add, of Ezekiel's prophecy that the gate must remain *shut* (Ezekiel 44:2). A crane had been set up outside the gate and air-hammers had been laid inside the gate. Work was to commence on June 7 but the Israeli move into Jerusalem on June 6 pre-empted Hussein's plans. The gate stayed shut.

The re-unification of Jerusalem is viewed by religious Jews as a fulfillment of the prophecy found in Psalm 122. *Our feet shall stand within thy gates, O Jerusalem. Jerusalem is builded as a city that is compact together* [reunited] (vv. 2-3). Some see the Six Day War as a fulfillment of the *times of the gentiles,* a prophecy given by Jesus Who said, ... *Jerusalem shall be trodden down of the Gentiles, until the times of the Gentiles be fulfilled* (Luke

21:24). Since that historic war in 1967, Jerusalem has been
declared the eternal and indivisible capital of Israel. Therefore,
the taking of Jerusalem points up the importance of Psalm 67 and
its call for joy.

PSALM 68

*Let God arise, let his enemies be scattered: let them also that
hate him flee before him.*
*As smoke is driven away, so drive them away: as wax melteth
before the fire, so let the wicked perish at the presence of God*
(vv. 1-2).

On May 17, 1967, President Nasser demanded the removal of
United Nations peace keeping forces from the Sinai. (He had
thrown out the British and French before the ill-fated war over
the Gaza Strip in 1956.) He then moved large military forces in
parade-like fashion through the streets of Cairo amongst the
cheers of the masses. The troops were enroute to the Sinai. By
May 20 about 100,000 troops organized in seven divisions (with
over 1,000 tanks) were amassed along Israel's southwest border.
As in 1956, he closed the Straits of Tiran for Israeli shipping.[1]
Beginning on May 21, Israel waited as participants in a wake.
Two young lions, Moshe Dayan, Minister of Defense and Yitzhak
Rabin, Chief of Staff of the Israeli Defense Forces chomped at the
bits for a pre-emptive strike. Dayan's autobiography devotes four
chapters to the following fourteen days. The chapters are entitled: "The Long Wait I;" followed by "The Long Wait II;" then
"Decisions;" and finally "Explosion."[2] Yitzhak Rabin, in his
MEMOIRS devotes two chapters to this long two-week waiting
period.[3] Their minute-by-minute recollections read like an exciting suspense novel.
On May 26 Nasser told the Arab Trade Union Congress, "If
Israel embarks on an aggression against Syria or Egypt ... our
basic objective will be to destroy Israel."[4] King Hussein of Jordan
patched up his differences with Nasser and flew to Cairo and signed a defense pact with Egypt on May 30. Arab forces built up to
250,000 troops, two thousand tanks and seven hundred aircraft.
Israeli forces were prepared for a pre-emptive strike and sat

nervously waiting while Prime Minister Eschol parlayed with the major powers. He depended on President Johnson to counter-balance Premier Kosygin. Diplomatic negotiations dragged on and on while Generals Dayan, Yadin, Rabin and Air Force Commander Motti Hod could hardly restrain themselves. Egyptian bombers were fueled and loaded on Egyptian airstrips. If someone didn't act soon those bombs would be killing Israeli civilians.

The Israeli leadership estimated it would take from three to five days to beat the Arabs. It took six. Motti Hod figured it would take three hours for Israeli planes to destroy the Egyptian Air Force. It took less than three hours.[5]

Who can forget the big grin on Ariel Sharon's face in 1967 as his forces crossed the Suez Canal and headed toward Cairo — or the Israeli dash toward Damascus after taking the Golan Heights? At this point in time, the power of the Arabs could have been completely demolished.

However, Israel did not destroy their enemies. God has reserved the destruction of all wicked for Himself alone. Once again the young lions of Israel were forbidden to pre-empt God's prize and were ordered to "destroy not."

> *O God, when thou wentest forth before thy people, when thou didst march through the wilderness; Selah:* (v. 7).

Again, this reference to Israel's ancient exodus from Egypt not only stands to remind us who their enemy was in the Six Day War, but reminds us that the confrontation should continue until a peace treaty would be signed in 1979 and Anwar Sadat would be assassinated in 1981 (see comments in Psalm 66).

PSALM 69

> *I am weary of my crying: my throat is dried: mine eyes fail while I wait for my God.*
> *They that hate me without a cause are more than the hairs of my head: they that would destroy me, being mine enemies wrongfully, are mighty: then I restored that which I took not away* (vv. 3-4).

This psalm resounds with the pathos of Jeremiah. The commentary in THE CENTURY BIBLE says it "should be read throughout with Jeremiah in mind.¹ Whether he wrote it or not, his history gives the key to its meaning. "There were plenty of reasons for weeping in Israel in the years following the Six Day War. Between June 1967 and July 1969, terrorist activity claimed 1,952 Israeli victims. Of these, 401 were killed.² It seems the Jews had no respite even to mourn for their war dead.

Nasser's War of Attrition intensified. The Al-Fatah group harassed and killed people in the Gaza Strip almost daily. Bombs were exploded in public places like the Tel Aviv bus station and the Hebrew University in Jerusalem. In Zurich, an El Al plane was attacked. A TWA plane was hijacked to Damascus. The PLO and Al-Fatah merged under the leadership of Yassar Arafat with a combined fighting force of 25,000 troops. These forces received financial aid from the Arab League, China and private contributions funneled through Arab governments.²

Hardly had the dust settled from the Six Day War before the Arab leadership began regrouping. Never admitting defeat, they referred to the Israeli victory merely as "The Setback." At a summit conference in Khartoum, Sudan, thirteen Arab leaders met and formulated a joint statement regarding Israel. The statement, known as the "three no's" affirmed: "No peace with Israel, no negotiations with Israel, no recognition of Israel."⁵ They created a $392 million fund to assist damages done to the economies of Egypt and Jordan in the Six Day War. The Soviet Union rushed new planes and military equipment to Egypt so that by late 1968 all losses had been made up.⁵

The United Nations passed "Resolution 242" outlining a peaceful framework for settlement of the Arab-Israel dispute. It did not call for the returning of territory. However, Israel did turn much of the captured territory over to UN peace-keeping forces. Indeed, Psalm 69 seems prophetically to describe the mood of Israel in 1969.

There was yet another reason for weeping. Prime Minister Levi Eschol died. Golda Meir, who replaced him recalled: "Then, on February 26, 1969, my dear friend, Levi Eschol, with whom I had worked for so many years, had a heart attack and died. I was at home alone when the news reached me, and I was stunned. I sat by the phone for several minutes in a state of shock, unable to pull myself together enough to find someone to drive me to

Jerusalem. It seemed impossible that Eschol was gone. I had talked to him only the night before ... I could not imagine what would happen now or who would take his place ... As I sat in someone's office and waited ... [to learn] what had been decided about the funeral arrangements ... an Israeli newspaperman came in. 'I know how you must feel,' he said to me, 'but I have just come from the Knesset. Everyone says there is but one solution. Golda must come back.' "[6] She was sworn in as the fourth person to lead modern Israel on March 17, 1969.

> *They that sit in the gate speak against me; ... (v. 12).*

Eschol had demonstrated great statesmanship, particularly in fielding criticisms and reproaches from western leaders. For example, French President Charles de Gaulle openly denounced Israel's behavior in the Six Day War. "France condemns the opening of hostilities by Israel," de Gaulle proclaimed. "France accepts as final none of the changes effected on the terrain through military action."[7] Did the psalmist cryptically prophesy anti-Israel world opinion in 1969 by saying, *They that sit in the gate speak against me?*

> *For God will save Zion, and will build the cities of Judah: that they may dwell there, and have it in possession.*
> *The seed also of his servants shall inherit it: and they that love his name shall dwell therein* (vv. 35-36).

Here is a promise fulfilled since 1969. Jerusalem has been proclaimed the eternal indivisible capital of Israel — not open for negotiation. The West Bank has become known by its ancient names, Judea and Samaria. The Messianic promises of these verses must also surely come to pass.

PSALM 70

> *Let them be ashamed and confounded that seek after my soul: let them be turned backward, and put to confusion, that desire my hurt;* (v. 2).

This psalm is excerpted from Psalm 40, verses 14-18. In 1940 the

Jews were destined to suffer many casualties over the next few years. In 1970 a similar fate hung over the nation. In a few years Israel would be caught off-guard and three thousand of her finest soldiers would die.

"David may be likened to the shepherd who grazed the flocks of the king. The king became vexed by the shepherd and so he chased away the flock, tore down the animal shed, and dismissed the shepherd. After a time, the king gathered in the sheep and rebuilt the shed, but he did not restore the shepherd to his position. The shepherd lamented, 'Behold the sheep are gathered in, the shed is rebuilt, but I am not remembered.' "[1] The sheep (the Jews) are being gathered into the rebuilt shed (Israel) before our very eyes. Soon the Great Shepherd (Messiah), the offspring of David will return to rule and reign forever.

> *Let them be turned back for a reward of their shame that say,*
> *Aha, aha* (v. 3).

Meanwhile, in 1970 there were many who wagged their heads and said "Aha! Aha!" In Lebanon "Fatahland" was established as a "state within a state" to train and equip terrorists. A SwissAir plane enroute to Israel was blown from the sky by a bomb planted on board. Three other planes were hijacked. Russian made planes challenged Israeli aircraft and SAM 3 missiles were used against Israeli planes.[2] It was not a good year for Israel.

On September 29, 1970, Gamal Abdel Nasser died. But the Jews of Israel dared not breathe a sigh of relief. As it turned out, they were correct. For Anwar Sadat, Nasser's successor, carefully laid plans for another invasion. This time it would be a sneak attack to take place on the most holy of all Jewish observances — Yom Kippur, 1973.

PSALM 71

Be thou my strong habitation, whereunto I may continually resort: thou hast given commandment to save me; for Thou art my rock and my fortress; (v. 3).

It had been thirty-five years since David made his first flight from danger as his father-in-law, King Saul, pursued him (Psalm 31). Now, as an old man, he was fleeing again. This time from his own son, Absalom. It seems significant that he uses the same phrase on both occasions, *thou art my rock and my fortress.* On the former occasion he cried for personal safety in the rock of habitation. Here, he cries for a "sheltering rock" literally, "a rock of a palace." His concern here is for the nation of Israel.

Deliver me, O my God ... out of the hand of the unrighteous and cruel man (v. 4).

It is no coincidence that the Jews of the Soviet Union were stirred to action in 1971. Awakening from the long night of exile, they began to demand the right to emigrate. The Soviets allowed a trickle of Jewish emigration to Israel which has continued on a token basis.[1] At this writing, though, the mass of Russian Jewry is still held in the Diaspora.

I am as a wonder unto many ...; (v. 7).

From the conquest of Israel by the Romans in 70 A.D. until the British Mandate of 1917, Eretz (the land of) Israel was under the domination of Oriental and Eastern influence. Ironically, the British did little to westernize the region. However, when Israel became a reborn nation in 1948, her ties instinctively fell toward Western and democratic values. Even today, Israel is the only genuine democracy in the Middle East. Two modern nations are unique as allies of the United States. They are Japan, "the most western of Eastern nations" while Israel is the most "eastern of Western nations."[2] In this sense, Israel is a "wonder to many."

For mine enemies speak against me; and they that lay wait for my soul take counsel together,

Saying, God hath forsaken him; for there is none to deliver him (vv. 10-11).

The Arab liberation movement spent much of 1971 regrouping and expanding. Its center of operation was the so-called "Fatahland" in Lebanon. Rearmed by Russia and to a lesser degree by China, through Syria and Algeria the movement began to accelerate.[3] It was as though they really felt that a jihad, or holy war, could be successful in exterminating the Jews from Palestinian soil.

PSALM 72

Give the king thy judgments, O God, and thy righteousness unto the King's son.
He shall judge thy people with righteousness, and thy poor with judgment.
The mountains shall bring peace to the people, and the little hills, by righteousness.
He shall judge the poor of the people, he shall save the children of the needy, and shall break in pieces the oppressor.
They shall fear thee as long as the sun and moon endure, throughout all generations.
He shall come down like rain upon the mown grass: as showers that water the earth.
In his days shall the righteous flourish; and abundance of peace so long as the moon endureth.
He shall have dominion also from sea to sea, and from the river unto the ends of the earth (vv. 1-8).

With Psalm 72, we reach the final psalm depicting specific events in the personal and public life of David. Here, as before, mystical and wonderful innuendos unfurl as the king relinquishes his throne officially to his son, Solomon. Apparently, David was aware that Solomon's rule was but a shadow of events to come. Undoubtedly he recognized that Messiah may not come in Solomon's days. Assuredly, He would come in due time. So David entered Paradise and rested peacefully (see I Kings 2:10). Could this also depict events in 1972 as David Ben-Gurion would die the following year in 1973? Though Ben-Gurion was not called king, the prophetic references to the title may simply be a 3,000 year old assessment of the political power of that highest office in the Israeli government.

The promise of Messiah is apparent. It "forms a complete vision of Messiah's kingdom ... The emphatic word is righteousness."[1] This psalm concludes the Exodus book with a promise of the coming of Messiah to rule *from sea to sea*. The next Messianic psalm (89) will conclude the Leviticus portion of the psalter.

The Exodus period of Israel's modern history is thus concluded as the "Chosen People" are back in their "Promised Land." With the next psalm (73) Israel will turn to its most important mandate — restoration of Temple worship. It will not come overnight, but movement in that direction is clear as the next several psalms progress. The priesthood must eventually be revived to herald and welcome the Messiah when He comes. This psalm, therefore, is filled with hope, perhaps because the next year will see a devastating war and the loss of 3,000 of Israel's finest men in the Yom Kippur War.

> *There shall be an handful of corn in the earth upon the top of the mountains; the fruit thereof shall shake like Lebanon: and they of the city shall flourish like grass of the earth* (v. 16).

With the establishment of Fatahland in Lebanon, it became inevitable that civil strife and destruction would descend upon that land. Even after the Israelis ferreted out the PLO in the Litani War of 1978 and the Lebanon War of 1982, the government of Lebanon still waved in the breeze like a patch of fruited grain before the wind.

> *And blessed be his glorious name for ever: and let the whole earth be filled with his glory; Amen, and Amen* (v. 19).

Two *Amen*s conclude this Exodus portion just as two *Amen*s also conclude the Genesis section (Psalm 41:13) and the Leviticus book (Psalm 89:52). In each case, they represent events both historical and prophetic. The word *Amen* means "so be it." Two of them together imply that events will continue into the next period. The Genesis period will continue to develop into the Exodus period; the Exodus period into the Leviticus period and the Leviticus period into the Numbers period. But when we come to the end of the Numbers section of the Psalms (106:48) there is only one prophetic *Amen* coupled with a concluding **Hallelujah**. (*Praise ye the LORD.*) It is **Hallelujah** because the Messiah has finally come to set up His kingdom and there are no more prophecies to be fulfilled. (See the chapter, The Prophetic Amen.)

THE
LEVITICUS
PSALMS

INTRODUCTION TO
THE LEVITICUS PSALMS

The third book of the Psalms (73-89) corresponds with Leviticus, the third book of Moses. Its theme alludes to a development toward reviving the priesthood and Temple worship. Psalms 73-83 are ascribed to Asaph, a Levite of the family of Gershom who was chosen to preside over the service of praise in the reigns of David and Solomon (I Chronicles 16:5). It was he who sounded cymbals before the Ark of the Covenant as it was brought to Jerusalem's Temple Mount.[1]

Twelve psalms are credited to him (50,73-83), perhaps strategically placed as a prophetic prelude to the return to Jerusalem of the ancient Ark. Asaph's first psalm (50) follows the birth of the nation (48) and the introductory message by the Lord for the new state (49). His message is apocalyptic. *Our God shall come ... a fire shall devour before him ... that he may judge his people ... Gather my saints together unto me: those that have made a covenant with me by sacrifice ...* (Psalm 50:3-5). He thus prepares the Jewish nation for a return to Temple worship and offers hope in the coming Armageddon: *Call upon me in the day of trouble: I will deliver thee, and thou shalt glorify me* (v. 15). In his other eleven psalms (73-83), Asaph continues preparing the nation for tribulation and their return to Temple service.

Twelve psalms (42-49, 84-85, 87-88) are also credited to the three sons of Korah: Assir, Elkanah, and Abiasaph (Exodus 6:24). They fathered that part of the priesthood who carried the Ark of the Covenant (Numbers 4:15). Are they placed strategically in the Psalms (84-85, 87-88) to oversee the return of the long lost Ark? Do we now live in the time which will see that ancient artifact brought back to the Temple Mount? The sons of Korah are also credited with the writing of eight earlier psalms (42-49). These contain uncanny descriptions of the Holocaust, World War II and the birth of Israel. They seemed to be strategically placed in the Psalms to correspond with the very years in this century which witnessed the fulfillment of those predicted events (1942-49). Not knowing the future, we can only wait and see what prophetic purpose they will have in following the Psalms of Asaph.

Psalms 73-89 were compiled by Solomon (the builder of the Temple) and compare with Leviticus. They were arranged in such a way as to resemble the processional of taking the Ark of the Covenant up to Jerusalem. This is most remarkable and may be prophetic of a future return of that ancient artifact. The implications for the discovery of the long lost Ark within the foreseeable future at least warrants a closer look at these psalms in light of this prophetic possibility.

Psalms 73-83 were written by Asaph. Psalms 84, 85, 87, and 88 were credited to the sons of Korah. Psalm 86 was a prayer of David. Psalm 88 was written by Heman and Psalm 89 (the last in this series) was written by Ethan the Ezrahite. Asaph, David, the sons of Korah, Heman, and Ethan played important roles in bringing the Ark to Jerusalem. When King David organized the procession, he chose Asaph and his brethren to provide the music. They led the processional, with musical instruments (cymbals, psalteries, harps, and trumpets) going before the Ark of the Covenant. This precious symbol of God's throne was borne upon the shoulders of the Kohathites of whom the sons of Korah were descended. David accompanied the procession. It was the highlight of his life. The Ark was coming to Jerusalem for the first time! It had never before been to the sacred city. Joshua had conquered the Promised Land and taken the Ark to Shiloh along with the Tabernacle of Moses. It was preserved there throughout the early history of the twelve tribes.

Under the priestly administration of Eli, Israel fought a war with the Philistines and lost the Ark to their enemies. But the judgment of God fell upon Philistia and the Ark was returned to Israel upon a cart pulled by milk cows. After the destruction of Shiloh the emptied Mosaic Tabernacle was moved to the city of Nob, a priestly community thought to be located on Mount Scopus, along the northern ridge of the Mount of Olives. After a time, the Tabernacle was moved again — to the city of Gibeon, six miles northwest of Jerusalem where it remained until Solomon built the Jerusalem Temple.

The return of the Ark from the Philistines excited the children

of Israel and 50,070 men gathered in the Sorek Valley below the
city of Beth Shemesh to see the Ark. Unfortunately, someone
opened it — a violation of the law of God. Their resulting deaths
frightened the nation (I Samuel 6:19). Priests were called to take
the dangerous artifact to Kirjath Jearim, another Gibeonite city,
for safekeeping. The Ark was never returned to the Mosaic
Tabernacle at Gibeon. It never again graced the Holy of holies
after its loss to the Philistines.

Many years later, David decided to bring the Ark to the capital
city of Israel, Jerusalem. The Ark represented the throne of God,
and David recognized the Lord as being the all powerful ruler of
the Chosen People. He prepared a special tent for the Ark,
erected it in the City of David *which is Zion* (I Kings 8:1) and
organized the procession. David retrieved the Ark and ignorantly
had it placed on a cart pulled by oxen. This violated God's law.
The Ark should only have been carried upon the shoulders of the
Kohathites. They were commanded in the Mosaic book of
Numbers to walk as they bore the contents of the Tabernacle.
When Aaron and his sons have made an end of covering the sanc-
tuary, and all the vessels of the sanctuary, as the camp is to set
forward; after that, the sons of Kohath shall come to bear it: but
they shall not touch any holy thing, lest they die. These things are
the burden of the sons of Kohath in the tabernacle of the congrega-
tion (Numbers 4:15).

David failed to follow the prescribed course laid out in the law.
Instead of commissioning the Kohathites to carry the Ark, he had
it placed on a new cart — just as the Philistines had done several
years before. Along the road to Jerusalem the Ark almost tipped
over. Uzzah, an attendant to the Ark, reached up to steady it and
was immediately killed by the strange power resident within the
golden box (II Samuel 6:6-7).

David, fearing the judgment of God, stopped the procession and
placed the Ark in the home of Obededom until he could reconsider
the situation. Over the following three months, David learned
what went wrong. He was told of God's blessings upon the house of
Obededom and realized it was time to fetch the Ark. *David was*
clothed with a robe of fine linen, and all the Levites that bare the
ark, and the singers, and Chenaniah the master of the song with
the singers: David also had upon him an ephod of linen. Thus all
Israel brought up the ark of the covenant of the LORD with

shouting, and with sound of the cornet, and with trumpets, and with cymbals, making a noise with psalteries and harps (I Chronicles 15:27,28).

Imagine the joy of the people as they gathered along the road to Jerusalem to get a glimpse of the Ark passing by. Asaph and his brethren sang processional songs and played the instruments. Following them were the Kohathites bearing the famous Ark. David danced around the Ark and rejoiced in the momentous occasion. This remarkable procession can be observed in the arrangement of Psalms 73-89. It may well represent a prophetic scenario to be fulfilled in the twentieth century. Psalms 73-83 were written by Asaph. It is as if they led the procession for the return of the Ark to Jerusalem.

Psalms 84-88 describe that part of the processional which carried the Ark itself. Imagine four sons of Korah (Kohathites) bearing the precious artifact — two in front as seen in Psalms 84 and 85, and two behind the Ark as seen in Psalms 87 and 88, while the Ark itself is borne between them as seen in Psalm 86. David prays in Psalm 86:17, *Shew me a token for good; that they which hate me may see it, and be ashamed: because thou, LORD, hast holpen me, and comforted me.* Could that *token* be the Ark of the Covenant? The word *token* is a translation of the Hebrew word "oth" translated in other places as "sign." Could it represent the famous insignia of the nation — the Ark of the Covenant?

Please note: along with Asaph, another musician, Ethan, was appointed to ring the cymbals. He may be the same Ethan (the Ezrahite) who wrote Psalm 89, the last psalm in the Leviticus portion. *And David spake to the chief of the Levites to appoint their brethren to be the singers with instruments of music, psalteries and harps and cymbals, sounding, by lifting up the voice with joy. So the Levites appointed Heman, the son of Joel; and of his brethren, Asaph the son of Berechiah; and of the sons of Merari their brethren, Ethan the son of Kushaiah. So the singers, Heman, Asaph, and Ethan, were appointed to sound with cymbals of brass;* (I Chronicles 15:16,17,19).

Ethan was called the son of Kushaiah (also called Kishi in I Chronicles 6:44). That may be related to "Kush," a Hebrew word for Ethiopia. The possibility may be prophetically important. Today's Ethiopian Jews are being rescued by Israel and though we have not yet been told, they may bring the Ark of the Covenant with them. There is an Ark in the Church of St. Mary of Zion in Aksum, said to be the original Ark taken by Menelik, the son of Solomon by the Queen of Sheba.

But there is another use of the term Ethan which we should consider. When Solomon finished the Temple, he organized the same kind of processional as David his father. *Then Solomon assembled the elders of Israel, and all the ... fathers of the children of Israel, unto king Solomon in Jerusalem, that they might bring up the ark of the covenant of the LORD out of the city of David, which is Zion. And all the men of Israel assembled themselves unto king Solomon at the feast in the month Ethanim, which is the seventh month* (I Kings 8:1,2).

The term Ethanim (a plural of Ethan) is used to date the processional. Solomon had the Ark taken into the Holy of holies of the new Temple *at the feast,* most probably the Feast of Trumpets. That would be on Rosh Hashanah, the Jewish New Year. The word Ethan means "enduring, long-lived." The plural term, Ethanim, means "continual, permanent, ever-flowing." Psalm 89, therefore, may refer to the Ark of the Covenant as an enduring and long-lived object. It could refer to a reappearance of it in this generation. It may also be an indication of when the Ark will be taken to the Temple Mount. If it is brought to Jerusalem on a Passover as some religious Jews expect, it may be transfered to the Temple site on a later Rosh Hashanah. Some time may be necessary to strike a deal with Moslems to divide the Temple site.

Psalm 89 actually has a reference to the Feast of Trumpets. *Blessed is the people that know the joyful sound: ...* (Psalm 89:15). According to Rabbi Rashi, the *joyful sound* describes the "teruah" blast of the shofar trumpet. Rashi, an eleventh century rabbi, wrote that when God hears the "teruah" on Rosh Hashanah and sees the Jews' repentance, He rises from His throne of Strict Justice and sits on His throne of Mercy.[2] But do we have a Scripture which specifically predicts the return of the Ark in the last generation? Yes! It is found in Hezekiah's Psalms of Ascent.

In the Deuteronomy portion of Hezekiah's psalms we have a prophecy of the appearance of both the Messiah and the Ark of the Covenant. *Arise, O LORD, into thy rest; thou, and the ark of thy strength* (Psalm 132:8). Here is a verse which clearly predicts the return of the long lost Ark in the days when Messiah shall establish His kingdom. The implication is that He will make it His throne. In Psalm 99, a psalm of rejoicing over the coming of Messiah, Moses wrote: *The LORD reigneth; let the people tremble: he sitteth between the cherubims; ...* (v. 1). The implication is that the Ark of the Covenant with its cherubims will be in Jerusalem when Messiah comes.

Now let us return to David and the processional. *So they brought the ark of God and set it in the midst of the tent that David had pitched for it: Then on that day David delivered first this psalm to thank the LORD into the hand of Asaph and his brethren* (I Chronicles 16:1,7). This historic psalm delivered by David has a clear reference to Psalm 86. *For great is the LORD, and greatly to be praised: he also is to be feared above all gods. For all the gods of the people are idols: but the LORD made the heavens* (I Chronicles 16:25,26).

The gods referred to are the planets and stars. They are the luminaries created by the LORD and worshiped as idols by the people. The same reference is made in Psalm 86. *Among the gods there is none like unto thee, O LORD; neither are there any works like unto thy works* (Psalm 86:8). The psalm delivered by David in honor of the golden Ark is akin to David's prayer in Psalm 86, which is positioned between the four psalms (84, 85, 87, and 88) written by the sons of Korah of the Kohathites who carried the Ark.

Among the many psalms written by David, only two are recorded as "prayers of David" — Psalm 86 and Psalm 17. The first prayer appears to have a prophetic reference to 1917 and the taking of Jerusalem by the British general, Allenby. It was both a prophetic and historic war — a special fulfillment of the deliverance of Jerusalem in preparation for the return of the Jews. Perhaps Psalm 86 was designated as a prayer for similar prophetic and historic reasons.

Will that golden insignia of Israel be returned? If so, where is the Ark? Is the artifact in Ethiopia the original Ark? Ethiopian history recounts that King Solomon had a duplicate made of the Ark for his son Menelik, who switched them the night before he left for Ethiopia, taking the real one with him. I met an ex-catholic priest in 1977 who said he had seen the Ark in the underground vaults of the Vatican — four stories under the west wing. His descriptions were quite impressive. Also, a few years ago, a group from Winfield, Kansas, claimed they found the Ark in a cave beneath the monastery on Mount Nebo. They can't all be the Ark. However, there are at least two and maybe three recorded in Jewish history. It is reported by some that one Ark was made to house the tables of stone and another was made to house the broken tables of stone.

If the Ark is returned to Israel it would spark a revival among Jews and Christians all over the world. Perhaps that is why David wrote: *All nations whom thou hast made shall come and worship before thee, O Lord; and shall glorify thy name* (Psalm 86:9). In light of its prophetic possibilities, the Leviticus portion of the Psalms (73-89) becomes a fascinating study.

PSALM 73

Truly God is good to Israel, ... (v. 1).

Asaph begins Psalm 73 with a declaration of God's goodness to Israel. Even when God brings judgment upon the nation, He is good. The punishments administered are "goodness in disguise" (Midrash Shocher Tov).[1] God appears to be preparing the Chosen People for a spiritual revival — a return to the Temple Mount! *Until I went into the sanctuary of God; ...* (v. 17). This verse was given to remind us that we have entered upon a new development — the Leviticus portion of the Psalms. In 1973 a symbolic "half shekel" offering was received from Jews around the world with which to build the first central house of worship for the Jewish world since the Temple was destroyed almost 2,000 years ago. Plans were announced for the construction of the Jerusalem Great Synagogue.

In the years since 1973 a marked turn in the development of the State of Israel can be noted. A world center for Judaism (the Jerusalem Great Synagogue) has been built. A school has been established for the training of the priesthood (the Yeshiva Torah Ha Cohenim). Jewish groups (the Faithful of the Temple Mount, the Jerusalem Temple Foundation and others) have organized campaigns to demand their rights to worship on the Temple site. They hope eventually to erect a sanctuary on the Temple Mount. Their campaigns could result in the fulfillment of a prophecy in Amos 9:11,12 — the raising of the Tabernacle of David. Do not lose sight of this theme as we approach the next several psalms for they (73-81) also reveal a continued confrontation and negotiation with Egypt.

The opening psalm (73) in this Leviticus section seems to present a description of the Yom Kippur War in 1973. Israel was caught off-guard in a surprise attack. In those first few days it looked as if Israel would not survive.

*But as for me, my feet were almost gone; my steps had well
nigh slipped ...
For all the day long have I been plagued, and chastened every
morning* (vv. 2,14).

The nation was at rest on that historic day, October 6, 1973, as
observing Jews were fasting in commemoration of the Biblical
"Day of Atonement." Only a few soldiers were on duty along the
southern and northern borders of Israel. It was a few minutes
before two in the afternoon. In a coordinated attack, Egyptian
tanks began their move toward the Mitlav Pass in the Sinai while
Syrian tanks rumbled up the roads which led through the Golan
Heights. The feet of Israel were nearly snatched from the Promised Land. Within a few hours they could have met in Tel Aviv for a
victory celebration. However, because of an unexplained hesita-
tion by the Egyptians and Syrians, Israel was able to rally its
forces on both fronts. After two weeks of fierce fighting Israeli
forces turned what looked like certain defeat into a decisive victory.

The Israelis knew days in advance that there would be a two-
front assault by the Arabs. On the very day of the invasion, Prime
Minister Golda Meir was briefed. She decided against a pre-
emptive strike by Israel because of world opinion. She thought if
Israel were the aggressor, the United States might not provide
arms needed to win the war.[2] The United States did airlift arms
and munitions to Israel just in a nick of time. On the day
American C-5A Galaxies touched down at Lydda Airport, Mrs.
Meir learned that 656 Israelis had already fallen in battle. "I
cried for the first time since the war began," she said.[3]

By the end of the first week of the war it was obvious that Israel
would win. Since the War of Independence in 1948, the Israeli
fight-plan had been to carry the war into enemy territory. "A
canal crossing would have to be made."[4] Not only was the Suez
Canal crossed in pursuit of the retreating Egyptians but the very
city of Cairo was at the mercy of the Israelis. "We could be in
Cairo for late lunch," Bill Marmon (a TIME magazine correspondent) quoted an Israeli soldier in the West Central Suez. As he
stood on top of his armored personnel carrier and scanned the
road ahead, he said, "There is nothing to stop us ..."[5] On the northern front Israeli forces neared the town of Sassa about twenty
miles from Damascus.[6] It would be relatively easy to destroy both

cities.

> *Verily, I have cleansed my heart in vain, and washed my
> hands in innocence* (v. 13).

This sounds like the commemoration of Yom Kippur when
Israel as a nation repents.

> *Until I went into the sanctuary of God; then understood I their
> end. Surely thou didst set them in slippery places: thou castedst
> them down into destruction. How are they brought into desola-
> tion, as in a moment!* (vv. 17-19).

Over the centuries Jews had learned of the ultimate destruction
of their enemies. This knowledge came through the study and
teaching of Torah scholars.[7] As in previous wars with the Arabs
the Israelis did not destroy their enemies. That judgment is
reserved for the Messiah when He comes.

In the ancient Yom Kippur (Day of Atonement) liturgy a high
priest would take the blood of a sacrificed goat into the Holy of
holies as an atonement for the sins of the nation. Ironically,
perhaps even prophetically, 3,000 Israeli soldiers were killed during the 1973 Yom Kippur War. Was their blood shed for prophetic
reasons? The number appears to be quite significant. It was in the
wilderness that 3,000 people died for worshiping the golden calf
(Exodus 32:28). Samson killed 3,000 Philistines (Judges 16:27).
The great Laver which stood in the courtyard of Solomon's Temple held 3,000 baths of water (II Chronicles 4:5), and in like manner 3,000 converts to Christianity went down in the watery graves
of baptism on the day of Pentecost (Acts 2:41). These 3,000 symbols of sacrifice may compare in some uncanny way to the 3,000
Israeli soldiers who were killed in the Yom Kippur War. Perhaps
God was introducing the "Leviticus period" on the Day of Atonement by allowing the sacrifice of 3,000 men — Israel's finest. *Until
I went into the sanctuary of God; then understood I their end* (v.
17).

> *... my heart was grieved, and I was pricked in my reins* (v. 21).

Could this passage refer to the heartache of Israel upon learning of the death of David Ben-Gurion? In addition to their wounded and the deaths of 3,000 soldiers in battle, the beloved "Old

Man'' died on November 29, 1973. He had lived to see his dream fulfilled. Israel could defend herself no matter what the odds. He died peacefully.

Psalm 73 also assures God's judgment upon the super-rich who take advantage of others. Ironically, in 1973 the world's oil barons raised the price of crude and held the world hostage. In the years following, the world's economies have crumbled. Every nation on earth faces impossible national debts to an international banking cartel. It is the opinion of some theologians that the ultimate goal of these people is to bring about a one-world government based upon a unified monetary system, called in the Bible *the mark ... of the beast* (Revelation 13:17).

PSALM 74

O GOD, why hast thou cast us off for ever? why doth thine anger smoke against the sheep of thy pasture? (v. 1).

In the preceding psalm a frustrated Asaph questions the wealth of wicked people. In this psalm he discusses the equity of extreme Jewish suffering. Is God guilty of forsaking the Chosen People or have they forsaken him? "The first (Babylonian) Exile was limited to seventy years; but this second (Roman) Exile still continues, with no end in sight (Sforno)."[1]

This mind-set could explain why 1974 was such a bitter year for Israel. After the Yom Kippur War, Golda Meir was accused of being guilty of the deaths of Israeli soldiers and for not guarding the nation's borders more carefully. Israel should never allow itself to be caught off-guard when surrounded by hostile Arab nations. She was called a murderer and two of her generals argued in public. It was a time for recriminations and introspection. The divided nation resented Meir's administration. Saddened, Golda resigned in April 1974. Shortly thereafter, Yitzhak Rabin became the fifth person to rule the modern State of Israel.

Thine enemies roar in the midst of thy congregations; ...
They said in their hearts, Let us destroy them together: ...
Remember this, that the enemy hath reproached, O LORD,
and that the foolish people have blasphemed thy name.

> *Forget not the voice of thine enemies, the tumult of those that*
> *rise up against thee ... continually* (vv. 4,8,18,23).

Just as Psalm 46 reflects upon the conflict which ended in 1945
and Psalm 68 alludes to the military aspects of the 1967 war,
Psalm 74 strongly suggests the behavior of Egypt and Syria during the Yom Kippur War. Shortly before two o'clock on October 6,
1973, 222 Egyptian jets roared into Israeli held territory in the
Suez region. Two thousand guns blazed while hundreds of tanks
and thousands of foot soldiers moved toward Israel. The Egyptian
front was 110 miles in length. The area was being manned by only
436 Israeli soldiers who had only three tanks at their disposal.[2]

Simultaneously, Syrian fighter planes flew over the Golan
Heights in the north while their tanks rumbled southward toward
Galilee. "The Israelis at home never knew or felt how great was
the danger nor how bloody was the battle. Eight hundred tanks
had broken onto the heights. The pride of Syrian armor was only a
few miles from (Israel). Late on Sunday afternoon (the second
day of battle), the Israelis thought for two hours that they had
lost.[3]

The Syrians were armed with surface to air missiles supplied
by the Soviet Union. Early on in the war they were invincible
against Israeli jets. However, the missiles were programmed to
intercept the planes similar to the way a quarterback leads his
receiver in American football. Within hours Israeli pilots learned
to out-maneuver them.

> *We see not our signs: there is no more any prophet: neither is*
> *there among us any that knoweth how long.*
> *O God, how long shall the adversary reproach? shall the*
> *enemy blaspheme thy name for ever?* (vv. 9-10).

The Talmud quotes an ancient Jewish belief that after the death
of the last prophets, Haggai, Zechariah, and Malachi, no man was
granted the knowledge of when the redemption would come. They
can only wait for the coming of Elijah to announce the Messiah,
but Rabbi Radak said, "We eagerly await the advent of Elijah,
the prophet of Redemption, who will appear before the Messiah;
but even he tarries."[4] Though the writings of those prophets still
exist, the exact date of the redemption cannot be determined. God
purposely concealed it even from the early prophets. This rabbinical concensus is important in light of those religious Jews in

Jerusalem who set the date for the coming of Messiah in 1974. Some reported that the Yom Kippur War was the Battle of Gog and Magog. They must have been disappointed when the Messiah did not appear.

Rabbi Avrohom Feuer wrote, "The Talmud (Sanhedrin 97a) lists numerous signs which herald the imminent arrival of Messiah; among these are cataclysms, crises, wars, and plagues. However, concludes the Talmud, there is really none in our midst who knows until when the Exile will endure, for all these signs have appeared, yet Messiah tarries."[5]

> *Thou didst divide the sea by thy strength: thou brakest the heads of the dragons in the waters.*
> *Thou brakest the heads of leviathan in pieces, and gavest him to be meat to the people inhabiting the wilderness* (vv. 13-14).

This reference to their first exodus points up the prophetic nature of Egypt's final attempt to destroy Israel in the Yom Kippur War. There are several scriptures from Psalms 47-81 which allude to Israel's confrontation and negotiation with Egypt. Anwar Sadat would ask for peace in 1977, sign the treaty in 1979, and be assassinated in 1981. The destruction of a many-headed dragon or leviathan alludes to the future many-headed Hydra of the end-time Tribulation Period. He is described in the New Testament book of Revelation as representing a ten-nation confederation, believed to be the Revived Roman Empire. Such a dragon was not included in the original narrative given in the book of Exodus.

Its inclusion in this psalm must be prophetic of the geo-political climate in 1974 as oil prices escalated and the nine-nation European Common Market helped to give rise to the Trilateral Commission — a financial group whose purpose is to merge the economies and monetary systems of three hemispheres (including Japan, the United States, and Europe) into a global network issuing a world currency. Could this emerging global system be the fulfillment of the many-headed serpent? Usury (interest charged on loans), in the Scriptures, is translated from the Hebrew word, "nashak" meaning "bite of the serpent." Certainly, 1974 saw major strides toward the development of a world government based on a global financial structure.

PSALM 75

To the chief Musician, Al-taschith, A Psalm or Song of Asaph
(introduction).

Here is another "Do not destroy!" psalm, a term used also in
Psalms 57-59. It seems that Israel is not allowed to destroy its
enemies for that should be left to God's vengeance. In the Yom
Kippur War, the IDF (Israeli Defense Forces) had ample opportunity to destroy Cairo and Damascus, yet did not. Captured territory in the Sinai was held only for future negotiations. Eventually, it was to be given back to Egypt.

In 1975 "Do not destroy!" took on new meaning. For in the wake
of the Yom Kippur War, terrorists step up actions against
defenseless Jews all across Israel and in Europe. In January,
Israeli airline (El Al) planes were attacked by Arab terrorists
twice in Paris. In March, the Savoy Hotel in Tel Aviv was invaded
and hostages were taken. In April, the Rashi Synagogue in Paris
was destroyed. In June, PLO terrorists hit a moshav near the
Lebanon border killing two. On July 4, fourteen people were killed
in Jerusalem's Zion Square by a terrorist bomb. In September,
the Chief Rabbi of France escaped as his home was bombed. In
November, six Israelis were killed by a bomb planted on Jaffa
Road in Jerusalem. Three days later Arab terrorists killed three
students in the Golan Heights. Finally in December, the Israeli
Defense Force began to strike back by bombing terrorist targets
in Lebanon.[1]

Rabbinic scholars commenting on Psalm 75 wrote that
"Israel's anguish will intensify as the end of the exile draws near.
At that time, calamities will befall Israel in rapid succession. The
world will be engulfed in the colossal conflict of Gog and
Magog."[2]

Could the world in 1975 have been witnessing a political unrest
building toward that future final conflict? Have we reached the
generation which will see the enemy's destruction and Israel's
complete redemption from Exile with the coming of Messiah?
Radak said, "This psalm is dedicated to the final era of the Exile,
the period of the ingathering of the exiles." It is also noted in the
Talmud (Sanhedrin 97a) that this final period of the Exile will be

especially difficult.[3] Since Jewish theologians believed this psalm to be a prophecy for "the period of the ingathering of the exiles" then 1975 must have been a part of that period.

> I said unto the fools, Deal not foolishly: and to the wicked, Lift not up the horn:
> Lift not up your horn on high: speak not with a stiff neck.
> For promotion cometh neither from the east, nor from the west, nor from the south.
> But God is the judge: he putteth down one, and setteth up another (vv. 4-7).

Could these words of advice be intended for the Soviet Union in 1975? The 100,000th Russian Jew arrived in Israel on January 15th. Though a milestone, it was no great victory as millions of Jews remained at the mercy of the "fools" of Russia. Remember that the Scriptures define the meaning of "fool" (Psalm 14:1 and 53:1). *The fool hath said in his heart, There is no God.* These two passages already have been attributed to Stalin in our discussions of Psalms 14 and 53.

In March the Russians stopped Passover services in the Moscow synagogue. Later that month they sentenced two Jewish "activists" to five years exile in Siberia. In May the Russians announced plans to build a monument at Babi-Yar without special mention of the Jews massacred there. On August 5 they raised the amount of tax that Jews would have to pay prior to exiting the Soviet Union. In September the Soviets interrupted Jewish observances of Succoh.[4] And so it was that the Soviets, with stiff necks, refused to release God's Chosen People. In 1975 it seemed that the Jews were begging God not to allow the destruction of their brethren in communist lands.

> For in the hand of the LORD there is a cup, and the wine is red; it is full of mixture; and he poureth out of the same: but the dregs thereof, all the wicked of the earth shall wring them out, and drink them.
> All the horns of the wicked also will I cut off; but the horns of the righteous shall be exalted (vv. 8,10).

This is the cup of God's wrath which the nations will be made to drink at the final Tribulation Period. The prophet Zechariah referred to Jerusalem as a *cup of trembling* [poison] (Zechariah

12:2) at the final siege of the city. Mystery Babylon holds a cup in her hand (Revelation 17:4) full of the *filthiness of her fornication.* Though the cup is bitter, it gets even more bitter just below the surface of the drink. The dregs will be fed to wicked nations at Armageddon. "This is an allegory alluding to the full force of Divine retribution, unrestrained by any mercy or compassion."[5] The cup is so full it runs over so that the wicked will get their full share of God's wrath. In Revelation 16, seven angel's bear seven bowls of wrath to be poured out upon the wicked. In 1975 world events were developing toward that future final war.

PSALM 76

Surely the wrath of man shall praise thee: the remainder of wrath shalt thou restrain.
Vow, and pay unto the LORD your God: let all that be round about him bring presents unto him that ought to be feared (vv. 10-11).

The ebb and flow of these psalms seem to be centered on Egypt and its contention with Israel. The wrath of the enemy would soon be turned into a peace initiative. Anwar Sadat, hater of the Jews would soon come to Jerusalem to speak to the Israeli Knesset. Wrath will be turned into praise. Egypt shall *vow a vow unto the Lord and perform it* (Isaiah 19:21).

The entire scenario is predicted also in Isaiah 19. It compares perfectly with these psalms. The opening verses predict the political climate in Egypt beginning in 1948, the year Israel was born. In fact, all prophecies of end-time events are centered around the birth of Israel. Note the failure of King Farouk and the resulting civil war in Isaiah's account of verses 2-4: *And I will set the Egyptians against the Egyptians: and they shall fight every one against his brother, and every one against his neighbour.*

Gamal Abdel Nasser took over the reigns of power according to verse 4: *And the Egyptians will I give over into the hand of a cruel lord; and a fierce king shall rule over them.*

The foolish adventure of building the Aswan Dam and its resulting problematic effects on the Nile are recorded in verses 5-8: *And the waters shall fail from the sea, and the river shall be wasted and dried up. And they shall turn the rivers far away.*

The Six Day War is described in Isaish 19:16-18: *In that day shall Egypt be like unto women: and it shall be afraid and fear because of the shaking of the hand of the LORD of hosts, which he shaketh over it. And the land of Judah shall be a terror unto Egypt, ... In that day shall five cities in the land of Egypt speak the language of Canaan, and swear to the LORD of hosts; one shall be called, The city of destruction.* Al Arish (*city of destruction*) was among five captured cities in the Sinai desert captured and held by the Israelis until the territory was returned under the terms of the peace treaty. The language of Hebrew was spoken in those Egyptian cities from 1973 to 1982.

Anwar Sadat was the subject of Isaiah 19:19-21. There is the prediction of his rise to power: *... he shall send them a savior, and a great one, and he shall deliver them.* The peace treaty is predicted: *... the Egyptians shall ... vow a vow unto the LORD, and perform it.* Sadat's death was implied in verse 21: *... the Egyptians ... shall do sacrifice and oblation.* Even the tomb of the Unknown Warrior (where Sadat was buried) appears in verse 19: *In that day shall there be an altar to the LORD in the midst of the land of Egypt.* Sadat, the *saviour* was *sacrificed* at the *altar ... in the midst of Egypt.* Furthermore, the *highway* in verse 23 was made a part of the provisions of the peace treaty between Egypt and Israel. One can now travel by bus from Israel to Egypt.

A step-by-step prediction of events are given in Isaiah 19. But just as amazing are the predictions in the Psalms concerning Egypt as President Anwar Sadat contemplated the possibility of making peace with Israel. Even Talmudic scholars say that Psalm 75 speaks of the final days of Jewish exile and that Psalm 76 continues that theme and describes the War of Gog and Magog "which will be waged at the end of the exile."[1] One can be certain that 1976 places us within that time frame — the end of Israel's exile and the upcoming War of Gog and Magog. That final war has not yet come, but it will. The ebb and flow of these psalms predict it.

Also, there is a rabbinical prediction that the War of Gog and Magog is destined to take place in the month of Tishri (September/October) in conjunction with the Feast of Tabernacles. Therefore, Psalm 76 is designated as the Song of the Day for the first day of the Feast of Tabernacles."[2]

*He shall cut off the spirit of princes: he is terrible to the kings
of the earth* (v. 12).

In December, 1976, Prime Minister Yitzhak Rabin, perhaps the
most qualified and brilliant of all Israeli prime ministers to date,
was forced to resign due to financial mismanagement. He was the
first since King David to master both military and diplomatic
portfolios. Perhaps, it is as he insinuated in his MEMOIRS that
the press seemed to have tried and sentenced him and his
cabinet.[3]

Rabin tells that Egyptian President Anwar Sadat had begun to
make unprecedented overtures toward a peace initiative.[4]
Nonetheless, Rabin was out and Begin began his belated rise to
power. The Egyptian-Israeli peace initiative took place under
Begin's administration, as we shall see.

PSALM 77

I have considered the days of old, the years of ancient times
(v. 5).

It was in 1977 when Egyptian President Anwar Sadat expressed
an unprecedented desire for peace. "I am ready to go to the end of
the world to get a settlement," he announced to the Egyptian
Parliament, "I am even ready to go to Israel, to the Knesset, and
speak to the Israeli Parliament there and negotiate with them
over a peace settlement." Amidst applause from the Egyptian
Parliament he added, "The Israelis are going to be stunned when
they hear I am ready to meet them in their home."[1]

Menachem Begin, who had just become Prime Minister of
Israel, extended the invitation for the Egyptian leader to do just
that. On November 19, 1977, Egypt's presidential plane touched
the runway in Tel Aviv. It was an historic occasion of monumental proportions. Both leaders could have met the criteria of this
verse, *I have considered the days of old, the years of ancient
times.* Israel's confrontation with Egypt is the theme of the
psalm.

According to rabbinic scholars the psalm reaches back to note
how God delivered Israel out of their first exile, only to ignore
them in their last exile. The prophet-psalmist wonders why God
does not perform miracles to help them now?

> *Will the Lord cast off for ever? and will he be favourable no
> more?*
> *Is his mercy clean gone for ever? doth his promise fail for
> evermore?*
> *Hath God forgotten to be gracious? hath he in anger shut up
> his tender mercies? Selah.*
> *And I said, This is my infirmity: ...* (vv. 7-10).

As 1977 commenced, the Jewish people could fit the description
of these verses. A gloom had spread over Israel after the Yom
Kippur War. It had left them with a bleak future. They were
disappointed in their government. Political unrest had brought
the Likud party to power with Menachem Begin at the helm. It
was time for a change. The socialist philosophy of Begin's
predecessors was blamed for the instability of the nation. A
strong democratic prime minister would be given a chance to bring the country out of the doldrums.

Has God forever forsaken Israel? Are there no more miracles
in His arsenal? Many of the Jewish people were just about to give
up. More were leaving the country than were coming there to live.
The population was not growing. But, in 1977, God came through
with another miracle! The pharoah wants peace! No longer is his
heart hardened. He walks into the midst of Israel's leaders, takes
the podium, and talks of treaties.

This same question is addressed by the Apostle Paul in the New
Testament book of Romans. *Hath God cast away his people? God
forbid* (Romans 11:1). *I say then, Have they stumbled that they
should fall? God forbid: ...* (Romans 11:11). History bears out the
fact of Israel's longest exile, but Paul predicted the day when
Israel would be received again. The Jew is not forever forsaken.
Reconciliation will come when the *fulness of the Gentiles be come
in* (Romans 11:25). We are fast approaching that time. Since 1948
we have been in the transition period. The last Gentile convert
will soon be redeemed. At that time, God will renew His covenant

with Israel. The Creator is already moving on behalf of Israel. He has given them military supernatural abilities. He has endowed their politicians with vision. He has crowned their scientific minds with inventions undreamed of a century ago. *Thou are the God that doest wonders: ...* (v. 14).

PSALM 78

> *Give ear, O my people, to my law: incline your ears to the words of my mouth.*
>
> *I will open my mouth in a parable: I will utter dark sayings of old* (vv. 1-2).

The Temple Scroll was among the first eight scrolls found in the Qumran cave in 1947, but was hidden away by its Arab owner. It was recovered in 1967, turned over to Yigael Yadin, son of Professor Sukenek (the man who bought the first set of scrolls in 1947). The Temple Scroll was carefully preserved and studied over the next 10 years. A Hebrew commentary was published in 1978. Could that be why a reference is given in Psalm 78 about *dark sayings of old*? (See a discussion on the Dead Sea Scrolls in our commentary on Psalm 49.) The Temple Scroll contains information for the establishment of Temple worship,[1] and fits perfectly the modern Leviticus Period (which began in 1973), corresponding with the Leviticus Psalms.

> *We will not hide them from their children, shewing to the generation to come the praises of the LORD, and his strength, and his wonderful works that he hath done.*
>
> *That the generation to come might know them, even the children which should be born; who should arise and declare them to their children* (vv. 4,6).

What generation would have the *dark sayings* opened up to them? The answer lies in the birth of the nation of Israel in 1948. That must surely be the generation referred to here. May we also be reminded that Jesus said, *This generation shall not pass, till all these things be fulfilled* (Matthew 24:34).

> *That they might set their hope in God, and not forget the works of God, but keep his commandments:*

*And might not be as their fathers, a stubborn and rebellious
generation; a generation that set not their heart aright, and
whose spirit was not stedfast with God* (vv. 7-8).

On the political front, negotiations with Egypt continued
throughout 1978. They were long and difficult. It seemed at times
there would be no peace. It was such an important year for
Israel's talks with Egypt that it seems, in Psalm 78, that the Lord
spent a full seventy-two verses on the subject.

*Marvellous things did he in the sight of their fathers, in the
land of Egypt, ...* (v. 12).

As God performed those great miracles of the past, so it would
be in 1978. Israel had the opportunity to be part of another miracle
— a modern miracle! The message seemed to be, "Don't miss
this chance. Don't turn your backs on what God is doing for you in
1978."

*So that he forsook the tabernacle of Shiloh, the tent which he
placed among men;* (v. 60).

The goal of this generation should be to restore Temple worship. The prophetic admonition seems to be for Israel not to
jeopardize the future by refusing peace with Egypt.

*He gave his people over also unto the sword; and was wroth
with his inheritance* (v. 62).

On March 11, 1978, Arab terrorists infiltrated from the sea.
They commandeered a passenger laden bus and sped along the
Haifa-Tel Aviv highway shooting and killing at random. Then
they exploded the vehicle. In all, thirty-seven Israelis were
murdered and eighty-two wounded.[2] Four days later Israel began
Operation Litani. Israeli Defense Forces swept into Southern
Lebanon and cleared a narrow zig-zag security belt driving out
PLO terrorists. Up to that time Palestinian guerrillas had been
within sight of Northern Israeli villages and made life miserable
along the border.[3] Also, Golda Meir died at the age of 80 in
December, 1978.

PSALM 79

O GOD, the heathen are come into thine inheritance; thy holy temple have they defiled; they have laid Jerusalem on heaps.
We are become a reproach to our neighbours, a scorn and derision to them that are round about us (vv. 1,4).

Asaph, of the tribe of Korah, was worried about his forefather's rebellion against Moses. Korah had been swallowed by an earthquake (Numbers 16:31-33). Upon learning that the Temple would someday be destroyed and its gates swallowed beneath the Temple Mount, he rejoiced, and wrote this psalm in hopes that whoever descends into the bowels of the earth to retrieve the gates will also raise [his father].[1]

The psalm rehearses the exiles of Israel, giving the real reason for Gentile oppression. The nations have directed all their hatred at the place where God had chosen to dwell among His people. All persecution of Jews is in reality an attempt to rid the planet of Israel's God.

All Jewish hearts long for the day when the Temple will be rebuilt and the shekinah returns. They wait. Years turn into centuries. The Egyptian exile lasted 210 years. The Babylonian exile was concluded after 70 years. But this Roman exile has continued until the twentieth century. When will it end?

How long, LORD? wilt thou be angry for ever? shall thy jealousy burn like fire? (v. 5).

Back in their land, in 1979, Israel waited with baited breath for a sign from heaven that God will redeem Israel — that their national identity would be recognized by their cousins, the Arabs and that they can proceed with plans for reviving Temple worship. And it came! Anwar Sadat and Menachem Begin signed an historic peace treaty on the White House lawn in Washington D.C. The ranks of Arab solidarity were broken. Israel was at last recognized by an Arab neighbor. The world was moving closer to the predicted last great war. God is about to pour out His wrath upon a wicked and sinful world.

Pour out thy wrath upon the heathen that have not known thee, and upon the kingdoms that have not called upon thy name (v. 6).

An important step toward the *day of vengeance* (Isaiah 61:2) occurred with the signing of the treaty. The Sinai would be given back to Egypt. Israel's attention would then be focused on the north. The PLO in Lebanon would be the next target. Syria would push for war. A Russian invasion must be anticipated. But through the rough years ahead, Israel will never forget the promise that the Messiah will appear to save the day and set up His kingdom. This verse is a request for God to pour the vials of His wrath upon the nations. It is a prayer to hasten Armageddon and deliverance. The seven vials (bowls or cups) are explained in Revelation 16.

Let the sighing of the prisoner come before thee: ... (v. 11).

Early in January, 1979, the Israeli Parliament voted to accept 100 Vietnamese refugees. Within three weeks 101 boat people arrived in Israel. In October, another 197 destitute Vietnamese were resettled. It seems that the tiny nation of Israel heard *the sighing[s] of the prisoner.*

In March, seventy-six Palestinian terrorists were exchanged for only one Israeli soldier. One month later, the Soviets unexpectedly released seven Soviet Jewish Prisoners of Zion. Meanwhile in New York more than 100,000 Jews turned out for Solidarity Sunday in a march urging the release of Soviet Jewry.[2] It seems that 1979 was a year to attend to the *sighing of the prisoner.*

And render unto our neighbours sevenfold ... (v. 12).

This could be a reference to the future seven years of Tribulation, which, if allowed to continue any longer, *... there should no flesh be saved:* (Matthew 24:22).

So we thy people and sheep of thy pasture will give thee thanks for ever: we will shew forth thy praise to all generations (v. 13).

This verse alludes to the millennial reign of Christ. He will save the world from destruction at the conclusion of those seven dreadful years, set up His kingdom and rule over the earth for a thousand years. Jerusalem will be His capital, and Israel will be set at the head of the nations. Grateful Israel will show forth His praises to each succeeding generation.

PSALM 80

O LORD God of hosts, how long wilt thou be angry against the prayer of thy people?
Thou feedest them with the bread of tears; and givest them tears to drink in great measure.
Thou makest us a strife unto our neighbours: and our enemies laugh among themselves (vv. 4-6).

If Israel and Egypt thought they would be able to enlarge their peace treaty to include other Arab nations, they were mistaken. The PLO were enraged that Sadat could sign a treaty with the Jews. They vowed to continue their fight and to assassinate the Egyptian president. These verses seem to record the consternation of Israel and point up their frustration with another record of the question, *How long?* (See our discussion in the chapter entitled, How Long?)

Thou hast brought a vine out of Egypt: ... (v. 8).

In Psalm 80 Anwar Sadat appears to be represented through the symbol of a vine. He may well be the fulfillment of the implication — that vine whose life was cut short because he signed a peace treaty with the Jews. Please note what was to happen to the vine.

And the vineyard which thy right hand hath planted, and the branch that thou madest strong for thyself.
It is burned with fire, it is cut down: ... (vv. 15-16).

It was on the anniversary of the Yom Kippur War in 1981 that Sadat was viewing a military parade. Suddenly, a group of soldiers jumped out of an armored vehicle in front of the viewing stand brandishing automatic weapons. The Egyptian president thought it was part of a demonstration and stood to salute them. They opened fire, killing Sadat instantly (see Psalm 81).

What incredible descriptions are given in these psalms! Important prophetic implications are made concerning Israel's relationship with Egypt in Psalms 47-81.

The number 80, in the Hebrew alphabet, is a single letter "peh," signifying "a mouth"[2] and may represent a very important turn of events for Israel in the Leviticus period. Compare the number 40 "mem" meaning "water"[3] with 80 "peh" implying the "Spirit." Several examples of this come to mind. First, Jesus told Nicodemus, *Except a man be born of water and of the Spirit, he cannot enter into the kingdom of God* (John 3:5). Also, on the evening of the resurrection Jesus appeared to the disciples, told them about the prophecies in the Psalms, then *breathed on them, and saith unto them, Receive ye the Holy Ghost* (John 20:22). It is as if He were demonstrating that one day Israel would be born of water, then later, of the Holy Spirit!

The numbers 40 and 46 both mean "water" while 41 and 45 both mean "what?"[4] in the sense of frustration. It shows the consternation of the victims of the Holocaust. The 40 and 46 together drive home the importance of Israel's 1948 birth being like unto that of water. On the other hand, both 80 and 85 mean "mouth" while both 81 and 86 mean "to blow."[5] These numbers drive home the concept that Israel is about to be born of the Spirit!

Furthermore, the number 48 describes the condition of the baby born of water. The number 48 is the Hebrew word "meah" meaning "fat" and "rich."[6] The new baby, Israel, was both healthy and wealthy. It was "rich in that God had given them their inheritance — the land. Now, if Israel was born of water in 1948, just eight years after 1940, is one to consider the possibility that the nation may be born of the Spirit in the not too distant future? Only time will tell. Of one thing we can be sure. Israel is on the verge of a national spiritual revival.

Ezekiel prophesied to the valley of dry bones and they developed into a host of lifeless bodies. Then God said, *Prophesy unto the wind, prophesy, son of man, and say to the wind, Thus saith the Lord GOD; Come from the four winds, O breath, and breathe upon these slain, that they may live. So I prophesied as he commanded me, and the breath came unto them, and they lived, and stood up upon their feet, an exceeding great army* (Ezekiel 37:9-10).

The number 83 is comprised of two letters "peh" and "gimel." They make up the word "pag" meaning, "unripe figs."[7] In Psalm 48 the fig tree was planted and in Psalm 83 the unripe figs appear.

Is the nation about to bear fruit? The number 84 is comprised of two letters "peh" and "daleth." The resulting word, "pahdah" means "to loose, set free."[8] In 1984 a movement got underway to demand a place of worship on the Temple Mount. Perhaps it fulfills the connotation of setting the Temple site free for Jewish worship. Spiritual revival should come to the nation when Temple worship is resumed on the mountain. Will it be soon?

PSALM 81

This he ordained in Joseph for a testimony, when he went out through the land of Egypt: ...
I am the LORD thy God, which brought thee out of the land of Egypt: ... (vv. 5,10).

These verses contain the last reference to Egypt in this portion of the Psalms. It marks the conclusion of Israel's confrontation and negotiation with Egypt. Ironically, it alludes to the year of Sadat's death — thus ending an era.

It happened on October 6, 1981, at the annual commemoration of the Egyptian invasion of Israel. President Anwar Sadat, sixty-two, was not enthusiastic about attending and was urged by his Vice President to stay home and rest. Out of a sense of duty, Sadat decided to go. His elegant wife, Jehan, forty-eight, had brought the grandchildren and was watching from a glass enclosed booth at the top of the reviewing stand.

At about 12:40 P.M., midway through the parade, six Mirage jet fighters swept low overhead, trailing plumes of blue, yellow, red and white smoke across the sky. A truck stopped in front of the reviewing stand. Suddenly, three uniformed men started spraying the dignitaries with gunfire from the back of the truck. A fourth leaped from the passenger seat and hurled a grenade into the crowd. Several grenades followed, but all failed to detonate. Then all four men ran toward the reviewing stand unleashing a torrent of automatic-weapons fire.

The assassins encountered little resistance in the first minute as Sadat's bodyguards and security forces dived for cover. Chairs were thrown over Sadat in a futile attempt to protect his life. It was bloody chaos. Sadat took seven bullets. He didn't have a chance. Running out of ammunition, the attackers ran for the truck and the military police opened fire. In the end, one of the assassins was killed and the other three wounded. In the first moments, Jehan tried desperately to get to her husband but was forced down by security guards who feared for her life. A helicopter was summoned, arrived four minutes later, and Jehan accompanied her husband's body to Maadi Military Hospital, south of Cairo. "I knew he was finished," said Mubarak, who escaped with only cuts on his left hand. "I saw all the blood. I just couldn't believe it."[1]

Thus ended a epoch — Egypt had vowed *a vow unto the LORD* ... and made a *sacrifice* of the *great one* who delivered them (as predicted in Isaiah 19:20-21). In prophetic concurrence, Psalm 81 concludes all references to Egypt in the Leviticus section of the Psalms. Sadat was dead.

In the following Numbers division, there is a verse (Psalm 95:10) which says, *Forty years long was I grieved with this generation* ... but the subject of the verse is Israel's wilderness sojourn, not their confrontation with Egypt. Another verse in Psalm 99:7 says, *He spake unto them in the cloudy pillar: they kept his testimonies, and the ordinance that he gave them.* Yet again, the passage is not of Egypt, but Israel.

There is a passage in Psalm 105:17-41 which reminds Israel of their bondage and God's deliverance, *Israel also came into Egypt; and Jacob sojourned in the land of Ham* (v. 23). Finally, Psalm 106:7 reminds the Jews, *Our fathers understood not thy wonders in Egypt; ...*

These passages refer primarily to Israel's relationship to God rather than to their confrontation with Egypt. Psalm 81, therefore, rightly disposes of the subject until after the seven year Tribulation Period and the coming of God's Son to establish His kingdom as seen in Psalms 88-94.

Blow up the trumpet in the new moon, in the time appointed, on our solemn feast day (v. 3).

This verse refers to Rosh Hashanah, the Feast of Trumpets along with the blowing of the shofar. Prophetically, it looks forward to that future day when the heavenly trumpet will sound to raise the dead and set the judgment. According to rabbinical teachings, Resurrection day should come on a future Rosh Hashanah. Even the number 81 is comprised of two letters, "peh" and "aleph," root of the word, "paah" meaning, "to blow." On September 11, 1980, the Jewish people celebrated Rosh Hashanah (New Years Day) for the Jewish year 5741 (1980-81). It marked the end of a sabbatical year (shemittah) and pointed up the importance of its prophetic significance. Psalm 81 represented the first of the next seven years. Many dates were set for the Rapture in 1981 — perhaps more than any other year in history. Though it did not represent the beginning of the Tribulation Period, Rosh Hashanah did seem to mark a milestone in prophetic fulfillment. It showed that the Psalms are prophetically aligned with the sabbatical cycles of this century, and that there is something important to be learned by students of prophecy.

In a 1975 article entitled "Chrono-messianism," Rabbi Ben Zion Wacholder presented a Jewish perspective on the prophetic significance of the sabbatical year along with the jubilee. He reported that in ancient times, the rabbis believed that the Messiah would come in a post-sabbatical year and that Daniel's seventy weeks were actually seventy sets of seven-year cycles (shavuah), each concluding with a sabbatical year (shemittah). Further, he noted that they covered a total 490 years which included ten jubilees — the seventieth week of Daniel's prophecy would conclude with the final jubilee.[2] According to Christian theologians, the prophecy was interrupted after sixty-nine weeks by the rejection of Messiah. He was *cut off, but not for himself* (Daniel 9:26) at Calvary. The seventieth week (shavuah) was held in abeyance until the end of this dispensation of Gentile Christianity. It should become the seven year Tribulation Period.

Rabbi Wacholder also reported that the year of the Bar Kochba revolt (A.D. 132/33) happened to be the only jubilee recorded in history. The dates of all other jubilees did not survive. This one historical account, however, is enough to allow scholars to calculate the next jubilee.

Daniel's 69th week ended on the 42nd year of the jubilee cycle. The 70th week should comprise the 43rd through the 49th year and conclude with a jubilee. John the Baptist began preaching along the banks of the Jordan River at Passover in the year 28, which was a sabbatical year and the 42nd year of the jubilee cycle. It marked the end of Daniel's 69th week. Jesus was baptized six months later upon the conclusion of the sabbatical year and at the beginning of the 43rd year of the jubilee cycle. Following His death on Calvary, the year A.D. 34/35 was the 49th year of the cycle and the jubilee. Those who thought the Messiah would come in 1981 to set the judgment of the Tribulation were wrong because 1986/87 is not a jubilee.

Will the thinking of the rabbis who believe in chronomessianism or sabbatical-messianism prevail? Will the Messiah set the final judgment of seven years within the confines of a sabbatical cycle? And will it conclude with His personal appearance to inaugurate the jubilee? According to the Encyclopedia Judaica "Elijah told Judah, the brother of Sala Hasida, 'The world will endure not less than 85 Jubilees, and on the last jubilee the Son of David will come" (Sanhedrin 97b).[3] One should be cautious not to set dates in this regard. We cannot box in the LORD. He is sovereign.

One further note, though modern Israel celebrated the sabbatical year in 1980/81, the true sabbatical year may have actually been 1981/82. If Rabbi Wacholder's calculations are correct, and we have no reason to suspect them, then the trumpet of Psalm 81 should have opened the sabbatical year instead of closing it. "The difference among the Jewish authorities as to the correct shemittah year is due to the varied interpretation of the words 'closing of shebi'it,' as meaning either the last year of the cycle or the year after the cycle."[4] The burning of Herod's Temple in A.D. 70 was written as having been burned "in the closing of the shemittah." Some have even suggested that the destruction of the Temple occurred in A.D. 69.Maimonides gave the shemittah year occuring in his time as 1107 years (A.D. 1175) from the destruction of the Temple (4936 after creation in the Jewish calendar). Rashi determined that the destruction occurred at the closing of shemittah. He makes A.D. 70 to be in the first year of the new cycle.[5] Rabbenu Hananeel claimed that the closing of shemittah was the year after the destruction of the Temple. The year of the shemittah was finally settled according to the view of Maimonides.[6]

If Wacholder is right, Maimonides was wrong. Even though world Jewry celebrated the sabbatical year in 1980/81, perhaps it should have been observed the next year, 1981/82. Instead of 1986/87 being shemittah, 1987/88 could be the sabbatical year.

Further, instead of 1993/94 being the 49th year of the cycle and the jubilee, 1994/95 could be the correct year. Perhaps such problems with dates as these caused Jesus to say, ... *in such an hour as ye think not the Son of man cometh.*

PSALM 82

How long will ye judge unjustly, and accept the persons of the wicked? (v. 2).

Again, the question *How long?* appears. And why at this point? Perhaps because Israel had become exasperated with the PLO. (See the chapter, HOW LONG?.) Please note, the last place the question will appear is in Psalm 94, a passage which alludes to the appearance of Messiah on the day of his vengeance. It is a question first asked in Psalm 4 and leads the reader through twelve psalm passages to its final answer in Psalm 94.

Defend the poor and fatherless: do justice to the afflicted and needy.
Deliver the poor and needy: rid them out of the hand of the wicked (vv.3-4).

On June 6, 1982, the Israeli Army launched "Operation Peace for Galilee." They moved into Lebanon to disperse the PLO. Arafat's terrorists had continually harassed the Israeli nation. After a renewed round of Ketusha rockets, Menachem Begin decided the nation had suffered enough.

Under the leadership of Ariel Sharon the IDF moved into Lebanon. The attack began at 11:00 A.M. on Sunday and within forty-eight hours, many of the PLO's fixed positions and much of its long-range Soviet-built artillery had been eliminated from Southern Lebanon. By the time a cease-fire came at the end of the week, at least sixty thousand troops, led by more than five hundred tanks had swept across the sixty-three mile long Lebanese border, and pushed the PLO all the way to Beirut.[1]

Israel could have captured Yassar Arafat, but the U.S. Government asked them to halt on the outskirts of Lebanon's capital. That move proved to be expensive. Israel had to maintain the cost of occupation for several months, draining their economy and producing unparalleled inflation. Days dragged on into weeks as the PLO took their time evacuating Beruit.

The August 16, 1982, edition of TIME magazine brandished the headline "Beirut Goes Up in Flames," though Israel tried to explain that their attack was not "the real thing."[2] TIME gave a dismal picture of Israel's blitz, but at least reported Israel's battle strategy. Above the first paragraph in the TIME article they quoted the cliche: "... Joshua fought the battle of Jericho, and the walls came tumbling down."[3]

What really happened, says Hal Lindsey, was that the IDF wanted to help Arafat speed up his schedule for leaving Beriut. Weeks had gone by while the PLO had dragged their feet on evacuating the country. Arafat was stalling. Demands were being negotiated for a pull-out, but it was obvious that Arafat was making the most of the situation. Israeli supersonic jets began to circle the city throughout the day breaking the sound barrier with every turn.

The noise of explosions sounded fierce, but were created by those aircraft traveling faster than the speed of sound. They dropped a few bombs in strategic locations for aesthetic effect and completely unnerved Arafat's PLO. The intensive bombardment lasted for eleven hours, from 6:00 A.M. until 5:00 P.M.. More than sixty Israeli warplanes took part. According to Beirut reports, "Israel dropped their payloads of death and destruction on the besieged city, making some 220 bombing runs. The jets were flying so low that their markings were clearly visible, their noise a deafening howl," wrote the Western correspondent for TIME.[4] The PLO dropped their demands and began leaving two days later. Israel explained that they weren't really bombing Beriut off the map, they were just marching around the walls of Jericho making a lot of noise!

Israel was getting a bad press. It was reported that UPI had sold to Arab oil interests just a few weeks before the June 6 invasion. They weren't about to report the story straight. Also, the news media received most of its information from Arafat's brother (head of the Red Cresent, an Arab division of the Red Cross) — exaggerated out of all proportions. They reported lies about Israel killing innocent civilians by the tens of thousands. According to some reports, Israel supposedly killed more civilians than the entire population of Southern Lebanon.

Menachem Begin came to the UN General Assembly to explain that they went after the PLO to rid the world of all terrorism. However, many of the delegates walked out on his speech. The world refused to understand Israel's need to break up the training bases for terrorists who operated in several countries around the world. There were more than just Palestinians involved. The Lebanon bases were providing training and materials for terrorism in every hemisphere. Also, Israel found underground storage areas with enough military supplies to last the PLO for ten years. Records and files were found to determine that Russia was planning an invasion of Israel and the Middle East for the near future. Israel had put a dent into Russian war plans.

Unfortunately, Israel was not allowed to finish the job. The conflict continued into 1983, as we shall see in Psalm 83.

PSALM 83

> For, lo, thine enemies make a tumult: and they that hate thee have lifted up the head.
> They have taken crafty counsel against thy people, and consulted against thy hidden ones.
> They have said, Come, and let us cut them off from being a nation; that the name of Israel may be no more in remembrance.
> For they have consulted together with one consent: they are confederate against thee (vv. 2-5).

The war dragged on into 1983. Arafat met with Jordan's King Hussein in an effort to rally support for his dispersed PLO. The enemies of modern Israel included almost the entire Arab world. As a matter of fact, the enemy is named in verses 6-8:

> The tabernacles of Edom, and the Ishmaelites; of Moab, and the Hagarenes;
> Gebal, and Ammon, and Amalek; the Philistines with the inhabitants of Tyre;
> Assur also is joined with them: they have holpen the children of Lot (vv. 6-8).

Please note, the country of Jordan is described by the ancient tribes listed in these verses — Edom, Moab, and Ammon. The Ishmaelites, children of Ishmael, make up the bulk of the modern

Arab world. The Hagarenes were children of Hagar. Gebal was
an ancient city on the Mediterranean, twenty-five miles north of
Beruit. In Greek and Roman times it was called Biblos because of
the manufacture of papyrus there. Today the city is called
Jebeil.¹ It was listed along with the inhabitants of Tyre in
Lebanon.

The Philistines or Palestinians are listed. Also, there is some
evidence that among the Palestinians are descendants of ancient
Edom. Amalek and Assur also have offspring among the Arabs
today! Incredible, but there it is. It seems to be a 3,000 year-old
description of Israel's modern enemies along with their attempt
to destroy God's Chosen People in 1983! Verses 14-16 indicate that
the conflict will continue. The psalmist wrote:

> As the fire burneth a wood, and as the flame setteth the moun-
> tains on fire;
> So persecute them with thy tempest, and make them afraid
> with thy storm.
> Fill their faces with shame; that they may seek thy name, O
> Lord (vv. 14-16).

The ultimate fulfillment of this passage will come at Armageddon (which Jews call the Battle of Gog and Magog). The ebb and
flow of the psalm continues in Psalm 86:14, *O God, the proud are
risen against me, and the assemblies of violent men have sought
after my soul; ...* The conclusion of the conflict will come in
Psalm 94:23. *... he shall bring upon them their own iniquity, and
shall cut them off in their own wickedness; yea, the LORD our
God shall cut them off.*

In the years since 1982-83 we can follow the continuation of the
strife. We cannot say that it will end in 1994, only that Psalm 94
describes the conclusion of the conflagration with the coming of
Messiah to establish His kingdom.

The number 83 is made up of the letters "peh" and "gimel."
They comprise the Hebrew word, "pag," meaning, "unripe
figs."² How exciting! The fig tree put forth its leaves in 1948, but
now the fruit appears. They are still unripe, but we can be sure
Israel is about to bear fruit. Psalm 1:3 reminds us, *he* [Israel]
shall be like a tree planted [replanted] *by the rivers of water, that
bringeth forth his fruit in his season.*

The Song of Solomon tells the story of the bridegroom coming to
catch away his bride. He arrives at night and says, *Rise up, my*

*love, my fair one, and come away. For, lo, the winter is past ... the
fig tree putteth forth her green figs, ... Arise, my love, my fair
one, and come away* (Song of Solomon 2:10-11,13). The bride
speaks, *My beloved is mine, and I am his: ... Until the day break,
and the shadows flee away, ...* (Song of Solomon 2:16-17).

One day, soon, Christ will come to snatch away His bride, New
Testament Christianity, because the fig tree has put on its unripe
figs! Christians will disappear from the earth and seven dreadful
years will set in — years of judgment for wicked nations and
years of fruitbearing for Israel. At the end of the seven years, we
shall return from the heavenly "hoopah" (bridal chamber) for a
thousand year honeymoon and Israel will be placed at the head of
the nations!

PSALM 84

How amiable are thy tabernacles, O Lord of hosts!
*My soul longeth, yea, even fainteth for the courts of the
Lord: ...*
Blessed are they that dwell in thy house: ...
*For a day in thy courts is better than a thousand. I had rather
be a doorkeeper in the house of my God, than to dwell in the tents
of wickedness* (vv. 1-2,4,10).

Psalm 84 is the highlight psalm of the Leviticus section. It
follows a series of Psalms written by Asaph and is the first of a second group (84-85, 87-88) attributed to the sons of Korah. They also
wrote Psalms 42-49.

Radak suggested that the theme was inspired by David's sojourn in the land of the Philistines while running from Saul. Rabbi
Feuer wrote that David, while on foreign soil, "yearned to return
to the Holy Ark and to the sacrificial altar." In this psalm, he
described the longing of all "lonely exiles in future generations."[1]

The tenor of the psalm certainly describes devout Jews in 1984.
After so many long years excluded from the Temple Mount and
content with praying at the Western Wall, certain "Faithful of the
Temple Mount" began to call for a Jewish presence within the
confines of the Moslem-held Temple site. It was as if the pent-up
cry burst forth, *My soul longeth, yea, even fainteth for the courts
of the LORD.*

Even the number 84 lends to the mood of the year. The number is comprised of the letters "peh" and "daleth," making up the word "pedah," meaning, "to ransom, to release, to set free."[2] This was certainly the cry of the religious Jews who desire to establish a place of worship on the mountain. The Moslems are in control of the Holy site and it's time for the Jews to redeem it.

In March of the previous year, a group of twenty-nine men attempted to enter the Solomon's Stables area under the pavement where the El Aksa Mosque stands. It was reported that they had hoped to establish a synagogue. Their attempt failed, however, and they were arrested. When the trial concluded in September, all twenty-nine were acquitted and the police were reprimanded for their handling of the case.

On January 25, 1984, two men were seen just before sunrise carrying explosives toward the Dome of the Rock. Again, police were called and eventually both were arrested. One received a ten year prison term. When asked why he wanted to blow up the Moslem mosque, he replied that he wanted to cleanse the Temple Mount for the rebuilding of a Jewish Temple.

Also in January of 1984, Yigael Yadin published his commentary on the famous Temple Scroll in English. According to Yadin the scroll was drafted "with the object of establishing that it is God Himself who is the speaker."[3] Should the religious Jew then consider this scroll to be an end-time message from God? Instructions are given in the ancient document on rebuilding the Temple! The subject of these events point up the theme of Psalm 84. It is as if Psalm 84 were a prophecy under development in 1984.

In the April, 1984 issue of BAR Magazine, archeologist Asher Kaufman discussed at length the site of the ancient Temples and suggested that both Solomon's and Herod's were built on a site which lies to the north of the Dome of the Rock directly west of the Eastern Gate. A small cupulo stands some three hundred feet north of the mosque. It is called the "Dome of the Tablets" and covers a rock suggested to be the foundation stone for the Ark of the Covenant. The spot marks the possible location of the Holy of holies in both Temples.

And whatever happened to the Ark of the Covenant? According to Jewish history, Jeremiah took the hangings of the Tabernacle, along with the Ark of the Covenant, and hid them in a cave in the country of Moab almost 2,600 years ago. The account is recorded in the apocryphal book of II Maccabees:

"The document also described how the prophet, warned by an oracle, gave orders for the Tabernacle and the Ark to go with him when he set out for the mountain which Moses had climbed to survey God's heritage.

"On his arrival Jeremiah found a cave dwelling, into which he brought the tabernacle, the Ark, and the altar of incense, afterwards blocking up the entrance.

"Some of his companions came to mark out the way, but were unable to find it.

"When Jeremiah learned this, he reproached them: 'The place is to remain unknown,' he said, 'until God gathers His people together again and shows them His mercy.

"'Then the Lord will bring these things once more to light, and the glory of the Lord will be seen, and so will the cloud, as it was revealed in the time of Moses and when Solomon prayed that the Holy Place might be gloriously hallowed'" (II Maccabees 2:4-8).

According to the ancient account, Jeremiah declared that the Tabernacle would be discovered in that day when "God gathers His people together again and shows them His mercy." Furthermore, Jeremiah predicted the return of the shekinah glory. The fire will fall from heaven to bless the old tent with the presence of God, just as it did in the days of Moses and Solomon.

Can you imagine the excitement worldwide if the Ark of the Covenant were found in a cave on Mount Nebo, returned to Jerusalem and set up on the Temple Mount? Imagine the astonishment if the glory were to fall again from heaven to grace the Ark of the Covenant with the presence of God? Can you imagine how exciting it would be not only for the Jewish world, but also for Christianity?

Does Psalm 84 contain possible references to the ancient tabernacles. If and when they are discovered, the Jewish people could set up the Tabernacle of David on the Temple Mount — perhaps on the north side of the Mosque of Omar. The prophecies of Ezekiel seem to concur. Though the Battle of Gog and Magog is predicted in Ezekiel 38, the last three verses of chapter 37 allude to the return of the Tabernacle: *Moreover I will make a covenant of peace with them; it shall be an everlasting covenant with them: and I will place them, and multiply them, and will set my sanctuary in the midst of them for evermore. My tabernacle also shall be with them...* (Ezekiel 37:26,27).

The Hebrew word used in Ezekiel 37:27 and Psalm 84:1 for *tabernacle* is "Mishkon." It is used exclusively in the Old Testament for the Mosaic Tabernacle built of acacia wood, overlaid with gold, comprising two rooms — the holy place and the Holy of holies. Ezekiel referred to both a sanctuary and a "Mishkon." Psalm 84 makes the term plural (tabernacles) which implies at least two places of worship.

In the days of King David, a tent was built to house the Ark of the Covenant on Mount Moriah. It was called *the tabernacle of David*. The Mishkon of Moses during that time was set up at Gibeon about 6 miles northwest of Jerusalem. The Hebrew term used for David's *tabernacle* was "Ouhel" meaning simply a tent. The implication seems to be that both the "Mishkon" of Moses and the "Ouhel" of David may be found with the Ark of the Covenant and returned to Jerusalem. The "Ouhel" of David could house the Ark of the Covenant on the Temple Mount while the "Mishkon" of Moses could be housed elsewhere.

There are also reports of an Ark of the Covenant hidden in the Church of Saint Mary of Zion in Aksum, Ethiopia. According to Ethiopian history, Menelik, son of Solomon and the Queen of Sheba stole the Ark, leaving a duplicate in its place.

An ex-catholic priest has also reported seeing the Ark of the Covenant in the underground vaults of the Vatican — four stories under the West Wing of the complex in Rome. We may not have long to wait until the real Ark is returned to Jerusalem. Then, we will know.

Perhaps the most exciting event of 1984 was the rediscovery of the ancient "Techelet" — the blue-purple die once used in the ribbons along the borders of Jewish prayer shawls (Tallits). In the September 8, 1984, edition of SCIENCE NEWS OF THE WEEK the headline read, "Blue-purple dye of antiquity reborn."[4] A biochemist in Jerusalem pieced together historical, scriptural and scientific evidence to conclude that he had rediscovered the formula for the ancient dye used by Moses to color the tapestries of the Tabernacle and the "ribbons of blue" on the tallits of ancient Judaism. God had told Moses to obtain the dye from a small sea creature which lived in the Red Sea and the Mediterranean. This purple dye eventually became the color for the royalty of Europe.

In the days of the New Testament, Lydia was a "seller of purple" (Acts 16:14). The industry maintained its popularity until the seventh century when the Moslems overran the Holy Land. They killed the manufacturers of the dye and the formula died with them. For the past 1,500 years, Jewish Tallits have been adorned with black ribbons. It seemed that God had turned their day into night — until 1984! The shell fish, called a Banded Dye Murex grows in abundance in the Mediterranean Sea. *How amiable* [friendly] *are thy tabernacles* [tallits?], *O LORD!* God is about to turn the Jewish night back into day.

PSALM 85

LORD, thou hast been favorable unto thy land: thou hast brought back the captivity of Jacob (v. 1).

In January of 1985 the world learned of "Operation Moses."[1] Israel had been airlifting Ethiopian Jews from refugee camps in Sudan. Over ten thousand black Jews (Falashas) had escaped persecution under Ethiopia's communist regime. They had journeyed over the mountainous border into Sudan. Though Sudan is an Arab country and had no official relations with Israel, certain government personnel had permitted European airliners, hired by Israel, to rescue the refugees.

Living conditions in the camps were deplorable. Several hundreds of the Falashas, perhaps thousands had died for lack of food or proper medical attention. Most, however, had managed to survive and were rescued. It is quite remarkable that the first verse of Psalm 85 alludes to the *captivity of Jacob* returning to the Promised Land.

Trans European Airways, a Brussels-based charter airline made 35 flights from November 1984 to January 1985, airlifting black Jews out of refugee camps in Sudan. The flights were canceled after Israeli officials confirmed newspaper reports that a rescue mission was under way. Embarrassed Sudanese government officials halted the flights once news leaked out. Their Arab neighbors were furious that Sudan would help Israel. Some 7,000 Falashas remained stranded in refugee camps in Sudan. Perhaps as many as 10,000 were still in Ethiopia. Prime Minister Peres vowed, "we shall not rest until all our brothers and sisters from Ethiopia come safely back home."[2]

Who are these Ethiopian Jews? Some claim descent from the tribe of Levi by Moses and his Ethiopian wife (Numbers 12:1). Others claim descent from the tribe of Judah by Solomon and the Queen of Sheba. According to Ethiopian history, the Queen of Sheba had a foot disorder and heard that Solomon had knowledge of medicines and herbs. In the weeks following her arrival in Jerusalem, she fell in love with Solomon. From their union came a son, Menelik — the first of the dynasty of whom Hali Salasi was generation number 225.

When Menelik was nineteen years old, having received his education in Jerusalem, he was ready to make his journey to Ethiopia. Solomon had a duplicate made of the Ark of the Covenant and presented it to his son. However, according to Ethiopian history, having some of the wisdom of his father, Menelik threw a farewell party the night before he left. He served several rounds of wine to the priesthood. While they were preoccupied and inebriated, he sneaked into the Holy of holies, switched Arks and took the real Ark of the Covenant back to Ethiopia.

That Ark is kept today in the Church of St. Mary of Zion in Aksum, Ethiopia. Will the rescue of Ethiopian Jews eventually bring about its return to Jerusalem? Hali Salassi claimed it was the real Ark. Encyclopedia Britanica in 1934 reported the Ark being in the church. Bnai Brith, a Jewish publication said it was taken to the mountain strongholds of Abyssinia in Northern Ethiopia for safekeeping when Mussolini invaded the country in 1934.

I interviewed Aradom Tedla in 1985 about his years in Ethiopia. He served in the office of Minister of Law and Justice under the Hali Salassi administration and escaped the communists by being smuggled over the mountains into Sudan. He now lives in the United States. When I asked him if the Ark was really in Aksum, he replied, "Yes," and added, "The table of stone upon which the Ten Commandments was written is also there."

Isaiah 18 records a prophecy about the rescue of Jews from Ethiopia and their bringing a *present* to the Temple Mount. *Woe to the land shadowing with wings, which is beyond the rivers of Ethiopia:* (Isaiah 18:1). The headwaters of the Nile River begin in

Northern Ethiopia and flow through Sudan. The designation is obvious. The passage refers to Ethiopia. The *wings* could be a picture of those airplanes airlifting the black Jews to safety. *Woe to the land* could be a reference to Ethiopia's destruction in the Battle of Gog and Magog (Ezekiel 38:5). Ethiopia will accompany Russia against Israel.

Isaiah 18:2 speaks of *vessels of bulrushes*. Such boats are still used in the land unto this day. There are only two places in the Bible where bulrushes are mentioned — here, and in Exodus 2:3, a story of the rescue of Moses. The *vessels of bulrushes* may be God's way of predicting that the rescue of Ethiopian Jews would be called "Operation Moses."

Isaiah 18 continues, ... *Go, ye swift messengers, to a nation scattered and peeled, to a people terrible from their beginning hitherto; a nation meted out and trodden down, whose land the rivers have spoiled!* (v. 2). The *swift messengers* could be the air rescue team. The term *scattered* could refer to the displaced people and *peeled* refers to the color of their skin — a black skinned people who look as if their skin has been baked in the sun. *Meted out and trodden down* describes the communist overthrow of the country since 1974 and their oppressive actions against the populace. *Whose land the rivers have spoiled* compares with the drought which has devastated the land in recent years.

With all of these descriptions of modern Ethiopia, I am convinced the chapter is talking about events which are taking place in that land. The next verse reveals a message to Gentile Christianity all over the world. *All ye inhabitants of the world, and dwellers on the earth, see ye, when he lifteth up an ensign on the mountains; and when he bloweth a trumpet, hear ye* (Isaiah 18:3). The *ensign* may be the *Holy Ark* brought back to the Temple Mount and the *trumpet* refers to the shofar sounded on Rosh Hashanah.

The concept that the Ark of the Covenant will be returned to the Temple site on Rosh Hashanah is given in the "Tehillim" commentary of Rabbi Avrohom Feuer on Psalm 47. Talmudic rabbis say that this sounding of the trumpet has a reference to the Ark of the Covenant, which was concealed as the era of the First Temple drew to a close. "In the future, when the great horn of redemption is blown, this Ark will ascend from its concealment."[3]

The rabbi's believe the blast will occur on Rosh Hashanah heralding not only the appearance of the Ark of the Covenant, but the time when the "Dispenser of Strict Justice" sets His judgment and raises the dead. "When the Jew hears the sound of the teruah (trumpet), he realizes that he deserves shattering punishment for his sins and is inspired to repent. Having felt remorse for his sins, he is forgiven and the verdict is nullified. Thus, God ascends and departs because of the Teruah blast."[4]

What magnificent picture of the rapture of Gentile Christianity at the beginning of the Tribulation Period. The religious Jews retrieve their Holy Ark and repent, having been left behind as "God ascends and departs" taking Christians with Him! Question: Will the return of the Ark of the Covenant to the Temple Mount occur on a future Rosh Hashanah? Will Russia invade on that day as the divine judgment is set? Will the dead be raised and the saints raptured during that judgment? Will the conversion of 144,000 Jews occur as a result of those events? Rabbinic thought leans in that direction.

Isaiah 18:5 alludes to the Battle of Gog and Magog: *For afore the harvest, when the bud is perfect, and the sour grape is ripening in the flower, he shall both cut off the sprigs with pruning hooks, and take away and cut down the branches.* Just before *the harvest* (rapture and resurrection) when the *bud is perfect* (the last sinner is converted) and *the sour grape is ripening* (the wicked are ready to be thrown into God's winepress of judgment) *God will cut down the branches* (bring on the Battle of Gog and Magog).

Ezekiel's prophecy compares with this passage. Just as Ezekiel 39:17-20 offers an invitation to ... *every feathered fowl, and to every beast of the field,* ... to eat the flesh of the slain on the battlefield, Isaiah 18:6 says, *They shall be left together unto the fowls of the mountains, and to the beasts of the earth: and the fowls shall summer upon them, and all the beasts of the earth shall winter upon them.*

Isaiah 18:7 returns to the most important subject of the chapter. *In that time shall the present be brought unto the LORD of hosts of a people ... to the place of the name of the LORD if hosts, the mount Zion.* Could that *present* be the Ark of the Covenant? The poor Ethiopian Jews have no money. The only thing of value is that Ark kept in the Church of St. Mary of Zion in Aksum.

The minor prophet Zephaniah offers a further prophecy. Zephaniah was an Ethiopian Jew, *the son of Cushi* (Zephaniah

1:1) and in chapter 3, verse 10 the prophet wrote, *From beyond the rivers of Ethiopia my suppliants, even the daughter of my dispersed, shall bring mine offering.* The word *suppliants* is used only one time in the Bible. It means "a multitude of worshipers." This multitude of Ethiopian Jews is called *the daughter of my dispersed.* These people are the *daughter* (offspring) of the Jews (my dispersed). The reference is unmistakable. They are Jews who will come from Ethiopia. Furthermore, they will bring *mine offering.* This may be another reference to the Ark of the Covenant since they have no other offering to bring. The Zephaniah passage is placed in the time frame of *that day* (v. 11) *at that time ... [when] I gather you: for I will make you a name and a praise among all people of the earth, when I turn back your captivity before your eyes, saith the LORD* (Zephaniah 3:20).

This is why Psalm 85 is so important as a reference to the rescue of Ethiopian Jews. Their rescue is not yet complete and the Holy Ark has not yet been returned. But perhaps it will in the near future.

According to rabbinic scholars, the psalm originally predicted Israel's return from the Babylonian exile to rebuild the Temple.[5] Ultimately, however, the psalm projects a future time when Jews would return to open the Third Temple period. In 1985 a movement was already underway in Israel with demands by religious Jews for a place to worship on the Temple Mount. The prophetic aspect of the psalm is most significant when considered with the preceding psalm (84) wherein David "yearned to return to the Holy Ark and to the sacrificial altar."[6] Both Rashi (an eleventh century rabbi) and Radak (a twelveth century rabbi) interpret this psalm as "a prophecy describing Israel's eventual redemption from the present exile."[7]

> *Wilt thou not revive us again: that thy people may rejoice in thee?*
> *Surely his salvation is nigh them that fear him; that glory may dwell in our land.*
> *Righteousness shall go before him; and shall set us in the way of his steps* (vv. 6,9,13).

The fulfillment of these verses was already under development in 1985. Israel will be spiritually *revive*[d] *again.* Reconciliation will be made with God. His shekinah *glory* will return. The people will become *righteous* as a prelude to the *steps* (coming) of

Messiah. Even in 1985, one could observe that God's salvation was *nigh them.*

Future events which may lead to Israel's revival includes a return of the Ark of the Covenant, an appointment of 144,000 to raise the Tabernacle of David and a restoration of Temple worship on the Sacred Mount.

Rabbi Avrohom Feuer wrote in his commentary on the Psalms, "In the future, God's glory will return to the land and to the Holy Temple. In the Second Temple, however, this glory was absent. The Talmud (Yoma 21b) relates that five Divine manifestations which were present in the First Temple were absent in the Second Temple. These were: 1) The Holy Ark, along with its cover, and the cherubim; 2) the heavenly fire which descended upon the altar; 3) the Shekinah [manifestation of the Divine Presence]; 4) Ruach HaKodesh [the Divine Spirit of prophecy]; and 5) Urim V'Tumim [the breastplate of the High Priest, which relayed prophetic messages]. All of these phenomena will be present when the Third Temple is built (Radak; Meiri)."[8]

The number 85 is made up of the letters "peh" and "he" and constitutes the word "peh" with two uses: 1) It means "mouth in the sense of blowing or breathing," and 2) It means "here, in this place."[9] Again, like the numbers 80 and 81, we have a moving of the Spirit. God is about to birth the nation with the Holy Spirit. Remember the words of Jesus, *Except a man be born of water and of the Spirit, he cannot enter into the kingdom of God* (John 3:5). Israel was born of water in 1948. Soon the nation will be born of the Spirit — where? Here, in this place! On the Temple Mount!

Though 1985 did not see the ultimate conclusion of the prophecy, development was definitely underway for an eventual fulfillment. The trend is apparent.

PSALM 86

A Prayer of David.
Bow down thine ear, O LORD, hear me: for I am poor and needy.
Preserve my soul; for I am holy: O thou my God, save thy servant that trusteth in thee.
Be merciful unto me, O Lord: for I cry unto thee daily (introduction, vv. 1-3).

"It is significant that this psalm of David has been placed in the middle of a series of works composed by Korah's sons" (Ayalah Sheluchah).[1]

Psalms 84-88 compare with that part of the processional which carried the Ark of the Covenant up to Jerusalem. Imagine four sons of Korah (Kohathites) bearing the long-lost Ark of the Covenant — two in front as seen in Psalms 84 and 85, and two behind the Ark as seen in Psalms 87 and 88, while the Ark itself is borne between them as seen in Psalm 86.

On the day of the processional, David delivered a Psalm to commemorate the occasion. Some parts of it are similar to passages in Psalm 86. *Declare his glory among the heathen; his marvellous works among all nations* (I Chronicles 16:24) compares with Psalm 86:9, *All nations whom thou hast made shall come and worship before thee, O Lord; and shall glorify thy name* (v. 9). Another passage in the Ark Psalm also alludes to Psalm 86: *For great is the LORD, and greatly to be praised: he also is to be feared above all gods. For all the gods of the people are idols: but the LORD made the heavens* (I Chronicles 16:25-26). It's companion verse in Psalm 86 says, *Among the gods there is none like unto thee, O Lord* (v. 8). These comparable passages may designate Psalm 88 as an Ark Psalm situated between the Sons of Korah, bearers of the Ark.

Among the gods there is none like unto thee, O Lord; neither are there any works like unto thy works (v. 8).

The *gods* refers to the luminaries or stars of heaven. They are called gods because ancient civilizations worshipped them as gods. However, long before the perverted idolatry of astrology was developed, God made the stars *for signs* (Genesis 1:14). Could the appearance of Halley's Comet in 1986 be a fulfillment of this verse? Has God prepared the fly by as a *sign* in the heavens (Luke 21:25)?

> *All nations whom thou hast made shall come and worship before thee, O Lord; and shall glorify thy name* (v. 9).

Not only would there be a Jewish revival if the ancient Tabernacle of David were erected on the Temple site, there would also be a worldwide interest stirred among New Testament Christians.

If this is the prophetic implication of Psalm 86, then it concurs with the prophecy of Amos, who predicted that God would restore the Tabernacle of David. *In that day will I raise up the tabernacle of David that is fallen, and close up the breaches thereof; and I will raise up his ruins, and I will build it as in the days of old: That they may possess the remnant of Edom, and of all the heathen, which are called by my name, saith the Lord that doeth this.* (Amos 9:11-12)

The prophecy was repeated in Acts 15 when a question was raised by the Pharisees over the conversion of Gentiles. The Pharisees were quite upset because converted Gentiles were not keeping Jewish law. After hearing the testimonies of Peter and Paul, James drew the conclusion of the matter: *Simeon hath declared how God at the first did visit the Gentiles, to take out of them a people for his name. And to this agree the words of the prophets; as it is written, after this I will return, and will build again the tabernacle of David, which is fallen down; and I will build again the ruins thereof, and I will set it up: that the residue of men might seek after the Lord, and all the Gentiles, upon whom my name is called, saith the Lord, who doeth all these things.* (Acts 15:14-17)

What began at the house of Cornelius with the conversion of the first Gentile will be concluded one day when the Tabernacle of David is returned to the Temple site. When the prophecy is fulfilled, there will be a worldwide revival of interest among Jews and Christians. On the following Sabbath, synagogues will probably be filled with the devout who seek after the Lord. On Sunday morning, churches also may be filled with Christians seeking the face of God. From around the world, Jews and Christians may crowd into Jerusalem to see the Tabernacle and the Ark in fulfillment of verse 9.

According to Jewish rabbinical thought, the verse can only be fulfilled at the time of Messiah. "Only in the Messianic Era will God's omnipotence be evident to all and there will be no room for error (Radak; Meiri). The nations that surround Israel will see that God will release His People from their strangle hold in a miraculous manner. Amazed and overwhelmed, they will spread the word of the marvels to all other nations, who will then hasten to pay homage to ..." God.[2]

Do comparable events in 1986 represent at least a partial fulfillment of Psalm 86? There was trouble over Jerusalem's Temple Mount in January, 1986. Certain members of Israel's government asked and received permission from Moslem authorities (Wakf) to make an inspection tour of the Solomon's Stables area along the southern end of the Temple Mount (under the Al-Aksa Mosque).

The committee wanted to investigate charges that illegal construction was going on. The group of twenty-five, however, included Jewish members of the Knesset who were not on the committee — such as Geula Cohen who introduced legislation some years ago making Jerusalem the "indivisible capital of Israel" and Gershon Solomon who is known for his many attempts to organize Jewish worship services on the Temple Mount.

After visiting the Al-Aksa Mosque, the group started down the stairs into the basement area called Solomon's Stables. Suddenly, a group of masons and plasterers ran up the stairs toward the group and pushed them back shouting, "No cameras! No cameras!" The workmen punched and slapped members of the committee. Other workmen brandished tools for weapons and shouted obscenities. Meanwhile the Wakf guards and police rushed from behind and there was pandemonium. The group of Jewish Knesset members were thrust up and out of the stairs onto the pavement. Hundreds of young Arabs crowded around shouting and cursing while the loudspeakers blared that the Jews were taking over the Moslem shrines. Over forty policemen, officers and border patrolmen controlled the crowd with clubs and tear gas during the two-hour altercation.

Mayor of Jerusalem, Teddy Kollek, urged the group not to

return to the Temple Mount, and to use restraint so as not to spoil the delicate balance of coexistence. In the weeks that followed, Jerusalem's Rabbinical Council voted to refuse permission for Jews to enter the Temple Mount.

As January 1986 came to a close, Arab delegates meeting in Morocco, called for all Islamic countries to "wage jihad [holy war] in all its forms" until the liberation of Jerusalem and Arab territories occupied by Israel since 1967. The fourteen nation "Jerusalem committee" made the call after discussing the incident on the Temple Mount. They accused the Jews of planning to destroy the Al-Aksa Mosque.

At a February meeting of Jerusalem's Rabbinical Council, Rabbi Mordicai Eliahu suggested the building of a synagogue on the Temple Mount, either to the northeast or to the southeast of the Moslem area. The council discussed fund raising and considered what would happen to the money for the project "if Messiah should come before construction was begun." In the event that Messiah comes, perhaps the money could be diverted toward the erection of a sanctuary or temporary Temple north of the Dome of the Rock.

The prophet Ezekiel wrote that measurements were made of the northern half of the area and that a wall was built across the grounds from the Eastern Wall to the Western Wall just south of the Eastern Gate *to make a separation between the sanctuary and the profane place* (Ezekiel 42:20). Could Ezekiel's profane place be the Dome of the Rock?

The current situation may not see much progress unless or until the Ark of the Covenant is returned — perhaps from the Church of St. Mary of Zion in Aksum, Ethiopia. Though some 15,000 Ethiopian Jews have been rescued no word had yet been received on the Ark.

> *O God, the proud are risen against me, and the assemblies of violent men have sought after my soul; ...* (v. 14).

This verse appears to be a prophetic reference to an impending battle — perhaps an invasion by Syria, leading to the future Battle of Gog and Magog. The battle is brewing as attested by Psalm 87:4 which declares, *Behold Philistia, and Tyre, with Ethiopia ...* These are nations confederate with Russia (Ezekiel 38:5-6). Just when the battle will erupt is not certain, but in 1986 one can easily see war clouds brewing once again in the Middle East.

> *Shew me a token for good; that they which hate me may see it, and be ashamed: because thou, LORD, hast holpen me, and comforted me.* (v. 17).

Could that *token* be the Ark of the Covenant? The word *token* is a translation of the Hebrew "oth", translated in other places as "sign." Could it represent the famous insignia of the nation — the Ark of the Covenant?

Among the many psalms written by David, only two are recorded as "prayers of David" — Psalm 86 and Psalm 17. The first prayer appears to have a prophetic reference to 1917 and the taking of Jerusalem by the British general, Allenby. It was both a prophetic and historic war — a special fulfillment of the deliverance of Jerusalem in preparation for the return of the Jews. Perhaps Psalm 86 is designated as a prayer for similar prophetic and historic reasons. Is Jerusalem being prepared for the return of the Ark along with the Tabernacle of David?

The number 86 is made up of the letters "peh" and "vav" making the words "poh" and "puwah," both with the same meanings given of "peh" (85). They both mean "to blow" and "in this place."[3] This must be a double emphasis that Israel is nearing the time when Temple worship will be restored on the Temple Mount and God will bless the place with His Spirit. With 80, 81, 85, and 86 meaning the same thing, there can be little doubt that a spiritual revival is about to break out in Israel. Born of water in 1948, Israel is about to experience the glory that came in the days of Moses and Solomon! Jeremiah predicted that when the Ark returns, the glory will return.

PSALM 87

> *His foundation is in the holy mountains.*
> *The LORD loveth the gates of Zion more than all the dwellings of Jacob.*
> *Glorious things are spoken of thee, O city of God* (vv. 1-3).

The sons of Korah extolled the beauty of Jerusalem as the *city of God.* Their psalms reflect a love for the Temple Mount. Psalm 48 also compares with the Korahites' dedication to the mountains of Jerusalem as they wrote, *Great is the LORD, and greatly to be praised in the city of our God, in the mountain of his holiness. Beautiful for situation, the joy of the whole earth, is mount Zion, on the sides of the north, the city of the great King* (Psalm 48:1,2).

The sons of Korah refused to agree with their father when he rebelled against Moses and (wrote the rabbis) penned this psalm to show that God loved the Promised Land better than the wilderness where they sojourned.[1] The story is told that when the earth opened up and swallowed Korah, his sons fell upon a ledge near the top of the ground and were rescued.

Upon writing this psalm, they prophetically referred to the gates of the Temple which were also swallowed up by the earth and lie preserved underground. Someday, according to rabbinical thought, the Temple gates will be retrieved, and along with them, Korah will be rescued![2]

The prophecies of Psalm 87 do not necessarily have to be fulfilled in 1987. We can only say that the psalm seems to set a trend for those events which will someday come to pass. The earlier 86 psalms appear to contain prophetic passages which allude to events seemingly fulfilled during the twentieth century — many even in the year numbered according to each psalm. Yet they also contain prophetic portions which point to the future coming of Messiah and events which have not yet been fulfilled. Which, if any, of the many prophetic implications of Psalm 87 will come to pass in 1987 is not presently known.

> *I will make mention of Rahab and Babylon to them that know me ...* (v. 4).

The psalmist referred to Rahab, a notorious harlot in the days of Joshua, connecting her with the mystery religion of ancient Babylon. It seems that God has thus promised to reveal the harlot Babylon to those who desire to know the mystery. The Apostle John called her *MYSTERY, BABYLON THE GREAT, THE MOTHER OF HARLOTS AND ABOMINATIONS OF THE EARTH* (Revelation 17:5). To this day, *BABYLON THE GREAT* has remained a mystery. Perhaps soon, however, she will be revealed!

According to Unger's Bible Dictionary, the term Rahab as used in this passage refers also to a "sea monster."[3] Nelson's Illustrated Bible Encyclopedia calls it "Rahab the Dragon — a mythological sea monster or dragon representing the evil forces of chaos ... as it occurs in Job 9:13 (NIV), Job 26:12 (NIV), Psalm 87:4, Psalm 89:10, and Isaiah 51:9 ..."[4]

The Old Testament usage compares perfectly with *MYSTERY, BABYLON THE GREAT* who is seen by John as a harlot riding upon a seven-headed dragon (Revelation 17:3-5).

Isaiah's prophetic description makes it clear: *Awake, awake, put on strength, O arm of the LORD; awake, as in the ancient days, in the generations of old. Art thou not it that hath cut Rahab, and wounded the dragon?* (Isaiah 51:9). Obviously, *Rahab and Babylon* in Psalm 87 refers to the Revived Roman Empire predicted to dominate the world under the leadership of the antichrist during the Tribulation Period.

The mystery city will be destroyed as related in Psalm 89! Ethan completes the picture of God's judgment upon the harlot city as he wrote, *Thou hast broken Rahab in pieces, as one that is slain; thou hast scattered thine enemies with thy strong arm. The heavens are thine, the earth also is thine: ...* (Psalm 89:10,11). This is the same kind of prophetic description as given in Revelation 17-19. The wicked city is destroyed and Messiah becomes King of kings.

... behold Philistia, and Tyre, with Ethiopia; ... (v. 4).

As a prophecy, it could be noted that Ethiopia is listed in Ezekiel 38:5 as an ally of Magog in that future invasion. Tyre is mentioned as giving the location of the invasion route (from the north). Philistia is an ancient name for the modern Palestinians and may refer to the PLO. The verse alludes to the prophetic Battle of Gog and Magog which also may be described in the previous psalm: *O God, the proud are risen against me, and the assemblies of violent men have sought after my soul; ...* (Psalm 86:14). This is not to say that the Russian invasion of Israel will take place in 1987, only that our attention is drawn to the alliance which is building against Israel.

... this man was born there.

> *And of Zion it shall be said, This and that man was born in her: and the highest himself shall establish her.*
> *The LORD shall count, when he writeth up the people, that this man was born there* (vv. 4-6).

When the time has come for Mystery Babylon to be revealed and for the Battle of Gog and Magog to ravage the world, God shall appoint and seal 144,000 Jews for a special ministry. When 12,000 from each of the twelve tribes are chosen, they will need to present their genealogies. Each must prove his tribal ancestry. Therefore, it is written, *this man was born there,* ... A prophetic reference seemingly is made to the choosing of the 144,000 as the sons of Korah wrote, *The LORD shall count.*

After a study of the number 88 (See Psalm 88), a friend pointed out the Hebrew definition of the number 87. The two Hebrew letters "peh" and "zayin," which make up the number 87, also happen to make up the Hebrew word "pahz," meaning, "refined gold." The ordinary Hebrew word for gold is "zahab." But, according to the Gesenius Hebrew-Chaldee Lexicon to the Old Testament, "pahz" means, "purified, pure, a epithet [metaphor] of gold, Song of Solomon 5:11; hence purified, pure gold, Psalm 21:3; Lamentations 4:2; Isaiah 13:12. It is distinguished from common gold ..."[5]

"Pahz" comes from a root word "pahzaz" meaning, "to separate, to distinguish... specifically, to separate and purify metals from dross, by means of fire." Pahzaz also means "to leap for joy, leaping and dancing, to bound, to be light, agile, to flee as a gazelle."[6] This ancient rendering, however, seems to have almost fallen into disuse among the Hebrews. These meanings are all important when considering the future Jewish remnant (144,000) who will be separated and sealed in their foreheads, as opposed to the "mark of the beast" in the foreheads of wicked men (representing the ordinary gold of Mystery Babylon). The Jewish remnant will be tried in the fires of the Tribulation Period. When they restore Temple worship, they will "leap for joy," but when the "abomination of desolation" occurs, they will "flee as a gazelle." By the way, the melting point of gold is 1948 degrees Fahrenheit!

> *As well the singers as the players on instruments shall be there: all my springs are in thee* (v. 7).

The processional for bringing the Ark of the Covenant must include the singers and players of instruments. Just when the Ark will be returned or taken to the Temple Mount is not known, but the general feeling is that the momentum is building for that predicted event. The sons of Korah were members of the Kohathites who carried the Ark. Psalms 73-89 are positioned is such a way as to present the processional. It may be the duty of the 144,000 to return the Ark to the Temple site, set up the Tabernacle of David and restore the Priesthood at or near the beginning of the Tribulation Period.

The year 1987 is regarded as a sabbatical year and the 42nd year of the jubilee cycle, though, according to other Jewish sources, 1987/88 could be the sabbatical year. For a study on the prophetic significance of the sabbatical and jubilee cycles, see our notes on Psalm 81.

PSALM 88

A Song or Psalm for the sons of Korah, to the chief Musician upon Mahalath Leannoth, Maschil of Heman the Ezrahite (introduction).

Though the psalm was accompanied by the sons of Korah, its author was Heman. He was appointed along with Asaph and Ethan to sound cymbals (I Chronicles 15:19) in the processional for bringing the Ark of the Covenant to Jerusalem. Psalm 88 was delivered to the chief Musician, Chenaniah (I Chronicles 15:22), who instructed the psalm to be played upon "Mahalath", a term meaning "sickness" (Rashi) or "forgiveness" (Midrash Shocher Tov). "Meiri identifies Mahalath as a special musical instrument that moves the listener to anguish and tears"[1] Leannoth means "afflicted". Its music served "to afflict and upset the listener so much that he is prepared to repent with utter sincerity."[2]

Maschil refers to the psalm as one of instruction. It means that the composer has prepared himself to be the recipient of a prophetic inspiration. As the spirit of prophecy came to the composer, he gave the message to the orator, who repeated it aloud to the assembly (Rashi).[3]

> *For my soul is full of troubles: and my life draweth nigh unto*
> *the grave.*
> > *Thy wrath lieth hard upon me, ...*
> > *I am afflicted and ready to die ...*
> > *Thy fierce wrath goeth over me; thy terrors have cut me off*
> (vv. 3,7,15,16).

"On one matter all commentators who deal with Psalm 88 are fully agreed: IT IS THE GLOOMIEST PSALM FOUND IN THE SCRIPTURE"[4] The random verses above point out the utter despair of the Jews whose lives have been "an endless chain of tragedy ..."[5] They feel that every type of punishment inflicted upon the world has smitten them.

Psalms 88-94 seem to describe the future seven years of *Jacob's trouble* in chronological order. This is not to say that the Tribulation Period will begin in 1988. These psalms do, however, seem to set a trend for those events which someday will come to pass.

> *Thou hast put away mine acquaintance far from me; thou*
> *hast made me an abomination unto them ...* (v. 8).

Some Jewish "commentators maintain that this refers to the Gentiles."[6] Since many students of prophecy believe in a pre-tribulation Rapture, the verse may well be descriptive of Gentile Christianity. We are historically the only true friends of Israel. Devout Christians appear to have disappeared from the earth as the Jewish nation is thrown into tribulation.

> *Lover and friend hast thou put far from me ...* (v. 18).

Lover, according to the rabbis, is Israel's dearest friend — "the eagerly awaited Messiah."[7]

It is as if the Rapture has occurred and Christians are gone! If true, then a verse must be found in Psalm 88 which prophetically describes the Resurrection. That *blessed hope* must occur simultaneously with the Rapture of living saints. It is incredible that such a verse should be found, but indeed it appears in verse 10!

> *Wilt thou show wonders to the dead? Shall the dead arise and*
> *praise thee?* (v. 10).

There could be no more powerful a passage to convince the skeptic of a pre-tribulation Rapture and Resurrection than Psalm

88!

What a psalm! Not only does it contain cryptic references to the world's most devastating period of history, it also appears to contain prophetic references to the Resurrection and Rapture of Gentile Christianity. Even Jewish commentators agree that the *acquaintance* of verse 8 and the *friend* of verse 18 refers to Gentiles and that the *Lover* of verse 18 refers to the Messiah.

Another Jewish rabbi (the Apostle Paul) described the event in his New Testament epistle to the church at Thessalonica: *For the Lord himself shall descend from heaven with a shout, with the voice of the archangel, and with the trump of God: and the dead in Christ shall rise first: Then we which are alive and remain shall be caught up together with them in the clouds, to meet the Lord in the air: and so shall we ever be with the Lord* (I Thessalonians 4:16,17).

What a powerful prophecy! The Jewish people will be thrust into the midst of *Jacob's trouble*. They will suffer for seven dreadful years. At or before the beginning of it the dead in Christ will be raised, living believers will be raptured, and the Jewish nation will be left behind.

Psalms 88-94 prophetically describe the coming of Elijah and Moses, the abomination of desolation, the fleeing of the remnant to the wilderness, and world conditions as Armageddon approaches. Psalm 94 culminates with the appearance of Messiah to judge the wicked and set up his glorious kingdom.

I asked a Jewish friend one day to decipher the Hebrew number for 88. I was curious about Psalm 88 and the possibility of a mystical significance of the number. Hebrew numbers are taken from their alphabet, unlike English. Our numbers have no relationship with the letters of the English alphabet. But in many of the more ancient alphabets, numbers are derived from their letters.

For example, Roman numerals correspond to certain letters in Latin. "I" becomes one, "V" becomes five, "X" becomes ten, "L" becomes fifty, "C" becomes one hundred, etc. In a similar fashion, Hebrew numbers are taken from their alphabet. The first ten letters become 1 through 10. The eleventh letter becomes 20, the twelfth becomes 30, etc. A special procedure is used by which Hebrew letters are turned into numbers.

As you may recall, in the Roman alphabet, a bar placed at the top and bottom of a Latin letter makes that letter a number. If the letter "V" has a bar across the top and bottom of it, it becomes the number five. In a similar fashion, the Hebrew numbering system also has a special method by which letters are made to represent numbers. Sometimes the symbol has the appearance of an apostrophe and at other times quotation marks. Often both are used. These marks are called in the Hebrew language "avi-ka-dabar," meaning "as my father would have said it." Perhaps you do not recognize the term "avi-ka-dabar," but are familiar with its more modern pronunciation — abra-ca-dabra.

So I asked my friend to remove the "abracadabra" from Psalm 88 and tell me what that Hebrew number would be if it were a word instead. He reached into his desk, pulled out his Hebrew copy of the Psalms (Tehillim), and turned to Psalm 88. After a moment, he looked at me and said, "It is the word 'pach.'" I asked him, "What does it mean?" and he replied, "It is how you say a trap — like a pit. It is like a man who dug a pit for a trap and then fell in it." He was quoting a verse of Scripture. It is a phrase repeated several times throughout the Old Testament. Psalm 7:15 says: *He made a pit, and digged it, and is fallen into the ditch which he made.* Psalm 57:6 says: *They have prepared a net for my steps; my soul is bowed down: They have digged a pit before me, into the midst whereof they are fallen themselves.* Proverbs 26:27 says: *Whoso diggeth a pit shall fall therein:* ... Psalm 141:9-10 says: *Keep me from the snares which they have laid for me, and the gins of the workers of iniquity. Let the wicked fall into their own nets* ... And Proverbs 28:10 says: *Whoso causeth the righteous to go astray in an evil way, he shall fall himself into his own pit:* ...

These and other similar Scriptures appear to be prophecies of the antichrist, who will lay a trap for the Jewish people during the Tribulation Period, but will himself fall into his own trap. Here's a word of caution: just because the term used for 88 refers to a trap does not mean the trap will be laid in 1988.

When my friend told me that the Hebrew word for 88 was "pach," which means "a trap or pit," I reminded him that a similar theme was used in Psalm 88: *For my soul is full of troubles: and my life draweth nigh unto the grave. I am counted with them that go down into the pit* ... (vv. 3-4).

The meaning is obvious. The Jewish people will one day enter upon a seven-year period of unparalleled trouble. There has never been anything like it before in history. The life of the Israeli nation will draw near to the grave. Their souls will be filled with trouble — a key word from which comes the term "tribulation." A world dictator will arise upon his platform of peace, but it will be a pseudo-peace through which he will plot the enslavement of humankind. This antichrist will lay a trap through which he will plan the genocide of the Jews. In a manner similar to that of Adolf Hitler, he will deceive the whole world.

It is my opinion that he will make his debut following the Battle of Gog and Magog. In the aftermath of the failed Russian invasion, the antichrist will offer what appears to be a perfect plan for world peace. But beware! It will be a "pach" — a trap by which he will attempt to ensnare not only Israel, but the entire world.

Psalm 91 has a reference to the abomination of desolation, which will occur in the middle of the Tribulation Period. The antichrist will enter Jerusalem, go to the Temple site, desecrate the place, and declare himself to be the savior of the world. When the antichrist commits that abomination of desolation, the Jewish remnant will flee to the mountains for safety. Psalm 91 describes it in this manner: *Surely he shall deliver thee from the snare of the fowler, ...* (Psalm 91:3). Could that snare be another description of this trap laid by the antichrist? I asked my friend (who had just deciphered the number 88), "What Hebrew word is used in Psalm 91:3 which is translated 'snare' of the fowler?" He turned to it in his Hebrew Scriptures, then looked up excitedly and said, "It is pach! It is the same word!"

Not only was he excited, I was elated! It is a theme which appears to be laid in Psalm 88 and sprung in Psalm 91. But that's not the end of it, for you see, the one who laid the trap will fall into his own trap, and that is found in Psalm 94, the last of these seven psalms, the theme of which is built around the "pach" — the trap, the snare, the pit. Psalm 94 describes the Battle of Armageddon on the day of God's vengeance. It begins by saying: *O God, to whom vengeance belongeth, show thyself* (Psalm 94:1). That will occur in the midst of history's most devastating war. Christ will appear in the heavens with vengeance and the antichrist will fall into his own pit: *That thou mayest give him rest from the days of adversity, until the pit be digged for the wicked.* (Psalm 94:13). There is the pit dug by the wicked and used for the wicked. He who digs the pit will fall into it himself: *And he shall bring upon them their own iniquity, and shall cut them off in their own wickedness; ...* (Psalm 94:23). The antichrist, who lays the trap in Psalm 88 and springs his snare in Psalm 91, will himself fall into the pit in Psalm 94.

When the "man of sin" enters Jerusalem in the middle of the Tribulation Period, his purpose will be to establish a world kingdom with Jerusalem as his capital city. Two men will oppose him. They are the leaders of the Jewish remnant — the 144,000 who have re-established Temple worship by setting up the Tabernacle of David on the Temple Mount just north, I think, of the Moslem Mosque of Omar.

These two leaders of the Jewish remnant are described in the prophecies of the Bible as fulfillments of a prophetic Moses and Elijah. They will be a thorn in the side of the antichrist. But when Mr. 666 makes his triumphal entry onto the Temple site to declare himself deity, he will have these two men killed. Their bodies will lie in the streets of Jerusalem unattended for three and a half days.

Their followers, the Jewish remnant, will flee in fear. The remnant will escape the *snare of the fowler* — the trap of the antichrist — and will make their way south and east to the wilderness area of Petra, site of an ancient city forty miles south of the Dead Sea. Petra was once the capital of the Edomite empire. Today, it is a ghost town with enough caves hewn out of the mountains to accommodate the fleeing Jewish people. It's just sitting there waiting for the Jewish remnant — the 144,000 and their converts. Here's why I think the remnant will flee to Petra. There is a mountain overlooking the city of Petra in the formation of an eagle. It is easy to distinguish the head and the wings of the natural stone formation. The huge eagle has become the symbol of the ancient city down through history and can be seen in many places in the Bible.

Psalm 91 calls this trap the *snare of the fowler*. It is the description of one who lays a trap for a bird. But God has promised that the Jewish remnant will not be caught in the trap: *He* [God] *shall cover thee with his feathers, and under his wings shalt thou trust* ... (Psalm 91:4). The bird will not be caught, for God will gather His remnant and bring them to a place of safety, *as a hen gathereth her chickens* when the storm approaches. That was the terminology used by Jesus Christ as He wept over Jerusalem. He wanted to save the Jewish people. He wanted to set up the kingdom. In the days following His triumphal entry, He had a prophetic word about a future time when the antichrist will make his triumphal entry into Jerusalem. Jesus said, *O Jerusalem, Jerusalem, thou that killest the prophets, and stonest them which are sent unto thee, how often would I have gathered thy children together, even as a hen gathereth her chickens under her wings, and ye would not!* (Matthew 23:37). One day, however, when the antichrist makes his triumphal entry into the city of Jerusalem, the Jewish remnant will realize the prophetic significance of it and flee to safety.

Isaiah described it in a similar manner: *Send ye the lamb to the ruler of the land from Sela* [Petra] *to the wilderness, unto the mount of the daughter of Zion* (Isaiah 16:1). Let me pause here to say that the *lamb* is descriptive of the Lamb of God, and the *ruler of the land* appears to be a reference to the antichrist. Isaiah describes the Second Coming of Jesus Christ to destroy satan's "man of the hour" and throw him into his own trap. Isaiah said that the Lamb will be sent from Petra in the wilderness. This is the place where the 144,000 will hold up in the last half of the Tribulation Period. They will flee there when the antichrist springs his trap and commits the abomination of desolation. Three and a half years later in the height of the Battle of Armageddon, Jesus Christ will come — first to Petra in the country of Edom to rescue His remnant, and then will proceed on to Jerusalem with vengeance.

Isaiah 63 describes the scene even more vividly: *Who is this that cometh from Edom, with dyed garments from Bozrah? this that is glorious in his apparel, traveling in the greatness of his strength? I that speak in righteousness, mighty to save. Wherefore art thou red in thine apparel, and thy garments like him that treadeth in the winefat? I have trodden the winepress alone ... For the day of vengeance is in mine heart, and year of my redeemed is come.* (Isaiah 63:1-4). When Christ returns in power and great glory, He will come from the east — from Edom and Petra in the wilderness — to conquer the antichrist, destroy the armies of the world, and establish His own throne in Jerusalem. In Isaiah 16:2, we are taken back to the abomination of desolation: *For it shall be, that, as a wandering bird cast out of the nest,*

... In the original Hebrew, it is a fleeing bird cast out of the nest. Isaiah uses the same terminology which is followed consistently in Scripture. The believing Jewish remnant is described as a bird fleeing from the snare of the fowler.

They will hasten to the wilderness area of Petra, where they will be protected during the last half of the Tribulation. In Isaiah 16:3-4, God has a message for Moab and Petra: *Take counsel, execute judgment; make thy shadow as the night in the midst of the noonday; hide the outcasts; bewray not him that wandereth. Let mine outcasts dwell with thee, Moab; be thou a covert to them from the face of the spoiler: for the extortioner is at an end, the spoiler ceaseth, the oppressors are consumed out of the land.* The message to Moab and Petra is to allow the 144,000 and their converts to safely escape the trap of the antichrist. Petra will make a good hideaway until the Lamb appears to establish His throne in Jerusalem.

Another description of the Jewish remnant fleeing the city of Jerusalem for the wilderness area of Petra is given in the New Testament book of Revelation: *And the woman fled into the wilderness, where she hath a place prepared of God, that they should feed her there a thousand two hundred and threescore days* (Revelation 12:6). The woman is symbolic of Israel, who will flee into the wilderness of Petra for 1,260 days or three and one-half years: *And to the woman were given two wings of a great eagle, that she might fly into the wilderness, into her place, where she is nourished for a time, and times, and half a time, from the face of the serpent* (Revelation 12:14). The symbol of the bird is consistent with the psalmist who wrote of the snare of the fowler and promised the Jews, *He shall cover thee with his feathers and under his wings shalt thou trust* (Psalm 91:4). It is consistent with Isaiah who described the fleeing remnant as a wandering bird cast out of the nest. It is consistent with the message of Christ, Who said, *How often would I have gathered thy children together, even as a hen gathereth her chickens, and ye would not* (Matthew 23:37). Here, however, in Revelation 12:14 the Jewish remnant will accept God's offer. *As a hen gathering her chickens,* the two wings of a great eagle will assist the 144,000 with their flight into the wilderness where they will be nourished for a time (meaning one year) and times (meaning two years) and half a time (meaning one-half year) — or three and one-half years — from the face of the serpent.

Now the question is: Why did the psalmist use the term *snare of the fowler* when referring to the abomination of desolation perpetrated by the antichrist? What is it about the antichrist which will be so deceiving to the Jewish people, and why is the symbolism of the bird used to describe him? It is my conclusion that the antichrist will be from the tribe of Dan, whose ancient symbol was an eagle. When Jacob was dying, as recorded in Genesis 49, he gathered his children around him and gave prophecies of that which would befall each of his sons in the last days. As he came to Dan, he ascribed to him the symbol of a snake, a many-headed Hydra. It is the same symbolic seven-headed, ten-horned serpent or dragon seen in Revelation.

In later years, when the Tabernacle was built at Sinai, the tribe of Dan changed their symbol from a many-headed serpent to an eagle.[8] Thus began a deception which has continued down through history. The tribe of Dan disappeared from the pages of history a thousand years B.C. But the psalmist warned the Jewish nation to beware the snare of the fowler, for one day, under the symbol of the Danite eagle, the antichrist will spring his trap.

When the antichrist enters Jerusalem, he will do so, I think, under the symbol of an eagle. But beware! It's a trap! The eagle is not really an eagle; it's a snake! The symbolism is deceptive. The many-headed snake, symbolic of the tribe of Dan, was changed into a many-headed eagle. But when the book of the Revelation begins to unfold and the prophecies are fulfilled, the eagle will be transformed back into the many-headed serpent of Revelation.

The year 1987/88 could be a sabbatical year and the 42nd year of the jubilee cycle, though, according to the calculations of Maimonides, world Jewry set the sabbatical year in 1986/87. For a study on the prophetic significance of the sabbatical and jubilee cycles, see our notes on Psalm 81.

PSALM 89

Maschil of Ethan the Ezrahite (introduction).

Ethan was listed along with Heman as a wise man. Only Solomon was considered wiser (I Kings 4:31).[1] Ethan means "enduring, long-lived." He may be the same Ethan, son of Kushaiah, named in I Chronicles 15:17 where Heman is again named as an associate. Heman and Ethan were chosen to sound cymbals in the processional to bring the Ark of the Covenant to Jerusalem.

For Asaph, Heman, and Ethan to be positioned as they are in the Leviticus portion of the Psalms (73-89) certainly lends to the prophetic possibility that the Ark of the Covenant may once again become the central theme of a restored priesthood.

> *I will sing of the mercies of the LORD for ever: with my mouth will I make known thy faithfulness to all generations.*
> *For I have said, Mercy shall be built up for ever: thy faithfulness shalt thou establish in the very heavens* (vv. 1,2).

Psalm 89 is the last chapter in the Leviticus section. The Mosaic book of Leviticus dealt with sacrificial worship, the consecration of the priesthood, moral laws of purity, the meanings of the holy days, and God's promised chastisements for wickedness. God promised disobedient Israel a future captivity and warned that if the Chosen People did not then repent, He would multiply their judgments *seven times more* (Leviticus 26:18).

Psalms 73-89 are a counterpart to the Mosaic Leviticus and correspond with its general theme. These psalms appear to pick up where Moses left off. It seems the divine punishment of *seven times more* is about to be concluded and the priesthood restored just in time to bring on the last seven years of judgment.

> *I have made a covenant with my chosen, I have sworn unto David my servant* (v. 3).

Psalms 89 and 90 seem to present the messages of two future witnesses, Elijah and Moses, who will come to lead the 144,000 during the first half of the Tribulation Period. Though we do not have the name of Elijah in Psalm 89, the message appears to be the kind Elijah would give to the Jews. First of all, he reminds them of the covenant made with David.

> *Thy seed will I establish for ever, and build up thy throne to all generations* (v. 4).

Here the Jewish people are reminded that God has chosen one of the offspring of David to be the Messiah.

> *Thou hast broken Rahab in pieces as one that is slain; thou hast scattered thine enemies with thy strong arm* (v. 10).

It should be noted that the destruction of Mystery Babylon is implied here. God's judgment upon the *great city which reigneth over the kings of the earth* is given in Revelation 17-18 (Also see our comments on Psalm 87).

> *For the Lord is our defense; and the Holy One of Israel is our King.*
> *I have found David my servant; with my holy oil have I anointed him.*
> *Also I will make him my first-born, higher than the kings of the earth* (vv. 18,20,27).

This could well be the message of the coming Elijah. He is reminding the Jewish people that God has chosen the offspring of David to be His *first-born, higher than the kings of the earth,* obviously a Messianic prophecy. Furthermore, they are told that God will yet keep His word:

> *My covenant will I not break, nor alter the thing that is gone out of my lips.*
> *Once have I sworn by my holiness that I will not lie unto David.*
> *His seed shall endure for ever, and his throne as the sun before me.*
> *It shall be established for ever as the moon, and as a faithful witness in heaven* (vv. 34-37).

This is a confirmation of the covenant made with David. God has promised that the throne of David will be established and that the Son of God will sit upon it. He came 2,000 years ago and was presented to the Jewish people as their King. He rode into the city of Jerusalem on the back of a donkey, and in so doing, came as the Prince of Peace — not as a military conqueror. At this point, the fiery Elijah indicts the Chosen People for rejecting their Messiah.

> *But thou hast cast off and abhorred, thou hast been wroth with thine anointed.*
> *Thou hast made void the covenant of thy servant: thou hast profaned his crown by casting it to the ground* (vv. 38-39).

One can imagine the future Elijah declaring to the 144,000, "Instead of presenting Him with a golden diadem, you gave Him a crown of thorns!''

> *Thou hast made his glory to cease and cast his throne down to the ground* (v. 44).

Again, it seems the evangelist proclaims, "Instead of a throne, you gave Him a cross!"

> *The days of his youth hast thou shortened: thou hast covered him with shame* (v. 45).

Elijah declares, "He died when He was only 33!" What a powerful indictment! They rejected their Messiah and cast His crown and throne to the ground. They crowned Him with thorns instead of gold. They gave Him a cross on which to hang instead of a throne upon which to sit.

> *Wherewith thine enemies have reproached, O LORD; wherewith they have reproached the footsteps of thine anointed* (v. 51).

Psalm 89 may be the message to be delivered by Elijah to the sinful nation of Israel, whose forefathers had long ago rejected the Messiah and nailed Him to a cross. Such a message will be delivered in the Tribulation Period when the enemies of God are preparing for world government — bringing discredit and disgrace upon the very footsteps of the Messiah as the time for His arrival approaches.

> *Blessed be the LORD for evermore. Amen, and Amen* (v. 52).

We have come to the conclusion of the Leviticus Psalms. The two *Amen*[s] seem to be both historic and prophetic. What has occurred in the past to inspire the writings of these psalms may be indicated by the first *Amen* while those future events which will fulfill their prophetic scenario may be indicated by the second *Amen*. (See the chapter, The Prophetic Amen.)

THE
NUMBERS
PSALMS

INTRODUCTION TO THE NUMBERS PSALMS

A study of the two numbers (87 and 88) set my mind to thinking. What about the numbers 90 through 106? How many of them are made up of words in the Hebrew language? Do they tell the story of the Tribulation Period and the Second Coming of Christ?

Are you ready for this? They do! Out of 17 chapters in the **NUMBERS** division of the Psalms, there are 12 numbers which make up words in the Hebrew Lexicon. Six of them describe Armageddon and the glory of Christ's return, followed by another six which portray God's vengeance upon the wicked! No wonder this section of the Psalms is called NUMBERS! And no wonder Moses wrote in Psalm 90:12, *So teach us to NUMBER our days, that we may apply our hearts unto wisdom.*

Of 17 psalms, five of them are simply numbers. They are not words which can be found in the Hebrew Lexicon. They are 90, 93, 97, 99, and 103. Perhaps these five numbers represent the Dispensation of Grace. Five is the number of grace. And perhaps they have no meanings because all believers from the Dispensation of Grace will be raptured before the Tribulation Period begins. Furthermore, if we pick up the two numbers preceding the Numbers book (Psalms 88 and 89) which, even though they are part of the Leviticus period for setting up Temple worship, are obviously descriptive of the numbers period as well, then we can note that one has a meaning (88) and one does not (89).

They remind me of the five loaves and two fish used to feed the 5,000. After the meal there were twelve basketsfull left over. Five psalms represented by five loaves of bread (the gospel — 90, 93, 97, 99, and 103) and two psalms represented by two fish (Judaism and Christianity — 88 and 89) add credence to the possibility of a pre-tribulation Rapture. If we add 88 plus 89 plus 90 plus 93 plus 97 plus 99 plus 103 plus 7 (for the seven numbers) we get a total of 666. The twelve basketsfull left over from the Dispensation of Grace (depicted by the number 5,000) may, in turn, represent the twelve psalms whose numbers have meanings. These twelve have a fantastic story to tell.

Psalm 91 prophetically portrays the abomination of desolation — an abominable act committed by the antichrist on the Temple Mount in the midst of the Tribulation Period, at which time the 144,000 will flee to the mountains. The number 91 is made up of two Hebrew letters, "tzade" and "aleph." They comprise part of a root word "tsaw" meaning, "to go out, or to be cast out."[1]

Psalm 92 continues with an assessment of the antichrist, *a brutish man* and a description of the approaching armies for the Battle of Armageddon. The number 92 is made up of two Hebrew letters "tzade" and "beth." They make up the word "tsawb" with three possible meanings: 1) "a litter, a covered and curtained couch provided with shafts and used for carrying a single passenger." Here is a perfect description of the triumphal entry of the antichrist onto the Temple Mount. 2) "To establish, a canopy (as a fixture)." The antichrist will enter the Sanctuary on the Temple Mount and offer himself as the Messiah of Israel. 3) "a species of lizard." Could this allude to the dragon of Revelation? There is yet another word derived from the number 92. If we add an additional "Aleph" it becomes "Tsawba" meaning "to muster soldiers for war." The war clouds of Armageddon appear to be brewing.[2]

Psalm 94 records the dreadful Battle of Armageddon, Christ's appearing on the day of His vengeance, and His judgment meted out. The number 94 is comprised of two Hebrew letters, "tzade" and "daleth." They make up the word "tsad" having two meanings: 1) "side" and 2) "adversary." The Lexicon explains the "side" with a reference to Psalm 91:7, *a thousand shall fall at thy side* and Judges 2:3, *thorns in your sides.* Both are references to Armageddon. "Adversary" certainly smacks of the enemies of Israel who come to destroy the Jewish race. "Tsadaw" is a word meaning, "to lay snares." It is descriptive of the trap into which the antichrist will fall. Psalm 94:13 says, ... *the pit be digged for the wicked.*[3]

Psalm 95 rejoices over the appearance of Christ to save the day. The number 95 is comprised of two Hebrew letters "tzade" and "he." They are part of a combination of several exciting words. As "tsahab" they mean "glitter, be golden in color." As "tsahal" they mean "to shout for joy." As "tsohar" they mean 1) "to appear, to come forth, to reveal oneself, splendor" and 2) "to squeeze out oil (in a press)." When Christ reveals himself in splendor and glitter, to tread the winepress of His wrath, Israel will shout for joy![4]

Psalm 96 describes His coming to ... *judge the world with righteousness, and the people with His truth* (Psalm 96:13). The number 96 is made up of two Hebrew letters, "tzade" and "vav." They form a two-letter word "tsav" meaning "precept, injunction, commandment." The Revelation account says, ... *out of his mouth goeth a sharp sword* (Revelation 19:15). The Apostle Paul described the day, ... *then shall that Wicked be revealed, whom the Lord shall comsume with the spirit of his mouth, and shall destroy with the brightness of his coming* (II Thessalonians 2:8).[5]

Psalm 98 describes His spectacular appearance, ... *all the ends of the earth have seen the salvation of our God* (Psalm 98:3). The number 98 is made up of two Hebrew letters, "tzade" and "cheth." They spell the word "tsach" meaning "dazzling, bright white" another magnificent description of the glorious appearing of Messiah. Another meaning, "clear heat", is a term used in Isaiah 18:4 alluding to the Battle of Gog and Magog.[6] It describes the judgment, as *clear heat* shrivels the plants, so will the Saviour destroy the antichrist *with the brightness of His coming* (II Thessalonians 2:8). The prophet Zechariah described the scene most vividly, ... *this shall be the plague wherewith the LORD will smite all the people that have fought against Jerusalem; Their flesh shall consume away while they stand upon their feet, and their eyes shall consume away in their holes, and their tongue shall consume away in their mouth* (Zechariah 14:12).

Psalm 100 happens to be the 19th letter of the Hebrew alphabet and thus concludes the 19 hundreds! (Don't miss that combination of 19 and 100 which makes **nineteen hundred**). The number 100 is made up of a single Hebrew letter "koph" and denotes "the hole of an axe."[7] Perhaps it has a reference to the description, ... *out of his mouth goeth a sharp sword, that with it he should smite the nations* (Revelation 19:15). By the way, please note that Christ's appearance in Revelation happens to be in chapter number 19! Could that also refer to the 1900's? At this point there is a turn in the meanings of the next six numbers. The earlier six (91, 92, 94, 95, 96, and 98) describe the glory of His coming, but the latter six (100, 101, 102, 104, 105, 106) reveal His judgment upon a sinful world.

Psalm 101 refers to judgment, *I will early destroy all the wicked out of the land* (Psalm 101:8). The number 101 is made up of two Hebrew letters "koph" and "aleph." They comprise the word "kay" meaning "to vomit."[8] What a description of judgment! It was to the wicked apostate church of Laodicea that Christ promised, *I will spue thee out of my mouth* (Revelation 3:16).

Psalm 102 denotes a similar connotation. Christ will hear the cry of the oppressed Chosen People and will come to avenge them. The number 102 is made up of two Hebrew letters "koph" and "beth." As the word "kab" they refer to a "scoop" used to measure dry things. The wicked will be measured in God's scales. As the word "kabab" meaning "to curse" the wicked will be *weighed in the balances, and ... found wanting* (Daniel 5:27).[9]

Psalm 104 extols the majesty and power of God and the humility of man while saying, *Let the sinners be consumed out of the earth ...* (Psalm 104:35). The number 104 is comprised of the Hebrew letters "koph" and "daleth" root of the word "kadad" meaning "to bow the head, to bow before God."[10] In that day, ... *every knee shall bow, and every tongue shall swear* ... allegience to Him! In that day, *all that are incensed against Him shall be ashamed* (Isaiah 45:23,24).

Psalm 105 reminds Israel of the Abrahamic Covenant — God's oath to give them the Promised Land and declares, *He* [God] *hath remembered his covenant* (Psalm 105:8). The number 105 is made up of "koph" and "he." As "kawhaw" meaning "to be blunted" we are reminded of Isaiah's prophecy, ... *they shall beat their swords into plowshares, and their spears into pruninghooks: nation shall not lift up sword against nation, neither shall they learn war any more* (Isaiah 2:4). As "Kawhal" meaning "assembly, congregation, multitude," we are reminded of the group of nations who will be judged and of those who will inherit the new kingdom of Christ.[11]

Psalm 106 concludes the Numbers portion of the Psalms with a humbling reminder of how the Chosen People have provoked the anger of the Lord, only to be forgiven and avenged. The number 106 denotes the conclusion of judgment upon the wicked. It is comprised of two letters, "koph" and "vav" which make up the word "kav" meaning "a rule for measuring." Men will be judged by the rules. There will be a basis or rule of law by which Christ will judge. As the word "kavkav," judgment will be "meted out." As "kow," another word for "vomit," the judgment will be concluded and the Messiah will get on with the job of setting up the kingdom as depicted in the Deuteronomy book, Psalms 107-150![12]

The number 90 has no apparent meaning in the Hebrew Lexicon. It is one of those few numbers whose Hebrew letters make no words. It seemed rather strange to me that this portion of the Psalms which reveals so much prophecy should begin with such a number. "Perhaps the meaning lies even deeper," I thought. So I looked in the Lexicon at the two root numbers that comprise the number 90 — 9 and 10. I found that the number 9 is made up of a single letter "teth" meaning "a serpent!" The number 10 is made up of a single letter "yod" meaning "a hand!"

I immediately remembered the prophecy of Amos: *Woe unto you that desire the day of the LORD! to what end is it for you? the day of the LORD is darkness, and not light. As if a man did flee from a lion, and a bear met him; or went into the house, and leaned his hand on the wall, and a serpent bit him* (Amos 5:18-19).

In 1948 Israel dispensed with the *lion* (Great Britain). Soon Israel will face the *bear* (the Soviet Union). Israel will also raise up the *house* (Tabernacle of David on the Temple site) and will be bitten on the hand by a *serpent* (the abomination of desolation committed by the antichrist). This is an amazing prophecy hidden in the component numbers that make up the number 90. The nineties tell the story of the serpent. We could call them the Serpent Psalms.

Someday, a world dictator will usurp the throne of God. His symbol is the serpent. It is important to note that the number 9 means "a serpent" whose story is covered in Psalms 90-100! Moses wrote those eleven psalms and dedicated each to a tribe, leaving out the tribe of Simeon. It is remarkable that the name Simeon means, "hearing." Any encyclopedia will confirm that serpents are deaf!

That may be the reason why Revelation 13:9 says, *If any man have an ear, let him hear.* The verse is found in chapter number 13 (a number of ill omen) and in verse number 9 (which in Hebrew means a serpent) — in the chapter which describes the dragon or serpent. Serpents are deaf!

What an incredible set of numbers we have in the **Numbers book** of the Psalms! Even the **numbers** of these psalms tell the same prophetic story. No wonder Psalms 90 through 106 correspond to the book of Numbers! And no wonder Moses wrote in Psalm 90 (in verse 12! no less!), *So teach us* [the 12 tribes] *to NUMBER our days, that we may apply our hearts unto wisdom.*

PSALM 90

A Prayer of Moses the man of God (introduction).

Just as Psalm 89 compares with the message of Elijah, Psalm 90 contains *A Prayer of Moses the man of God*. These are the two witnesses referred to in Revelation 11. According to that prophetic passage, one of the witnesses will have power to *turn water to blood*. That is characteristic of Moses. The other will have power to *shut up heaven, that it rain not in the days of their prophecy* (Revelation 11:6). Only Elijah displayed such power in the days of his ministry. These are also the two men who met with Jesus on the Mount of Transfiguration which, according to the passage, is a prophetic picture of those future events which will attend the Second Advent of Christ. Further, Malachi closed the Old Testament with an admonition to *Remember ye the law of Moses* ... and promising to ... *send you Elijah the prophet before the coming of the great and dreadful day of the LORD* (Malachi 4:4-5). Moses represents the Law and Elijah represents the Prophets.

Thou turnest man to destruction; and sayest, Return, ye children of men (v. 3).

Psalm 90 was dedicated to Reuben. "Midrash Schocher Tov demonstrates how the theme of each of the eleven psalms relates to a specific tribe. The theme of each follows the Mosaic blessing given on the Lawgiver's last day of his life (Deuteronomy 33). Psalm 90 speaks of repentance, as indicated in the third verse: Thou turnest man to destruction; and sayest, Return (repent), ye children of men. Reuben introduced the principle of complete repentance to the world."[1] Repentance will bring about the conversion of Israel in the predicted Tribulation Period.

For a thousand years in thy sight are but as yesterday when it is past, and as a watch in the night (v. 4).

Could these psalms (90-100) be the song of Moses referred to in

Revelation 15? The vision of John takes us into heaven to see the 144,000 around the throne of God, having been delivered from the Tribulation Period: *And I saw another sign in heaven, great and marvelous, seven angels having the seven last plagues; for in them is filled up the wrath of God. And I saw as it were a sea of glass mingled with fire: and them that had gotten the victory over the beast, and over his image, and over his mark, and over the number of his name, stand on the sea of glass, having the harps of God. And they sing the song of Moses ... (vv. 1-3).*

Are these psalms (90-100) the song they sing? Why not? Moses referred to the *New Song* in Psalm 96:1 and 98:1. It is this series of songs which deals with the Tribulation Period and with the great judgment of God about to be poured out upon an unbelieving human race.

There are two verses in Psalm 90 which deal with great prophetic numbers — verses 4 and 10. In verse 4, Moses implies that the six days of creation represent 6,000 years of human history and that the seventh day of creation represents the seventh millennium of human history — the Great Sabbath Rest. Peter made reference to this verse when he wrote in his second epistle, *But, beloved, be not ignorant of this one thing, that one day is with the Lord as a thousand years, and a thousand years as one day* (II Peter 3:8).

We are approaching the end of the sixth millennium of human history. The Great Sabbath Rest should be just ahead. To be more specific, however, Moses wrote of the last generation in verse 10:

> *The days of our years are threescore years and ten; and if by reason of strength they be fourscore years, yet is their strength labor and sorrow ... (v. 10).*

The passage implies that the last generation should be somewhere between seventy and eighty years, and those years after seventy will be filled with labor and sorrow. Perhaps those are the years of tribulation.

> *So teach us to number our days, that we may apply our hearts unto wisdom (v. 12).*

This is not a message for Gentile Christianity. Dates cannot be calculated before the predicted seven years begins. However, it should not be difficult for the Jewish people to count the days once the Tribulation Period sets in. When the abomination of desolation occurs in the middle of those predicted seven years, the faithful can reckon that Messiah will come in another three and a half years. During that time, the remnant will rely heavily on the prophecies recorded in Scripture.

> *Return, O LORD, How long?* (v. 13).

This is the cry of repentant Israel. The remnant will realize that Messiah has already come once (two thousand years ago) so they pray, *Return!* The question, *How long?* is asked eighteen times in the Psalms. The question was posed in the previous psalm (89) and is repeated here. The final *How Long?* will be found in Psalm 94 which describes the appearing of Messiah on the day of His vengeance.

Psalm 90 is one of eleven psalms written by Moses (Psalms 90-100). They were each dedicated to one of the 12 sons of Jacob. Only Simeon was excluded from the list. Why was Simeon left out? It is the opinion of scholars that Simeon was a prophetic characteristic of the children of Israel. His name means "hearing." That trait has been missing from among the Jews for two thousand years. Isaiah wrote concerning unbelieving Israel, *Hear ye indeed, but understand not; and see ye indeed, but perceive not. Make the heart of this people fat, and make their ears heavy, and shut their eyes; lest they see with their eyes, and hear with their ears, and understand with their heart, and convert, and be healed* (Isaiah 6:9-10).

Jesus Christ invoked this prophecy against his generation. He said, *And in them is fulfilled the prophecy of Esaias, which saith, By hearing ye shall hear, and shall not understand ...* (Matthew 13:14). Later, the Apostle Paul repeated the prophecy against the elders of the synagogue in Rome. He said, *... Well spake the Holy Ghost by Esaias the prophet unto our fathers, Saying, Go unto this people and say, Hearing ye shall hear, and shall not understand ...* (Acts 28:25-26). In his epistle to the Romans, Paul addressed the unbelief of Israel in Jesus their Messiah. He wrote, *Israel hath not obtained that which he seeketh for; but the election hath obtained it, and the rest were blinded (According as it is written, God hath given them the spirit of slumber, eyes that they should not see,* *and ears that they should not hear;) unto this day* (Romans 11:7-8).

Paul did not leave his people in despair, however, but promised their redemption at the end of the fulness of the Gentiles. He continued, *Have they stumbled that they should fall? God forbid: but rather through their fall salvation is come unto the Gentiles, for to provoke them to jealousy. Now if the fall of them be the riches of the world, and the diminishing of them the riches of the Gentiles; how much more their fulness? ... For if the casting away of them be the reconciling of the world, what shall the receiving of them be, but life from the dead?* (Romans 11:11-12,15).

When Joseph, governor of Egypt, sent his brothers back to fetch Benjamin, he kept Simeon in prison to assure their return. Prophetically, Joseph represents the rejected Messiah, who in the end, will be revealed to his repentant brethren. Simeon was detained as a prophetic type of Israel's refusal to hear and consider their true Savior.

Also, Psalms 90-100 are the "serpent" psalms and serpents are deaf! Any encyclopedia will explain that serpents cannot hear sounds which are transmitted through the air. They are deaf. Well, why are these psalms related to the serpent? The number 9 is made up of a single letter "teth" meaning "a serpent!"[2] The number 10 is made up of a single letter "yod" meaning "a hand!"[3]

Please note the prophecy of Amos: *Woe unto you that desire the day of the LORD! to what end is it for you? the day of the LORD is darkness, and not light. As if a man did flee from a lion, and a bear met him; or went into the house, and leaned his hand on the wall, and a serpent bit him* (Amos 5:18-19).

In 1948 Israel dispensed with the *lion* (Great Britain). Soon Israel will face the *bear* (the Soviet Union). Israel will also raise up the *house* (Tabernacle of David on the Temple site) and will be bitten on the hand by a *serpent* (the abomination of desolation committed by the antichrist). This is an amazing prophecy hidden in the component numbers that make up the number 90.

PSALM 91

*He that dwelleth in the secret place of the Most High shall
abide under the shadow of the Almighty.*
*I will say of the LORD, He is my refuge and my fortress: my
God; in him will I trust.*
*Surely he shall deliver thee from the snare of the fowler, and
from the noisome pestilence.*
*He shall cover thee with his feathers, and under his wings
shall thou trust* ... (vv. 1-4).

Psalm 91 brings us to the middle of the Tribulation Period — to
the abomination of desolation when the remnant of believing
Jews flee to the mountains to escape the wrath of the antichrist.

Moses dedicated this psalm to the tribe of Levi.[1] It is they who
will lead the 144,000 to restore Temple worship. The Levites will
recoil in horror when the antichrist enters the Temple precinct
and declares himself to be Israel's Messiah. In the New Testament epistle of II Thessalonians, Paul predicts that the *man of sin*
will sit *in the temple of God showing himself that he is God* (II
Thessalonians 2:4). The Levitical priesthood will know enough to
reject the usurper and lead the escape of the remnant from
Jerusalem.

Jesus warned, *When ye therefore shall see the abomination of
desolation, spoken of by Daniel the prophet, stand in the holy
place, (whoso readeth, let him understand:) Then let them which
be in Judea flee into the mountains: Let him which is on the
housetop not come down to take any thing out of his house:
Neither let him which is in the field return back to take his
clothes. And woe unto them that are with child, and to them that
give suck in those days! But pray ye that your flight be not in the
winter, neither on the sabbath day: For then shall be great
tribulation, such as was not since the beginning of the world to
this time, no, nor ever shall be. And except those days should be
shortened, there should no flesh be saved* (Matthew 24:15-22).

Daniel's prediction places the abomination of desolation in the
midst of a seven-year cycle (Shavu'a), the seventieth week of the
series given by Gabriel (Daniel 9:24-27). The angel prophesied a
series of seventy sets of seven year cycles (490 years) *to make an
end of sins, and to make reconciliation for iniquity, and to bring in*

everlasting righteousness, and to seal up the vision and prophecy, and to anoint the most Holy (v. 24). The general consensus of scholars places a gap between the 69th and 70th weeks. The first 69 weeks concluded with the first advent of Christ and his rejection. The destruction of Herod's Temple in 70 A.D. was predicted in verse 26, followed by an indeterminant period of time. ... *the people of the prince that shall come shall destroy the city and the sanctuary; AND THE END thereof shall be with a flood, and unto the end of the war desolations are determined* (v. 26).

Already nineteen centuries have transpired, but events are preparing this generation to see the conclusion of the prophecy. The rebirth of Israel makes the following prediction possible. *He shall confirm the covenant with many for one week: and in the midst of the week he shall cause the sacrifice and the oblation to cease, and for the overspreading of abominations he shall make it desolate, even until the consummation, and that determined shall be poured upon the desolate* (v. 27).

According to the account given in the New Testament book of Revelation, the antichrist will make war with the two witnesses (Moses and Elijah) and will kill them. *Their dead bodies shall lie in the street of the great city, which spiritually is called Sodom and Egypt, where also our Lord was crucified. And they of the people and kindreds and tongues and nations shall see their dead bodies three days and an half, and shall not suffer their dead bodies to be put in graves* (Revelation 11:8-9). Those horrifying events will cause the remnant to flee from the city of Jerusalem.

With his reference to the wings in verse 4, the psalmist alludes to the city of the eagle — the rose-red mountains of Petra, ancient capital of Edom 40 miles south of the Dead Sea. The remnant of the Jews will leave Jerusalem when the antichrist commits the abomination of desolation described in v. 3 as the *snare of the fowler*. The trap is sprung. The *mark of the beast* will be implemented. Revelation 13 describes it as a mark in the right hand or forehead. *He causeth all, both small and great, rich and poor, free and bond, to receive a mark in their right hand, or in their foreheads: and that no man might buy or sell, save he that had the mark, or the name of the beast, or the number of his name* (Revelation 13:16-17).

Today's plans for a one-world monetary system will some day culminate in the attempted enslavement of every person on the planet. The various currencies of the nations are now being prepared for the merger. Credit cards and debit cards are introducing an age of plastic money. Computers are advancing the concept of marks upon commodities — the Universal Product Code (UPC). Someday, a mark will be required upon the consumer! Present plans for a unified monetary system are laying the trap which will be sprung by the antichrist at the abomination of desolation.

> *Thou shalt not be afraid for the terror by night; nor for the arrow that flieth by day;*
> *Nor for the pestilence that walketh in darkness; nor for the destruction that wasteth at noonday.*
> *A thousand shall fall at thy side, and ten thousand at thy right hand; but it shall not come nigh thee.*
> *Only with thine eyes shalt thou behold and see the reward of the wicked.* (vv. 5-8).

Not only will the LORD save the Jewish remnant from the *snare* [trap] *of the fowler,* He will also save them from the *noisome pestilence* [raging epidemic]. As indicated, there will be a world-wide epidemic raging out of control. Moses went on to explain that the disease was a *terror by night* (v. 5) and that it *walketh in darkness* (v. 6). Further, he promised the remnant safety from the disease saying, *Only with thine eyes shalt thou see the reward of the wicked* (v. 8). The passage seems quite descriptive of a new disease, first diagnosed in 1981 called "Acquired Immune Deficiency Syndrome" (AIDS).

AIDS could decimate the population of our planet by the year 2000 if the big bomb doesn't get us first. According to an Associated Press report, "By 1991 everyone will know someone with AIDS." The AP reporter was not aware of Psalm 91 when he wrote his story. In a TIME magazine article dated February 17, 1986, it was reported that 17,000 Americans had contracted the disease and that half of then had died.[2] But on November 3 some eight and one half months later TIME reported 15,000 dead.

The disease had doubled its death toll and was continuing to grow on an exponential curve. The TIME report said, "the figure is expected to rise to nearly 180,000 in five years"[3] By 1991 145,000 Americans with AIDS will need health and other services costing between $8 billion and $16 billion annually.[4] Beyond that, the disease will continue to double about every six months until, within one generation, there should be no one left on the planet.

An ABC Television report said that 27,000 people were infected as of November 1986 and that by 1991 the number will be ten times that amount — 270,000!

I am not suggesting that the psalm demands fulfillment in 1991, but the date of 1991 has been cited by the Associated Press, ABC-TV and by TIME magazine who, in turn, was quoting the U.S. Surgeon General, C. Everett Koop. I believe the prophecy will come to pass as it is predicted in Psalm 91 and is already under development. AIDS is a disease which travels in *darkness* and at *night* and is *a reward of the wicked.* It can only be considered as the judgment of an offended Holy God.

More than half of all diagnosed victims are dead and there is no hope for the other half. It is an absolutely fatal disease running rampant among homosexuals and prostitutes and drug users. Present reports claim that one in every 100 Americans is already infected. The number of victims is doubling every six months. If that continues, then all immoral people in the world will be dead by the turn of the century. Soon all the people who are going to be affected will be.

Jewish rabbis interpret the "destruction that wasteth at noon-day" to be by demonic forces. The Talmud (Shavuos 15b) records that the psalm was used to drive out demons when the Temple Mount was cleansed or expanded. Some call it the "Song of the Demons" because verse 7 reads that thousands and ten thousands of demons will fall. Others call it the "Song of Plagues" because verse 10 promises protection from any plague. This psalm was recited by the Levites during the Temple period in order to cleanse the hitherto unsanctified area of all impure and evil forces."[5] With the psalm used for cleansing the Temple site centuries ago, one can see how the psalm would refer to that ultimate desecration of the holy place.

> *For he shall give his angels charge over thee, to keep thee in all thy ways.*
> *They shall bear thee up in their hands, lest thou dash thy foot against a stone* (vv. 11-12).

Since this is considered a "Song of Demons" who desecrate the Temple site, it is easy to understand how the prince of demons could take Jesus to the pinnacle of the Temple and urge him to jump off. It was the devil, himself, who recited a portion of this psalm. He must have been especially familiar with it. It is this particular psalm which deals with his plans to commit the future abomination of desolation.

With long life will I satisfy him, and shew him my salvation (v. 16).

The Talmudic scholar, Radak, believed that this verse will be fulfilled "at the advent of the Messiah, at the time of the revival of the dead, and at the salvation of the World to Come."[6] Even Jewish scholars view the psalm as a prophecy to be fulfilled at the Second Advent of Messiah.

Psalm 91 prophetically portrays the abomination of desolation — an abominable act committed by the antichrist on the Temple Mount in the midst of the Tribulation Period, at which time the 144,000 will flee to the mountains. The number 91 is made up of two Hebrew letters, "tzade" and "aleph." They comprise part of a root word "tsaw" meaning "to go out, or to be cast out."[7]

PSALM 92

It is a good thing to give thanks unto the LORD, and to sing praises unto thy name, O most High (v. 1).

Psalm 92 portrays a believing remnant who rejoice in the soon-coming destruction of the antichrist and his crumbling world system. Rabbinic sources agree that redemption approaches at this point. The Messianic Era is about to begin. Therefore, this psalm was dedicated to the future world, a "day which is completely Sabbath, for ordinary weekdays will not exist in that totally sacred world."[1] Talmudic scholars have commented on this psalm with the following assessment: "Human history is God's masterpiece. Physical creation was completed at the end of the sixth day, but the spiritual development of mankind will continue until this world ends, at the close of the sixth millennium ... When the panorama of human history is completed, the seventh millennium will be ushered in as the day of everlasting Sabbath. At that time all Adam's descendants will look back and admire God's completed masterpiece."[2] This psalm is designated as the Song of the Day for the Sabbath. It is the third song of Moses and dedicated to Judah, the tribe through which the Messiah will come.

Christian clergy are not alone in believing the world will welcome the kingdom of heaven at the end of six thousand years of human history. Jewish scholars believe it, too. The evidence is overwhelming for a Divine intervention into human affairs. The Son of God will soon appear to establish a heavenly throne on earth. The next thousand years will be paradise!

> *O LORD, how great are thy works! and thy thoughts are very deep.*
> *A brutish man knoweth not; neither doth a fool understand this* (vv. 5-6).

Though he does not understand, the antichrist incurs the wrath of the world when he moves his throne to Jerusalem and demands to be worshipped as God. When his new monetary system is implemented and mankind is forced to accept a mark in the flesh of the right hand or forehead, those who have not been brainwashed by his propaganda machine will balk. I believe the *kings of the east* (Revelation 16:12) will rebel and marshall their forces against the antichrist and his crumbling world government. The greatest war of history will be in the making — Armageddon!

> *When the wicked spring as the grass, and when all the workers of iniquity do flourish; it is that they shall be destroyed for ever*
> *The righteous shall flourish like the palm tree: he shall grow like a cedar in Lebanon* (vv. 7,12).

The wicked flourish like grass and are soon withered. On the other hand, *the righteous flourish like the palm tree* and the *cedar in Lebanon.* God allows the wicked to prosper so they will suffer all the more when they are punished. An example is Haman. Jewish folktales say that his original treachery occurred when he advised Ahasuerus to halt the construction of the Second Temple. At that time he was only a minor official. If God had punished him then, no one would have noticed. Therefore God "caused Haman to prosper and succeed so that he could hang and teach the world a lesson in Divine retribution."[3] That reflects the thinking of scholars about the antichrist as well. The world ruler will be allowed enough proverbial rope to hang himself.

Psalm 92 continues with an assessment of the antichrist, *a brutish man* and a description of the approaching armies for the Battle of Armageddon. The number 92 is made up of two Hebrew letters "tzade" and "beth." They make the word "tsawb" with three possible meanings: 1) "a litter, a covered and curtained couch provided with shafts and used for carrying a single passenger." Here is a perfect description of the triumphal entry of the antichrist onto the Temple Mount. 2) "To establish, a canopy (as a fixture)." The antichrist will enter the sanctuary on the Temple Mount and offer himself as the Messiah of Israel. 3) "A species of lizard." Could this allude to the dragon of Revelation? There is yet another word derived from the number 92. If we add an additional "aleph" it becomes "tsawba" meaning "to muster soldiers for war." The war clouds of Armageddon appear to be brewing.[4]

PSALM 93

The floods have lifted up, O LORD, the floods have lifted up their voice; the floods lift up their waves.
The LORD on high is mightier than the noise of many waters, yea, than the mighty waves of the sea (vv. 3-4).

There are two possibilities for the fulfillment of Psalm 93. Either or both could be under development in the sixth year of the Tribulation Period and conclude in the seventh year. First, the *flood* could be indicative of the world's most overwhelming war. Rashi wrote a thousand years ago that the term is a metaphor for the "enemy hordes who seek to sweep Israel away. They raise their voices and threaten Israel with extinction."[1] Even today, Jewish scholars say this refers to the Gentile nations; who will gather outside the gates of Jerusalem for the final war of Gog and Magog.[2]

The LORD ... is mightier than the noise of many waters, is the subject of Isaiah's prophecy concerning that future war. In describing the battle which introduces the Tribulation Period, Isaiah wrote, *Woe to the multitude of many people, which make a noise like the noise of the seas; and to the rushing of nations, that make a rushing like the rushing of mighty waters! The nations shall rush like the rushing of many waters: but God shall rebuke them, and they shall flee far off, ...* (Isaiah 17:12-13).

On the other hand, the description may well be that of a worldwide flood — not as devastating as Noah's deluge, but global, nevertheless. Such a flood could occur in the last half of the Tribulation Period when God pours out His seven vials of wrath upon an unbelieving world. You may recall Jesus said, *But as the days of Noe* [Noah] *were, so shall also the coming of the Son of man be* (Matthew 24:37). Furthermore, the angel Gabriel spoke of a flood to Daniel when he said: *... and the end thereof shall be with a flood, ...* (Daniel 9:26).

The Revelation account of seven angels pouring out the vials of God's wrath could produce a flood which would inundate all of the coastal areas of the world. As the fourth angel pours out his vial of wrath upon the sun, men are scorched with fire. This could be a nova or explosion of our sun. If such a thing were to occur, it is estimated that temperatures could get as high as six hundred degrees. The heat of the sun could melt the polar caps thus raising the levels of the oceans fifteen to twenty feet. This would produce a worldwide flood.

As the fifth angel pours out his vial of wrath, darkness covers the earth. This could be the result of the same nova. Were our sun to explode, the brilliance would last only a short time, then darkness. Joel described such a scene. *The sun shall be turned into darkness, and the moon into blood, before the great and the terrible day of the LORD come* (Joel 2:31). Isaiah put it this way, *The light of the moon shall be as the light of the sun, and the light of the sun shall be sevenfold ...* (Isaiah 30:26). Yet in another passage, Isaiah depicted the opposite, *... the sun shall be darkened in his going forth, and the moon shall not cause her light to shine* (Isaiah 13:10).

Thus the fourth and fifth vials become clear. When the sun explodes, there could be a short period of heat to melt the polar caps, dry out the rivers (including the Euphrates), and create huge clouds around the world producing hurricanes, tornadoes, and hail stones weighing a hundred pounds apiece. Tectonic pressures will cause earthquakes, level mountains, and move coastlines as described in Revelation 16. One thing is certain, Psalm 93 prepares the world for the day of God's vengeance.

This psalm is a direct continuation of the Psalm 92 and is designated as the "Song of the Day" for the sixth day of the week because on that day God completed His work and donned the grandeur of His creation. The footsteps of Sabbath begin to be heard.[3] It is the fourth psalm of Moses and is dedicated to Benjamin, in whose territory (Jerusalem) the Temple was built. Indeed, the Temple will be rebuilt — apparently in the near future.

PSALM 94

O Lord God, to whom vengeance belongeth; O God, to whom vengeance belongeth, show thyself (v. 1).

This is the day of vengeance when Christ will appear in power and great glory. The term "vengeance" is the key. It was the word used by Isaiah to describe the Second Advent of the Messiah. Jesus quoted from the passage as He stood in the synagogue in Nazareth (Luke 4:18). However, he did not read the concluding phrase. Jesus read, *The Spirit of the Lord GOD is upon me; because the LORD hath anointed me to preach good tidings unto the meek; he hath sent me to bind up the brokenhearted, to proclaim liberty to the captives, and the opening of the prison to them that are bound; To proclaim the acceptable year of the Lord, ...* (Isaish 61:1-2). He did not read, *and the day of vengeance of our God; to comfort all who mourn.*

Why did he not finish reading the passage? Because His First Coming fulfilled the first part of the prophecy; His Second Coming will fulfill the last part of the passage. He will come in vengeance at Armageddon to judge the wicked armies who converge upon Israel. And He will come to comfort the Jews — those who mourn under the world's proposed genocide of the Jewish race.

This is also the term used by Isaiah to describe the glorious appearing of Christ on that day when he comes to judge the world and save Israel: *Who is this that cometh from Edom, with dyed garments from Bozrah? this that is glorious in his apparel, travelling in the greatness of his strength? I that speak in righteousness, mighty to save. Wherefore art thou red in thine apparel, and thy garments like him that treadeth in the winevat? I have trodden the winepress alone; ... For the day of vengeance is*

in mine heart, and the year of my redeemed is come (Isaiah
63:1-4). Isaiah wrote of the coming of Christ to tread the
winepress of the fierceness and wrath of Almighty God on the
DAY OF VENGEANCE. That is the theme of Psalm 94.

> LORD, how long shall the wicked, how long shall the wicked
> triumph?
> How long shall they utter and speak hard things? and all the
> workers of iniquity boast themselves? (vv. 3-4).

The question "How long?" is asked eighteen times in the
Psalms. We have finally arrived at the conclusion of the query.
Why have we reached the end of the questioning? Because the day
has arrived! The answer is come! The Son of God appears in the
clouds of glory with the armies of heaven to establish the kingdom
on planet earth.

Whether this will occur in 1994 is by no means certain. We cannot set dates for future events. We can only note that 1993/94 happens to be a sabbatical year and the 49th year of a Jubilee cycle,
which normally should bring on a Jubilee. According to rabbinical authorities, however, Jubilee has not been observed by
Jews for centuries. Their prayer is for the restoration of all of
Israel and of Temple worship so that they may return to the
observance of Jubilee. For further study on the sabbatical and
Jubilee cycles, see our notes on Psalm 81.

According to Daniel's 70 weeks, the Messiah was cut off after
the 69th week, leaving the 70th week for a future time. Someday,
when that final 70th week concludes, the Messiah will appear to
declare a Jubilee. Whenever, in the future, the Messiah finally
comes, it should be on a Jubilee. One further note, if 1993/94 was
recognized in Israel as a Jubilee, it would be the 40th Jubilee since
Calvary.

As the end of the seven years approaches, the Gentile nations
will seek to destroy the Jewish race. What Hitler attempted, the
world will try to finish. Why? It is not out of reason to consider the
possibility that the antichrist will be of Israelite descent. If the
Son of God came from the tribe of Judah then the man of sin could
emerge from one of the other tribes. Even the rabbis suggested
2,150 years ago that the lost tribe of Dan might produce the antichrist.[1] If so, then the world will blame all of the Jewish race
under a blanket condemnation. Nevertheless, mankind will final-

ly believe the devil's lie that all of the world's ills were caused by the Jews.

God's Chosen People have always been the whipping boy of nations. The only plausible reason for such action by the Gentiles is that satan has them deceived. He is determined to destroy God's plan for paradise on this planet. The devil has been trying to usurp the throne of God ever since his fall. But the final hour will arrive at the end of a seven year Tribulation Period.

> *That thou mayest give him rest from the days of adversity, until the pit be digged for the wicked* (v. 13).

The pit or trap was laid by the antichrist to enslave the human race and destroy Israel. It was introduced in Psalm 88, enacted in Psalm 91, and here the trap backfires. Those who prepared the pit fall into it themselves (see Psalm 88).

> *For the LORD will not cast off his people, neither will he forsake his inheritance* (v. 14).

Israel is not forever forsaken. God's Chosen People were only set aside temporarily because of unbelief that the Gospel might be taken to the Gentiles. All of the Old Testament prophets agree that Gentiles will be allowed to obtain eternal life. If Christianity had not offered salvation to the Gentile nations what would have happened to those millions of people over the past twenty centuries? One day Israel will have to face that question.

Because so much wickedness has been perpetrated upon the Jews in the name of Christ, the Chosen People have a tendency to blame all Christians for the sins of a few wicked men who, under the guise of Christianity, committed those crimes. Those who are quick to condemn all Christians are themselves victims of the same grand delusion that causes Gentiles to blame all Jews for the sins of a few.

Paul explained, *For I would not, brethren, that ye should be ignorant of this mystery, lest ye should be wise in your own conceits; that blindness in part is happened to Israel, until the fulness of the Gentiles be come in. And so all Israel shall be saved: as it is written, There shall come out of Zion the Deliverer, and shall turn away ungodliness from Jacob: For this is my covenant unto them, when I shall take away their sins* (Romans 11:25-27).

God has made covenants with Israel which He will not forsake. The Abrahamic covenant is just as viable today as it ever was. The Jew has been promised the heritage of Eretz (the land) Israel and God will keep His promise. Further, the Davidic Covenant will also be fulfilled. The Scion (offspring) of David will sit upon a throne in Jerusalem and rule the world. Gentile Christianity may not understand all of the spiritual ramifications of God's covenants, but neither do the Jews understand the New Covenant (Testament) made by Jesus Christ. One day soon, however, we all will understand.

This psalm, the fifth written by Moses, was dedicated to the tribe of Gad. According to Jewish tradition, Elijah descended from that tribe. It is he who is expected to come as a forerunner of Christ to prepare the Chosen People for their KING. It is said that Moses composed this psalm as a prayer to bring that day of Messianic redemption and retribution closer. The Talmud designates this psalm as the Song of the Day for the fourth day of the week.[2] Why the fourth? Perhaps because the number four represents the coming of the kingdom. Its meaning is consistent throughout Scripture.

In his book, NUMBER IN SCRIPTURE, E. W. Bullinger wrote: "The number four is made up of three and one... and it denotes... that which follows the revelation of God in the Trinity, namely, His creative works. He is known by the things that are seen. Hence the written revelation commences with the words, 'In-the-beginning God CREATED.' Creation is, therefore, the next thing — the fourth thing, and the number four always has reference to all that is created... It is the number of material completeness. Hence it is the world number..."

Then he listed some examples to show the relationship between the number four and the world. "Four is the number of the great elements — earth, air, fire, and water. Four are the regions of the earth — north, south, east, and west. Four are the divisions of the day — morning, noon, evening, and midnight. Four are the seasons of the year — spring, summer, autumn, and winter."[3]

The kingdom's number is four, as depicted in the four columns which held the veil covering the Holy of holies. How fitting that this psalm should be read on the fourth day of the week.

They gather themselves together against the soul of the

righteous, and condemn the innocent blood.
But the LORD is my defence; and my God is the rock of my
refuge.
And he shall bring upon them their own iniquity, and shall cut
them off in their own wickedness; yea, the LORD our God shall
cut them off (vv. 21-23).

As the armies of the nations gather for the world's worst war, Christ will come to save the day. Jesus said, ... *except those days should be shortened, there should no flesh be saved;* ... (Matthew 24:22). Without the intervention of Jesus Christ, the Jewish race would be brutally eliminated from among the nations. Furthermore, so fierce will be the battle, that if left to themselves, the armies would destroy each other. With the advent of the nuclear age it is easy to see how such a thing would be possible.

John described the arrival of Messiah in the last book of the Christian New Testament, Revelation. *I saw heaven opened, and behold a white horse; and he that sat upon him was called Faithful and True, and in righteousness he doth judge and make war. His eyes were as a flame of fire, and on his head were many crowns; and he had a name written, that no man knew, but he himself. And he was clothed with a vesture dipped in blood: and his name is called The Word of God. And the armies which were in heaven followed him upon white horses, clothed in fine linen, white and clean. And out of his mouth goeth a sharp sword, that with it he should smite the nations: and he shall rule them with a rod of iron; and he treadeth the winepress of the fierceness and wrath of Almighty God. And he hath on his vesture and on his thigh a name written, KING OF KINGS, AND LORD OF LORDS* (Revelation 19:11-16).

Psalm 94 records the dreadful Battle of Armageddon, Christ's appearing on the day of His vengeance, and His judgment meted out. The number 94 is comprised of two Hebrew letters, "tzade" and "daleth." They make up the word "tsad" having two meanings: 1) "side" and 2) "adversary." The Lexicon explains the "side" with a reference to Psalm 91:7, *a thousand shall fall at thy side* and Judges 2:3, *thorns in your sides.* Both are references to Armageddon. "Adversary" certainly smacks of the enemies of Israel who come to destroy the Jewish race. "Tsadaw" is a word meaning, "to lay snares." It is descriptive of the trap into which the antichrist will fall. Psalm 94:13 says, ... *the pit be digged for the wicked.*[4]

The year 1994/95 could be a sabbatical year and the year of the jubilee, though, according to calculations by Maimonides, world Jewry set the sabbatical year for 1993/94. For a study on the prophetic significance of the sabbatical and jubilee cycles, see our notes on Psalm 81.

PSALM 95

> O come, let us sing unto the LORD: let us make a joyful noise
> to the rock of our salvation.
> Let us come before his presence with thanksgiving, and make
> a joyful noise unto him with psalms (vv. 1,2).

The mood changes with Psalms 95-106 from tribulation to rejoicing. The kingdom has come! These twelve psalms follow the coming of the Messiah in Psalm 94. They seem to foreshadow the setting up the government of God. The number 12 represents governmental perfection throughout the Bible. Just as there are 12 tribes of Israel, 12 disciples of Christ, and 12 months to govern the seasons of the year, there are 12 psalms which complete the fourth division of the Psalms. They conclude that portion which compares with the book of Numbers.

In 1893 Dr. E. W. Bullinger published a classic work entitled NUMBER IN SCRIPTURE in which he explained the mystical significance of the number twelve:

"Twelve is a perfect number, signifying perfection of government, or of governmental perfection. It is found as a multiple in all that has to do with rule. The sun rules the day, and the moon and stars which govern the night, do so by their passage through the twelve signs of the Zodiac which completes the great circle of the heavens ... Twelve is the product of 3 (the number of heaven) and 4 (the number of the earth). While seven is composed of 3 added to 4, twelve is 3 multiplied by 4."[1]

It is hard to explain this spiritual concept in words, but at least we can appreciate the perfection of God's mathematical arrangement. For example, there were 12 patriarchs from Seth to Noah and his family. There were 12 generations from Shem to Jacob. There were 12 sons of Jacob which comprised the 12 tribes of Israel. And there were 12 judges after the days of Joshua until the kingdom was established under the reign of Saul.

The number 12 is associated with the great Temple of Solomon, in contrast to the Tabernacle which was associated with the number five. This agrees with **grace** which shines in the Tabernacle, and with the **glory** of the kingdom which is displayed in the Temple.

The New Testament follows the same principle. There were 12 Apostles, 12 foundations of the New Jerusalem, 12 gates, 12 pearls, and 12 angels. The measurement of the New Jerusalem will be 12,000 furlongs while the height of the wall will be 144 cubits (which is comprised of 12 x 12). Furthermore, 144,000 Jews will be made up of 12,000 men from the 12 tribes of Israel.''

These are but a few of the many examples in the Bible which underscore the number 12 to be of special spiritual significance. The 12 psalms which follow the coming of Christ point up the precision and magnificence to be found in the prophetic pattern.

Psalms 95-106 highlight certain aspects of His appearance and the establishment of His kingdom. They reflect upon the time when Jesus will judge the nations, rid the world of war, reorganize the government, remove the curse, and return paradise to the planet.

> *For the LORD is a great God, and a great King above all ... (v. 3).*

This is the sixth of eleven psalms composed by Moses. He dedicated it to Isaachar.[2] In Psalm 95, we can see the coming Redeemer as the same one who made the heavens and the earth.

> *In his hand are the deep places of the earth: the strength of the hills is his also.*
> *The sea is his, and he made it: and his hands formed the dry land.*
> *O come, let us worship and bow down: let us kneel before the LORD our maker (vv. 4-6).*

Then comes the admonition for the Jewish people to repent and declare Jesus Christ as their Messiah. The psalmist implores Israel not to be guilty of doing what their forefathers did.

> *Today if ye will hear his voice,*
> *Harden not your heart, as in the provocation,*
> *Unto whom I sware in my wrath that they should not enter into my rest (vv. 7,8,11).*

Armageddon is raging. The genocide of the Jewish race is imminent. Armies from around the world have converged upon Jerusalem to destroy every Jew from the face of the earth. No nation stands beside Israel. None come to their defense. In the darkness of the hour, the Israeli people will turn to the one person whom they had rejected. They will literally pray to the one who was nailed to a cross. When they do, they will be redeemed!

Psalm 95 rejoices over the appearance of Christ to save the day. The number 95 is comprised of two Hebrew letters "tzade" and "he." They are part of a combination of several exciting words. As "tsahab" they mean "glitter, be golden in color." As "tsahal" they mean "to shout for joy." As "tsohar" they mean 1) "to appear, to come forth, to reveal oneself, splendor" and 2) "to squeeze out oil (in a press)." When Christ reveals Himself in splendor and glitter, to tread the winepress of His wrath, Israel will shout for joy![3]

PSALM 96

O sing unto the LORD a new song: sing unto the LORD, all the earth.
Declare his glory among the heathen, ...
... for he cometh to judge the earth: he shall judge the world with righteousness, and the people with his truth (vv. 1,3,13).

Moses' seventh psalm was dedicated to Zabulon. The *new song* compares with Revelation 5. The Lamb approaches the throne, takes the title deed to earth and breaks the seals. The redeemed sing, *Thou art worthy to take the book, and to open the seals thereof: for thou wast slain, and hast redeemed us to God by thy blood out of every kindred, and tongue, and people, and nation; And hast made us unto our God kings and priests: and we shall reign on the earth* (Revelation 5:9-10).

Psalm 96 describes His coming to ... *judge the world with righteousness, and the people with his truth* (Psalm 96:13). The number 96 is made up of two Hebrew letters, "tzade" and "vav." They form a two-letter word "tsav" meaning "precept, injunction, commandment." The Revelation account says, ... *out of his mouth goeth a sharp sword* (Revelation 19:15). The Apostle Paul described the day, ... *then shall that Wicked be revealed, whom the Lord shall consume with the spirit of his mouth, and shall destroy with the brightness of his coming* (II Thessalonians 2:8).[1]

PSALM 97

The LORD reigneth; let the earth rejoice; ... (v. 1).

Moses dedicated this psalm to the children of Joseph — Ephriam and Manasses.[1] Christ is praised as Redeemer and King. The remaining verses describe the battle scene at Armageddon.

> *Clouds and darkness are round about him: righteousness and judgment are the habitation of his throne.*
> *A fire goeth before him, and burneth up his enemies round about.*
> *His lightnings enlightened the world: the earth saw, and trembled.*
> *The hills melted like wax ...*
> *... all the people see his glory ...*
> *... high above all the earth: ... (vv. 2-6,9).*

As the armies of the world converge upon Jerusalem for their deadly work, the sun will turn as black as sackcloth of ashes. In the darkened sky above Jerusalem, the clouds will roll back like a scroll — as a mighty curtain upon a stage — to reveal the majesty and glory of the ruler of the universe. Angels will attend His grand entrance. The armies of heaven will be gathered on His right and on His left. As He approaches the planet, the brilliance of His glory will dazzle the people. An angry world will be astounded as they see the mighty God of creation come to the defense of the Jewish people.

PSALM 98

> *O sing unto the LORD a new song; for he hath done marvellous things: ...*
> *With trumpets and sound of cornet make a joyful noise before the LORD, the King (vv. 1,6).*

According to Jewish writings, Moses, the author of this psalm, dedicated it to the tribe of Nepthalim. Again, the *new song* compares with Revelation 14:3 where the Jewish remnant praise the Lamb with a song which *no man could learn* but those who are redeemed.

> *He hath remembered his mercy and his truth toward the house of Israel: all the ends of the earth have seen the salvation of our God* (v. 3).

This verse compares with John's salutation to the Apocalypse. *Behold, he cometh with clouds; and every eye shall see him, and they also which pierced him: and all kindreds of the earth shall wail because of him* (Revelation 1:7).

> *Let the sea roar,*
> *Let the floods clap their hands:*
> *Before the LORD; for he cometh to judge the earth: with righteousness shall he judge the world, ...* (vv. 7-9).

When He comes, the Savior will establish His throne on Mount Moriah, site of the great Jewish temples. The seat of His world government will be the same mountain where the antichrist committed the abomination of desolation. There Christ will bring all nations before His bar of justice.

Psalm 98 describes His spectacular appearance, ... *all the ends of the earth have seen the salvation of our God* (Psalm 98:3). The number 98 is made up of two Hebrew letters, "tzade" and "cheth." They spell the word "tsach" meaning "dazzling, bright white" another magnificent description of the glorious appearing of Messiah. Another meaning, "clear heat," is a term used in Isaiah 18:4 alluding to the Battle of Gog and Magog.[1] It describes the judgment, as a *clear heat* which shrivels the plants. In like manner, the Savior will destroy the antichrist ... *with the brightness of his coming* (II Thessalonians 2:8). The prophet Zechariah described the scene most vividly, ... *this shall be the plague wherewith the LORD will smite all the people that have fought against Jerusalem; Their flesh shall consume away while they stand upon their feet, and their eyes shall consume away in their holes, and their tongue shall consume away in their mouth* (Zechariah 14:12).

PSALM 99

The Lord reigneth; let the people tremble: he sitteth between the cherubims; let the earth be moved (v. 1).

Moses dedicated his tenth psalm to the tribe of Dan. It speaks of the future Day of Judgment, "when God will call all of the depraved nations to task."[1] Scholars have speculated upon the possibility that Dan would produce the antichrist. The dying Jacob predicted that Dan would *judge his people* (Genesis 49:16). The symbol of a snake (many-headed Hydra) was attributed to him. It is the symbol used in Revelation to describe the kingdom of the antichrist. It is Rahab the Dragon of Psalm 87:4 and 89:10.

What is so remarkable about the number 99 is that it is comprised of two 9's. The number 9 is "tzade" meaning "a serpent." Two of them (9 and 9) represent a two-headed serpent! Though the number 99 has no meaning in the Lexicon, it still has a definite symbolic and prophetic significance.

The promise was made to Eve that the seed of the woman would bruise the serpent's head (Genesis 3:15). The kingdom is thus established as Christ takes His rightful place beneath the cherubim which once guarded the Ark of the Covenant.

PSALM 100

Make a joyful noise unto the LORD, all ye lands.
Serve the Lord with gladness: come before his presence with singing.
Enter into his gates with thanksgiving, and into his courts with praise: be thankful unto him, and bless his name (vv. 1,2,4).

"Rabbi Hirsch explains that this song of thanksgiving deals with the gratitude that will be due to God in the Messianic Age, when the world has reached perfection. Psalm 100 serves as a finale to the previous psalms concerning the approach of the Messianic Era[1]

Moses dedicated this eleventh and last psalm to the tribe of Asher. These verses declare the Kingship of Christ and the blessings of the kingdom age. Messiah sits upon the throne of this world to establish a golden age for the human race.

Psalm 100 happens to be the 19th letter of the Hebrew alphabet and thus concludes the 19 hundreds! (Don't miss that combination of 19 and 100 which makes **nineteen hundred**.) The number 100 is made up of a single Hebrew letter "koph" and denotes "the hole of an axe."[2] Perhaps it has a reference to the description, *out of his mouth goeth a sharp sword, that with it he should smite the nations* (Revelation 19:15). By the way, please note that Christ's appearance in Revelation happens to be in chapter number 19! Could that also refer to the 1900's? At this point there is a turn in the meanings of the next six numbers. The earlier six (91, 92, 94, 95, 96, and 98) describe the glory of His coming, but the latter six (100, 101, 102, 104, 105, 106) reveal His judgment upon a sinful world.

PSALM 101

I will sing of mercy and judgment: unto thee, O LORD, will I sing (v. 1).

The first six psalms (95-100) praise the appearance of the King of kings. The next six psalms (101-106) set about to establish the law of God in His new government — making a total of twelve psalms. Just as there are twelve months to govern the year, twelve sons of Israel, and twelve disciples of Christ, there are twelve psalms which oversee the establishment of the kingdom.

I will behave myself wisely in a perfect way ... I will walk within my house with a perfect heart.
I will set no wicked thing before mine eyes: ...
A froward heart shall depart from me: I will not know a wicked person (vv. 2-4).

David seems to lift himself above the realm of time and into the future — to the kingdom age where he describes the perfection of the human race. He not only shuns the company of the wicked, but is simply ignorant of evil. His heart has no knowledge of it. According to rabbinic scholars, "this resembles Adam before the sin. He was totally oblivious of evil and could not even imagine it."[1]

> *Mine eyes shall be upon the faithful of the land, that they may dwell with me: he that walketh in a perfect way, he shall serve me* (v. 6).

The inhabitants of earth's population determine to live righteously in a new and godly world. No longer will men plot to deceive. No longer will wickedness be tolerated. All will determine to live holy and godly lives — pleasing to Christ the King.

> *He that worketh deceit shall not dwell within my house: he that telleth lies shall not tarry in my sight. I will early destroy all the wicked of the land* (vv. 7-8).

The Jewish Targum maintains that this refers to the "world to come." The kingdom will be established by Christ. He will judge the nations and eliminate evil. A mighty angel will remove satan from the scene by casting him into the *bottomless pit* (Revelation 20:3). Men will no longer be tempted to sin.

Psalm 101 refers to judgment, *I will early destroy all the wicked out of the land* (Psalm 101:8). The number 101 is made up of two Hebrew letters "koph" and "aleph." They comprise the word "kay" meaning "to vomit."[2] What a description of judgment! It was to the wicked apostate church of Laodicea that Christ promised, *I will spue thee out of my mouth* (Revelation 3:16).

PSALM 102

> *Hear my prayer, O LORD, and let my cry come unto thee.*
>
> *Hide not thy face from me in the day when I am in trouble; incline thine ear unto me: in the day when I call answer me speedily.*
>
> *For my days are consumed like smoke, and my bones are burned as an hearth.*
>
> *My heart is smitten, and withered like grass; so that I forget to eat my bread.*
>
> *By reason of the voice of my groaning my bones cleave to my skin. I am like a pelican of the wilderness; I am like an owl of the desert.*
>
> *I watch, and am as a sparrow alone upon the housetop.*

> *Mine enemies reproach me all the day; and they that are mad against me are sworn against me.*
> *For I have eaten ashes like bread, and mingled my drink with weeping,*
> *Because of thine indignation and thy wrath: for thou hast lifted me up, and cast me down.*
> *My days are like a shadow that declineth; and I am withered like grass* (vv. 1-11).

The psalm was written as a prophecy of the far future. It is called *a prayer of the afflicted when he is overwhelmed.* Note the heart-cry of this prophetic prayer, and keep in mind that its fulfillment has come in this generation.

These verses appear to describe the suffering of the Jewish people from 1939 through 1945. Verse 3 is especially descriptive: *For my days are consumed like smoke, and my bones are burned.*

During the days of Nazi Germany, Jewish people were rounded up and sent off to concentration camps where they were unmercifully slaughtered. Six million Jews (a third of the world's Jewish population) were burned in the gas furnaces of Hitler. Their days were consumed like smoke, and their bones were burned! What a description of this generation! Remember please, the psalmist wrote, *This shall be written for the generation to come* (v. 18). Further, he said it will be in an appointed time — a *set time* (v. 13).

> *But thou, O LORD, shalt endure forever; and thy remembrance unto all generations.*
> *Thou shalt arise, and have mercy upon Zion: for the time to favor her, yea, the set time, is come* (vv. 12,13).

After the prophecy of the Holocaust (described in the first eleven verses) the psalmist wrote that the Lord will have mercy upon Zion, and upon her people. That must surely be this generation, for the first eleven verses (almost half of the chapter) is spent describing the terrible plight of the Jew before he begins to describe the events which follow.

When this appointed time is come men will begin to dig in the rubbish heaps to uncover the ancient building stones, pottery, utensils, inscriptions, coins, and tools. This, we have seen with the development of archaeology.

> *Thou shalt arise, and have mercy upon Zion: for the time to*

*favor her, yea, the set time, is come. For thy servants take
pleasure in her stones, and favor the dust thereof* (vv. 13,14).

In 1798 Napoleon Bonaparte led his army into the valley of the
Nile conquering the land of Egypt. In August of the following
year, while the French army was repairing some fortifications
north of the town of Rosetta, one of the workers digging in the
sand, unearthed a stone with some strange writing on it.

Napoleon, delighted with the find, had it brought to Cairo to
have it copied. There were three languages engraved upon the
tablet. The first section contained Egyptian hieroglyphics. The
second contained a type of Egyptian script, and the third was
written in Greek. It was the decree of an ancient Egyptian
priesthood honoring Ptolemy Epiphanes, who lived and reigned
200 years before the birth of Christ.

For the first time in modern history a clue was found to help
historians read the ancient language of Egyptian hieroglyphics.
Napoleon called it, "the Rosetta Stone." When the British
defeated Napoleon in 1802, it was taken to the British Museum,
where it is kept to this day. With the discovery of the Rosetta
Stone, the science of archaeology was born.[1]

By digging up the rubbish heaps of the past — the ruins of ancient cities — historians can get a glimpse of the language, the
culture, the coins, the economic system, the customs, and the
religion of ancient civilizations.

The science of archaeology was conceived in the womb of world
history less than 200 years ago. It was not until this century that
archaeology was perfected with a system of charting and catalog-
ing the various levels of a dig. Archaeology is a relatively new
science. Yet, it was predicted in the Bible 3,000 years ago! A
perfect description is given in Psalm 102.

> *Thou shalt arise, and have mercy upon Zion: for the time to
> favour her, yea, the set time is come.*
> *For thy servants take pleasure in her stones, and favour the
> dust thereof.*
> *When the LORD shall build up Zion, he shall appear in his
> glory.*
> *This shall be written for the generation to come: ...* (vv.
> 13,14,16,18).

According to the psalmist, these verses were written as prophecies of that which would occur in the far future, when God

shall have mercy upon Zion, and is designated for a time in the future, *yea,* wrote the psalmist, *the set time* (v. 13). The incredible prophecy describes that future generation when God shall arise and have favor upon Zion. *For thy servants take pleasure in her stones, and favour the dust thereof.* That is a perfect description of the science of archaeology.

These verses designate the century in which we live as that special time — that *set time* — when God will arise and have mercy upon Jerusalem. In fact, verse 16 says that the Lord will *build up Zion.* Furthermore, in that generation, *he shall appear in his glory!* All of this — the building up of the city of Jerusalem (Biblical Zion) and the appearing in His glory will be at a time when men will *take pleasure in her* [Jerusalem] *stones, and favour the dust thereof.*

According to STRONG's CONCORDANCE, the Hebrew word for stones is pronounced "eh-ben."[2] It refers to a building stone! Gesenius wrote that it was "a stone of any kind, whether rough or polished, very large or very small, used of the foundation stone of a house."[3] The psalmist looked forward to a day when the Jewish people would take pleasure in the ancient building stones of old Jerusalem.

How do we know this refers to archaeology? The last part of the sentence says that they will *favour the dust thereof.* According to STRONG's CONCORDANCE, the word *dust* is "aw-fawr" which refers to "clay, earth, mud, ashes, ground, mortar, or [most important] rubbish."[4]

What a perfect description of the digging sites for the science of archaeology! Frankly, the archaeologist delights in digging in the rubbish heaps of the ancient past.

According to Gesenius, "aw-fawr" (translated dust) refers to "clay or loam, of which walls are made — a heap of rubbish, very rarely of fine dust, such as is blown by the wind."[5]

The psalmist wrote of a generation in the far future, when the Lord would appear in His glory. It will be at a time when the Lord shall build up Zion. It is described as a generation when men will take pleasure in her ancient building stones, and favor the very clay and rubbish from which those ancient buildings were made.

Yes, the science of archaeology was predicted 3,000 years ago. Psalm 102:14 was to see its fulfillment in the 19th and 20th centuries. It all began, quite by accident, when a French soldier, digging in the sand near Cairo, uncovered an ancient stone with a message written in three languages, giving the world a window into the past.

In the years following, there were hundreds of groups organized to dig at various sites throughout the Middle East.

Jews stand before the ancient stones at the Western Wall uncovered by the archaeologists and pray for the coming of Messiah. One day, God will *regard the prayer of the destitute, and not despise their prayer* (v. 17). He will *hear the groaning of the prisoner* and will *loose those that are appointed to death* (v. 20). The Savior will come in power and great glory to establish the kingdom of heaven on planet earth.

He shall reign for a thousand years. No king has ever lived so long. But, according to the psalmist, His *years are throughout all generations* (v. 24).

The last four verses of the chapter deal with those events which will take place after the millennial reign of Christ. The psalmist wrote:

> *Of old hast thou laid the foundation of the earth: and the heavens are the work of thy hands.*
> *They shall perish, but thou shalt endure: yea, all of them shall wax old like a garment; as a vesture shalt thou change them, and they shall be changed:*
> *But thou art the same, and thy years shall have no end.*
> *The children of thy servants shall continue, and their seed shall be established before thee* (vv. 25-28).

The earth and the heavens will not always be as they are. Succombing to the laws of thermodynamics, the elements will need to be changed. Isaiah wrote, *I create new heavens and a new earth: and the former shall not be remembered, nor come into mind* (Isaiah 65:17). John wrote, *I saw a new heaven and a new earth: for the first heaven and the first earth were passed away* (Revelation 21:1). Though the earth and the heavens pass away, God's Chosen People will endure. *The children of thy servants shall continue, and their seed shall be established* (v. 28).

I believe we have reached that momentous time in history when the Lord *shall appear in his glory* (v. 16). According to the psalmist, four major predictions will attend that glorious event —

the unmerciful suffering of the Jewish people; their deliverance and return to Israel; His building up of Jerusalem; and the development of archaeology. We live in that generation when men *take pleasure in her stones, and favour the dust thereof* (v. 14).

Psalm 102 denotes a similar connotation. Christ will hear the cry of the oppressed Chosen People and will come to avenge them. The number 102 is made up of two Hebrew letters "koph" and "beth." Together they make the word "kab," which refers to a "scoop" used to measure dry things. The wicked will be measured in God's scales. They are also used in the word "kabab," meaning "to curse." The wicked will be *weighed in the balances, and ... found wanting* (Daniel 5:27).[7]

PSALM 103

> *Bless the LORD, O my soul: and all that is within me, bless his holy name.*
> *Bless the LORD, O my soul, and forget not all his benefits:*
> (vv. 1-2).

The *soul* of man makes him different from all other creatures. The foundational principles of Christianity make us aware of the soul — that we might nurture this precious possession. We desire to be worthy to stand before God and praise Him.

David repeats the refrain five times in Psalms 103 and 104, *Bless the LORD, O my soul.* They are found in Psalm 103:1, 2, and 22; also in Psalm 104:1, and 35. They compare with the five books of Moses and in turn depict the five stages of development for a soul.[1]

The Genesis refrain (Psalm 103:1) compares with the gestation period of the fetus. Only God could form such a miraculous thing inside its mother and prepare the soul for independent existence.[2]

The Exodus refrain (Psalm 103:2) compares with birth when the soul is released from its mother's womb to discover God's creation.[3]

The Leviticus refrain (Psalm 103:22) compares with the spiritual development of the soul. Life is a struggle between good and evil. The body becomes a temple, complete with a Holy of holies.[4]

The Numbers refrain (Psalm 104:1) compares with the struggle between good and evil. This is manifested in the heartaches and tribulations of life. The soul gains strength to resist evil.[5]

The Deuteronomy refrain (Psalm 104:35) compares with the fifth and final stage when the soul is released from the body at death and returns to God who made it.[6]

This refrain concludes with a **Hallelujah** the first of four which ends the Numbers section of the Psalms. They, in turn, compare with the four **Hallelujahs** of Revelation 19:1,3,4, and 6. (These are discussed at length in the chapter, The Hallelujah Psalms.)

> *Who forgiveth all thine iniquities; who healeth all thy diseases;*
> *Who redeemeth thy life from destruction; who crowneth thee with lovingkindness and tender mercies;*
> *Who satisfieth thy mouth with good things; so that thy youth is renewed like the eagle's* (vv. 3-5).

We can see a continued development in the kingdom age as the Lord forgives all sins and heals all diseases:

> *As far as the east is from the west, so far hath he removed our transgressions from us* (v. 12).

The kingdom age will be a glorious time of spiritual ecstasy. Heaven will come to earth. We *shall reign with him* [Christ] for *a thousand years* (Revelation 20:6). The term *removed* is "nasa" in Hebrew and means "to lift away." One suspicions more than a coincidence in America's space program being dubbed "NASA" for the National Aronautics and Space Administration.

> *The Lord hath prepared his throne in the heavens; and his kingdom ruleth over all* (v. 19).

The throne of God is established upon this planet and the Messiah sets about to declare His kingdom.

> *Bless the LORD, ye his angels, that excel in strength, that do
> his commandments, hearkening unto the voice of his word.*
> *Bless ye the LORD, all ye his hosts; ye ministers of his, that do
> his pleasure.*
> *Bless the LORD, all his works in all places of his dominion:
> bless the LORD, O my soul* (vv. 20-22).

We are told that the angels will assist in setting up the kingdom;
we, His ministers, will do His pleasure; and His works will show
forth His praise. This Leviticus refrain *bless the LORD, O my
soul* concludes Psalm 103, but a comparable refrain opens on the
very next verse — Psalm 104:1 and moves directly into the
Numbers refrain (as suggested).

PSALM 104

> *Bless the Lord, O my soul. O Lord my God, thou art very
> great; thou art clothed with honour and majesty* (v. 1).

This fourth occurrence of the phrase, *Bless the LORD, O my
soul* (v. 1) compares with the Mosaic book of Numbers and
describes the coming of Christ at the conclusion of the Tribulation
Period with power and great glory. This Numbers refrain (v. 1)
also compares with the soul's struggle between good and evil. It is
manifested in the trials and difficulties of life.

> *Who coverest thyself with light as with a garment: who stret-
> chest out the heavens like a curtain:*
> *Who layeth the beams of his chambers in the waters: who
> maketh the clouds his chariot: who walketh upon the wings of
> the wind:*
> *Who maketh his angels spirits; his ministers a flaming fire:*
> *Who laid the foundations of the earth, that it should not be
> removed for ever* (vv. 2-5).

David describes the beauty of Eden and predicts the glory of the
kingdom age. The six days of creation with all of its activity brings forth praise to God. It is a magnificent planet made in
perfect harmony.

> *He appointed the moon for seasons: the sun knoweth his going
> down* (v. 19).

Psalm 104 was chosen to be the "Song of the Day" — used on Rosh Chodesh, the first day of each month. Perhaps it was picked because David made a reference to the new moon in verse 19. Each month in the Jewish calendar begins with the new moon.

> *The glory of the LORD shall endure for ever: the LORD shall rejoice in his works.*
> *He looketh on the earth, and it trembleth: he toucheth the hills, and they smoke.*
> *I will sing unto the LORD as long as I live: I will sing praise to my God while I have my being.*
> *My meditation of him shall be sweet: I will be glad in the LORD* (vv. 31-34).

It is believed that David's very purpose for existing was to sing praises to God. In the kingdom age all of the redeemed will praise Him.

> *Let the sinners be consumed out of the earth, and let the wicked be no more. Bless thou the Lord, O my soul. Praise ye the Lord* [**Hallelujah**] (v. 35).

This fifth occurrence of the phrase *Bless the LORD, O my soul* (v. 35) compares with the Mosaic book of Deuteronomy and implies the fifth and final stage of the soul's development. The soul is released from the body at death and returns to God who made it.

These five refrains in Psalms 103 and 104 also compare with the prophetic scenario laid out in the five books of the Psalms. The fifth of which depicts the kingdom age:

> *Let the sinners be consumed out of the earth, and let the wicked be no more. Bless thou the LORD, O my soul. Praise ye the LORD* [**Hallelujah**] (v. 35).

Here begins the first in a series of four **Hallelujahs** which declare the end of this section of the Psalms — that portion called the Numbers book. These **Hallelujahs** compare with the four **Hallelujahs** of Revelation 19:1,3,4, and 6. Psalm 104 concludes with **Hallelujah**. Psalm 105 concludes with **Hallelujah**, and the last psalm of the section, Psalm 106, both begins and ends with **Hallelujah**.

Psalm 104 extols the majesty and power of God and the humility

of man while saying, *Let the sinners be consumed out of the earth
...* (Psalm 104:35). The number 104 is comprised of the Hebrew
letters "koph" and "daleth" root of the word "kadad" meaning
"to bow the head, to bow before God."[1] In that day, *... every knee
shall bow, and every tongue shall swear* ... allegiance to Him! In
that day, *all that are incensed against him shall be ashamed*
(Isaiah 45:23,24).

PSALM 105

> *O GIVE thanks unto the LORD; call upon his name: make
> known his deeds among the people.*
> *Sing unto him, sing psalms unto him: talk ye of all his won-
> drous works.*
> *Glory ye in his holy name: let the heart of them rejoice that
> seek the LORD.*
> *Seek the LORD, and his strength: seek his face evermore* (vv.
> 1-4).

"This psalm was composed on the day King David brought the
Holy Ark from its temporary quarters in the home of Obed Edom
to the holy city of Jerusalem, where it was installed with great
ceremony and honor ... The Levites sang Psalm 105 each morning
and Psalm 96 each evening while the Holy Ark was housed in a
temporary tent in Jerusalem. When Solomon built the Temple
and the Ark was placed in its permanent abode, a perpetual order
of songs was established. These were the Songs of the Day which
were related to the respective days of the week and to each
special festival."[1]

> *He hath remembered his covenant for ever, the word which he
> commanded to a thousand generations.*
> *Which covenant he made with Abraham, and his oath unto
> Isaac;*
> *And confirmed the same unto Jacob for a law, and to Israel for
> an everlasting covenant:*
> *Saying, Unto thee will I give the land of Canaan, the lot of your
> inheritance:* (vv. 8-11).

David began with the story of Abraham and followed the history
of the children of Israel with the stories of Joseph, the plagues
upon Pharoah, the Exodus and the wilderness journey. In the

following psalm (106) he picked up the story of Israel's unbelief at Sinai and followed the history of their rebellion through to the great Diaspora — the dispersion of the nation to live among Gentiles. He concludes the Numbers book with a prayer for deliverance (Psalm 106:47) from among the Gentiles. This will be fulfilled at Armageddon with the coming of Messiah.

When Christ returns He will establish His throne in Jerusalem; complete His restoration of the land of Israel as an inheritance for the Jewish people; and extend His kingdom throughout the world. At this point, He reminds the Chosen People that His covenant with Abraham will continue to a thousand generations.

We do not understand nor can we comprehend the vast implications of this promise. We see only 1,000 years for the millennial reign of Christ, yet He will keep His promise to the Jewish nation for at least 1,000 generations. That could extend anywhere from 20,000 to 100,000 years. And beyond that, who knows? ... *Eye hath not seen, nor ear heard, neither have entered into the heart of man, the things which God hath prepared for them that love him* (I Corinthians 2:9).

> *For he remembered his holy promise, and Abraham his servant.*
> *And he brought forth his people with joy, and his chosen with gladness:*
> *And gave them the lands of the heathen: and they inherited the labour of the people;*
> *That they might observe his statutes, and keep his laws. Praise ye the Lord* (vv. 42-45).

He concludes Psalm 105 with **Hallelujah** and immediately opens Psalm 106 with the same word, **Hallelujah** — Praise ye the Lord.

Psalm 105 reminds Israel of the Abrahamic Covenant — God's oath to give them the Promised Land and declares, *He* [God] *hath remembered his covenant* (Psalm 105:8). The number 105 is made up of "koph" and "he." As "kawhaw" meaning "to be blunted" we are reminded of Isaiah's prophecy, ... *they shall beat their swords into plowshares, and their spears into pruninghooks: nation shall not lift up sword against nation, neither shall they learn war any more* (Isaiah 2:4). As "Kawhal" meaning "assembly, congregation, multitude," we are reminded of the group of nations who will be judged and of those who will inherit the new kingdom of Christ.[11]

PSALM 106

Praise ye the LORD [Hallelujah] *O give thanks unto the Lord; for he is good: for his mercy endureth for ever* (v. 1).

This refrain compares with Psalm 100:5. *For the LORD is good; his mercy is everlasting; and his truth endureth to all generations.* This passage concludes the first six psalms (95-100) while the above refrain (v. 2) concludes the last half of these twelve psalms (95-106). They both represent the King of kings who will establish the kingdom of heaven in Jerusalem.

Who can utter the mighty acts of the LORD? who can shew forth all his praise?
Blessed are they that keep judgment, and he that doeth righteousness at all times.
Remember me, O LORD, with the favour that thou bearest unto thy people: O visit me with thy salvation;
That I may see the good of thy chosen, that I may rejoice in the gladness of thy nation, that I may glory with thine inheritance (vv. 2-5).

Psalm 106 concludes the Numbers section of the psalms which deal with the tribulations of the Israeli nation leading up to the coming of the Messiah and the establishment of His glorious kingdom.

Many times did he deliver them: but they provoked him with their counsel, and were brought low for their iniquity (v. 43).

These verses reflect upon the sins of Israel during those forty years in the wilderness and discuss the reasons why God had scattered them throughout the nations of the world. It is an explanation of why the Jewish people have had to suffer those judgments found in the Numbers section of the Psalms.

Save us, O LORD our God, and gather us from among the heathen, to give thanks unto thy holy name, and to triumph in thy praise.
Blessed be the LORD God of Israel from everlasting to everlasting: and let all the people say, Amen. Praise ye the LORD (vv. 47-48).

Here is the concluding *Amen* of the seven to be found in the Psalms (see the chapter, The Prophetic Amen) and the concluding **Hallelujah** of the four (see the chapter, The Hallelujah Psalms) which concludes the Numbers section.

Twelve psalms (95-106) follow the coming of the Messiah at Armageddon. They declare the setting up of the government of God. Remember, "twelve" represents governmental perfection throughout the Bible. Just as there are twelve tribes to the children of Israel, twelve disciples who carried out the great commission of our Lord, and twelve months to govern the seasons of the year, there are twelve psalms which represent the establishment of the kingdom of heaven. It must be no coincidence that twelve psalms follow the coming of Christ at Armageddon to declare the establishment of His government.

Psalm 106 concludes the Numbers portion of the Psalms with a humbling reminder of how the Chosen People have provoked the anger of the Lord, only to be forgiven and avenged. The number 106 denotes the conclusion of judgment upon the wicked. It is comprised of two letters, "koph" and "vav" which make up the word "kav" meaning "a rule for measuring." Men will be judged by the rules. There will be a basis or rule of law by which Christ will judge. As the word "kavkav," judgment will be "meted out." As "kow," another word for "vomit," the judgment will be concluded and the Messiah will get on with the job of setting up the kingdom as depicted in the Deuteronomy book, Psalms 107-150! [1]

THE
DEUTERONOMY
PSALMS

INTRODUCTION TO
THE DEUTERONOMY PSALMS

The Psalms were compiled into five books corresponding with the Pentateuch — namely the Genesis book (covering Psalms 1-41), the Exodus book (covering Psalms 42-72), the Leviticus book (covering Psalms 73-89), the Numbers book (covering Psalms 90-106), and the Deuteronomy book (covering Psalms 107-150).

Furthermore, we have taken note that David compiled books one and four, while Solomon, his son, compiled books two and three. The fifth book was probably compiled by Ezra after the Babylonian captivity. Each psalm was written separately and compiled into their various divisions.

Psalm 1 introduces that special generation which would see the birth of the man-child, Israel (*Blessed is the man*) and the budding of the fig tree, Israel (*... he shall be like a tree ...*).

Psalm 2 seems to imply year two, Psalm 3, year three, etc., with each successive psalm appearing to describe the plight of the Jewish people in each succeeding year of the twentieth century (at least to the present). Again, it is not our purpose to set dates. We can only say that the future psalms seem to set a trend for those spectacular events which we feel will someday come to pass.

We must say that the seven-year Tribulation Period appears to be vividly described in Psalms 88 through 94, but hasten to add, we are not suggesting that the Tribulation must occur in those years corresponding with the number of each psalm. It is an astounding study, to say the least!

The next twelve psalms (95-106) give a detailed account of the judgments of Armageddon, the appearance of Christ and the establishment of His kingdom. They refer to a time when the Savior will come to judge the nations, rid the world of war, reorganize the government, remove the curse, and return paradise to the planet.

The fifth book of the Psalms was compiled after the Babylonian captivity (some five hundred years after David and Solomon). However, there was a period of five centuries separating the gathering of the first four books of the Psalms from the compilation of the fifth book. It was, nevertheless, necessary that a fifth book should be compiled to correspond with the fifth book of Moses, called Deuteronomy.

This last set is comprised of forty-four psalms which declare the glory of His kingdom. In them are references to various events which were recorded in the first 106 psalms. It seems a group of psalms would be collected which would enlarge upon certain aspects of the last century. Psalms 107-112 reveal an expression of gratitude by those who endured the dangers of the Tribulation Period and were rescued. Psalm 113 adds praise to the theme and is also included in the Hallel (praise) psalms (113-118).

Psalms 113-118 are referred to in the Talmud as the Hallel (praise). They reveal the character of God's mercy upon His repentant people. Psalm 119 is a mini-commentary of Israel's deliverance along with an exhaltation of the great "Dabar" — the Word! (Greek, Logos).

Psalms 120-135 outline the last generation from the viewpoint of Hezekiah's Psalms of Degrees, with Psalms 136-137 offering praise over their deliverance by the Messiah who comes to set up the kingdom. Psalms 138-145 give the story of the 144,000 and their ministry during the Tribulation Period, with Psalm 144 especially descriptive of the 144,000. Psalms 146-150 conclude the Deuteronomy book with yet another appraisal of the last century as it corresponds to the five books of Moses — an incredible forty-four psalms!

The number four is most significant, for it is distinctly the number associated with the millennial reign of Christ on earth. Forty-four psalms represent the ultimate fulfillment of the mystical meaning found in the number four.

In his book, NUMBER IN SCRIPTURE, published in 1893, Dr. E. W. Bullinger discussed the number four at some length and gave its mystical meaning:

"The number four is made up of three and one and denotes the number of material completeness. Hence, it is the world number. Four is the number of the great elements — earth, air, fire, and water. Four are the regions of the earth — north, south, east, and west. Four are the seasons of the year — spring, summer, autumn, and winter."

The number four points to the establishment of the throne of God on planet earth. This can be seen prophetically in its use throughout the Bible. For covering the Holy of holies. Woven into the veil were the images of four cherubim. In like manner, Revelation 7 describes *four angels standing on the four corners of the earth, holding the four winds of the earth,* ... (Revelation 7: 1). The number four, then, is associated with the kingdom when the throne of God will be established upon the earth.

Moses' fifth book was originally named "Dabar" after the statement in the first verse of the book, *These be the words* ... (Deuteronomy 1:1). In the third century B.C., however, the translators of the Septuagint changed the name of the book to "Deuteronomy" after the statement in chapter 17, verse 18, *a copy of this law* (Deuteronomy 17:18).

The Septuagint was a Greek translation of the Old Testament made in Alexandria, Egypt, by seventy Jewish scholars. The manuscript is usually referred to by the Roman numeral LXX (70). Their Greek copy of the law was just that — a **copy**, hence the name **Deuteronomy.** However, had they translated the Hebrew name of the book directly into Greek, the fifth book of Moses would have been called, LOGOS! — the WORD! No wonder Jesus Christ was introduced in John's Gospel as the WORD! *In the beginning was the Word, and the Word was with God, and the Word was God. The same was in the beginning with God. And the Word was made flesh, and dwelt among us, (and we beheld his glory, the glory as of the only begotten of the Father,) full of grace and truth* (John 1:1-2,14). Also, John described his Second Coming in Revelation 19 with the same affirmation, ... *and his name is called The Word of God* (Revelation 19:13).

Moses' fifth book was written, not only about the establishment of the government of God among His Chosen People, but prophetically about the future government which would be established by the Messiah, Himself. Jesus is the great "Dabar" depicted in the fifth Mosaic book and is the theme of the fifth book of the Psalms as well. It is Jesus, the WORD, who will come to establish the kingdom of heaven on earth!

PSALM 107

*O give thanks unto the LORD, for he is good: for his mercy en-
dureth forever.*
*Let the redeemed of the LORD say so, whom he hath redeem-
ed from the hand of the enemy;*
*And gathered them out of the lands, from the east, and from
the west, from the north, and from the south* (vv. 1-3).

Psalm 107 opens with praise, the theme of which is indicative of
the entire Deuteronomy book (Psalms 107-150). Verse 2 tells why.
Israel has been redeemed in the midst of Armageddon. Messiah
has come to save the day and set up the long-awaited kingdom.
After 2,000 years or more of dispersions, the Chosen People are
gathered back into the Promised Land to receive their inheritance — a promise made to Abraham. It is said that David
composed this psalm after bringing the Ark of the Covenant to
Jerusalem. Prophetically, it may represent Israel's joy over a
future return of the Ark.

Psalms 107-113 make up a set of seven psalms which reflects
upon the suffering of Israel over the centuries and their final
deliverance at the coming of Messiah. Psalm 107 considers the
plight of His people through 3,000 years of suffering and predicts
that they will return to their land. In Psalm 108 He adds to the territory of Israel the area called Gilead, which is Northern Jordan,
Moab, which is Central Jordan, and Edom, which is Southern Jordan.

Psalm 109 alludes to the rise of the antichrist, and in Psalm 110
we have the glorious return of the Messiah to establish His
kingdom, followed by four **Hallelujahs** found in Psalms 111, 112,
and 113. In these three **Hallelujah Psalms** we have the same
theme given in the other **Hallelujah Psalms**, namely His judgment upon the wicked, His redemption of Israel, and the
establishment of His kingdom. Oh the perfection of our Lord's

grand design!

In Psalm 107 the Deuteronomy book is introduced with a keynote declaration which is repeated four times. (Please note again the use of the number four.)

In verse 8 the psalmist wrote:

> *Oh that men would praise the LORD for his goodness, and for his wonderful works to the children of men! (v. 8).*

Again in verse 15 he wrote:

> *Oh that men would praise the LORD for his goodness, and for his wonderful works to the children of men! (v. 15).*

Again in verse 21 he wrote:

> *Oh that men would praise the LORD for his goodness, and for his wonderful works to the children of men! (v. 21).*

And yet again in verse 31 he wrote:

> *Oh that men would praise the LORD for his goodness, and for his wonderful works to the children of men! (v. 31).*

This grand declaration is repeated four times and provides us with a key to the understanding of the mystery represented in the number four. It indicates the redemption of Israel's land and of the entire planet when Christ returns. Psalm 107 opens the Deuteronomy book by reminding us of how the Lord punished the people for their sins and then delivered them when they repented.

> *They wandered in the wilderness in a solitary way; they found no city to dwell in.*
> *Hungry and thirsty, their soul fainted in them.*
> *Then they cried unto the LORD in their trouble, and he delivered them out of their distresses (vv. 4-6).*

These verses are typical of Psalm 107. They describe the suffering of the Jewish people over the past 3,000 years:

> *Because they rebelled against the words of God, and contemned the counsel of the most High: (v. 11).*

Throughout Israel's history there were times of rebellion

against God, followed by punishment, which led to repentance and deliverance. The process can be seen in verses 12-14:

> *Therefore he brought down their heart with labour; they fell down, and there was none to help.*
> *Then they cried unto the LORD in their trouble, and he saved them out of their distresses.*
> *He brought them out of darkness and the shadow of death, and brake their bands in sunder* (vv. 12-14).

This process of chastening began in the life of Abraham and has continued upon his offspring throughout succeeding generations. For example, the Lord called Abraham out of the Ur of the Chaldees: *Get thee out of thy country, and from thy kindred, and from thy father's house, unto a land that I will shew thee: And I will make of thee a great nation* ... (Genesis 12:1-2). Abraham did not completely obey. The taking of his nephew, Lot, resulted in the Sodom dilemma and the births of Moab and Ammon (the incestuous children of Lot), whose offspring eventually became the perennial enemies of Israel.

The second problem came when Abraham married Hagar, the Egyptian. The resulting birth of Ishmael created an even greater enemy to the descendants of Isaac. The offspring of Ishmael includes most of the Arab world.

Another major problem can be seen in the ill treatment of Joseph by the other sons of Jacob. Though it resulted in their deliverance from the famine, the sin was eventually exacted upon the children of Israel after the death of Joseph. They suffered years of bondage in Egypt.

Yet another example may be noted in the years following their exodus. Because of unbelief God punished them with a 40-year sojourn in the wilderness. These chastenings by the Lord are just a few examples which bear out the truth of Psalm 107 and are typical of God's dealing with Israel down through the centuries. There was the Assyrian captivity of 721 B.C., the Babylonian captivity of 606 B.C., the Roman domination of Israel during the time of Christ, the destruction of the Temple in 70 A.D., and the final dispersion of the Jews to the slave markets of the world in 135 A.D.

Over and over again when Israel would rebel against *the words of God, and contemned* [condemned] *the counsel of the most*

High, He would bring *down their heart with labour.* Each time, however, there was the promise of deliverance if they would only repent.

> *He turneth rivers into a wilderness, and the watersprings into*
> *dry ground;*
> *A fruitful land into barrenness, for the wickedness of them*
> *that dwell therein* (vv. 33-34).

Here is a vivid description of these continual chastenings upon Israel down through the centuries. After the Babylonian captivity, the Jewish people were allowed to return to their desolated land, to rebuild their cities, and reclaim their fields. God had allowed the land to lay out for seventy years. No crops had been planted; no harvest had been gathered. The land had become a barren wilderness. This is typical of God's careful chastening of His wayward people.

> *He turneth the wilderness into a standing water, and dry*
> *ground into watersprings.*
> *And there he maketh the hungry to dwell, that they may*
> *prepare a city for habitation;*
> *And sow the fields, and plant vineyards, which may yield*
> *fruits of increase.*
> *He blesseth them also, so that they are multiplied greatly; and*
> *suffereth not their cattle to decrease* (vv. 35-38).

In these verses we have a description of God's restoration of the land. They also remind us of the desolation of the land over the past twenty centuries. After the Bar Kochba revolt in 135 A.D., the Romans emptied the land of Israel of its people. They were dispersed to the slave markets of the world to spend the next 1,813 years scattered among the nations. The fertile hills and valleys became a barren wasteland.

In this century, however, the Lord has restored the nation and reclaimed the land. Since 1948 the Israelis have planted 150 million trees, drained the swamps in the Valley of Jezreel, removed the rocks from fertile Galilee, washed the salt out of the soil along the western shore of the Dead Sea, and watered the deserts in the Negev. They can grow pumpkins several feet in diameter and cabbages as big as a bushel basket. The incredible nation has become one of the major exporters of fruits and vegetables to

Europe and the Middle East.

> *Whoso is wise, and will observe these things, even they shall understand the lovingkindness of the LORD* (v. 43).

The psalmist concludes in verse 43 with a reference to the predictions found in this psalm. Throughout these psalms there is a reminder of the difficulties of the past with the purpose of declaring the glory and joy of the future kingdom.

PSALM 108

> *O GOD, my heart is fixed; I will sing and give praise, even with my glory.*
> *Awake, psaltery and harp: I myself will awake early.*
> *I will praise thee, O LORD, among the people: and I will sing praises unto thee among the nations.*
> *For thy mercy is great above the heavens: and thy truth reacheth unto the clouds.*
> *Be thou exalted, O God, above the heavens: and thy glory above all the earth* (vv. 1-5).

These verses are copied after Psalm 57:7-11. The earlier psalm (57) relates a dilemma David faced when he ran from King Saul. This later rendering of the passage (108) predicts a time when Israel will face similar circumstances.

Psalms 108-110, composed by David, present an overview of the Tribulation Period and Israel's future deliverance. This first psalm (108) relates to those events occurring as the Tribulation begins — namely, the restoration of Temple worship and the conquering of Israel's Arab neighbors. Psalm 109 alludes to those events occurring in the midst of the seven years — as the antichrist commits the abomination of desolation. And Psalm 110 describes the coming of Christ at the end of the Tribulation Period to establish His kingdom. These are followed by three psalms of praise (111-113). They contain four **Hallelujahs** — comparable to the four **Hallelujahs** of Revelation 19. (See the chapter, The Hallelujah Psalms.)

In the first five verses David alludes to the Resurrection (*I myself will awake early*) and the welcome of Gentile Christianity (*among the nations*) at the erection of the Tabernacle of David

(*Be thou exalted, O God*). In the last part of the chapter (vv. 6-13) David reminds Israel of their conflict with the Arabs — a prophecy which we are presently observing in the Middle East.

> That thy beloved may be delivered: save with thy right hand, and answer me.
> God hath spoken in his holiness; I will rejoice, I will divide Shechem, and mete out the valley of Succoth.
> Gilead is mine; Manasseh is mine; Ephraim also is the strength of mine head; Judah is my lawgiver:
> Moab is my washpot; over Edom will I cast out my shoe; over Philistia will I triumph.
> Who will bring me into the strong city? who will lead me into Edom?
> Will not thou, O God, who hast cast us off? and wilt not thou, O God, go forth with our hosts?
> Give us help from trouble: for vain is the help of man (vv. 6-13).

These verses are basically a repetition of Psalm 60:5-12. Prophetically, they represent an overview of the conflict between Israel and the Palestinians. These verses will ultimately be fulfilled as the Messianic Era develops. The processes for their fulfillment are underway today. Shechem Nablaus represents an area in Northern Israel occupied since the Six Day War in 1967. It is a part of that territory once known as the West Bank. Gilead is a mountainous area east of the Jordan River Valley. It lies in the territory of Northern Jordan. Half the tribe of Manesseh lived in the Gilead region, and the other half, along with Ephraim, lived in the area around Shechem. All of this, writes David, will one day be given to Israel and Judah, for *Judah,* he said, *is my lawgiver.*

Verse 9 puts a prophetic claim upon Moab, Edom, and Philistia. Moab and Edom represent the territory of modern Jordan, south of the capital city, Amman. Philistia, on the other hand, may represent not only the acquisition of the Gaza Strip, but also a victory over the militant Palestinian Liberation Organization.

Moab is my washpot, said the Lord — indicating a boiling cauldron. It may refer to a coming conflict between Israel and Jordan. *Over Edom will I cast out my shoe,* may be a reference to the Mosaic covenant wherein a kinsman-redeemer has the option to restore the land of a brother in need. The children of Esau (twin brother to Jacob) consistently refused to help the Jews in those early centuries.

The offspring of those people may comprise at least part of the Palestinians of this generation. The PLO are actually fighting to deprive Israel of its Promised Land. The doctrine of casting off the shoe may be a prophecy that Israel's cousins will fall under God's judgment for their unkind actions. In fact, the Jewish remnant will occupy Edom's ancient capital city of Petra during the last half of the Tribulation Period.

Who will bring me into the strong city? who will lead me into Edom? (v. 10). This verse seems to refer to the flight of the 144,000 who will witness the abomination of desolation perpetrated by the antichrist. The strong city must surely represent the ancient capital of Edom. The rose-red city of Petra carved out of solid rock high in the mountains of Edom may well be the destination of the 144,000.

PSALM 109

Hold not thy peace, O God of my praise;
For the mouth of the wicked and the mouth of the deceitful are opened against me: they have spoken against me with a lying tongue.
They compassed me about also with words of hatred; and fought against me without a cause (vv. 1-3).

This is the second of three psalms of David which give an overview of the Tribulation Period. The previous psalm depicts the beginning of the Tribulation, while this psalm concentrates on the antichrist and his provocative abomination of desolation. The third psalm of David (110) alludes to the glorious appearing of Christ at Armageddon.

David sees into the far future and addresses the generation in which anti-Semitism will flourish. Jew hatred will reach its peak during the Tribulation Period. The Jews will be blamed once again for the ills which beset mankind.

One is tempted to think that the future antichrist could follow in the footsteps of Hitler. Psalm 109 contains a vivid reference to the antichrist. David wrote:

Set thou a wicked man over him: and let satan stand at his right hand (v. 6).

The *wicked man* will become the dictator of those people who hated and persecuted the Jews. This *wicked man* will have *satan* standing at his right hand and could be none other than the antichrist.

> But do thou for me, O GOD the Lord, for thy name's sake: because thy mercy is good, deliver thou me (v. 21).

The remainder of this psalm is a prayer for deliverance from the enemies of Israel. We are reminded of the escape of the Jewish remnant to the wilderness — there to stay for the last half of those seven dreadful years. As the end approaches, Armageddon rages — bringing us to David's prophetic Psalm 110.

PSALM 110

> The LORD said unto my Lord, Sit thou at my right hand, until I make thine enemies thy footstool (v. 1).

Psalm 110 declares the coming of Christ to establish His kingdom. Verse one refers to the past 2,000 intervening years between His First Coming and His Second Coming. Christ has been in heaven at the right hand of the Father. The following verses declare His glorious return:

> The LORD shall send the rod of thy strength out of Zion: rule thou in the midst of thine enemies.
> Thou art a priest for ever after the order of Melchizedek.
> The Lord at thy right hand shall strike through kings in the day of his wrath.
> He shall judge among the heathen, he shall fill the places with the dead bodies; he shall wound the heads over many countries (vv. 2,4-6).

This is a picture of Armageddon when the Savior comes to deliver Israel and destroy the antichrist. Not only will Christ become the King of kings and Lord of lords, he will also reveal His priesthood. He is the altogether unique High Priest established, not after the order of the Levitical priesthood, but after the order

315 of Melchizedek.This is

of Melchizedek.This is most important in relation to Israel. The Levitical priesthood was uniquely Jewish. On the other hand, the priesthood of Melchizedek represented an all-encompassing order of worship. Here enters the legitimate claim of Gentile New Testament Christianity found right in the middle of a Jewish book! This one little verse represents a proverbial bomb in the midst of an exclusive Judaism. Christ is High Priest of all!

The religious Jew emphatically denies the legitimacy of Gentile Christianity. He denies the authority of Jesus Christ as the Messiah of Israel and Savior of the rest of the world. As this dispensation closes, however, the religious Jewish community will recognize our claim to the Jewish Christ! The New Testament book of Hebrews contains an explanation for the Chosen People. Being the 19th book of the New Testament, like its counterpart, the Psalms (19th book in the Old Testament), the treatise to the Hebrews is actually a message based upon the Psalms. It is as if the treatise was written for Israel in this generation!

PSALM 111

Praise ye the LORD [**Hallelujah**]. *I will praise the LORD with my whole heart, in the assembly of the upright, and in the congregation* (v. 1).

Psalms 111-113 follow the return of Christ with four **Hallelujahs**, comparable to the four **Hallelujahs** of Revelation 19. Furthermore, they describe His wrath at Armageddon, His deliverance of the Jewish people, and His establishment of the kingdom.

... he will ever be mindful of his covenant.
He hath shewed his people the power of his works, that he may give them the heritage of the heathen (vv. 5-6).

The Abrahamic covenant will be fulfilled at the coming of Christ. God promised Abraham's seed certain borders for their Promised Land. Thus, the nation will be established at the head of the nations in the Messianic kingdom.

The works of his hands are verity and judgment; ... (v. 7).

The Palestinian people will be made to understand that God is not a harsh and ruthless taker of their land. He is, instead, a keeper of His promises made in the book of Genesis. The seven dispossessed nations will know that the works of God's hands are truth and justice.

The fear of the LORD is the beginning of wisdom: a good understanding have all they that do his commandments: his praise endureth for ever (v. 10).

God's purpose for prophecy is to instill a holy fear in His people. An awesome and reverential respect causes men to live circumspectly. It was the motivating force behind the ministry of the Apostle Paul who wrote, *Knowing therefore the terror of the Lord, we persuade men; ...* (II Corinthians 5:11). Isaiah, inspired of the Holy Spirit, was led to record a heavenly message from the Creator, Himself: *Remember the former things of old: for I am God, and there is none else; I am God, and there is none like me, Declaring the end from the beginning, and from ancient times the things that are not yet done, ...* (Isaiah 46:9-10). We would do well to govern our conduct with great care, knowing that we must stand before Christ one day and give an account of ourselves. In that day, when He establishes His kingdom, we should want to hear Him say, "Well done!"

PSALM 112

Praise ye the LORD [Hallelujah]. *Blessed is the man that feareth the LORD, that delighteth greatly in his commandments* (v. 1).

The opening words of this psalm are taken from the final words of the preceding one. "The fear of God is so important that Solomon, the wisest of all men, concluded two of his books with this very theme."[1] ... *a woman that feareth the LORD, she shall be praised* (Proverbs 31:30). And also, *Let us hear the conclusion of the whole matter: Fear God, and keep his commandments: for this is the whole duty of man* (Ecclesiastes 12:13).
Verse one begins with the second **Hallelujah** of this series which

follows the coming of Christ the King in Psalm 110. There are four **Hallelujahs** in these three Psalms 111-113. (See the chapter, The Hallelujah Psalms.) Psalms 113-118 are regarded by rabbinic scholars as the Hallel (Praise) Psalms. Why Psalms 111 and 112 were not included by the rabbis in the Hallel Psalms (113-118) is not known. But the **Hallelujahs** in Psalms 111 and 112 certainly lead into the following burst of praise and concluding with the establishment of the reign of Messiah (The Word) in Psalm 119.

Unto the upright there ariseth light in the darkness: ... (v. 4).

The hope of the Messianic kingdom is given for the Jewish people. In the midst of Armageddon, Israel's darkest hour, the light of God's glory will shine forth. As the sun turns into darkness, Jesus Christ will appear in power and great glory!

... the righteous shall be in everlasting remembrance.
The wicked shall see it, and be grieved; he shall gnash with his
teeth, and melt away: the desire of the wicked shall perish (vv.
6,10).

The fulfillment of this prophecy can only come at the Second Advent of the Messiah. The righteous will be restored and the wicked will be judged.

PSALM 113

Praise ye the LORD [**Hallelujah**]. *Praise, O ye servants of the*
LORD, praise the name of the LORD.
Blessed be the name of the LORD from this time forth and for
evermore.
From the rising of the sun unto the going down of the same the
LORD'S name is to be praised (vv. 1-3).

Psalm 113 is the first of the Hallel (Praise) Psalms (113-118). The group is designated "Hallel" throughout rabbinic literature. They are also known as the "Egyptian Hallel" to distinguish them from Psalm 136 which is referred to as the "Great Hallel."[1]

They are called the "Egyptian Hallel" because their theme includes the exodus out of Egypt, the parting of the Red Sea, and the

events at Mount Sinai. They also include the future resurrection
of the dead and the coming of the Messiah.

> *The LORD is high above all nations, and his glory above the*
> *heavens.*
> *Who is like unto the LORD our God, who dwelleth on high,*
> *Who humbleth himself to behold the things that are in heaven,*
> *and in the earth!* (vv. 4-6).

At His First Advent, Christ humbled Himself, took on the form
of man, and walked among His creation. His Calvary experience
was an act of redemption for all people of all ages — for all who
call upon Him. At His Second Advent, Christ will be exalted above
all nations as King of kings and Lord of lords. His kingdom will
last for a thousand years.

> *He raiseth up the poor out of the dust, and lifteth the needy out*
> *of the dunghill;*
> *That he may set him with princes, even with the princes of his*
> *people.*
> *He maketh the barren woman to keep house, and to be a joyful*
> *mother of children. Praise ye the LORD* [Hallelujah] (vv. 7-9).

In His coming kingdom, the human race will be redeemed and
the earth restored to its pristine state — as it was in the Garden of
Eden.

Rashi (an eleventh century rabbi) suggested that the barren
woman was Israel — unable to populate Jerusalem through the
long years of exile. This is certainly the theme of the Psalms —
the return of the Jews to their Promised Land and the birth of the
nation of Israel. Isaiah was one among many who predicted the
marvelous event. *Before she travailed, she brought forth; before*
her pain came, she was delivered of a man child. Who hath heard
such a thing? who hath seen such things? Shall the earth be made
to bring forth in one day? or shall a nation be born at once? for as
soon as Zion travailed, she brought forth her children (Isaiah
66:7-8).

There are six Hallel psalms (113-118) followed by Psalm 119
which features the "WORD." Psalm 119 is the longest chapter in
the Bible, perhaps because the great "WORD," Himself, will
establish a kingdom which will be the longest continuous reign in
history. The kingdom of Christ will last a thousand years. In the

Gospel of John (1:1-14) and in his later writing (Revelation 19:13), Jesus Christ is referred to as the "Word of God." How fitting then, that Psalm 119 should follow the Hallel (Praise) Psalms.

PSALM 114

When Israel went out of Egypt, the house of Jacob from a people of strange language;
Judah was his sanctuary, and Israel his dominion (vv. 1-2).

Psalm 114 discusses the first three of five themes highlighted in the Hallel (Praise) Psalms — the exodus from Egypt, the splitting of the sea, and the revelation at Mount Sinai. The fourth theme, the resurrection of the dead, is addressed in Psalm 116:3-9 and the fifth theme, the coming of the Messiah, is given in Psalm 118:26. These are Israel's most revered events both past and future. They constitute the reasons for praise.

This psalm (second of the Hallel) carries the same theme as Psalm 113 — God lifts the needy and destitute and gives them nobility. The Chosen People attained this exaltation by their willingness to plunge into the Red Sea. According to verse 1, Israel refused to assimilate themselves into the culture of the Egyptians. *When Israel went out* indicates that the Jewish nation remained *Israel*, retaining their Jewish names. They maintained their distinct and holy language, refusing to use the language of Egypt. After 210 years, they could still refer to the Egyptians as *a people of strange language.*

God singled out the tribe of Judah to be royalty. They became His sanctuary because, it is said, they led the way to jump into the Red Sea. At first, Benjamin's people ran toward the sea and the royal tribe of Judah cried out, "You are committing suicide by jumping into these waters. You deserve to be stoned for this crime." But Benjamin argued, "God commanded the Children of Israel, to descend into the sea. The forerunners of the other tribes were born while our father was still called Jacob. Only Benjamin was born after Jacob was awarded the title, Israel. Thus, only we Benjaminites are the true Children of Israel and only we are fit to lead the Jewish people triumphantly across the sea."[1] Though the psalm states that Judah is God's sanctuary, the Temple was built on Mount Moriah at the border between Judah and Benjamin — just inside the territory of Benjamin. Could the fact that Benjamin was born to Jacob after his name was changed to Israel be the reason why?

The sea saw it, and fled: Jordan was driven back (v. 3).

Here, God turned the water into stone. Later, He turned stone into water as is recorded at the conclusion of this psalm, *Which turned the rock into a standing water, the flint into a fountain of waters* (v. 8). The Red Sea parted at the beginning of their forty year sojourn in the wilderness and the Jordan River parted at the end of it.

The mountains skipped like rams, and the little hills like lambs.
What ailed thee, O thou sea, that thou fleddest? thou Jordan, that thou wast driven back?
Ye mountains, that ye skipped like rams; and ye little hills, like lambs?
Tremble, thou earth, at the presence of the Lord, at the presence of the God of Jacob (vv. 4-7).

Some believe that the entire earth trembled at the splitting of the Red Sea and that every person on the planet felt the tremor. Possible as that might be, we are not told such in Scripture. The story of the tremor is recorded, however, when God appeared on Mount Sinai. Someday, the earth will again tremble — at the appearance of the Messiah!

PSALM 115

Not unto us, O LORD, not unto us, but unto thy name give glory, for thy mercy, and for thy truth's sake.
Wherefore should the heathen [Gentiles] say, Where is now their God?
But our God is in the heavens: he hath done whatsoever he hath pleased (vv. 1-3).

This psalm (third in the Hallel or Praise Psalms) shows the long-term effect of the miracles given in the preceding psalm. The Gentiles soon forget God's goodness. Gentile nations have taunted the Jews saying, *Where is now their God.* The gods of the Gentiles are idols made of silver and gold. They cannot answer in the day of distress. They have eyes and cannot see, ears and cannot hear. The Chosen People of Israel plead for deliverance from their long exile, not for their sakes, or for the sake of their forefathers, but for God's holy name's sake. This deliverance began in the twentieth century with the return of the Jews to the land of their forefathers and will see its ultimate fulfillment with the Second Advent of the Messiah.

> *O Israel, trust thou in the LORD: he is their help and their shield.*
> *O house of Aaron, trust in the LORD: he is their help and their shield.*
> *Ye that fear the LORD, trust in the LORD: he is their help and their shield* (vv. 9-11).

Three groups are given in these verses — Israel, the house of Aaron, and Gentile Christianity, — *ye that fear the LORD.* Israel will be brought back into the Promised Land at the close of this sixth millennium and the house of Aaron will lead the nation in restoring Temple worship while Gentile Christianity will be invited to join in the Great Hallel (Praise Celebration). Not only is the birth of the nation in 1948 a major fulfillment of prophecy, but just as important will be the restoration of the priesthood and the revival of Temple worship.

PSALM 116

> *I love the LORD, because he hath heard my voice and my supplications* (v. 1).

This fourth Hallel psalm predicted the day when the exiled Jews return to their Promised Land to prepare for the coming of Messiah. After so many long years God hears the *voice* and *supplications* of the wandering Jew. As this psalm proceeds, one can observe not only the fulfillment of this verse leading to the birth of the nation in 1948, but the progress of the following verses as the coming of the Messianic Age approaches.

> *The sorrows of death compassed me, and the pains of hell gat*
> *hold upon me: I found trouble and sorrow.*
> *Then called I upon the name of the LORD; O LORD, I beseech*
> *thee, deliver my soul.*
> *Gracious is the LORD, and righteous; yea, our God is mer-*
> *ciful.*
> *The LORD preserveth the simple: I was brought low, and he*
> *helped me* (vv. 3-6).

These predicted events preceded the birth of the nation. The Chosen People suffered the Holocaust of World War II. They found *trouble and sorrow*. But God heard their cries as He did 3,430 years ago in Egypt and *helped them*.

> *Return unto thy rest, O my soul; for the LORD hath dealt*
> *bountifully with thee.*
> *For thou hast delivered my soul from death, mine eyes from*
> *tears, and my feet from falling.*
> *I will walk before the LORD in the land of the living* (vv. 7-9).

Following the defeat of the Nazis, many of the surviving Jews left for Palestine where, in 1948, they officially regained their national identity. God had delivered their souls from death (the death camps), their eyes from tears (the tears of the Holocaust) and their feet from falling (the Jewish race was saved from annihilation). Today, they walk before the Lord in the land of the living (Eretz Israel).

> *I believed, therefore have I spoken: I was greatly afflicted.*
> *I said in my haste, All men are liars.*
> *What shall I render unto the LORD for all his benefits toward*
> *me?*
> *I will take the cup of salvation, and call upon the name of the*
> *LORD* (vv. 10-13).

These verses relate a phenomenon presently under development. Because of their afflictions at the hands of Gentiles (many of those persecutions were under the guise of Christianity), the Chosen People in their *haste* placed a blanket condemnation upon all Christians. They were as quick to condemn all believers in Christ as some Gentiles are to condemn all Jews for the political problems faced by their nations. However, there will come a day when the Jews will realize that the vast majority of Christians love the Chosen People and are not guilty of persecuting them. Today, Christians are the only true friends Israel has.

The Jews will eventually recognize this and turn to Christ as their Messiah. They will *call upon the name of the LORD.* This is not to say they will become a part of some Christian denomination, thus losing their national and religious identity. They will, however, believe and call upon Christ for salvation — at least 144,000 of them. How this will come about is not known, but the following verses reveal a revival of Temple worship, the return of the Ark of the Covenant, and the presence of a world of Gentiles who, likewise, have called *upon the name of the LORD.*

The Apostle Paul addressed this question of Israel's salvation in his epistle to the Romans and referred to Psalm 116:13 and 17 as he wrote, *For whosoever shall call upon the name of the Lord shall be saved* (Romans 10:13).

> *I will pay my vows unto the LORD now in the presence of all his people.*
> *Precious in the sight of the LORD is the death of his saints.*
> *O LORD, truly I am thy servant; I am thy servant, and the son of thine handmaid: thou hast loosed my bonds.*
> *I will offer to thee the sacrifice of thanksgiving, and will call upon the name of the LORD.*
> *I will pay my vows unto the LORD now in the presence of all his people,*
> *In the courts of the LORD's house, in the midst of thee, O Jerusalem. Praise ye the LORD* [**Hallelujah**] (vv. 14-19).

The Talmud (Rosh HaShanah 16b-17a) explains how this psalm decribes the day of Final Judgment at the time of the Resurrection of the Dead.[1] The events of these verses are thus placed at the end of this dispensation of Gentile Christianity. Two thousand years ago Israel as a nation was set aside by the Messiah for the purpose of bringing salvation to Gentiles. This is a mystery spoken of by Paul who wrote to the Romans, ... *I would not, brethren, that ye should be ignorant of this mystery, lest ye should be wise in your own conceits; that blindness in part is happened to Israel, until the fulness of the Gentiles be come in* (Romans 11:25).

It was in the will of God to temporarily set aside His Chosen People in order to enlarge His plan of salvation to include Gentiles. Paul explained, *Have they* [Israel] *stumbled that they* should fall? God forbid: but rather through their fall salvation is come unto the Gentiles, for to provoke them to jealousy. Now if the fall of them be the riches of the world, and the diminishing of them the riches of the Gentiles; how much more their fulness ... For if the casting away of them be the reconciling of the world, what shall the receiving of them be, but life from the dead? (Romans 11:11,12, 15).

The Jewish nation was not forever forsaken. Their blindness in part was only for the purpose of bringing the Gospel to the Gentiles. However, the day will come when the fulness of the Gentiles will have arrived. At that time, Israel will be reconciled to God. Once that occurs, Resurrection and Rapture will take place. How these events will happen is a matter of speculation, but they will center around the return of the Jews to the top of Mount Moriah to set up the Tabernacle of David and return the Ark of the Covenant as related in the last three verses of Psalm 116.

Talmudic scholars say that I will pay my vows unto the LORD means they will invoke the ineffable Name of the LORD. This is the Name which Jews reverence to be so holy they will not pronounce it or write it. They refer to God only as HASHEM (The Name). Jewish publications render God as "G-d" for fear they will be guilty of taking the Name in vain, thus breaking the Third Commandment. On the day of their reconcilation, however, they will speak the Holy Name. Sforno (a Jewish sage) says it will be in the presence of the Gentile nations, called in verses 14 and 18 as all his people. This is a most important admission by Talmudic scholars that Gentile Christians are indeed children of God through faith in Jesus Christ. Furthermore, this recognition will come in the future when Israel pays their vows to God in the courts of the LORD's house, that is in Jerusalem on the Temple Mount. "The vows will be paid in the location of the Holy Ark, where Hashem's Presence resides (Radak)."[2] "Jerusalem was ordained as the permanent resting place of the Holy Ark. Therefore, it is most appropriate that God be praised in the midst of this holy city (Abarbanel)."[3]

That Gentile Christianity will observe this praise celebration of the Great Hallel is also noted in the next psalm which is both the shortest chapter and middle chapter in the Bible, O praise the LORD, all ye nations (Psalm 117:1). The prophet Amos gave an indication of how and when this great PRAISE celebration will take place: *In that day will I raise up the tabernacle of David that is fallen, and close up the breaches thereof; and I will raise up his ruins, and I will build it as in the days of old: That they may possess the remnant of Edom, and of all the heathen* [Gentiles] *which are called by my name, saith the LORD that doeth this* (Amos 9:11-12). Implications are that someday the Ark of the Covenant will be returned to Jerusalem. The Jews will secure a place on the Temple Mount (perhaps north of the Mosque of Omar) and raise the Tabernacle of David. Gentile Christianity will be invited to join Israel in a great praise celebration as the processional brings the Ark back to its resting place on the Holy Mount. This prophecy records the concluding event which closes the *fulness of the Gentiles.* Rapture and Resurrection will come when Israel is reconciled to God.

Also, during the Tribulation Period which follows the Rapture, many of the Jewish remnant may be martyred. That could be the reason for the verse, *Precious in the sight of the LORD is the death of his saints* (v. 15). This passage is alluded to in the Revelation as the faithful martyrs refuse the mark of the beast, *Blessed are the dead which die in the Lord* (Revelation 14:13).

Finally, it should be noted that C. I. Scofield referred to the prophetic aspects of the psalms in his footnote comments on Romans 11:5. He wrote, "Many of the psalms express, prophetically, the joys and sorrows of the tribulation remnant."[4] Paul's epistle to the Romans (9-11) discusses the mystery of the *casting away* of Israel and of *the receiving of them* at the close of this dispensation.

PSALM 117

O praise the LORD, all ye nations: praise him, all ye people.
For his merciful kindness is great toward us: and the truth of
the LORD endureth for ever. Praise ye the LORD (vv. 1-2).

This psalm (fifth in the Hallel) is the shortest chapter in the Bible. Prophetically, it symbolizes the "simplicity of the world order which will prevail after the Advent of the Messiah."[1] Presently, the world is filled with many different groups and nations but in the Messianic Era, there will be only two groups — Gentile nations who will serve the Lord and the Children of Israel who will be exalted at the head of the nations.

Both the shortest chapter (Psalm 117) and the longest chapter (Psalm 119) are located here, right in the middle of the Christian Bible. Psalm 117 is both the shortest chapter and the middle chapter with 594 chapters before it and 594 chapters after it. There are 39 Books in the Old Testament and 27 in the New Testament. When these psalms were compiled, no one knew that they would end up in the middle of the Bible. The rest of the Christian Bible was completed a thousand years later. Furthermore, Psalm 118 contains the middle verse of the entire Christian Bible. There are 1189 verses, making a total of 1188 verses apart from the middle verse. It must be more than a coincidence that Psalm 118:8 is that middle verse. Even the number 1188 compares with uncanny accuracy. This undisputed fact must be a product of Divine inspiration.

CHEIRO'S BOOK OF NUMBERS takes note of this remarkable product of Divine design. "These three psalms were purposely planned to come together for a definite reason — that reason evidently being that the relation of such coincidences would sooner or later strike some searcher of truth, as an illustration of Divine design and consequently proof of the Divine inspiration that guided not only the writer of the Psalms, but thousands of years later, the translators of this book into other languages."[2]

PSALM 118

It is better to trust in the LORD than to put confidence in man
(v. 8; the middle verse of the Christian Bible).

The 118th psalm is located between the shortest chapter (Psalm 117) and the longest chapter (Psalm 119) in the Bible and it contains the middle verse. There are 1189 chapters in the Christian Bible, 594 chapters before and 594 chapters after Psalm 118:8. It is remarkable to note that 594 plus 594 make a sum total of 1188 — which is the number of the chapter and verse which contains the middle verse. It must be more than a coincidence. Yet, the design could not have been made by the psalmist who compiled this portion of the Psalms centuries before the New Testament was written or by the others who organized the order of the books. The Old Testament was compiled in its accepted form hundreds of years before the New Testament was compiled in its accepted order. The Geneva Bible, printed in the sixteenth century, was the first Bible to be printed with verse divisions. By then, it was too late to arrange the books in such an order as to make Psalms 117-119 fit into the center of the Scriptures. By that time they were already there. Only Divine design could have ordered this phenomenon.

CHEIRO'S BOOK OF NUMBERS comments on this unusual construction, "The actual form and division of the Bible is the work of different minds, widely separated by time, by countries, and by training. There can, therefore, be no question of collusion in the carrying out of the evident design that underlies the construction of the Bible."[1]

This middle verse actually sets the theme of the entire Bible. It's teaching is the epitome of all Scripture, *It is better to trust in the Lord than to put confidence in man* (v. 8).

> *They compassed me about like bees; they are quenched as the fire of thorns: for in the name of the LORD I will destroy them* (v. 12).

Two symbols are used in this verse which typify the antichrist — bees and thorns. Midrash Shocher Tov described the bees as typical of that final war when God gathers all the nations of the world and brings them against Jerusalem.[2]

The symbol of the bees was first used in the riddle of Samson the Danite (Judges 14:14). His bees made honey in the carcass of a lion. Prophetically, they are believed to represent the tribe of Dan killing the Lion of Judah, then producing a utopian world government, represented by the honey. At least 2,150 years ago, rabbis considered the possibility that the lost tribe of Dan might produce the antichrist.[3] Could his symbol be the bee?

For example, Joseph Smith, founder of the Mormon Church had a group of bodyguards who called themselves "Danites." When the state of Utah was founded, the Mormon state adopted the honeybee as its symbol.[4]

The historic tie goes back to the Spartans of Southern Greece and their cousins, the Trojans. Honey was used as a sacrifice to their gods. Furthermore, Flavius Josephus recorded a letter from the king of the Spartans to the High Priest in Jerusalem claiming descent from the "stock of Abraham."[5] Could the Spartan king have been a Danite? According to Homer's ILIAD, the first Spartan king was named Danaus. He came by boat from Phoenicia with his fifty daughters who were called Danades. They invented the cult of the mother goddess known as Diana! The people loved their king so much they called themselves Danaans before they were called Spartans.[6] History records that they wore their hair long as a symbol of their magical power — just like Samson.

The first Trojan was Dar-DAN-us (another use of Dan) who built the city of Troy along the Dar-DAN-elle waterway leading from the Aegean Sea to the Black Sea. Four rivers empty into the Black Sea — Danube, Danister, Danieper, and the Don. Such uses of the word Dan may be clues to tracing the lost tribe. That is not to say that the ten lost tribes became the Europeans. But such heresy may have been used to obscure the real identity of the one lost tribe of Dan. In the year A.D. 448, a Frankish king named Merovee claimed descent from the Trojans and wore his hair long as a symbol of magical power.[7] His symbolic bees were retrieved from the tomb of his son in 1653. Those three hundred bees became the motif of Napoleon's reign. They belonged to the Hapsburg Dynasty, who in turn were of Merovingian descent.[8] This famous family provided the emperors of the Holy Roman Empire for five hundred years. In fact, all European royalty are cousins. Could the future world dictator come from European royalty? Will his symbol be the bee?

The thorns take us back to a parable given by Jotham, son of Gideon (Judges 9:8-15). His wicked brother, Abimelech, became king in Israel and killed almost all of Gideon's seventy sons. Only Jotham escaped to stand before the elders of Israel on Mount Gerizim where he compared Abimelech to a bramble bush of thorns. The story is a prophetic scenario of the future dictator who will seek the extermination of all Jews. When Micah described the future *day* of God's visitation, he wrote, *The best of them is as a brier: the most upright is sharper than a thorn hedge: the day of thy watchmen and thy visitation cometh; now shall be their perplexity* (Micah 7:4). The wicked *thorn hedge* will attempt to enslave the world. That is why Jesus was made to wear a humiliating crown of thorns on the day of his crucifixion. The true Messiah was rejected as an antichrist!

PSALM 119 — LONGEST IN THE BIBLE

Thy word have I hid in mine heart that I might not sin against thee (v. 11).

Psalm 119 is the longest chapter in the Bible (176 verses). It is located in the fifth book of the Psalms corresponding to the fifth book of Moses — Deuteronomy. You may recall the Hebrew title of Deuteronomy is "Dabar" (meaning Word) taken from Deuternonomy 1:1, *These be the words.*

The emphasis is upon the *Word* — the great "Dabar." Prophetically, it points to Jesus Christ who was introduced in the Gospel of John as the *Word* of God! Psalm 119, then, seems to be the highlight psalm among the Deuteronomy psalms for it emphasizes "Dabar" — the *Word!* The term is used forty-two times (6x7) to highlight the significance of this great psalm. It must represent the Lord Jesus Christ. It was He, who on the evening of resurrection day said, *all things must be fulfilled which were written in the law of Moses, and in the prophets, and in the Psalms, concerning* me (Luke 24:44).

In the Gospel of John, chapter 1, the Savior was introduced as the unique *Word* of God. *In the beginning was the Word, and the Word was with God, and the Word was God. And the Word was made flesh, and dwelt among us, (and we beheld his glory, the glory as of the only begotten of the Father,) full of grace and truth* (John 1:1,14). And it was the same author, John, who described His Second Coming in the New Testament book of Revelation. *And he was clothed with a vesture dipped in blood: and his name is called the Word of God* (Revelation 19:13).

Psalm 119, then, follows the theme of the great "Dabar" as He would be called in the Hebrew, or "Logos" as He is called in the Greek. Both are terms translated into English as *Word.*

As we have noted, the term is found 42 times in this psalm. What a perfect number! It is a multiple of both 6 and 7 — six representing the number of man and seven representing the number of God. Jesus Christ is both man and God — pointed up by the 42 times the psalm refers to the great Dabar — the Word!

There is another reason why I believe Psalm 119 prophetically implies the incomparable *Word* Himself, the Lord Jesus Christ. These 176 verses are divided into 22 portions, each containing 8 verses, and named according to the 22 letters of the Hebrew alphabet.

"Each section is subdivided into 8 verses, each verse being an iambic tetrameter, namely 16 syllables alternately short and long (in the Hebrew language). Still more extraordinary is the fact that every one of the 8 verses of the first section begins with the first letter of the Hebrew alphabet: Aleph. Each of the 8 verses of the second section begin with the second letter of the Hebrew alphabet: Beth. Each of the 8 verses of the third section begin with the third letter of the alphabet: Gimel. This extraordinary precision continuing until all the 22 letters of the Hebrew alphabet are employed."[1]

Not only do they declare the *Word* 42 times, they are subtitled according to the letters which make up those words. May we be reminded that our Savior referred to Himself as the great author of all things when He used the first and last letters of the alphabet to represent all that He is and all that He does. *I am Alpha and Omega, the beginning and the ending, saith the Lord, which is, and which was, and which is to come, the Almighty ... I am Alpha and Omega, the first and the last ...* (Revelation 1:8,11). It is obvious that our Savior is the prophetic fulfillment of the fifth book of Moses along with the fifth book of the Psalms — and in particular, Psalm 119. There are 22 divisions of the psalm, each named according to a letter in the Hebrew alphabet with emphasis upon the "Word of God."

There is yet another reason why I believe Psalm 119 prophetically points to Jesus Christ. There are 8 verses to each of these 22 divisions of the psalm. The number 8 is uniquely a number of "new beginning" referring to none other than Jesus Christ. The very name Jesus (in the Greek language) has a numerical value of 888, as opposed to the number of the antichrist which is given in Revelation 13:18 as 666.

Furthermore, Psalm 119 is an acrostic, each division is named according to the letters of the alphabet, and there are 8 acrostic songs in the Psalms — 9, 10, 25, 34, 37, 111, 112, 114, and 119. Psalm 119 is the eighth and final acrostic psalm in the great songbook of the Bible. Finally, there are two basic numbers found in Psalm

119. There is a nineteen and there is a hundred. Again our attention is focused on nineteen — hundred! Perhaps the psalm was juxtaposed at this position in the Psalms to prophesy the coming of the **WORD**, himself, toward the close of the 1900's! How perfect is our God! He never misses an opportunity to emphasize the mathematical precision of His great design!

> *Blessed are the undefiled in the way, who walk in the law of the Lord.*
> *Blessed are they that keep his testimonies, and that seek him with the whole heart* (vv. 1-2).

Now let us consider the prophecies of this longest chapter in the Bible. To begin with, the psalm opens with the word, *Blessed*, which, in itself, offers a great prophetic significance. The term is used twice, and points up the introduction of the psalm as being both highly significant and prophetic. It stands along side those other prophetic passages of the Bible which are likewise introduced with the word *blessed*. For example, the entire series of Psalms is introduced by the term, *Blessed is the man that walketh not in the council of the ungodly, nor standeth in the way of sinners, nor sitteth in the seat of the scornful.*

We must not underestimate the use of the term, for it implies far more than just the emotional state of the those who serve the Lord. It is distinctly prophetic. It is used, not only to introduce the Psalms (including Psalm 119), but also to introduce the book of the Revelation. *Blessed is he that readeth, and they that hear the words of this prophecy, and keep those things which are written therein: for the time is at hand* (Revelation 1:3). These prophetic introductions will find their ultimate fulfillment in the Second Coming of Jesus Christ.

One day, our Savior stood before an unbelieving Jerusalem. He wept over the city and cried, *O Jerusalem, Jerusalem, thou that killest the prophets, and stoneth them which are sent unto thee, how often would I have gathered thy children together, even as a hen gathereth her chickens under her wings, and ye would not! Behold, your house is left unto you desolate. For I say unto you, Ye shall not see me henceforth, till ye shall say, Blessed is he that cometh in the name of the Lord* (Matthew 23:37-39). There it is! — the ultimate fulfillment of the term. Jesus said, I will not come again until the Jewish people are made to say, **Blessed!** *Blessed is* *he that cometh in the name of the Lord!* The term must surely be indicative of the Second Coming of Jesus Christ. Perhaps that is the reason the Apostle Paul was prompted to write to Titus, *Looking for that blessed hope, and the glorious appearing of the great God and our Saviour Jesus Christ* (Titus 2:13). What a prophetic fulfillment of the term *blessed!*

Perhaps we can see it most pointedly as it was used by our Savior in Matthew, chapter 5, when he introduced the prophetic "Sermon on the Mount" with the beautiful Beatitudes. Over and over again, our Savior declared:

Blessed are the poor in spirit: for theirs is the kingdom of heaven.

Blessed are they that mourn: for they shall be comforted.

Blessed are the meek: for they shall inherit the earth.

Blessed are they which do hunger and thirst after righteousness: for they shall be filled.

Blessed are the merciful: for they shall obtain mercy.

Blessed are the pure in heart: for they shall see God.

Blessed are the peacemakers: for they shall be called the children of God.

Blessed are they which are persecuted for righteousness' sake: for theirs is the kingdom of heaven.

Blessed are ye, when men shall revile you, and persecute you, and shall say all manner of evil against you falsely, for my sake.

Rejoice, and be exceeding glad: for great is your reward in heaven (Matthew 5:3-12).

Please note that all of those promises are for the future. They all look forward to the Second Coming of Christ. It is said that the word *blessed* means "happy" or "to be envied," but the term refers to far more than that. It is distinctly prophetic and implies that the ultimate blessing will be seen at the Second Coming of Jesus Christ.

"What a day that will be! When my Savior I shall see. When I look upon His face, the one who saved me by His grace. Then He'll take me by the hand, and lead me to the Promised Land, What a day, glorious day, That will be!"[2]

That is the blessed hope! and the ultimate fulfillment of the term *blessed* in the Bible. When Jesus gave the great "Beatitudes," He used them to introduce His "Sermon on the Mount." It seems to be highly significant as an introductory term and when our Savior returns to planet earth to fulfill the *blessed hope*, His coming will be an introduction to an eternity of never ending blessings.

The next major emphasis in Psalm 119 can be seen in the repetition of the promise that the Jewish people will keep the precepts, statutes, and the commandments of His law.

> *Thou hast commanded us to keep thy precepts diligently* (v. 4).
> *I will meditate in thy precepts, and have respect unto thy ways* (v. 15).
> *I will delight myself in thy statutes* (v. 16).
> *Give me understanding, and I shall keep thy law* (v. 34).
> *Behold, I have longed after thy precepts* (v. 40).
> *And I will delight myself in thy commandments* (v. 47).

Over and over again, the promise is made to keep the law of God. Such was the case in those early centuries from Moses through David and the prophets. And such appears to be the case today for the Chosen People. This keeping of the law seems to be like a schoolmaster to bring them to Christ.

> *I will praise thee with uprightheousness of heart, when I shall have learned thy righteous judgments* (v. 71).

According to this verse, the Jewish people will suffer the righteous judgments of God before they will be able to praise Him with uprightheousness of heart. These judgments appear to be described in Psalm 119.

> *Princes also did sit and speak against me ...* (v. 23).
> *The proud have had me greatly in derision ...* (v. 51).
> *The bands of the wicked have robbed me ...* (v. 61).
> *Before I was afflicted, I went astray ...* (v. 67).
> *The proud have forged a lie against me ...* (v. 69).

Why have the Jewish people been made to suffer? That they might learn, said the psalmist, *the statutes of the Lord.* This is the reason for their suffering and why Israel will yet suffer both the Tribulation Period and Armageddon.

> *Thy hands have made me and fashioned me: give me understanding, that I may learn thy commandments.*
> *They that fear thee will be glad when they see me; because I*

have hoped in thy word.
I know, O Lord, that thy judgments are right, and that thou in
faithfulness hast afflicted me (vv. 73-75).

Verses 73 through 75 seem to describe the birth of Israel in this generation along with the suffering they will have to endure. *Thy hands have made me and fashioned me,* wrote the psalmist. That could well refer to the birth of the baby — Israel. Further, the psalmist wrote, *that thou in faithfulness hast afflicted me.* God's judgment upon the Chosen People has not been the result of vindictive hatred, but has instead come from a loving God who has presented, through the suffering of Israel, the gift of eternal life to a Gentile world. Yet, through it all, He is preparing His Chosen People for the blessings of the coming kingdom.

Mine eyes fail for thy word ... (v. 82).

Here the Lord's affliction upon His people is described as blinded eyes. In fulfillment of that prophetic passage, the Apostle Paul wrote, *For I would not, brethren, that ye should be ignorant of this mystery, lest ye should be wise in your own conceits; that blindness in part is happened to Israel, until the fulness of Gentiles be come in* (Romans 11:25).

Christ was rejected, persecuted, and crucified by His people that Gentiles might have the benefit of that sacrifice. Throughout the following verses in Psalm 119, there is a continuing description of the suffering of the Tribulation Period and a prayer for deliverance.

The proud have digged pits for me ... (v. 85).
... they persecute me wrongfully (v. 86).
They had almost consumed me upon earth (v. 87).
Unless thy law had been my delights, I should then have
perished in mine affliction (v. 92).
The wicked have waited for me to destroy me (v. 95).
I am afflicted very much (v. 107).
The wicked have laid a snare for me (v. 110).
I have inclined my heart to perform thy statutes alway, even
unto the end (v. 112).

Here is a reference to the time frame predicted in these verses. The religious Jew declares that he will perform the statutes of the Lord, *even unto the end* — meaning, I think, the end of this dispensation which will conclude with the glorious appearing of the Messiah to establish the kingdom.

> *Quicken me after thy loving-kindness; so shall I keep the testimony of thy mouth* (v. 88).

Here is an unusual juxtaposition. The verse speaks of resurrection and it is happens to be in verse 88. It seems to compare with another verse about resurrection found in Psalm 88, *Wilt thou shew wonders to the dead? shall the dead arise and praise thee?* (Psalm 88:10). When the resurrection comes, the dead will be *quicken*[ed].

> *Let my soul live, and it shall praise thee; and let thy judgments help me.*
> *I have gone astray like a lost sheep; seek thy servant; for I do not forget thy commandments* (vv. 175-176).

As the persecution intensifies in the midst of Tribulation, and as the awesome Armageddon approaches, the Jewish people will pray in earnest for deliverance. They will finally admit that they have gone astray like lost sheep and beg the Lord to find them. This verse compares in a prophetic way with Isaiah, *All we like sheep have gone astray; we have turned everyone to his own way; And the LORD hath laid on him the iniquity of us all''* (Isaiah 53:6).

Yes, there will come a day, when the Jewish people will realize that the suffering of the Savior on the cross of Calvary had a purpose. The Father in heaven laid upon His own Son the iniquity of Israel and the sins of the world.

> *Order my steps in thy word* (v. 133).

That appears to be exactly what was done — Psalm 1 representing step 1, Psalm 2 for step 2, Psalm 3 for step 3, — as each successive psalm describes, step-by-step, the plight of the Jewish people in the last century. In previous studies, we have considered the prophetic nature of the Psalms. In Psalm 1, we seem to have an introduction to this century. It appears that Psalm 1 may correspond to 1901 with its reference to the replanting of the tree. Psalm 2 may represent 1902, Psalm 3 for 1903, etc. At least the first 86 psalms appear to be amazingly accurate when compared to the first 86 years of this century. Could that be the meaning of verse 133 of Psalm 119? Again, I repeat, the psalmist wrote, *Order my steps in thy word.* That may well be the prophecy laid out in the Psalms!

PSALMS 120-134
THE PSALMS OF ASCENT

It was seven hundred years before the birth of Christ. A veil of sadness hung over the city of Jerusalem. There was no singing in the Temple. There was no joy in the streets. The beloved King Hezekiah was dying. He had been a godly ruler and had brought spiritual revival to the country. Idolatry had been put away, and the worship of Jehovah had been encouraged.

Some months before, Jerusalem had been under siege by Sennacherib, the Assyrian king. But because of the prayer life of King Hezekiah, God had destroyed the Assyrian forces and had kept the nation free. Now Hezekiah was sick, and the prophet Isaiah had the difficult task of telling the king to set his house in order, for he would not live.

The sadness over the sickness of the king was compounded by the fact that he did not have a son to succeed him on the throne. With the death of Hezekiah would come an end to the royal lineage of the house of David. But Hezekiah was a godly king, and he knew how to pray.

When news of his impending death reached him, he turned his face to the wall and with tears called upon the God who had sustained him through some of the most dramatic moments in the history of the kingdom. He reminded the Lord of his faithfulness and asked that he might be granted a miracle. He wanted to live.

Isaiah left the bedside of Hezekiah with a feeling of helplessness. But he had hardly reached the court of the palace when the word of the Lord came to him saying: *Turn again, and tell Hezekiah the captain of my people, Thus saith the LORD, the God of David thy father, I have heard thy prayer, I have seen thy tears: behold, I will heal thee: on the third day thou shalt go up unto the house of the LORD* (II Kings 20:5).

God had granted the godly king another fifteen years to live! As was the custom in the days of the prophets, Hezekiah asked for a sign to prove the word of the Lord. Isaiah said, *... shall the shadow go forward ten degrees, or go back ten degrees? ... It is a light thing,* said Hezekiah, *for the shadow to go down ten degrees: ... but let the shadow return backward ten degrees* (II Kings 20:9-10).

Miracle of miracles! The magnificent Creator of the universe literally shifted the earth in its course about the sun to cause the great sun dial in the court of Hezekiah to move ten degrees backward. It is believed from that day forward, to the astonishment of all the world, the length of the year was changed from 360 days to 365 ¼ days.

The rabbis wrote that Hezekiah changed the calendar in the fifteen remaining years of his life, adding one month to the calendar every six years. It has also been recorded that the Romans and the Egyptians changed their calendars to account for the lengthened year.[1]

The healed and happy Hezekiah composed ten songs to compare with the ten degrees on the sun dial and added to them four songs written by David and one by Solomon to set the total number at fifteen, to compare with the fifteen years which the Lord had added to his life.

The LORD was ready to save me: therefore we will sing my songs to the stringed instruments all the days of our life in the house of the LORD (Isaiah 38:20).

Those fifteen songs chosen by the recovered Hezekiah are recorded in Psalms 120-134. They are called the Songs of the Degrees, so named because of the ten degrees of the sun dial. They are sometimes called the Psalms of Ascent, for they were sung by the priesthood as they ascended the fifteen steps of the Temple each year during the Feast of Tabernacles.

Though the Songs of Degrees were compiled by the king, they contain far more than just the joy of the healed Hezekiah. It is believed that the Songs of Degrees also contain five prophetic prayers of a dispersed Israel.

First, there is a prayer for the restoration of the land to the Jews which corresponds with Genesis.

Second, there is a prayer for the restoration of the Jews to their land which corresponds with Exodus.

Third, there is a prayer for the restoration of Temple worship which corresponds with Leviticus.

Fourth, there is a prayer for deliverance from tribulation which corresponds with Numbers.

And fifth, there is a prayer for the coming of the Messiah to establish a kingdom of peace which corresponds with Deuteronomy.

These five prayers (recorded in Hezekiah's Songs of Degrees) appear to be in the process of fulfillment in this twentieth century.

The fifteen psalms are compiled in five sets of three psalms each. The first psalm in each group offers a cry of distress; the second psalm declares a trust in the Lord; and the third psalm promises deliverance, blessing, and peace. Furthermore, these five sets follow an outline given in the five divisions of the Psalms:

Psalms 120, 121, and 122 represent a Genesis period.
Psalms 123, 124, and 125 represent an Exodus period.
Psalms 126, 127, and 128 represent a Leviticus period.
Psalms 129, 130, and 131 represent a Numbers period.
Psalms 132, 133, and 134 represent a Deuteronomy period.

In so doing, they offer a prophetic overview of the events of the last generation — even of the twentieth century!

THE GENESIS PERIOD
PSALM 120

In my distress I cried unto the LORD, and he heard me.
Deliver my soul, O LORD, from lying lips, and from a deceitful tongue (vv. 1-2).

Hezekiah began in Psalm 120 with a cry of distress on behalf of the Jewish people.

Woe is me, that I sojourn in Mesech,
My soul hath long dwelt with him that hateth peace.
I am for peace: but when I speak, they are for war (vv. 5-7).

This is a prophecy to open the twentieth century showing the distress of the Jewish people who were suffering under the "pogroms," or massacres, of the Russian czar. *Woe is me, that I sojourn in Mesech ...* Mesech is an ancient word for Moscow, the capital of Russia. The massacres of Russian Jews in the early part of this century led to the Bolshevik Revolution. Under those conditions, the prophetic psalm declares, *I am for peace: but when I speak, they are for war.*

This introduces the Genesis period for the Psalms of Degrees. It seems to represent the early years of this century when God chose certain men to prepare the Promised Land for the Jewish people.

PSALM 121

I will lift up mine eyes unto the hills, from whence cometh my help.
My help cometh from the LORD, which made heaven and earth.
He will not suffer thy foot to be moved:
Behold, he that keepeth Israel shall neither slumber nor sleep (vv. 1-4).

In Psalm 121, the emphasis shifts from distress to trust. Prophetically, the psalm indicates that deliverance for the Jewish people will be found in a return to their ancient homeland. *I will lift up mine eyes unto the hills* — those are the hills around Jerusalem. Again, we can see the progression of the prophecy for this twentieth century. Remember, in these fifteen psalms there are five sets of three psalms each. In the first psalm the theme is distress, in the second psalm the theme is trust, and in the third psalm the theme is deliverance. Therefore, in Psalm 122, Hezekiah inserted a psalm of David to show a prophetic future deliverance for the Jewish people.

PSALM 122

*I was glad when they said unto me, Let us go into the house of
the LORD.
Our feet shall stand within thy gates, O Jerusalem.
Jerusalem is builded as a city that is compact together:* (vv.
1-3).

The ultimate conclusion for a deliverance of the Jewish people
was to come one day when their feet would stand within the gates
of Jerusalem. Furthermore, he said in verse 3 that Jerusalem
would be built as a city that is compact together. The Hebrew
word for compact is "khaw-bar," meaning "to join." It appears
to be a prophecy of what happened to the city of Jerusalem in
1967. Until the Six Day War, Jerusalem was a divided city, but in
June 1967, the Israeli Army overran East Jerusalem and reunited
the city under Jewish control. *Jerusalem is builded as a city that
is compact together.*
What a tremendous prophecy has been fulfilled as seen in
Hezekiah's first three Psalms of the Degrees.

*Pray for the peace of Jerusalem: they shall prosper that love
thee* (v. 6).

This is a prayer which leads us yet into the future, for as of now
it remains unfulfilled. Pray for the peace of Jerusalem, for one
day, when the Messiah comes, there will be peace. And when
shall we see peace in Jerusalem? Verse 1 of Psalm 122 indicates
that it will be after the restoration of Temple worship.

*I was glad when they said unto me, Let us go into the house of
the LORD* (v. 1).

These are the five basic prayers given in the Songs of Degrees
compiled by Hezekiah 700 years B.C. — prayer number one: for
the return of the land to the Jews; prayer number two: for the
restoration of the Jews to their land; prayer number three: for
the restoration of Temple worship; prayer number four: for
deliverance from tribulation; and prayer number five: for the
coming of the Messiah to set up His millennial kingdom. All five
of these prayers can be seen in the first set of songs — Psalms 120
through 122.

THE EXODUS PERIOD
PSALM 123

> *Have mercy upon us, O LORD, have mercy upon us: for we
> are exceedingly filled with contempt.*
> *Our soul is exceedingly filled with the scorning of those that
> are at ease, and with the contempt of the proud* (vv. 3-4).

The second set of these psalms (123-125) represents the Exodus
period. Once again, the first psalm in the set opens with the theme
of distress. These verses could well express the distress of the
Jewish people in Germany during the days of World War II. In the
following psalm there is a shift from the theme of distress to one
of trust.

PSALM 124

> *If it had not been the LORD who was on our side.*
> *... when men rose up against us:*
> *Then they had swallowed us up quick, when their wrath was
> kindled against us* (vv. 1-3).

This is another psalm of David chosen by Hezekiah. It expresses a trust in the Lord's deliverance which may have been
fulfilled in the return of the Jewish people to their ancient
homeland after the German Holocaust of World War II. The
following psalm completes the picture in this set of three depicting deliverance and blessing.

PSALM 125

> *They that trust in the LORD shall be as mount Zion, which
> cannot be removed, but abideth for ever.*
> *As the mountains are round about Jerusalem, so the LORD is
> round about his people from henceforth even for ever* (vv. 1-2).

Though these psalms were written seven hundred years before

the birth of Christ, they appear to have a logical fulfillment in this generation with the return of the land to the Jews in the Genesis period (Psalms 120-122) and the return of the Jews to their land in the Exodus period (Psalms 123-125).

THE LEVITICUS PERIOD
PSALM 126

> *When the LORD turned again the captivity of Zion, we were like them that dream.*
> *Then was our mouth filled with laughter, and our tongue with singing: then said they among the heathen, The LORD hath done great things for them.*
> *The LORD hath done great things for us; whereof we are glad* (vv. 1-3).

This brings us to the Leviticus period (Psalms 126-128), the time for the restoration of Temple worship. Psalm 126 begins with a prophetic picture of the new state of Israel and the joy expressed by Jews around the world since 1948.

PSALM 127

> *Except the LORD build the house, they labor in vain that build it* (v. 1).

With the return of the Jews to their land, the next natural development in the course of prophetic fulfillment is the restoration of Temple worship. Psalm 127 was written by Solomon and chosen by Hezekiah to be placed at this strategic spot in the Leviticus section because it concerns the rebuilding of the Temple. It is the center psalm around which the fifteen Psalms of Degrees revolve.

This is the key verse not only for this set of the Leviticus Psalms, but also for the entire set of fifteen psalms compiled by Hezekiah. *Except the LORD build the house ...* is a reference to the rebuilding of the Temple in Jerusalem. Prophetically, we are in the midst of this period today. Since 1973, a World Synagogue has been built. It was dedicated on August 4, 1982.

In March 1983, a group of religious Jews were arrested for trying to enter the Temple Mount area to establish Jewish worship. In the October 1, 1983, issue of the JERUSALEM POST an article on the subject stated that the twenty-nine men arrested for attempting to break into the Temple Mount were acquitted of the charges.

These are just a few of the developments toward establishing a Jewish presence on the Temple Mount which will eventually lead to the erection of a Jewish sanctuary on the Temple site.

PSALM 128

The LORD shall bless thee out of Zion: and thou shalt see the good of Jerusalem all the days of thy life (v. 5).

Psalm 128 (the third psalm in the Leviticus series) expresses the deliverance and blessing that shall be the result of this Leviticus period. Today, we are awaiting the ultimate fulfillment of this prophecy. One day soon, the Jewish people will erect a sanctuary on the Temple site and will restore Temple worship. When that happens, the world will be approaching the Numbers period — seven dreadful years of Tribulation.

THE NUMBERS PERIOD
PSALM 129

Many a time have they afflicted me from my youth.
... yet they have not prevailed against me.
The plowers plowed upon my back: they made long their furrows (vv. 1-3).

Psalms 129-131 represent the Numbers period. The key phrase, *many a time,* must be prophetic of the Tribulation when the Jewish people will undergo a designated seven-year period wherein the Lord will pour out His wrath upon an unbelieving world.

Psalm 129 is a prayer for deliverance in the midst of distress, which leads us to the next psalm in this series, a psalm of trust.

PSALM 130

Out of the depths have I cried unto thee, O LORD.
Lord, hear my voice: let thine ears be attentive to the voice of
my supplications (vv. 1-2).

By now the abomination of desolation seems to have taken place. The remnant has escaped to the mountains.

I wait for the LORD, my soul doth wait, and in his word do I
hope (v. 5).

Verse 5 gives another key to the understanding of this Numbers period, *I wait ...* What else can they do? The seven years must run its course. Yet, there is a trust in the Lord's ability to deliver them.

My soul waiteth for the Lord more than they that watch for the
morning: I say, more than they that watch for the morning (v.
6).

This verse describes the darkest hour of world history. Armageddon is raging, *but unto you that fear my name shall the Sun of righteousness arise with healing in his wings* (Malachi 4:2) *My soul waiteth for the Lord more than they that watch for the morning.*

The song writer put it so aptly, "Some golden daybreak Jesus will come. Some golden daybreak battles all won. Then shall the victory break through the blue. Some golden daybreak, for me and you!"[1]

Let Israel hope in the LORD: for with the LORD there is mer-
cy, and with him is plenteous redemption.
And he shall redeem Israel from all his iniquities (vv. 7-8).

What a confidence in the midst of their greatest suffering in history!

PSALM 131

LORD, my heart is not haughty, nor mine eyes lofty: neither do I exercise myself in great matters, or in things too high for me.
Surely I have behaved and quieted myself, as a child that is weaned of his mother: my soul is even as a weaned child.
Let Israel hope in the LORD from henceforth and for ever (vv. 1-3).

Psalm 131 is another psalm of David chosen by Hezekiah because of its strategic message. It gives the ultimate answer to their prayer for deliverance. It is the third psalm in the series on the Numbers period, and represents the humility of the Jewish people as a result of the Tribulation Period.

It seems amazing to me that Hezekiah compiled these psalms seven hundred years before the birth of Christ and was probably quite unaware of their prophetic design. Bear in mind that they comprise five basic prayers — 1) for the restoration of the land to the Jews; 2) for the restoration of the Jews to their land; 3) for the restoration of Temple worship; 4) for deliverance from the Tribulation; and 5) for the coming of the Messiah to establish His kingdom.

THE DEUTERONOMY PERIOD
PSALM 132

LORD, remember David, and all his afflictions: (v. 1).

Psalm 132 is a psalm of distress. It is the first psalm in the series of three and seems to represent the Jewish people in the midst of their great affliction — Armageddon. Psalms 132-134 represent the Deuteronomy period when Messiah will come to establish the kingdom.

Furthermore, in this psalm, an indication is given that the sanctuary established for Temple worship was none other than the ancient Tabernacle of David, which I believe will be discovered and set up on the Temple site.

> Surely I will not come into the tabernacle of my house, nor go
> up into my bed;
> I will not give sleep to mine eyes, or slumber to mine eyelids,
> Until I find out a place for the LORD, a habitation for the
> mighty God of Jacob.
> Lo, we heard of it at Ephratah: we found it in the fields of the
> wood.
> We will go into his tabernacles: we will worship at his
> footstool.
> Arise, O LORD, into thy rest; thou, and the ark of thy strength
> (vv. 3-8).

These verses speak of the Tabernacle and the Ark of the Covenant, which have been missing for 2,500 years. One day they will be returned to Jerusalem to await the coming of the Messiah and the establishment of His kingdom. This psalm of distress looks forward to the appearance of the Messiah. The *rest* referred to in this verse will be the Great Sabbath Rest in the millennial kingdom of Christ.

> This is my rest for ever: here will I dwell; for I have desired it
> (v. 14).

In the midst of their affliction at Armageddon, Jesus Christ, the Messiah, will return to this earth in power and great glory to establish the kingdom rest. The distress of Psalm 132 gives way to the trust of Psalm 133.

PSALM 133

> Behold, how good and how pleasant it is for brethren to dwell
> together in unity! (v. 1).

The problems of planet Earth will all be solved when Jesus comes. Brethren shall dwell together in unity, for ... *nation shall not lift up sword against nation, neither shall they learn war anymore* (Isaiah 2:4). This is another psalm of David chosen by Hezekiah and placed at this strategic spot in the series to reveal the joy and blessing provided by the offspring of David — the Messiah Himself.

PSALM 134

Behold, bless ye the LORD, all ye servants of the LORD,
which by night stand in the house of the LORD.
Lift up your hands in the sanctuary, and bless the LORD.
The LORD that made heaven and earth bless thee out of Zion
(vv. 1-3).

Psalm 134 is the third psalm in this Deuteronomy series, and
the final psalm to conclude the fifteen Songs of the Degrees. It is a
psalm of joy and prophetically indicates both deliverance and
blessing, for the kingdom has come. The psalm declares that the
Messiah created the heavens and the earth and that He, the Great
Creator, lives in Jerusalem to bless the world for a thousand
wonderful years.

What a set of psalms — fifteen of them — compiled by Hezekiah
after his miraculous healing in the year 701 B.C.! How amazing it
is that they contain five prophetic prayers to be fulfilled in that
special generation destined to see the return of the land to the
Jews, the return of the Jews to their land, the restoration of Temple worship, the suffering of the Tribulation, and the coming of
the Messiah.

It is also amazing that they follow a prophetic theme apparently designed for this twentieth century, depicted by the five books
of Moses — Genesis, Exodus, Leviticus, Numbers, and
Deuteronomy.

PSALM 135

Praise ye the LORD [**Hallelujah**] *Praise ye the name of the*
LORD; praise him, O ye servants of the LORD (v. 1).

As a fitting conclusion to Hezekiah's Songs of Degrees, Psalm
135 declares **Hallelujah** both at its beginning (v. 1) and conclusion
(v. 21). Both Psalms 135 and 136 cover the same theme. This is
typical of each prophetic segment of those psalms which predict
the coming of the Messianic Era.

After concluding each book of the Psalms with *Amen and Amen* the Numbers book (Psalm 106:48) ends with *Amen and Praise ye the LORD* [**Hallelujah**]. This is because the kingdom has come. In fact, the Numbers book concludes with **Hallelujah**.

The Deuteronomy book (Psalms 107-150) records 18 "**Hallelu-jahs**" (6+6+6) as a joyful series of praises over the establishment of the Messianic kingdom.

Psalms 146-150 contain 10 of those "**Hallelujah's**" (the number of Ordinal perfection). As a grand climax they review that special generation which sees the Genesis period in which God prepares the Promised Land for the Chosen People; the Exodus period when the Chosen People return to possess their land; the Leviticus Period wherein Temple worship is revived; the Numbers period when Israel suffers Tribulation; and the Deuteronomy period in which the kingdom comes.

Psalm 135 is a Messianic psalm looking forward to the kingdom age when all will praise the LORD. "In this chapter, the psalmist singles out notable events of Jewish history and calls upon all segments of the Jewish people to join together in this climactic Messianic hymn."[1]

> *Whatsoever the LORD pleased, that did he ...*
> *Who smote the firstborn of Egypt,*
> *Who smote great nations,*
> *Sihon ... Og ... and all the kingdoms of Canaan:*
> *and gave their land for ... a heritage unto Israel ...* (vv.
> 6,8,10-12).

The psalm reviews the mighty deeds of the LORD in the creation, the exodus, and the taking of the Promised Land. The same theme follows in Psalm 136, which, in the Talmud (Pesachim 118b), is called the Great Hallel (though the term Hallel-ujah is not used). The two Psalms (135 and 136) cover the same subject — God's work in creation and Israel's exodus to possess their Promised Land.

PSALM 136

> *O give thanks unto the LORD; for he is good: for his mercy en-*
> *dureth for ever* (v. 1).

The 26 verses of this psalm are said to praise the holy name of the LORD, which in Hebrew has a numerical value of 26. It is called the "Great Hallel" and is recited every Sabbath morning to commemorate the perfection of God's creation.

Talmudic scholars (Pesachim 118a) wrote that the phrase *for his mercy endureth forever* is repeated 26 times to correspond with the 26 generations between Creation and the giving of the Law at Sinai.[1]

It is also made a part of the Passover ritual because of its many references to the Exodus.

> *To him that by wisdom made the heavens ... To him that stretched out the earth above the waters ... To him that smote Egypt ... And brought out Israel from among them ...* (vv. 5-6,10-11).

The psalm starts out with the Creator making the universe — then the earth, etc. until He narrows the message down to the deliverance of Israel out of Egypt, and the giving of their heritage — the land of Israel. It is a psalm of thanksgiving — *for his mercy endureth forever.*

PSALM 137

> *By the rivers of Babylon, there we sat down, yea, we wept, when we remembered Zion.*
> *We hanged our harps upon the willows in the midst thereof.*
> *How shall we sing the LORD's song in a strange land?* (vv. 1-2, 4).

Psalm 137 appears to be written as a prelude to Psalms 138-145. The prophecy begins in Psalm 137 with the destruction of Mystery Babylon, thus introducing seven years of Tribulation and concluding with the glorious appearing of the Messiah in Psalm 144, followed by a psalm of praise (145). Psalms 138-145 were written by David. Though Psalm 137 was not authored by him, it nevertheless sets the stage for those events predicted in David's psalms (138-145). The prophetic implications appear to be both progressive and chronological.

This psalm addresses the subject of the Babylonian captivity following the destruction of Solomon's Temple with strong prophetic implications to Babylon's future mystery daughter,

Babylon the Great. Prophetically, the lament of the 144,000 can be seen in verses 5-7:

> *If I forget thee, O Jerusalem, let my right hand forget her cunning.*
> *If I do not remember thee, let my tongue cleave to the roof of my mouth; if I prefer not Jerusalem above my chief joy.*
> *Remember, O LORD, the children of Edom in the day of Jerusalem; who said, Rase it, rase it, even to the foundation thereof* (vv. 5-7).

The memory of the Temple's destruction is kept alive in every facet of Jewish life. A Jewish home has at least one unpainted brick or board. Every garment has one small part soiled. At every wedding a glass is broken — all to keep the remembrance of a destroyed Temple. Prophetically, a restoration of Temple worship will be forthcoming at or near the beginning of the Tribulation. The Tabernacle of David will be set up on the Temple site (Amos 9:11-12). According to the prophets there must be at least one more desecration of the Temple site — the abomination of desolation.

It is ironic that Edom is mentioned here, for that will be the destination of the fleeing 144,000 when Jerusalem is surrounded by armies and the antichrist commits the abomination that makes the Temple Mount desolate. The Babylonian Captivity set the stage for the "Times of the Gentiles" — a term used to describe the great world empires which, having begun with Babylon, will end with her mystery daughter, Babylon the Great. Verse 8 gives the prophecy of the passage:

> *O daughter of Babylon, who art to be destroyed; happy shall he be, that rewardeth thee as thou has served us* (v. 8).

Mystery Babylon will be the capital of the antichrist. The ... *great city, which reigneth over the kings of the earth* (Revelation 17:18), will be destroyed sometime during the Tribulation. By the middle of those seven years the antichrist will move to Jerusalem and take over the government. He will enter the Temple Mount, establish his throne, and claim to be the Messiah. He will demand a mark be accepted in the hand or forehead of every person on earth as a medium of exchange in the marketplace. From that point, however, his kingdom will began to deteriorate — ending in the Battle of Armageddon.

PSALM 138

*I will praise thee with my whole heart: before the gods will I
sing praise unto thee.*
*I will worship toward thy holy temple, and praise thy name for
thy lovingkindness and for thy truth: for thou hast magnified thy
word above all thy name* (vv. 1-2).

This is the first of eight psalms (138-145) written by David,
seven of which describe (year by year) the plight of the future
Jewish remnant during the seven years of Tribulation, followed
by an eighth psalm (145) — designated distinctly as a psalm of
praise at the coming of Messiah.

Prophetically, Psalm 138 reflects upon the time before the antichrist desecrates the Temple site. These first two verses tell of
those happy days just before Tribulation sets in. The first of seven
dreadful years is depicted in this first of seven dreadful psalms.
Each psalm (138-144) follows the course of the seven years of
Tribulation!

*Though I walk in the midst of TROUBLE, thou wilt revive me:
thou shalt stretch forth thine hand against the wrath of mine
enemies, and thy right hand shall save me* (v. 7).

Verse 7 gives a clue to let us know the dreadful hour has arrived. The key word is *trouble*. According to Jewish thought, the
psalm depicts the triumphant spirit of the Jewish nation at the
coming of Messiah. They will see the destruction of Gog and
Magog and will thrill to the renewal of Jewish sovereignty by the
royal offspring of David. In my opinion, however, the thought is a
little premature. Verse 7 places the time-frame at the beginning
of Jacob's trouble, for victory is yet in the future. *...thou WILT
revive me: thou SHALT* [future tense] *stretch forth thine hand.*

Perhaps the rejoicing in this psalm will come after the Russian
invasion and destruction (which I believe could occur at the
beginning of the Tribulation), wherein the antichrist will present
himself as a great peacemaker. Many in Israel will be so anxious
for Messiah to appear they will consider the wrong one. Israel
could also confuse the Russian invasion with the final battle of Armageddon. Rabbinic writings already bear out the Jewish con-

cept that the Battle of Gog and Magog constitutes the final war. Israel may not understand that another more devastating war lies seven years in the future.

PSALM 139

O LORD, thou hast searched me, and known me.
Thou knowest my downsitting and mine uprising, thou understandest my thought afar off.
Thou compassest my path and my lying down, and art acquainted with all my ways.
For there is not a word in my tongue, but, lo, O LORD, thou knowest it altogether.
Thou hast beset me behind and before, and laid thine hand upon me (vv. 1-5).

This is the second of eight psalms (138-145) written by David, seven of which describe the seven year Tribulation Period year by year, followed by an eighth psalm (145) — designated distinctly as a psalm of praise at the coming of Messiah.

No other psalm is quite so perceptive of God's reasons for creation as this one. David wrote that God had planned every minute detail of history before the beginning. *Behind* refers to the past and *before* (v. 5) speaks of the future.

Rabbi Yehudah (quoted in Midrash Shocher Tov) states that Adam gave the basic premise upon which this psalm was written — "the outline of all human history was etched into the flesh and bone of Adam ... All subsequent historical events conformed to a comprehensive primeval pattern, the original Divine plan. As every new generation enters the stage of history, it follows an ancient script, and a predetermined Divine drama unfolds."[1]

My opinion is that the psalm refers to the birth of Israel rather than Adam. I suggest the Psalms give an overview of the birth process for the nation in this century. For rabbinic thought to consider a similar theme points up the plausability of this suggestion.

Prophetically, Psalm 139 presents an overwhelming sense of awe — an amazement at the complexity of God's prophetic pattern.

Such knowledge is too wonderful for me; it is high, I cannot at-

tain unto it (v. 6).

Israel must be the baby born in these verses. Its birth was planned and prepared by the omnipotence of God.

> *I will praise thee; for I am fearfully and wonderfully made; marvellous are thy works; and that my soul knoweth right well.*
> *My substance was not hid from thee, when I was made in secret, and curiously wrought in the lowest parts of the earth.*
> *Thine eyes did see my substance, yet being unperfect; and in thy book all my members were written, which in continuance were fashioned, when as yet there was none of them* (vv. 14-16).

The eleventh century rabbi, Rashi, taught that "in His Book, God recorded the days that would be fashioned by the development of human history. All of this was predetermined and known in advance, although not one of them [the days] had yet passed."[2]

Under the inspiration of the Holy Spirit, David enlarged upon the subject when he wrote, "All the days ordained for me were written IN YOUR BOOK before one of them came to be" (Psalm 139:16 NIV).

This rendering of the verse in the New International Version (NIV) appears to be an accurate description of the prophetic purpose of this psalm.

Here is a verse which prophetically symbolizes Israel, declaring that "all the days" were written in the book! The Jerusalem Bible is equally astounding: "You had scrutinized my every action, all were recorded in your book, my days listed and determined, even before the first of them occurred."

In the King James translation, the words *my members* are in italics which means they were not part of the original Hebrew Scriptures. They were added by the translators. Other versions treat the phrase as "my days."

> ... *in thy book all my members* [my days?] *were written, which in continuance* [chronological order?] *were fashioned, when as yet there was none of them* (v. 16 KJV).

Those events leading up to the birth of Israel appear to be implied in the Psalms *in continuance* or chronological order, suggesting Psalm 1 for year 1, Psalm 2 for year 2, etc.

The symbol of the baby is used of Israel many times in the Bible. God said to Moses, ... *thou shalt say unto Pharaoh, Thus saith the LORD, Israel is my son, even my firstborn:* (Exodus 4:22). The symbol was used by Isaiah, Jeremiah, Micah, John, Paul, and Jesus. Also, down through the centuries, rabbis and Christian scholars have considered the symbolic baby as a picture of the rebirth of Israel. The commemorative coin for 1948 struck by the Israeli government shows a woman (Rachel) with a new baby boy — Israel!

The birth of Israel took place in 1948, but the spiritual rebirth of the Jewish people may come at the onset of the Tribulation Period. No wonder David, archetype of Israel, declared, *How precious also are thy thoughts unto me, O God! how great is the sum of them!* (v. 17).

The following verses seem to reflect upon the abomination of desolation which will be committed by the antichrist.

> *Surely thou wilt slay the wicked, O God: depart from me therefore, ye bloody men.*
> *For they speak against thee wickedly, and thine enemies take thy name in vain* (vv. 19-20).

"The Talmud (Yerushalmi, Shabbos 16:1) identifies these as the apostates and renegade Jews, whose heresy is especially virulent. They are far more dangerous than ordinary Gentiles and idolaters because they attempt to poison other Jews against God."[3] Perhaps the most virulent renegade will be none other than the antichrist.

The Temple was always connected with the exaltation of the name of Jehovah. It was built to honor His matchless name. When the antichrist commits the abomination of desolation, his main goal will be to take God's name in vain. His actions will represent the greatest blasphemy ever seen on the Temple Mount. Mr. 666 will take upon himself the very name of Deity.

> *Search me, O God, and know my heart: try me, and know my thoughts:*
> *And see if there be any wicked way in me, and lead me in the way everlasting* (vv. 23-24).

"David ... turns his gaze to the future and prays that his dynasty will consist of leaders of flawless character, people who would be loyal ... [and, or course] the Messianic king will culminate David's dynasty."

PSALM 140

Deliver me O LORD, from the evil man; preserve me from the violent man; (v. 1).

This is the third of eight psalms (138-145) written by David, seven of which describe the plight of the future Jewish remnant in the seven year Tribulation Period, followed by an eighth psalm (145) — designated distinctly as a psalm of praise at the coming of Messiah.

Rabbi Ibn Ezra stated that this psalm reflected David's bitter period while a fugitive from King Saul. "How difficult this period was for David! He was so close to leading the people of God, yet the Jewish people refused to recognize him."[1]

Another rabbi (Sforno) commented that "this difficult period in David's life will be repeated on a larger scale at the advent of David's scion, the Messiah. The enemies of Israel ... will attack Israel in the awesome War of Gog and Magog in which they will meet their final defeat. At that time, the prophetic words of the psalmist will be fulfilled."[2]

The *evil man* referred to in verse 1 appears to be the antichrist, who, after three and a half years of Tribulation, will come to the Temple Mount and desecrate the sanctuary. Jesus referred to that occasion in Matthew's gospel. *When ye therefore shall see the abomination of desolation, spoken of by Daniel the prophet, stand in the holy place (whoso readeth, let him understand:) Then let them which be in Judea flee into the mountains: Let him which is on the housetop not come down to take anything out of his house: Neither let him which is in the field return back to take his clothes. And woe unto them that are with child, and to them that give suck in those days! But pray ye that your flight be not in the winter, neither on the sabbath day: For then shall be great tribulation, such as was not since the beginning of the world to this time, no, nor ever shall be. And except those days should be shortened, there should no flesh be saved: ...* (Matthew 24:15-22).

The scene described here marks the middle of the Tribulation Period. It is believed the 144,000 will flee to the mountain strongholds of Petra, forty miles south of the Dead Sea. They will remain there for the next three and one-half years while the world faces its most devastating period in history. The great world wars of this century will seem trivial when compared to the destruction of the last three and one-half years of the coming Tribulation.

Psalm 140 contains a plea for deliverance from the reign of terror unleashed by the antichrist upon the 144,000.

> Keep me, O LORD, from the hands of the wicked; preserve me from the violent man; who have purposed to overthrow my goings.
> The proud have hid a snare for me ... (vv. 4-5).

"Ibn Yachya interprets this as an allusion to the exile of Israel. The Ishmaelites [Arabs] are described as the 'wicked' while Edom [Rome and Christianity] is the 'violent man.' "[3] Leaders of protestant Christianity over the past 400 years have also considered the possibility that Rome will be Mystery Babylon and that a pope could be the antichrist. Others say an Israelite from the lost tribe of Dan will be the antichrist. The *snare* alludes to the trap of the antichrist. (See notes on Psalm 88.)

> Grant not, O LORD, the desires of the wicked: further not his wicked device; lest they exalt themselves. Selah (v. 8).

Commenting on this verse, Rabbi Avrohom Chaim Feuer wrote, "In the future, colossal military forces will enter into head-on conflict in the War of Gog and Magog. Only Divine intervention will save people from the perils of this war."[4]

Rabbinic views point up the prophetic significance of these psalms as they relate to the plight of the Jewish remnant (144,000) in the Tribulation Period.

PSALM 141

> LORD, I cry unto thee: make haste unto me; give ear unto my voice, when I cry unto thee.
> Let my prayer be set forth before thee as incense ... (vv. 1,2).

This is the fourth of eight psalms (138-145) written by David, seven of which describe the plight of the Jewish remnant (144,000) in the seven year Tribulation Period, followed by an eighth psalm

(145) — designated distinctly as a psalm of praise at the coming of Messiah.

This fourth psalm is strategically placed in the middle of these seven Tribulation psalms to give a perspective on the abomination of desolation. The prayers of the fleeing remnant reveal their fears about the antichrist.

The incense upon the golden altar symbolizes prayer. According to the Talmud (Kerisus 6b) eleven ingredients made up the spices for incense, one of which produced a foul odor. It was used to show that all Jews must be united in prayer. They must lay aside all differences and seek the forgiveness and protection of God.[1] The incense must be crushed and burned upon the golden altar. So will the Jewish people be as though they were crushed and burned through the fiery trials of the Great Tribulation.

The antics of the antichrist will bring all Jewish factions together. They will flee to the mountains in the midst of those seven dreadful years — when the antichrist commits the abomination of desolation.

> *Keep me from the snares which they have laid for me, and the gins of the workers of iniquity.*
> *Let the wicked fall into their own nets, whilst that I withal escape* (vv. 9-10).

The *snares* of verse 9 allude to the abomination of desolation. (See Psalm 88.) The remnant will escape!

PSALM 142

> *I cried unto the LORD with my voice; with my voice unto the LORD did I make my supplication.*
> *I poured our my complaint before him; I shewed before him my trouble* (vv. 1-2).

This is the fifth of eight psalms (138-145) written by David, seven of which describe the plight of the future Jewish remnant in the seven year Tribulation Period, followed by an eighth psalm (145) — designated as a psalm of praise at the coming of Messiah. David wrote this psalm when he was in the cave. Prophetically, the Jewish remnant (at least 144,000) will be hiding in the cave dwellings of Petra in the fifth year of the Tribulation Period.

> *When my spirit was overwhelmed within me, then thou knewest my path. In the way wherein I walked have they privily laid a snare for me* (v. 3).

The *snare* refers to the trap set by the antichrist to deceive the Jewish remnant and the world into accepting him as the Messiah. (See Psalm 88.) When he enters the Tabernacle of David and declares himself to be Deity, the religious Jews will recoil in horror. They will recognize his action as the deplorable abomination predicted by Daniel the prophet. At that occasion the Jewish remnant will flee to the mountain wilderness stronghold of Petra, leaving the Temple site desolate.

As they arrive in Petra, the words of this psalm will come to mind, *thou knewest my path* (v. 3). And the warning of Jesus will burn in their hearts: ... *pray ye that your flight be not in the winter, neither on the sabbath day: For then shall be great tribulation* ... (Matthew 24:20-21).

> *I looked on my right hand, and beheld, but there was no man that would know me: refuge failed me; no man cared for my soul. Attend unto my cry; for I am brought very low: deliver me from my persecutors; for they are stronger than I* (vv. 4,6).

Israel will have no allies in that day. The European confederation of nations will confiscate Jerusalem for their world capital and place their leader upon the throne of David. The United States will either be a part of the European-based world government or else will not exist by that time. No nation will stand on the side of the Jewish people.

Psalm 142 follows the same line of thought as the previous psalm. These psalms are prayers for help in the days following the abomination committed by the antichrist. Psalm 140 begins, *Deliver me, O LORD ...*; Psalm 141 begins, *LORD, I cry unto thee ...*; Psalm 142 begins, *I cried unto the Lord ...*; and Psalm 143 begins with, *Hear my prayer, O LORD.* These four psalms declare the great sorrow and heartache of the Jewish remnant in the midst of their suffering. They flee to the mountains.

> *Bring my soul out of prison, that I may praise thy name: the righteous shall compass me about; for thou shalt deal bountifully with me* (v. 7).

This prayer for deliverance will be heard as Armageddon develops. The world will propose a genocide for all Jews, but the remnant will look to the true Messiah, Jesus Christ, to come and save the day.

PSALM 143

> *Hear my prayer, O LORD, give ear to my supplications: in thy faithfulness answer me, and in thy righteousness.*
> *And enter not into judgment with thy servant: for in thy sight shall no man living be justified* (vv. 1-2).

This is the sixth of eight psalms (138-145) written by David, seven of which describe the plight of the future Jewish remnant during the seven year Tribulation Period, followed by an eighth psalm (145) — designated as a psalm of praise at the approach of the Messianic kingdom. The psalm is typical of the prayers of the remnant in the sixth year of the Tribulation Period.

"This psalm continues the theme of the preceding one."[1] Psalm 142 records David's prayer in the cave. In like manner, the Jewish remnant hiding in the caves of Petra, will pray for deliverance.

> *For the enemy hath persecuted my soul; he hath smitten my life down to the ground; he hath made me to dwell in darkness, as those that have been long dead* (v. 3).

Here is a further description of the mountainous area of Petra. The reference to those *long dead* is descriptive of the tomb-like caves of Petra and the *darkness* corresponds with Isaiah's prophecy about Petra. *Take counsel, execute judgment; make thy shadow as the night in the midst of the noonday; hide the outcasts; bewray not him that wandereth* (Isaiah 16:3).

> *Deliver me, O LORD, from mine enemies: I flee unto thee to hide me* (v. 9).

At the abomination of desolation, the remnant will flee to the mountains where God will hide them as Psalm 91 says, *He that dwelleth in the secret place of the Most High shall abide under the shadow of the Almighty* (Psalm 91:1).

PSALM 144

Blessed be the LORD my strength, which teacheth my hands to war, and my fingers to fight: (v. 1).

This is the seventh of eight psalms (138-145) written by David which describe the seven year Tribulation Period.

Psalm 144 is very special. It must have been numbered 144 to express the great significance of the 144,000 Jews who will be chosen to restore Temple worship during the first part of the Tribulation, but who will be forced to flee to Petra for the last part of the seven year period. The psalm describes the 144,000 in at least three respects.

First, there is a prayer for the personal appearing of the Messiah!

Bow thy heavens, O LORD, and come down: ... (v. 5).

Christ will return at the end of seven years of Tribulation to destroy the enemy and establish His kingdom. The description is unmistakable. This seventh psalm in David's series fits perfectly with the seventh and final year of the Tribulation Period.

Secondly, the psalm speaks of a flood:

Send thine hand from above; rid me, and deliver me out of great waters, ... (v. 7).

This is the kind of picture given in Revelation 12:13-17. *And when the dragon saw that he was cast unto the earth, he persecuted the woman which brought forth the man child. And to the woman were given two wings of a great eagle, that she might fly into the wilderness, into her place, where she is nourished for a time, and times, and half a time, from the face of the serpent. And the serpent cast out of his mouth water as a flood after the woman, that he might cause her to be carried away of the flood. And the earth helped the woman, and the earth opened her mouth, and swallowed up the flood which the dragon cast out of his mouth. And the dragon was wroth with the woman, and went to make war with the remnant of her seed, ...* (Revelation 12:13-17).

This world-wide flood will occur in the last half of the Tribulation. Though it will not cover the mountains as in the days of Noah, it will nevertheless be a fulfillment of the prophecy given by Jesus when He said: ... *as the days of Noe* [Noah] *were, so shall also the coming of the son of man be* (Matthew 24:37).

When the antichrist persecutes the woman, Israel, she will flee to the mountains of Petra. The symbol of an eagle was used to pinpoint the place. Furthermore, he (satan) will *make war with the remnant of her seed.*

Thirdly, the significant description found in Psalm 144 predicts a time when the remnant will sing a new song.

I will sing a new song unto thee, O God: upon a psaltry and an instrument of ten strings will I sing praises unto thee (v. 9).

The new song is most significant. It is referred to again in the book of Revelation. *And I looked, and lo, a Lamb stood on the mount Sion, and with him an hundred forty and four thousand, having his Father's name written in their foreheads. And I heard a voice from heaven as the voice of many waters, and as the voice of a great thunder: and I heard the voice of harpers harping with their harps: And they sung as it were a new song* ... (Revelation 14:1-3).

The new song marks a highlight in the midst of their suffering, for here, the Lord prepares for the deliverance of Israel.

Happy is that people, that is in such a case: yea, happy is that people, whose God is the LORD (v. 15).

The rest of the psalm (verses 10-15) tells how wonderful the millennial kingdom will be. It is a beautiful prayer for the coming of Messiah to deliver Israel. It is followed by a psalm of praise, which is typical of the other places in the Psalms which depict the coming of Messiah.

PSALM 145

I will extol thee, my God, O king; and I will bless thy name for ever and ever (v. 1).

Psalm 145 is the "only composition in the entire Book of Psalms, which is actually entitled a PRAISE."[1] It is so designated to compare with the other **Hallelujah** Psalms (see Psalm 135) which rejoice in the return of Christ to establish His millennial kingdom. The prayer for deliverance in Psalm 144 is answered in Psalm 145.

It is indicative of the appearing of Christ in the height of Armageddon to destroy the enemy and establish the kingdom. The psalm begins with words of praise to none other than the KING, Himself! Messiah has become *King of kings* (Revelation 19:16)! Furthermore, it is a praise which will last forever.

One generation shall praise thy works to another ... (v. 4).

The kingdom of Christ will last for a thousand years. This seventh thousand- year period of human history will be the Great Sabbath Rest. ... *and they shall beat their swords into plowshares, and their spears into pruninghooks: nation shall not lift up sword against nation, neither shall they learn war any more* (Isaiah 2:4). *For the earth shall be filled with the knowledge of the glory of the LORD, as the waters cover the sea* (Habakkuk 2:14).

This psalm contains exactly 150 words in the original Hebrew language — to correspond with the 150 psalms. The theme of the entire book, introduced in Psalms 1 and 2, reaches its climax in the coming of the Messianic kingdom.

They shall speak of the glory of thy kingdom, and talk of thy power;
To make known to the sons of men his mighty acts, and the glorious majesty of his kingdom.
Thy kingdom is an everlasting kingdom, and thy dominion endureth throughout all generations (vv. 11-13).

Through these eight psalms, we have covered the Tribulation Period — the establishment of Temple worship, the suffering of the 144,000 Jewish believers, the abomination of desolation committed by the antichrist, the fleeing of the remnant to the wilderness, and the devastations of the last three and one-half years.

When the armies of the world surround Jerusalem for the last great battle, the Jewish people will feel totally rejected by the world. Two hundred million soldiers will converge upon the land of Israel for the express purpose of destroying the Chosen People from the face of the earth. With no one coming to their aid, the Jews will call upon the one Person their forefathers had rejected. They will cry out to Jesus Christ to save them. At that moment, God will hear their cry. Verses 19 and 20 complete the story.

> He will fulfill the desire of them that fear him: he also will hear their cry, and save them.
> The LORD preserveth all them that love him: but all the wicked will he destroy (vv. 19-20).

In the height of the battle, the sun will explode — blowing the earth out of orbit. After a few days of unparalleled disasters, the sun will turn to ashes. In the darkened sky above Jerusalem, the world will see the grand entrance of the great Messiah! Millions of angels will attend His descent. The armies of heaven will be flanked on His right and on His left. The devastating cloud which covers the earth will roll back like a scroll to frame, like a majestic curtain upon a stage, the glorious revelation of the King of kings.That is the message of these eight psalms (136-145). That is the story of the 144,000 Jewish believers and their suffering at the hands of antichrist. It is the story of a people who were *fearfully and wonderfully made.*

PSALMS 146-150

The last five psalms correspond with the five divisions of the Psalms, which in turn, compare with the five books of Moses — Genesis, Exodus, Leviticus, Numbers, and Deuteronomy. Also, as seen in our review of the twentieth century, these divisions appear to describe the restoration of Israel for the coming of

Messiah.

This prophetic progression is seen in the Torah, the five books of the Psalms, Hezekiah's Songs of Degrees, and in Psalms 146-150.

Psalm 146 compares with the Genesis period; Psalm 147 with the Exodus period; Psalm 148 with the Leviticus period; Psalm 149 with the Numbers period; and Psalm 150 with the Deuteronomy period.

Each of these five psalms begins and ends with the words, *PRAISE ye the LORD.* In the Hebrew language the term is pronounced, **Hallelujah.** These last five psalms contain ten such praises — a **Hallelujah Chorus.** They represent a tremendous climax to the great Psalms of the Bible.

THE GENESIS PERIOD
PSALM 146

Praise ye the LORD. Praise the LORD, O my soul.
While I live will I praise the LORD: I will sing praises unto my
God while I have any being (vv. 1-2).

Psalm 146 corresponds with the Genesis period of this century and contains a candid assessment of the lack of British integrity. Verse 3 gives a warning to the Chosen People.

Put not your trust in princes, nor in the son of man, in whom
there is no help (v. 3).

The British conquered the land of Palestine under the Balfour Declaration, which promised to make the land available for Jewish settlement. They eventually turned from their promise and made the country into a British colony, refusing Jewish immigration. *Put not your trust in princes.*

Which executeth judgment for the oppressed: which giveth
food to the hungry. The LORD looseth the prisoners: (v. 7).

The Jews of Russia and Germany were indeed oppressed in the early years of this century, but here is a promise of vengeance upon their enemies and deliverance for the Chosen People.

> *The LORD preserveth the strangers; he relieveth the fatherless and widow: but the way of the wicked he turneth upside down* (v. 9).

Again, the oppressed are promised deliverance. Those orphans and widows of the death camps will be *relieve*[d] and God will bring judgment upon the Nazi perpetrators of those crimes.

THE EXODUS PERIOD
PSALM 147

> *Praise ye the LORD: for it is good to sing praises unto our God; for it is pleasant; and praise is comely* (v. 1).

Psalm 147 compares with the Exodus period of this century leading up to the birth of the nation of Israel.

> *The LORD doth build up Jerusalem: he gathered together the outcasts of Israel* (v. 2).

It is a perfect prophecy of the years following World War II when the outcasts of Israel returned to the ancient homeland of their forefathers to give birth to their nation and build up Jerusalem.

> *He sheweth his word unto Jacob, his statutes and his judgments unto Israel.*
> *He hath not dealt so with any nation:* ... (vv. 19-20).

God is preparing the Jewish nation for the appearing of Messiah. No other nation in history has returned to their ancient homeland as have the Chosen People. No other race has had within their hearts such a desire to return to the land of their nativity after centuries of exile.

THE LEVITICUS PERIOD
PSALM 148

Praise ye the LORD ... (v. 1).

Psalm 148 represents the Leviticus period. The key word is *praise*. After the introductory **Hallelujah**, the psalmist wrote:

Praise ye the Lord from the heavens: praise him in the heights.
Praise ye him, all his angels: praise ye him, all his hosts.
Praise ye him, sun and moon: praise him, all ye stars of light.
Praise him, ye heavens of heavens, and ye waters that be above the heavens.
Let them praise the name of the LORD:
Let them praise the name of the LORD: for his name alone is excellent; his glory is above the earth and heaven (vv. 1-5,13).

The Leviticus period will be a time of spiritual revival for the nation — to exalt the name of the Lord. That is the theme of this psalm and is believed to prophetically represent that period of time when Israel will re-establish the priesthood and restore Temple worship.

THE NUMBERS PERIOD
PSALM 149

Praise ye the LORD. Sing unto the LORD a new song, and his praise in the congregation of saints (v. 1).

Psalm 149 represents the Numbers period and the time of God's wrath. The *new song* of this passage compares with the *new song* of Psalm 96:1, Psalm 98:1, and Revelation 14:3. It will be a song of praise and victory for the Messiah — the Lamb.

Let the high praises of God be in their mouth, and a twoedged sword in their hand;

> To execute vengeance upon the heathen, and punishments
> upon the people;
> To bind their kings with chains, and their nobles with fetters of
> iron;
> To execute upon them the judgment written: this honour have
> all his saints (vv. 6-9).

The key word is *vengeance* (v. 7). It is a prophecy of the Tribulation Period, when the judgment of God will be poured out upon an unbelieving world to *execute upon them the judgment written.* Throughout the Bible *vengeance* is used to describe the Great Tribulation Period. For example, Isaiah wrote, *For it is the day of the LORD'S vengeance* (34:8); *... your God will come with vengeance* (35:4); *... I will take vengeance* (47:3); *... he put on the garments of vengeance* (59:17); *... the day of vengeance of our God* (61:2); *... For the day of vengeance is in mine heart* (63:4).

Over and over again *vengeance* refers to the Tribulation Period. In fact, the New Testament book written specifically to the Hebrew people promises them: *Vengeance belongeth unto me, I will recompense, saith the Lord* (Hebrews 10:30).

It is a prophecy of the coming Tribulation. The Apostle Jude also described it as: *... the judgment of the great day. Even as Sodom and Gomorrha, and the cities about them in like manner, giving themselves over to fornication, and going after strange flesh, are set forth for an example, suffering the vengeance of eternal fire* (Jude 6-7).

The harmony of these five psalms corresponding to the five divisions of the entire book is both conspicuous and astounding. It is incredible to consider that Psalm 149 declares the vengeance of the Numbers period — a time of Great Tribulation.

THE DEUTERONOMY PERIOD
PSALM 150

Praise God in his sanctuary: ... (v. 1).

Psalm 150 represents the Deuteronomy period, and the praises of the kingdom. With this tremendous conclusion, the psalmist declares that God dwells among men in a millennial Temple (to be built in Jerusalem). It is a picture of the golden age when the kingdom of heaven is established on earth. These psalms (146-150) are indeed a great **Hallelujah Chorus.** They conclude the Psalms with joy and praise.

> ... *praise him in the firmament of his power.*
> *Praise him for his mighty acts: praise him according to his excellent greatness.*
> *Praise him with the sound of the trumpet: praise him with the psaltery and harp.*
> *Praise him with the timbrel and dance: praise him with stringed instruments and organs.*
> *Praise him upon the loud cymbals: praise him upon the high sounding cymbals.*
> *Let every thing that hath breath praise the LORD. Praise ye the LORD* [**Hallelujah**] (vv. 1-6).

He concludes with a great, climactic, **Hallelujah.**

What a tremendous set of psalms! They so perfectly present a prophetic design for the events of the last generation.

THE HALLELUJAH PSALMS

It seems that even the Hallelujahs have a prophetic story to tell. In this Deuteronomy section of the psalms (107-150) I found eighteen Hallelujahs. (The word "Hallelujah" is a Hebrew term translated into English, "Praise ye the LORD.")

Hallelujah (Psalm 111:1)
Hallelujah (Psalm 112:1)
Hallelujah (Psalm 113:1)
Hallelujah (Psalm 113:9)
Hallelujah (Psalm 116:19)
Hallelujah (Psalm 117:2)
Hallelujah (Psalm 135:1)
Hallelujah (Psalm 135:21)
Hallelujah (Psalm 146:1)
Hallelujah (Psalm 146:10)
Hallelujah (Psalm 147:1)
Hallelujah (Psalm 147:20)
Hallelujah (Psalm 148:1)
Hallelujah (Psalm 148:14)
Hallelujah (Psalm 149:1)
Hallelujah (Psalm 149:9)
Hallelujah (Psalm 150:1)
Hallelujah (Psalm 150:6)

Remember, the Deuteronomy section prophetically portrays the seventh millennium of human history — the Great Sabbath Rest wherein the kingdom of Jesus Christ will be established. There are eighteen Hallelujahs to declare the praises of God during this time (6+6+6) in perfect contrast to the curses found in the mark of the beast, which, according to Revelation 13:18, bears the number — 666. These eighteen Hallelujahs seem to nullify the curse of the antichrist.

Furthermore, in the Numbers section (Psalms 90-106), which represents the Tribulation Period, there are four **Hallelujahs**. The first one is found in the last verse of Psalm 104; the second is found in the last verse of Psalm 105; and the third and fourth **Hallelujahs** introduce and conclude Psalm 106. These four **Hallelujahs** correspond with Revelation 19:1-6, showing the divine continuity of prophetic Scripture. Why four at this point? Because the number four has a mystical meaning. It represents the world.

In his book, NUMBER IN SCRIPTURE, E. W. Bullinger wrote: "... the number four is made up of three and one ... and it denotes ... that which follows the revelation of God in the Trinity, namely, His creative works. He is known by the things that are seen. Hence the written revelation commences with the words, 'In-the-beginning God CREATED.' Creation is, therefore, the next thing — the fourth thing, and the number four always has reference to all that is created ... It is the number of material completeness. Hence it is the world number."[1]

Bullinger listed some examples to show the relationship between the number four and the world: "Four is the number of the great elements — earth, air, fire, and water. Four are the regions of the earth — north, south, east, and west. Four are the divisions of the day — morning, noon, evening, and midnight. Four are the seasons of the year — spring, summer, autumn, and winter."[2]

The four **Hallelujahs** which conclude the Numbers section of the Psalms and the four **Hallelujahs** in Revelation 19 declare a rejoicing on the part of God's people over the fact that the problems which have plagued the human race since the fall of Adam are now ended. Paradise is regained. The Garden of Eden is restored. Humankind is no longer plagued by the great tempter. Satan is bound in the bottomless pit and Christ sits upon the throne of this world.

These four **Hallelujahs** in the Numbers section added to the 18 **Hallelujahs** in the Deuteronomy section make a total of 22 **Hallelujahs** in the Psalms — one for each of the 22 letters in the Hebrew alphabet. It is so fitting since the book of Deuteronomy was originally called "Dabar," meaning, "Word," and since our Saviour was referred to as the Greek equivalent "Logos," as well as the *Alpha and Omega*! **Hallelujah!**

THE PROPHETIC AMEN

In our previous study we took note of certain prophetic implications found in the word **Hallelujah**. While preparing the chapter, I noticed the word **Amen** was used seven times in the presentation of the Psalms. As insignificant as it may seem on the surface, it is by no means trite. The word **Amen** was used very carefully in the Psalms and throughout the Old Testament to represent prophetic passages. The very word itself has a future tense. It means, "so be it." Wherever you see the term **Amen** in the Old Testament, it has a prophetic implication. It is saying, "Let the thing that is done or said come to pass in the future."

The Psalms are divided into five books which correspond with the five books of Moses. They, in turn, present an outline of future events. A Genesis period was predicted for the land of Palestine to be prepared for the Chosen People. An Exodus period was predicted when the Chosen People would return to their land. A Leviticus period was predicted for the restoration of Temple worship. A Numbers period was predicted for the world to suffer unparalleled tribulation. Finally, a Deuteronomy period was predicted for the Messiah to establish the kingdom.

The first forty-one psalms correspond with the book of Genesis, the last verse of which is closed with two **Amens** — declaring the Genesis section of the Psalms to be a prophecy.

> *Blessed be the Lord God of Israel from everlasting, and to everlasting. Amen, and Amen* (Psalm 41:13).

Psalms 42-72 corresponds to Exodus. Like the first book, it is also concluded with two **Amens** and is thus declared to be a prophecy.

> *And blessed be his glorious name for ever: and let the whole earth be filled with his glory. Amen, and Amen* (Psalm 72:19).

Psalms 73-89 make up the third book, corresponding with

Leviticus. Again the section is designated as a prophecy. The psalmist declared, "so be it, so be it."

> *Blessed be the Lord for evermore. Amen, and Amen* (Psalm 89:52).

Psalms 90-106 make up the fourth book of the Psalms, which compares with Numbers. It is a prophecy of seven dreadful years at the conclusion of this dispensation. It represents the time of God's wrath. At the end of the Tribulation Period Christ will return to this earth to establish a new golden age — the millennial reign of Christ. Therefore, the Numbers section of the Psalms concludes with a single **Amen**, followed by a **Hallelujah**.

> *Blessed be the Lord God of Israel from everlasting to everlasting: and let all the people say, Amen. Praise ye the LORD* [**Hallelujah**] (Psalm 106:48).

Though the previous prophetic Psalms conclude with **Amen** and **Amen**, the Numbers section ends with a single **Amen** followed by **Hallelujah**. By this the psalmist declares the section to be not only prophetic, but the final prophecy containing the judgment of God. "So be it," he wrote, but then adds a **Hallelujah**, for the fifth book of the Psalms (107-150) declares not the judgment of God, but the blessings of the millennial kingdom.

When we come to Psalm 150, which concludes all five books, we do not find the word **Amen**. Instead, we find the same word which followed the last **Amen** of the Numbers section. The last word of Psalm 150 declares, **Hallelujah**.

Now if all of this seems insignificant, please understand that it is not. It is quite profound. When I noticed these seven **Amens**, I began to search the Old Testament to discover the various places where the term might be used and whether or not each instance contains a prophecy. To my delight I found seven occasions in the Old Testament where **Amen** is declared. In each passage a prophecy is implied — seven prophetic portions pointing out the important events which will fulfill God's great plan of the ages. Remember, the word **Amen** is prophetic. It means "so be it." In each place where it is found in the Old Testament, it declares that portion to be prophetic.

The Curse of an Unfaithful Wife

The first **Amen** is found in Numbers 5:22. The account concerns the curse of an unfaithful wife. According to the story, if a Jewish husband accused his wife of unfaithfulness, she could be brought before a divorce court. There the judge could administer a test to find out whether she had indeed been unfaithful. He would give her bitter water to drink, and if she was guilty, the bitter water would have a devastating effect. As the woman prepared to drink the bitter water, she would declare, **Amen**, and **Amen**. She was saying, "So be it. If I am guilty, let me suffer the consequences and if not, let me be vindicated."

A prophecy can be found in that ancient ritual, for God declared His wife, the nation of Israel, to be unfaithful. Israel committed spiritual adultery and has been made to drink bitter waters. God sent them into Babylonian captivity to fulfill the curse of an unfaithful wife.

The Dispersion of Israel

The second set of **Amens** is found in Deuteronomy 27. Moses instructed the people to go to the mountains of Gerizim and Ebal for the reading of the blessings and the cursings — which in themselves are prophecies.

He instructed half of the people to gather on Mount Gerizim, and the other half on Mount Ebal. The words of the law were to be read, along with prophetic blessings and cursings. On that occasion the people were to be reminded that if they served God, they would be blessed; but if they did not serve Him, they would be cursed.

There are twelve curses found in the passage. At the end of each the people were instructed to declare, **Amen**, meaning "so be it." The twelve **Amens** chanted by the people make this portion a prophecy. I believe it has been fulfilled over the past 2,500 years. God's curse has been heavy upon the Jews. They were driven from their land to live among Gentile nations for two millennia. The wandering Jew has become an enigma among the nations. It was not until this century that they returned to the land of their ancient forefathers to re-establish the nation.

The Return of a Remnant

That brings us to another **Amen** found in Nehemiah 5:13. The occasion had to do with the remnant of the people who returned to their land after the Babylonian captivity. The story involved the financial problems of the returning remnant. Those who loaned mortgage money at high interest rates were creating financial chaos in the nation. When Nehemiah heard the complaint, he became angry and declared: *Restore, I pray you, to them, even this day, their lands, their vineyards, their oliveyards, and their houses, also the hundredth part of the money, and of the corn, the wine, and the oil, that ye exact of them* (Nehemiah 5:11).

This was Nehemiah's solution for solving their economic dilemma. The bankers replied, *We will restore them, and will require nothing of them; so will we do as thou sayest ...* (v. 12).

The problem developed because the money lenders had taken advantage of the returning refugees. They were charging outrageous interest rates on loans. To solve the problem Nehemiah demanded they return every mortgage, plus one percent of the payments collected. *Then I called the priests, and took an oath of them, that they should do according to this promise. Also I shook my lap, and said, So God shake out every man from his house, and from his labor, that performeth not this promise, even thus be he shaken out, and emptied. And all the congregation said, Amen, and praised the LORD. And the people did according to this promise* (Nehemiah 5:12-13).

The **Amen** makes this passage a prophecy. It is a picture of the nation of Israel in this generation. First of all, a remnant has returned. Almost four million Jewish people have emigrated from nations around the world to re-establish their homeland.

At this time the annual inflation rate in Israel is very high. You can imagine the resulting problems. Some years ago the Israeli government tried to curb inflation by changing the currency in Israel. They discontinued the lira, replacing it with the Biblical shekel. However, that did not solve the problem. Perhaps the final solution will be found in the wisdom of Nehemiah. Not until Israel returns to the financial pattern set forth in the Bible will they ever find a solution to what has become one of the worst inflation rates among the nations of the world.

Return to the Mosaic Covenant

Another Amen can be found in Nehemiah 8:6. The passage tells about Ezra and the returning Israelites who assembled in Jerusalem for a reading of the Mosaic Law. It is the story of a revival and return to Temple worship. *And all the people gathered themselves together as one man into the street that was before the water gate; and they spake unto Ezra the scribe to bring the book of the law of Moses, which the Lord had commanded to Israel. And Ezra the priest brought the law before the congregation both of men and women, and all that could hear with understanding, upon the first day of the seventh month. And he read therein before the street that was before the water gate from the morning until midday, before the men and the women, and those that could understand; and the ears of all the people were attentive unto the book of the law* (Nehemiah 8:1-3).

It happened in September, at the Feast of Trumpets (Rosh Hashanah), the Jewish New Year. The people gathered just south of the Temple Mount to restore the Mosaic Covenant. *And Ezra opened the book in the sight of all the people; (for he was above all the people;) and when he opened it, all the people stood up: And Ezra blessed the LORD, the great God. And all the people answered, Amen, Amen, with lifting up their hands: and they bowed their heads and worshiped the LORD with their faces to the ground* (Nehemiah 8:5-6).

Their declaration makes this occasion a prophecy, the fulfillment of which is developing in Israel today. Not only have the Jews returned to their land, they are also preparing for a return to the Mosaic Covenant — namely, the reinstatement of the priesthood and the restoration of Temple worship.

The fulfillment of this prophetic scenario can be seen in Revelation 7 as 144,000 are sealed for a special ministry during the coming Tribulation Period. They will revive their ancient form of worship established in the days of Moses.

Return of the Ark of the Covenant

That brings us to the next prophetic **Amen**, found in I Chronicles 16:36. It was shouted by the people upon the return of the Ark of the Covenant. The scene is set in the opening of the chapter. *So they brought the ark of God, and set it in the midst of the tent that David had pitched for it: and they offered burnt sacrifices and peace offerings before God* (I Chronicles 16:1).

David delivered a special psalm of thanksgiving to commemorate the occasion. Upon his conclusion of the psalm, the people declared: *Blessed be the Lord God of Israel for ever and ever. And all the people said, Amen, and praised the Lord* (I Chronicles 16:36).

When David set up his tent and placed the Ark of the Covenant in it, the people shouted **Amen** making this occasion a prophecy of that which will occur again someday in the future — perhaps the near future. The Ark of the Covenant, along with the Tabernacle of David, will be returned to Jerusalem and set up on the Temple Mount.

The Rise of the Antichrist

Another **Amen** can be found in Jeremiah 28:6. It happened during the days of Zedekiah, the hot-headed king of Judah. Here's the story. Zedekiah wanted to overthrow the Babylonian army and put an end to their occupation of the land. Jeremiah opposed his military plans upon the basis of a prophecy that Israel was to be in Babylonian captivity for seventy years. Zedekiah wanted to cut short that time by driving out the Babylonian army.

Hananiah, a false prophet, came before the king with a lying prediction. Hananiah declared that within two years Zedekiah could overthrow the king of Babylon and bring the captives home. Jeremiah came before the king wearing a wooden yoke, declaring that the yoke of bondage to Babylon would remain throughout the seventy years.

When the lying Hananiah predicted an overthrow of the Babylonians, Jeremiah said: *Amen: the Lord do so: the Lord perform thy words which thou hast prophesied, to bring again the vessels of the Lord's house, and all that is carried away captive, from*

Babylon into this place (Jeremiah 28:6). Jeremiah's **Amen** makes this story a prophecy. I believe it is a prediction of the antichrist, who will lie to the Jewish people. Perhaps Jeremiah was referring to the prophetic return of the Ark of the Covenant, the Tabernacle of David, and the restoration of Temple worship.

One day the antichrist will make a covenant with Israel for the restoration of Temple worship, but will desecrate that Temple in the middle of the Tribulation Period. That is referred to in the Bible as the abomination of desolation. Hananiah took the yoke of wood from Jeremiah's shoulders and broke it in the presence of the king, whereupon the Lord told Jeremiah to say to Hananiah: *Thou hast broken the yokes of wood; but thou shalt make for them yokes of iron ... thou makest this people to trust in a lie* (Jeremiah 28:13,15).

The prophetic **Amen** declared by Jeremiah makes the lying Hananiah a profile of the future false prophet.

The Coming of Messiah

There is one more prophetic **Amen** in the Old Testament. It is given in I Kings 1:36. The occasion concerned the coronation of Solomon as king to sit upon the throne of his father David. What a prophecy of the future Son of David who will come to be crowned King of kings — to sit upon the throne of David as Ruler, not only in Israel, but throughout the entire world. *And King David said, Call me Zadok the priest, and Nathan the prophet, and Benaiah the son of Jehoiada. And they came before the king. The king also said unto them, Take with you with the servants of your lord, and cause Solomon my son to ride upon mine own mule, and bring him down to Gihon: And let Zadok the priest and Nathan the prophet anoint him there king over Israel: and blow ye with the trumpet, and say, God save king Solomon. Then ye shall come up after him, that he may come and sit upon my throne; for he shall be king in my stead: and I have appointed him to be ruler over Israel and over Judah. And Benaiah the son of Jehoiada answered the king, and said, Amen ...* (I Kings 1:32-36).

Solomon was considered to be the wisest man who ever lived, but one greater than Solomon will come. As Solomon succeeded his father to the throne, Jesus Christ will return in power and great glory to sit upon the throne of David. He will establish the golden age of human history, one thousand years of peace on earth.

So there you have it — seven **Amens** found in the Psalms which declare them to be a prophetic design, and seven **Amens** found in the rest of the Old Testament to highlight the seven major events of prophecy: the curse of an unfaithful wife; the dispersion of Israel; the return of a remnant; the restoration of Temple worship; the return of the Ark of the Covenant; the rise of the antichrist; and the coming of the Messiah to be proclaimed King of kings and Lord of lords. Isn't it amazing? Even the **Amens** in the Bible have a prophetic story to tell.

NOTES

THE ADVENTURE BEGINS

1. H. C. Leupold, *Zondervan Pictorial Encyclopedia of the Bible,* vol. 4, (Grand Rapids, MI: Zondervan Publishing House, 1975) p. 931.

THE TORAH IN SONG

1. E. W. Bullinger, *Companion Bible,* "Introduction to the Psalms," (Grand Rapids, MI: Zondervan Bible Publishers, 1974) p. 720.
2. Ibid.
3. Ibid.
4. H. A. Ironside, *Studies on the Psalms,* (New York: Loizeaux Brothers, Inc., 1963) p. 4.
5. Ibid., p. 5.
6. Ibid., pp. 5-6.

HOW LONG?

1. Nathan Ausubel, *The Book of Jewish Knowledge,* (New York: Crown Publishers Inc., 1964) p. 315.
2. Ibid.
3. Rabbi Avrohom Chaim Feuer, *Tehillim,* Psalms — A New Translation with a Commentary Anthologized from Talmudic, Midrashic and Rabbinic Sources, (Brooklyn, NY: Mesorah Publications, Ltd., 1985) p. 766.

MYSTERY OF THE NUMBERS REVEALED

1. Samuel Prideaux Tregelles, trans., *Gesenius' Hebrew-Chaldee Lexicon of the Old Testament,* (Milford, MI: Mott Media, 1982) p. 670.

THE GENESIS PSALMS

PSALM 1

1. Feuer, *Tehillim,* p. 52.
2. Ibid., p. 65.
3. Ibid., p. 51.
4. International Hebrew Heritage Library, *The Illustrated History of the Jews,* vol. 2, (Miami: International Book Corp., 1969) p. 235.
5. Abraham Shulman, *Coming Home to Zion, A Pictorial History of Pre-Israel Palestine,* (Garden City, NY: Doubleday and Company, Inc., 1979) p. 3.
6. Ibid, p. 8.

PSALM 2

1. A. Cohen, *The Psalms*, Soncino Press, p. 1.
2. Feuer, *Tehillim*, p. 65.
3. Ibid.
4. Max Dimont, *Jews, God and History*, (New York: New American Library, Inc., 1962) p. 303.

PSALM 3

1. *Talmud*, Berachos 10a.
2. Feuer, *Tehillim*, p. 73.
3. Dimont, *Jews*, p. 304.
4. Ibid.

PSALM 4

1. *History of the Jews*, vol. 2, p. 237.
2. Michael Cohen, *Jewish Almanac*, p. 163.
3. *History*, op. cit., p. 239.

PSALM 5

1. Feuer, *Tehillim*, p. 92.
2. Ibid., p. 1406.
3. Michael Baigent, Richard Leigh, and Henry Lincoln, *Holy Blood, Holy Grail*, (New York: Dell Publishing Company, Inc., 1983) p. 237.
4. Feuer, p. 91.

PSALM 6

1. Feuer, *Tehillim*, p. 101.
2. Dan Kurzman, *Ben-Gurion Prophet of Fire*, (New York: Simon and Schuster, 1983) p. 74.

PSALM 7

1. Feuer, *Tehillim*, p. 110.
2. Jacob S. Hertz, "The Bund's National Program and its Critics in the Russian, Polish and Austrian Socialist Movements," *Studies in Modern Jewish History*, (New York: Ktav Publishing House, Inc., 1972) pp. 80-94.

PSALM 8

1. Feuer, *Tehillim*, p. 121.
2. Nigel Calder, *The Comet is Coming*, (New York: Viking Press, 1980) p. 124.
3. Ibid.

PSALM 9

1. Feuer, *Tehillim*, p. 132.
2. Shulman, *Zion*, p. 116.
3. Ibid., pp. 131-132.

PSALM 10

1. Professor Davison, *The Century Bible*, The Psalms 1-72.
2. Calder, *Comet*, pp. 25-26.

PSALM 11

1. *Encyclopedia Judaica*, vol. 14, (Jerusalem: Keter Publishing House, Ltd., 1972) p. 798.
2. *Great Jewish Statesmen*, p. 96.
3. Ibid., p. 48.
4. H. M. Blumberg, *Weizmann: His Life and Times,* (Tel Aviv: American-Israel Publishing Company, 1975) pp. 31-32.

PSALM 12

1. Feuer, *Tehillim*, p. 163.
2. Ibid.
3. Ibid., p. 166.

PSALM 13

1. Feuer, *Tehillim*, p. 172.
2. Ibid.

PSALM 14

1. *World Book Encyclopedia*, (1973) vol. 21, p. 364-365.
2. Gene Gurney, *Kingdoms of Europe, An Illustrated Encyclopedia of Ruling Monarchs from Ancient Times to the Present,* (New York: Crown Publishers, Inc., 1982) p. 297.
3. Baigent, Leigh, and Lincoln, *Holy Blood,* pp. 398-414.
4. Feuer, *Tehillim*, p. 181.

PSALM 15

1. Shulman, *Zion*, pp. 83-94.

PSALM 16

1. Homer Duncan, *Israel Past, Present and Future,* (Lubbock, TX: Missionary Crusader, 1972) pp. 19-20.
2. Feuer, *Tehillim*, p. 198.

PSALM 17

1. L. Sale-Harrison, *The Remarkable Jew — His Wonderful Future*, p. 78.
2. Ibid., p. 79.
3. Ibid., p. 77.
4. *Gesenius' Lexicon*, p. 25.

PSALM 18

1. *Coming Home to Zion*, pp. 158-159.
2. Feuer, *Tehillim*, p. 213.
3. Ibid., p. 211.

PSALM 19

1. Feuer, *Tehillim*, p. 251.
2. Ernest Main, *Palestine at the Crossroads*, (London: George Allen and Unwin, Ltd., 1937) p. 269.
3. Robert John and Sami Hadawi, *The Palestine Diary*, 2 vols., (New York: New World Press, 1970) p. 119.

PSALM 20

1. Feuer, *Tehillim*, p. 253.
2. Ibid., p. 255.
3. Blumberg, *Weizmann*, p. 73.
4. Ibid.
5. A. W. Kayyali, *Palestine: A Modern History*, (London: Croom Helm, Ltd., n.d.) p. 88.

PSALM 21

1. Feuer, *Tehillim*, p. 261.
2. Christopher Sykes, *Crossroads to Israel*, (New York: World Publishing Company, 1965) p. 41.
3. Shulman, *Coming Home to Zion*, p. 154.
4. Ibid., p. 155.
5. A. W. Kayyali, *Palestine, A Modern History*, pp. 90-94.
6. *Encyclopedia Judaica*, Yearbook, 1974, pp. 24-25.
7. Feuer, *Tehillim*, p. 266.
8. Ibid.
9. Ibid.

PSALM 22

1. Robert John and Sami Hadawi, *The Palestine Diary*, pp. 182-183.
2. Feuer, *Tehillim*, p. 269.

PSALM 23

1. Feuer, *Tehillim*, p. 269.
2. John and Hadawi, *Palestine Diary*, p. 191.

PSALM 24

1. Feuer, *Tehillim*, p. 295 and Cohen, *Psalms*, p. 69.
2. Michael Bar-Zohar, *Ben-Gurion: A Biography*, (New York: Delacorte Press, Inc., 1979) pp. 52-53.
3. Feuer, p. 302.

PSALM 25

1. Blumberg, *Weizmann*, p. 100.
2. Christopher Sykes, *Crossroads to Israel*, p. 82.

PSALM 26

1. Sykes, *Crossroads*, p. 85.

PSALM 27

1. Sale-Harrison, *Remarkable Jew*, p. 165.
2. Sykes, *Crossroads*, p. 95.

PSALM 28

1. Feuer, *Tehillim*, p. 340.

PSALM 29

1. Soncino Press, *Babylonian Talmud*, Berakoth 29a.
2. C. H. Spurgeon, *The Treasury of David*, vol. 1b, p. 29.
3. Max I. Dimont, *Jews, God and History*, p. 365.
4. Humphrey Bowman, *Middle East Window*, p. 288.
5. Joseph B. Schlectman, *The Mufti and the Fuehrer*, (New York: Thomas Yoseloff, 1965) p. 37.
6. Ibid., p. 35.
7. Joan Dash, *Summoned to Jerusalem*, (New York: Harper and Row Publishers, 1979) p. 211.
8. Edwin Samuel, *A Lifetime in Jerusalem*, (London: Abelard-Schuman, 1970) pp. 106-107.
9. Sykes, *Crossroads to Israel*, p. 108.
10. Samuel, op. cit., p. 103.
11. Blumberg, *Weizmann*, p. 120.

PSALM 30

1. Cohen, *Psalms*, p. 85.
2. John and Hadawi, p. 211.
3. Golda Meir, *My Life*, (New York: G. P. Putnam's Sons, 1975) p. 134.
4. Chaim Weizmann, *Trial and Error*, (New York: Schocken Books, 1949) p. 331.
5. Y. Porath, *The Emergence of the Palestinian-Arab National Movement 1918-1929*, vol. I, (London: Frank Cass, 1974) p. 277.
6. Weizmann, op. cit.

PSALM 31

1. Weizmann, *Trial* pp. 337-340.
2. Sykes, *Crossroads* p. 119.
3. Weizmann, op. cit., p. 335.
4. Nosson Scherman and Meir Zlotowitz, eds., *Reb Elchonon*, "Artscroll History Series," (New York: Mesorah Publications, Ltd., 1982) p. 53.
5. Nora Levin, *The Holocaust: Destruction of European Jewry 1933-1945*, (New York: Thomas Y. Crowell Company, 1968) pp. 42-43.

PSALM 32

1. Weizmann, *Trial*, p. 357.
2. Raul Hilberg, ed., *Documents of Destruction: Germany and Jewry 1933-1945*, (Chicago: Quadrangle Books, 1971) pp. 14-16.

PSALM 33

1. H. J. Zimmels, *The Echo of the Nazi Holocaust in Rabbinic Literature*, (Jerusalem: Ktav Publishing House, Inc., 1977) p. xvi.
2. Adolph Hitler, *Mein Kampf*, (Boston: Houghton Mifflin Company, 1943) pp. 329-362.
3. Ibid.

PSALM 34

1. Ginsberg, *Legends of the Jews*, vol. IV, p. 90.
2. Zimmels, *Echo*, pp. 83-86.

PSALM 35

1. Spurgeon, *Treasury of David*, vol. 1a, p. 140.
2. *Palestine Post*, October 28, 1935, p. 1.
3. Levin, *Holocaust*, p. 69.
4. Ibid., p. 71.

PSALM 36

1. Richard Gutteridge, *The German Evaneglical Church and the Jews 1879-1950,* (New York: Barnes and Noble, 1976) p. 164.
2. Ibid., p. 165.
3. Ibid., p. 166.
4. Ibid., pp. 231-232.

PSALM 37

1. Feuer, *Tehillim*, p. 450.
2. G. Campbell Morgan, *Notes on the Psalms*, p. 71.
3. Feuer, *Tehillim*, p. 450.
4. Levin, *Holocaust*, pp. 72-73.

PSALM 38

1. Feuer, *Tehillim*, p. 471.
2. Levin, *Holocaust*, p. 76.
3. *Palestine Post*, November 11, 1938, p. 1.
4. Ibid., November 13, 1938, p. 1.

PSALM 39

1. Feuer, *Tehillim*, p. 485.
2. Feuer, *Tehillim*, p. 485.
3. Gerald Fleming, *Hitler and the Final Solution,* (Berkeley, CA: University of California Press, 1984) p. 68.
4. Ibid.
5. Milton Meltzer, *Never to Forget - The Jews of the Holocaust,* (New York: Harper and Row, 1976) p. 131.
6. Raul Hilberg, *The Destruction of the European Jews,* (New York: Harper and Row, Publishers, 1961) p. 128.
7. Feuer, *Tehillim*, p. 491.
8. Norman and Helen Bentwich, *Mandate Memories 1918-1948,* (London: The Hogarth Press, 1965) pp. 163-165. Also see: Kurzman, *Ben-Gurion Prophet,* chapter 7.

PSALM 40

1. Feuer, *Tehillim*, p. 497.
2. *Bereishis,* Rabba 65:8.
3. Abraham I. Katsh, trans. and ed., *The Warsaw Diary of Chaim A. Kaplan,* (New York: Collier Books, 1965) p. 119.
4. Ibid.
5. Ibid., p. 135.
6. Ibid., p. 179.
7. Ibid., p. 225.
8. *Gesenius' Lexicon*, p. 443.
9. Ibid., p. 664.

PSALM 41

1. Finas J.Dake, *Dake's Annotated Reference Bible*, p. 566.
2. *Gesenius' Lexicon*, p. 444.
3. Meltzer, *Never*, p. 138.
4. Hilberg, *European Jews*, p. 288.
5. Christopher R. Browning, *The Final Solution and the German Foreign Office*, (New York: Holmes and Meier Publishers, Inc., 1978) pp. 8-9.
8-9.
6. Hilberg, op. cit, pp. 192-196.
7. Fleming, *Hitler*, p. 103.
8. Ibid., p. 102.
9. Browning, *Final Solution*, p. 9.

THE EXODUS PSALMS

PSALM 42

1. E. W. Bullinger, *Number in Scripture*, (Grand Rapids, MI: Kregel Publications, 1981) p. 253.
2. Jewish Black Book Committee, *The Black Book: The Nazi Crime Against the Jewish People*, (New York: Duell, Sloan and Pierce, 1946) p. 73.
3. Hilberg, *European Jews*, p. 264.
4. Browning, *Final Solution*, p. 77.
5. Ibid., p. 218.
6. Meltzer, *Never*, p. 198.
7. Feuer, *Tehillim*, p. 535.
8. *Gesenius' Lexicon*, p. 446.

PSALM 43

1. Meltzer, *Never*, p. 163.
2. Ibid.
3. Ibid.
4. *Gesenius' Lexicon*, p. 446.

PSALM 44

1. Feuer, *Tehillim*, p. 544.
2. Ibid., See footnote, p. 545.
3. Ibid., p. 545.
4. Ibid., p. 546.
5. Norman and Helen Bentwich, *Mandate Memories*, p. 166.
6. Feuer, *Tehillim*, p. 550.

7. Hilberg, *European Jews,* p. 209.
8. Meltzer, *Never,* p. 179.
9. Ibid., pp. 180-181.
10. Yehuda Bauer, *The Holocaust in Historical Perspective,* (Seattle: University of Washington Press, 1978) pp. 94-155.
11. Meltzer, *Never,* p. 182.
12. James Strong, *Strong's Exhaustive Concordance,* "Hebrew-Chaldee Dictionary" (Grand Rapids, MI: Associated Publishers and Authors, Inc., n.d.) p. 61.

PSALM 45

1. Dake, *Reference Bible,* p. 568.
2. Feuer, *Tehillim,* p. 560.
3. Ibid., p. 561.
4. Ibid., p. 563.
5. Ibid., p. 564.
6. Ibid., p. 573.
7. Kurzman, *Ben-Gurion Prophet,* pp. 258-259.
8. Ibid.
9. Ibid., p. 261.
10. *Gesenius' Lexicon,* pp. 451-452.

PSALM 46

1. Feuer, *Tehillim,* p. 577.
2. Ibid., p. 579.
3. Ibid., pp. 580-581.
4. *Gesenius' Lexicon,* pp. 454-455.
5. Robert Slater, *Golda: Uncrowned Queen of Israel,* (New York: Jonathan David Publishers, Inc., 1981).
6. Herbert L. Matthews, "Joint Palestine Body Bars a Jewish State, But Urges Entry of 100,000 Refugees," *The New York Times,* p. 1.
7. Kurzman, *Ben-Gurion Prophet,* p. 265.
8. Slater, op. cit., p. 58.

PSALM 47

1. Kurzman, *Ben-Gurion Prophet,* p. 275.
2. Ibid.
3. Jacques Derogy and Carmel Hesi, *The Untold History of Israel,* (New York: Grove Press, Inc., 1979) pp. 76-77.
4. Cohen, *Psalms,* p. 147.
5. Yitzhak Rabin, The Rabin Memoirs, (Boston: Little, Brown and Company, 1979) p. 19.
6. David Ben-Gurion, *Israel: A Personal History,* (New York: Funk and Wagnalls, Inc., 1971) p. 59.

7. Rabin, op. cit.
8. Feuer, *Tehillim*, p. 599.
9. Ibid., p. 593.
10. Ibid., p. 592.
11. Ibid., p. 592.
12. Ibid.
13. Ibid., p. 597.
14. *Strong's Concordance*, op. cit., p. 64.

PSALM 48

1. Feuer, *Tehillim*, p. 601.
2. Ibid.
3. Colonel Trevor Dupuy, *Elusive Victory - The Arab Israeli Wars, 1947-1974*, (Fairfax, VA: Hero Books, 1984) p. 67.
4. Ibid., p. 91.
5. Kurzman, *Ben-Gurion Prophet*, p. 301.
6. *Gesenius' Lexicon*, p. 462.

PSALM 49

1 *Gesenius' Lexicon*, p. 466.
2. Meir, *My Life*, p. 235.
3. Theodor Herzl, *Complete Diaries*, R. Patai, ed., II, pp. 580-581.
4. John Allegro, *The Dead Sea Scrolls*, (New York: Penguin Books, 1964) pp. 17-36.
5. Feuer, *Tehillim*, p. 616.
6. Ibid., p. 617.

PSALM 50

1. *Encyclopedia Judaica*, vol. IX, p. 378.
2. Ibid. Also see Martin Gilbert, *Atlas of Jewish History*, (New York: Dorset Press, 1985) p. 110.
3. Howard M. Sachar, *A History of Israel*, (New York: Alfred A. Knopf, 1976) p. 423.
4. *Gesenius' Lexicon*, p. 523.
5. E. W. Bullinger, *The Witness of the Stars*, (Grand Rapids, MI: Kregel Publications, 1983) p. 96.
6. Ibid., p. 93.

PSALM 51

1. Cohen, *Psalms*, p. 161.
2. Ginsberg, *Legends*, vol. II, p. 364.
3. Rev. C. I. Scofield, ed., *Scofield Reference Bible*, (New York: Oxford University Press, 1945) see footnote to Psalm 51, p. 623.
4. David Ben-Gurion, *Israel-A Personal History*, p. 398.

PSALM 52

1. Cohen, *Psalms*, p. 165.
2. Shirley Graham DuBois, *Gamal Abdel Nasser - Son of the Nile*, (New York: The Third Press, 1972) p. 78.
3. P. J. Vatikiotis, *Nasser and His Generation*, (New York: St. Martin's Press, 1978) p. 118.
4. Joachim Joesten, *Nasser - The Rise to Power*, (London: Oldhams Press Limited, 1960) p. 78.
5. Robert Stephens, *Nasser - A Political Biography*, New York: Simon and Schuster, 1971) p. 11.
6. Meir, *My Life*, p. 293.

PSALM 53

1. Feuer, *Tehillim*, pp. 675-682.
2. Robert Payne, *The Rise and Fall of Stalin*, pp. 43-59.
3. *Encyclopedia Judaica*, vol. XIV, p. 460.
4. Harry G. Shafer, *The Soviet Treatment of Jews*, p. 10.

PSALM 54

1. Robert St. John, *Ben-Gurion*, (New York: Doubleday and Company, Inc., 1971) pp. 256-276.
2. Meir, *My Life*, pp. 284-285.

PSALM 55

1. Joesten, *Nasser*, p. 113.
2. *Encyclopedia Judaica*, vol. X. pp. 1378-1379.
3. Ibid.
4. Meir, *My Life*, p. 288.

PSALM 56

1. David Hirst, *The Gun and the Olive Branch*, (New York: Harcourt, Brace, Jovanovich, 1977) p. 200.
2. Joesten, *Nasser*, pp. 153-164.
3. Robert Henriques, *100 Hours to Suez*, (New York: Viking Press, 1957) p. 66.

PSALM 57

1. Feuer, *Tehillim*, p. 718.
2. Kurzman, *Ben-Gurion*, pp. 393-398.
3. Ibid.
4. Ibid. See also Moshe Dayan, *Story of My Life*, (New York: William Morrow and Company, Inc., 1976) pp. 251-253.
5. *New York Times*, November 4, 1957, p. 1.

PSALM 58

1. Dana Adams Schmidt, *New York Times*, April 26, 1967, p. 1.
2. Meir, *My Life*, p. 318.
3. David Ben-Gurion, *My Talks with Arab Leaders*, p. 327.
4. Ibid.

PSALM 59

1. Hirst, *Olive Branch*, pp. 269-288.

PSALM 60

1. Feuer, *Tehillim*, p. 746.
2. Robert Slater, *Golda: Uncrowned Queen of Israel*, pp. 133-136.

PSALM 61

1. Cohen, *Psalms*, p. 192.
2. Bar Zohar, *Ben-Gurion*, p. 297.

PSALM 62

1. Bar Zohar, *Ben-Gurion*, p. 2.

PSALM 63

1. Kurzman, *Ben-Gurion Prophet*, pp. 442-443.
2. Meir, *My Life*, p. 348.

PSALM 64

1. Hirst, *Olive Branch*, p. 276.
2. Ibid.

PSALM 65

1. Ben-Gurion returned as Minister of Defense on February 21, 1955. He was re-elected Prime Minister in August and took oath of office in November.
2. David Ben-Gurion, *Israel A Personal History*, p. 730.
3. *Encyclopedia Judaica*, vol. IX, p. 404.
4. Aharon Cohen, *Israel and the Arab World*, (New York: Funk and Wagnalls, 1970) p. 526.

PSALM 66

1. Feuer, *Tehillim,* p. 805.
2. Cohen, *Psalms,* p. 204.
3. Winston Burdett, *Encounter with the Middle East,* (New York: Atheneum, 1969) pp. 168-169.

PSALM 67

1. Zola Levitt and Thomas McCall, *Satan in the Sanctuary,* (Dallas: Zola Levitt Ministries, 1983) p. 22.

PSALM 68

1. Chaim Herzog, *The Arab-Israeli Wars,* (New York: Random House, 1982) p. 149.
2. Dayan, *My Life,* pp. 287-357.
3. Yitzhak Rabin, *The Rabin Memoirs,* pp. 67-99.
4. Stephens, *Nasser,* p. 479.
5. Rabin, *Memoirs,* p. 104.

PSALM 69

1. *The Century Bible,* Psalm 69, footnote.
2. Hisham Sharabi, *Palestine Guerillas,* (Beirut: The Institute for Palestine Studies, 1970) p. 11.
3. Judy Bertelsen, *The Palestinian Arabs: A Non-State Nation,* (Beverly Hills, CA: Sage Publications, 1976) p. 52.
4. Stephens, *Nasser,* pp. 493-593.
5. Donald Neff, *Warriors for Jerusalem,* (New York: Linden Press/Simon and Schuster, 1984) p. 31.
6. Meir, *My Life,* pp. 376-377.
7. Neff, op. cit., p. 315.

PSALM 70

1. Feuer, *Tehillim,* p. 871.
2. *Encyclopedia Judaica,* Yearbook 1973, p. 11.

PSALM 71

1. Nathan Ausubel, *Pictorial History of the Jewish People,* p. 403.
2. Ibid., p. 406.
3. Thomas Kiernan, *Arafat,* (New York: W. W. Norton and Company, Inc., 1976).

PSALM 72

1. Scofield, *Scofield Bible,* p. 633.

THE LEVITICUS PSALMS

INTRODUCTION TO THE LEVITICUS PSALMS

1. Merrill Tenney, ed., *Zondervan's Pictorial Bible Dictionary*, (Grand Rapids, MI: Zondervan Publishing House, 1968) p. 75.
2. Feuer, *Tehillim*, p. 1106.

PSALM 73

1. Feuer, *Tehillim*, p. 910.
2. Meir, *My Life*, pp. 426-428.
3. Ibid., p. 431.
4. Peter Allen, *The Yom Kippur War*, (New York: Charles Scribner's Sons, 1982) pp. 193-194.
5. Harold H. Hart, *Yom Kippur Plus 100 Days*, (New York: Hart Publishing Company, Inc., 1974) p. 107.
6. Lester Sobel and Hal Kosut, eds., *Israel and The Arabs: The October 1973 War*, (New York: Facts on File, 1974) p. 108.
7. Feuer, *Tehillim*, p. 917.

PSALM 74

1. Feuer, *Tehillim*, p. 925.
2. Allen, *Yom Kippur War*, p. 57.
3. *London Sunday Times*, The Yom Kippur War, p. 1.
4. Feuer, *Tehillim*, p. 931.
5. Ibid., p. 932.

PSALM 75

1. *Encyclopedia Judaica*, 1975-76 Yearbook, pp. 14-18.
2. Feuer, *Tehillim*, p. 939.
3. Ibid., p. 940.
4. *Encyclopedia Judaica*, op. cit., pp. 14-18.
5. Feuer, *Tehillim*, p. 944.

PSALM 76

1. Feuer, *Tehillim*, p. 947.
2. Ibid.
3. Yitzhak Rabin, *The Rabin Memoirs*, pp. 301-314.
4. Ibid., p. 302.

PSALM 77

1. Anthony S. Pitch, *Peace*, (Englewood, NJ: SBS Publishing, Inc., 1979).

PSALM 78

1. Yigael Yadin, ed., *The Temple Scroll,* vol. 1, (Jerusalem: Ben Zvi Printing, Ltd., 1983) p. 40.
2. *Encyclopedia Judaica,* 1973-82 Yearbook, p. 32.
3. Eric Silver, *Begin, the Haunted Prophet,* (New York: Random House, 1984) p. 222.

PSALM 79

1. Feuer, *Tehillim,* p. 1003.
2. *Encyclopedia Judaica,* 1973-82 Yearbook, pp. 39-47.

PSALM 80

1. *Time* magazine, October 19, 1981, p. 17.
2. *Gesenius' Lexicon,* p. 664.
3. Ibid., p. 443.
4. Ibid., pp. 444, 451.
5. Ibid., pp. 664, 668.
6. Ibid., p. 462.
7. Ibid., p. 665.
8. Ibid., p. 666.

PSALM 81

1. *Time* magazine, October 19, 1981, pp. 15-17.
2. Rabbi Ben Zion Wacholder, "Chronomessianism," *Hebrew Union College Annual Yearbook,* (Cincinnati, 1975) pp. 201-218.
3. David Bridger and Samuel Wolk, "The Sabbatical Years and Jubilees," *The New Jewish Encyclopedia,* (New York: Behrman House, Inc., 1976) pp. 607-608.

PSALM 82

1. *Time* magazine, June 21, 1982, p. 14.
2. *Time* magazine, August 16, 1982, p. 14.
3. Ibid.
4. *Time* magazine, August 23, 1982, p. 28.

PSALM 83

1. *Zondervan Pictorial Bible Dictionary,* Merrill C. Tenney, editor, p. 302.
2. *Gesenius' Lexicon,* p. 665.

PSALM 84

1. Feuer, *Tehillim*, p. 1051.
2. *Gesenius' Lexicon*, p. 666.
3. Yigael Yadin, *The Temple Scroll*, vol. 1, p. 71.
4. *Science News of the Week*, September 8, 1984, p. 1.

PSALM 85

1. *Time* magazine, January 21, 1985, p. 39.
2. Ibid.
3. Feuer, *Tehillim*, p. 599.
4. Ibid.
5. Feuer, *Tehillim*, p. 1061.
6. Ibid., p. 1051.
7. Ibid., p. 1062.
8. Ibid., p. 1066.
9. *Gesenius' Lexicon*, p. 667-668.

PSALM 86

1. Feuer, *Tehillim*, p. 1072.
2. Ibid., p. 1076.
3. *Strong's Concordance*, p. 93.

PSALM 87

1. Feuer, *Tehillim*, p. 1083.
2. Ibid., p. 1084.
3. Merrill F. Unger, *Unger's Bible Dictionary*, (Chicago: Moody Press, 1966) p. 908.
4. Herbert Lockyer, ed., *Nelson's Illustrated Bible Dictionary*, (Nashville: Thomas Nelson Publishers, 1986).
5. *Gesenius' Lexicon*, p. 670.
6. Ibid.

PSALM 88

1. Feuer, *Tehillim*, p. 1090.
2. Ibid.
3. Ibid.
4. *Zondervan Pictorial Encyclopedia of the Bible*, vol. 4, p. 931.
5. Feuer, *Tehillim*, p. 1096.
6. Ibid., p. 1093.
7. Ibid., p. 1097.
8. *Unger's Bible Dictionary*, pp. 235-236.

PSALM 89

1. Feuer, *Tehillim*, p. 1100.

THE NUMBERS PSALMS

INTRODUCTION TO THE NUMBERS PSALMS

1. *Gesenius' Lexicon*, p. 698.
2. Ibid., p. 699.
3. Ibid., p. 701.
4. Ibid., p. 703.
5. Ibid., p. 704.
6. Ibid., p. 707.
7. Ibid., p. 720.
8. Ibid.
9. Ibid.
10. Ibid., p. 722.
11. Ibid., p. 726.
12. Ibid., p. 726.

PSALM 90

1. Feuer, *Tehillim*, p. 1121.
2. *Gesenius' Lexicon*, p. 316.
3. Ibid., p. 325.

PSALM 91

1. Feuer, *Tehillim*, p. 1133.
2. *Time* magazine, February 17, 1986, p. 90.
3. *Time* magazine, November 3, 1986, p. 76.
4. Ibid.
5. Feuer, *Tehillim*, p. 1138.
6. Ibid., p. 1143.
7. *Gesenius' Lexicon*, p. 698.

PSALM 92

1. Feuer, *Tehillim*, p. 1146.
2. Ibid., p. 1145.
3. Ibid., p. 1151.
4. *Gesenius' Lexicon*, p. 699.

PSALM 93

1. Feuer, *Tehillim*, p. 1159.
2. Ibid.
3. Ibid., p. 1157.

PSALM 94

1. James H. Charlesworth, Editor, *The Old Testament Pseudepigrapha*, Garden City, NY: Doubleday and Company, Inc., 1983) p. 809.
2. Feuer, *Tehillim*, p. 1163.
3. Bullinger, *Number*, p. 123.
4. *Gesenius' Lexicon*, p. 701.

PSALM 95

1. Bullinger, *Number*, page 253.
2. Feuer, *Tehillim*, p. 1175.
3. *Gesenius' Lexicon*, p. 703.

PSALM 96

1. *Gesenius' Lexicon*, p. 704.

PSALM 97

1. Feuer, *Tehillim*, p. 1193.

PSALM 98

1. *Gesenius' Lexicon*, p. 707.

PSALM 99

1. Feuer, *Tehillim*, p. 1207.

PSALM 100

1. Feuer, *Tehillim*, p. 1215.
2. *Gesenius' Lexicon*, p. 720.

PSALM 101

1. Feuer, *Tehillim*, p. 1221.
2. *Gesenius' Lexicon*, p. 720.

PSALM 102

1. *The Zondervan Pictorial Encyclopedia of the Bible*, vol. 1, p. 266.
2. *Strong's Exhaustive Concordance*, Hebrew and Chaldee Dictionary, (word #68), p. 8.
3. *Gesenius' Lexicon*, p. 8.
4. *Strong's Concordance*, (word #6083), p. 90.

5. *Gesenius' Lexicon*, pp. 645-646.
6. *Zondervan Encyclopedia*, pp. 266-277.
7. *Gesenius' Lexicon*, p. 720.

PSALM 103

1. Feuer, *Tehillim*, p. 1238.
2. Ibid.
3. Ibid.
4. Ibid.
5. Ibid.
6. Ibid.

PSALM 104

1. *Gesenius' Lexicon*, p. 722.

PSALM 105

1. Feuer, *Tehillim*, p. 1269.
2. *Gesenius' Lexicon*, p. 726.

PSALM 106

1. *Gesenius' Lexicon*, p. 726.

THE DEUTERONOMY PSALMS

PSALM 112

1. Feuer, *Tehillim*, p. 1355.

PSALM 113

1. Feuer, *Tehillim*, p. 1363.

PSALM 114

1. Feuer, *Tehillim*, p. 1371.

PSALM 116

1. Feuer, *Tehillim*, p. 1385.
2. Ibid., p. 1396.
3. Ibid.
4. Scofield, *Scofield Bible*, p. 1205.

PSALM 117

1. Feuer, *Tehillim,* p. 1397.
2. *Cheiro's Book of Numbers,* pp. 178-181.

PSALM 118

1. *Cheiro's Book of Numbers,* pp. 178-181.
2. Feuer, *Tehillim,* p. 1406.
3. James H. Charlesworth, ed., *The Old Testament Pseudepigrapha,* vol. 1, p. 809.
4. *World Book Encyclopedia,* vol. 20, p. 182.
5. William Whiston, trans., *The Works of Flavius Josephus,* "Antiquities of the Jews," (Grand Rapids, MI: Baker Book House, 1979) book XII, chapter IV, paragraph 10.
6. John Pinsent, *Greek Mythology, Library of the World's Myths and Legends,* pp. 44-46.
7. Gurney, *Kingdoms of Europe,* p. 56.
8. Baigent, Leigh, and Lincoln, *Holy Blood,* p. 237.

PSALM 119

1. *Cheiro's Book of Numbers,* p. 178.
2. Jim Hill, *What a Day That Will Be,* copyright 1955 by Ben L. Speer.

PSALMS OF ASCENT

1. Donald Patten, Ronald Hatch, and Loren Steinhauer, *The Long Day of Joshua and Six Other Catastrophes,* (Grand Rapids, MI: Baker Book House, 1977) pp. 23.

PSALM 131

1. Carl A. Blackmore, *Some Golden Daybreak,* The Rodeheaver Company.

PSALM 135

1. Feuer, *Tehillim,* p. 1597.

PSALM 136

1. Feuer, *Tehillim,* p. 1607.

PSALM 139

1. Feuer, *Tehillim,* p. 1633.

2. Ibid., p. 1642.
3. Ibid., p. 1644.
4. Ibid., p. 1646.

PSALM 140

1. Feuer, *Tehillim*, p. 1647.
2. Ibid.
3. Ibid., p. 1649.
4. Ibid., p. 1651.

PSALM 141

1. Feuer, *Tehillim*, p. 1655.

PSALM 143

1. Feuer, *Tehillim*, p. 1669.

PSALM 145

1. Feuer, *Tehillim*, p. 1687.

THE HALLELUJAH PSALMS

1. Bullinger, *Number*, p.123.
2. Ibid.

SPECIAL OFFER

Monthly Tabloid
"Todays news from a prophetic perspective"

THE ARMAGEDDON SYNDROME

$18 for
12 monthly issues
and receive this
BONUS BOOK

World leaders are infected by a cloud of political gloom spreading over our planet. Will this generation face the awesome Armageddon? This book sheds light on the darkening political maze facing our world and reveals the electrifying remedy.

ORDER FROM

PROPHECY IN THE NEWS
P.O. Box 7000
Oklahoma City, OK 73153